Foucault's Orient

FOUCAULT'S ORIENT
The Conundrum of Cultural Difference, from Tunisia to Japan

Marnia Lazreg

berghahn
NEW YORK • OXFORD
www.berghahnbooks.com

First published in 2017 by
Berghahn Books
www.berghahnbooks.com

© 2017, 2020 Marnia Lazreg
First paperback edition published in 2020

All rights reserved. Except for the quotation of short passages
for the purposes of criticism and review, no part of this book
may be reproduced in any form or by any means, electronic or
mechanical, including photocopying, recording, or any information
storage and retrieval system now known or to be invented,
without written permission of the publisher.

Library of Congress Cataloging-in-Publication Data

Names: Lazreg, Marnia, author.
Title: Foucault's Orient : the conundrum of cultural difference, from Tunisia to
 Japan / Marnia Lazreg.
Description: New York : Berghahn Books, 2017. | Includes bibliographical
 references and index.
Identifiers: LCCN 2017015944 (print) | LCCN 2017037524 (ebook) | ISBN
 9781785336232 (e-book) | ISBN 9781785336225 (hardback : alk. paper)
Subjects: LCSH: East and West. | Foucault, Michel, 1926–1984. | Philosophical
 anthropology.
Classification: LCC CB251 (ebook) | LCC CB251 .L364 2017 (print) | DDC
 128–dc23
LC record available at https://lccn.loc.gov/2017015944

British Library Cataloguing in Publication Data

A catalogue record for this book is available from the British Library

ISBN 978-1-78533-622-5 (hardback)
ISBN 978-1-78920-817-7 (paperback)
ISBN 978-1-78533-623-2 (ebook)

To the memory of my parents

For Ramsi and Reda

Contents

Acknowledgments	ix
Introduction	1
Chapter 1. The Chinese Encyclopedia and the Challenge of Difference	13
Chapter 2. Madness and Cultural Difference	45
Chapter 3. Foucault and Kant's Cosmopolitan Anthropology	62
Chapter 4. Foucault's Negative Anthropology	97
Chapter 5. Foucault's Anthropology of the Iranian Revolution	122
Chapter 6. The Heterotopia of Tunisia	159
Chapter 7. The Enigma of Japan	192
Chapter 8. Japan and Foucault's Anthropological Bind	226
Epilogue	245
Bibliography	255
Index	274

Acknowledgments

This book started in 2009 with a question that lingered in my mind each time I taught a course on Foucault at the Graduate Center of the City University of New York: why did he start *The Order of Things* with Borges's Chinese encyclopedia, and not some other equally provocative quotation? Soon I found myself retracing his intellectual journey prior to *The Order of Things*. I then realized that the question I started out with called for an examination of Foucault's positioning toward non-Western cultures. There began a long, challenging, and enriching research that compelled me to engage several fields of study. Although I still have many questions and doubts, I appreciate more than ever before the complexity of Foucault's work.

I could not have completed this book without the generous and gracious help of a number of people to whom I am deeply grateful for the time they devoted to sharing ideas, references, or information with me, whether in Japan, Tunisia, France, or the United States.

In the United States, Peter Paret and Marvin B. Scott read an earlier draft of the entire manuscript and encouraged me to forge ahead. Robert B. Louden read and commented on the first draft of chapters 3 and 4. He was immensely generous with sharing sources and answering questions. Zhengguo Kang enlightened me about the real Chinese encyclopedia of medieval times. Liu Xi shared with me his thoughts about the place of China in the Western imagination, as well as the Chinese encyclopedia. Stefan Tanaka read a first draft of chapter 7. Kazushige Shingu provided references as well as insights into Lacan's conception of Japanese culture. Charles Kurzman answered questions and helped with references on the Iranian Revolution. Thanks go to Behrooz Ghamari-Tabrizi; Jon Solomon; Evelyn Fishburn, who answered a query about Borges; and Claus Mueller for his assistance with key German concepts. Last, but not least, I owe a special debt to Ramsi A. Woodcock, who read parts of the manuscript, shared references, and supported me through the ups and downs of bringing this book to life in more ways than I can recount.

In Paris, Daniel Defert shared his knowledge of Foucault's work as well as his and Foucault's experiences in Tunisia and Japan. Simone Othmani Lellouche's assistance and knowledge of the students' revolt in Tunisia of the 1960s was invaluable. I cannot thank her enough. Ahmed Hasnaoui made time to recount his early encounters with Foucault in Tunis and later in Paris. Brahim Razgallah spent hours analyzing the 1968 Tunisian students' revolt and its significance for present-day Tunisia. In Tunis, Zeineb Ben Saïd Cherni offered keen insights into the students' revolt as well as Foucault's thought. Jélila Hafsia recounted her encounters with Foucault. Sadek Ben Mhenni and Lina Ben Mhenni entertained questions on the legacy of the students' revolt to the Tunisian Revolution.

In Tokyo, Moriaki Watanabe provided insights into Foucault's trips in 1970 and 1978 and opened up new angles on Foucault's view of Japanese culture. I am deeply indebted to Hidetaka Ishida for his selfless assistance in facilitating my research and for stimulating discussions. I greatly appreciated Yasuo Kobayashi's thoughtful answers to my questions. I am thankful to Yasuyuki Shinkai for sharing his invaluable knowledge. Christian Polak kindly provided new information on Foucault's 1978 trip to Japan.

Students at a graduate seminar I taught at the Graduate Center of CUNY in 2015 helped with their stimulating discussions of the ideas expressed in a draft of this book.

I am grateful for the support I received in getting access to manuscripts at IMEC, Saint-Germain-la-Blanche-Herbe (Caen), and the Bibliothèque Nationale de France, Richelieu site. Most welcoming and helpful was also the staff of the Bibliothèque Documentation Internationale Contemporaine of the University of Paris-Nanterre. At the Mina Rees library, Graduate Center, I deeply appreciate Jill Cirasella time and expertise. Thanks to Vita Rabinowitz, former Provost at Hunter College, I benefited from an out-of-cycle travel award in Spring 2014.

Although so many people have contributed to the completion of this book, I alone am responsible for all and any shortcomings.

Introduction

This book examines the role played by the "Orient," and non-Western cultures more generally, in Foucault's critical scholarship. It attempts to shed light on the puzzling gap between Foucault's powerful demystifying thought and his view of the Orient as an enigma beyond the grasp of Western reason. Foucault had a keen interest in non-Western countries. He lived in Tunisia in 1966–1968 and once considered moving to Japan, a country he visited twice, in 1970 and 1978. In defining his *reportage d'idées,* he expressed his commitment to exploring ideas produced "particularly among the minorities or people who historically have been bereft of the ability to speak or make themselves heard."[1] He went to Iran as a journalist to discover some of these ideas. Yet in spite of his interest and travels, Foucault constructed Western reason in contradistinction to the Orient, as explained in his 1961 original preface to *Folie et déraison: Histoire de la folie à l'âge classique,* in which he wrote: "the Orient is for the Occident everything that it is not"; it constitutes the "limit" of Western rationality.[2] The preface was removed from the 1964 French abridged edition. For decades, all foreign language translations (except for the Italian) were based on the abridged edition, and therefore did not contain the 1961 preface with the passage on the Orient.[3] The revised 1972 edition, under the abridged title, *Histoire de la folie à l'âge classique* (*History of Madness*), contains a new and very brief preface without the passage on the Orient–Occident divide. It was not until 2006 that a translation of the 1972 version reproduced the 1961 preface in its entirety in the English language.[4]

The removal of the preface does not mean that Foucault had had second thoughts about the exclusion of the Orient from the Western *ratio*. On the contrary, the preface to *The Order of Things (Les mots et les choses),* published five years later, introduced the book with a citation from Borges about a fictitious Chinese encyclopedia. Discussing the encyclopedia as if it were real, Foucault analyzed a bizarre Chinese enumeration of dogs as reflecting the peculiarities of Chinese culture and language as opposed to the scientific orderliness of Western culture. Foucault's foregrounding of the discussion of the Chinese encyclopedia in the book transcends his penchant for provocative literary examples; it is also hardly attributable to what Georges Canguilhem called Foucault's *espagnolisme* or predilection for things Spanish.[5] Indeed, the fiction in which *The Order of Things* found its inspiration is different from the works of literature such as those of Flaubert, or Robbe-Grillet, that he was prone to cite.[6] Furthermore, the epistemic significance of the Chinese encyclopedia has not been fully explored, although, as chapter 1 indicates, a number of analysts have cited it but ignored its role in Foucault's conception of the Orient.

At first glance, Foucault's view of an insurmountable divide between East and West is baffling, as it appears to be at odds with his political outlook. Indeed, he had been a member of the French Communist Party, even if only for two years. He had taken positions usually associated with the Left on a range of issues such as the rights of immigrants, prisoners in Tunisia as well as France, psychiatric patients, and Polish insurgents against Soviet rule. In retrospect, however, a number of factors indirectly point to the compatibility of Foucault's radical perspective on cultural otherness with his philosophical orientation: for instance, as a "specific intellectual," he carefully picked and chose among the issues of his time rather than availing himself of a universal principle of justice, freedom, or democracy to guide his stance. In explaining Foucault's understanding of his role as an intellectual, Bourdieu pointed out that Foucault wished to avoid being "the moral and political conscience, or the spokesman and entitled advocate (mandataire)"—a stance seen as typical of "the universal intellectual,"[7] as Sartre was. Furthermore, Foucault was critical of the French Left, to some extent justifiably, attributing its failings to Marxism. Informed by the Communist Party's initial support for Stalinism, his interpretation of Marx typically rested on an economic-deterministic viewpoint. Further, he was opposed to socialism in Europe as well as in the Third World societies, such as Vietnam, that had established socialist governments in the aftermath of wars of decolonization.

Whether in Tunisia, Iran, or Japan, Foucault never failed to mention Marx negatively. In Tunisia, he was astonished by the seriousness with which students, rebelling against Bourguiba's dictatorship, took Marx's ideas (which he had deemed obsolete), to the point of risking their lives. He also dismissed their knowledge of Marx. In Iran, he felt he had found a ringing refutation of Marx's conception of religion. Ironically, when faced in Japan with the president of the Socialist Party, who was not keen on cooperating with French socialists, he appealed to the universalistic impetus behind Marx's thought to exhort the president to change his mind. The significance of Foucault's persistent opposition to Marx's philosophical orientation is frequently obscured by his ties to the Gauche Prolétarienne, a Maoist organization founded in 1969, which organized factory workers, considered France an occupied territory, and called for a general people's uprising. Its charismatic leader, Pierre Victor, whose real name was Benny Lévy, ultimately renounced his politics and turned to Orthodox Judaism instead.[8] Victor and Foucault held a long discussion on popular justice, published in *Les Temps Modernes* in 1972.[9] Daniel Defert explained to me that *he* had been a militant of the Gauche Prolétarienne, as well as the initiator of the establishment of the Groupe d'Information sur les Prisons (GIP) to which he had asked Foucault to lend his name because of his notoriety.[10] A consequence of Foucault's opposition to Marx as well as of his on-and-off links to the Left was his embrace of the ideas of the new philosophe, André Glucksmann, as well as his intriguing appreciation of neoliberalism in the years before his death.[11] However, although Foucault was hardly alone in his wholesale criticism of Marx's thought, or his interest in neoliberalism, his dalliances with the Left, when considered together with his critical scholarship, give a surplus meaning to his conception of the Orient. It is not that adoption of historical materialism is a precondition to understanding cultural difference. Rather, opposition to Marx's thought was one aspect of Foucault's broader opposition to humanist philosophy in which Kant's cosmopolitan anthropology plays an essential role. There is no doubt that Foucault's critique of humanist philosophy and the social sciences it informs is valuable. Indeed, humanist philosophy frequently conflates the Western experience with the human experience; it also uses the Western experience as a standard against which to gauge other societies. Foucault's opposition to humanism's universalist claims does not necessarily mean that he could not have used Western rationality as a standard of reference in making sense of non-Western cultures. However, Foucault's critique failed to decenter his own view of humanist philosophy.[12] For experiencing other cultures necessarily brings the human being back to the forefront of understanding himself as a subject of culture.

It is against the backdrop of Foucault's critique of Kant's *Anthropology from a Pragmatic Point of View*[13] early in his career that this book traces the rationale as well as the consequences of Foucault's exclusion of the Orient from the Western *ratio*. It unravels the effects of this exclusion on his understanding of cultural difference as well as his encounters with non-Western cultures. Foucault's Introduction to Kant's *Anthropology* foreshadows the unresolvability of his cultural conundrum as initially expressed in *Folie et déraison*: although posited as the outer limit of the Western *ratio*, the Orient's reason remains unfathomable, and glimpsed only as "different," or "mysterious." Hence what this outside reason actually is, how it relates to the sundered interior of Western reason, is left till the end of his life unexplored as if for fear it might reveal the operation of the very same reason Foucault analyzed so precisely from the inside.

Having argued against Kant's *Anthropology,* did Foucault provide an alternative approach to understanding and explaining cultural difference-qua-Orient in terms other than as a limit-experience? Once Foucault dismissed humanist anthropology as an illusory attempt to understand "man," a creature he assumed to have vanished with the death of God as announced by Nietzsche, could Foucault write or speak about the Orient while dispensing with anthropological assumptions? Parenthetically, Foucault tinkered at times with structuralist anthropology in his study of Western culture. Assuming the posture of the anthropologist,[14] he wished to apply the ethnological method to the history of ideas, thus doing for Western culture what Claude Lévi-Strauss did for preliterate societies. Foucault's ethnological-qua-archaeological posture may have served him well in understanding the history of ideas in Western culture. However, the Orient remained a puzzle as the method so construed when applied to live people and events in non-Western cultures proved to be an obstacle to the intersubjective character of cross-cultural interaction, a necessary condition for comprehending social meaning. Nevertheless, did he ultimately develop an anti- or nonhumanist anthropology? Could there be a nonhumanist anthropology? To what extent did Foucault's view of the Orient as well as his *experience* of non-Western cultures, especially that of Japan, paradoxically reveal a version of the anthropology he had intended to go beyond? When in the "Orient," how did he grapple with the *human* in the culturally different? In other words, did Foucault's view and experience of the Orient–Occident "division" represent the limit(ation) of the anti-humanist and radical nominalist conception of cultural difference? The way in which Foucault expressed his experiences of non-Western cultures cannot be dismissed as mere travel impressions; they were indicative of the manner in which he thought of the Orient. From his perspective, any experience has a thought content. He argued that thought "can and must be analyzed in all the manners of speaking, acting, behaving in which the individual appears and acts as a subject of knowledge, ethics or law, as a subject conscious of himself and of others."[15]

Acknowledging the epistemic role of experience means also considering the interviews Foucault gave about his sojourns in Tunisia, Iran, and Japan as sources of meaningful information about his views of cultural otherness. Some of them were extensive[16] and probed significant questions about Foucault's work. Foucault's interviews provide an opportunity to grasp in concrete terms what his philosophical-theoretical approach often kept abstract; they can hardly be dismissed as irrelevant to understanding his thought. Indeed, Foucault's views of events were rarely ad hominem, but were informed by his philosophical orientation. For example, his pronouncements on Japan were part of lectures as well as recorded interviews with major scholars. They cannot be ignored on the grounds that they were not part of his written corpus. Concerned about the distortions of meaning, especially in translation of interviews whose recordings are not available, as was the case in some instances in Japan, Daniel Defert cautions against the use of interviews in analyzing Foucault's ideas. Raising a legitimate concern, he points out that interviews were generally oral and thus lacked the reflection and nuances that writing affords.[17] The multiple translations to which some of the interviews were subjected should not diminish their documentary value, although allowance must be made for the translations' distorting effects in analyzing them; this can be said of the translations of Foucault's books too. In general, interviews helped to disseminate Foucault's ideas and are a constitutive part of his legacy. Mindful of variations in translations, I cite to the French language texts of Foucault's works and provide corresponding page references in English translations of those works whenever possible.

The book adopts a multidisciplinary approach combining the insights of sociology, especially content analysis, anthropology, as well as the history of ideas. In addition to examining Foucault's written work and interviews he gave about his stays in Tunisia, Iran, and Japan, the book also analyzes supplemental interviews I carried out on his conception of the Orient. In Paris, France, interviews were held with Tunisian scholars who had known Foucault well in 1966–1968, or had been active in the social turmoil of 1967–1968. In Tunis, discussions were held with Zineb Ben Said Cherni, a philosopher who had attended Foucault's philosophy course; Jélila Hafsia, former journalist and cultural host; Sadek Ben Mhenni, a former participant in the students' revolt, as well as Lina Ben Mhenni, a leading figure in the movement that led to the 2011 Revolution. In Japan, meetings took place with several scholars and translators, specifically, Professors Moriaki Watanabe, who helped arrange Foucault's 1970 trip and took part in his 1978 visit as well as introduced Foucault's work to his country; Hidetaka Ishida, Yasuo Kobayashi, and Yasuyuki Shinkai, who translated, among other works, *Dits et écrits*; and the interpreter and organizer of Foucault's 1978 trip, Christian Polak.[18] Finally, an interview as well as phone discussions were held with Foucault's longtime companion, Daniel Defert. Research took place over several years at the Foucault Archives of the IMEC (Institut Mémoires de l'Edition Contemporaine) at St. Germain-la Blanche-Herbe, Caen, Normandy; the Bibliothèque Nationale de France, Richelieu; as well as François Mitterrand sites; and the Bibliothèque Interuniversitaire Sorbonne. At IMEC, during the first trip, the archival journey began with listening to a number of Foucault's recorded radio interviews and lectures given in Paris, Tunis, Tokyo, and Berkeley, among other places. Not having met Foucault in his lifetime, I intended to get a feel for the manner in which he lectured and answered questions. More important, I wished to re-place his statements in their theoretical and methodological context as I searched for the location of non-Western cultures in his theorizing.

Foucault's lifelong work was to lay bare the structure and functions of Western cultural knowledge as a way of studying how and why Western modernity in its manifold manifestations became what it is. However, he did not write a book or lecture on cultural difference at the Collège de France. Therefore, tracing the itinerary of his view of the Orient–Occident divide required placing him in conversation with himself, as well as with the people he met on his trips to non-Western countries. To place him in conversation with himself meant reading his work, at times symptomatically, in conjunction with interviews he gave to the media, his lectures, as well as his conferences. Foucault's *experience* of non-Western cultures forms the empirical site within which his philosophical view of the Orient–Occident divide can be assessed in its temporal and spatial deployment. It provides the advantage of concretizing the meaning of the "empirico-transcendental doublet"[19] he foregrounded in his critique of the "human sciences" in *The Order of Things*. In the world of cultural otherness in which Foucault flung himself, he was in a position to uncouple the "doublet" by suspending the "transcendental" (by which he meant the assumption of a universal human nature) and experimenting with a new way of making sense of cultural diversity. This book further seeks to determine whether he allowed his exposure to non-Western societies to transform his thought as well as methodological practice. What Foucault overlooked is the effect of his view of the Orient not only on the other side of Western rationality (which he left unexamined), but also on himself.[20]

There are variations in tone and character in Foucault's experience of non-Western cultures. Although diverse, the three countries under study have in common a moral geographical location in the Western map of the East (near and far); they also have in common cultural features traditionally interpreted as irremediably non-Western. In Tunisia Foucault mapped ancient Greece onto the local cultural present. Living in the (historical) heterotopia of the village of Sidi Bou Saïd, he missed the part of Tunisian culture that hid behind its French veneer. Tunisian culture formed a blank in Foucault's imagination. In Iran, Foucault felt freer to explore the local culture by delving into the significance of Shi'i Islam to explain the resistance and risk taking the anti-shah protesters exhibited. In Japan, he experienced the palpable "limit" of the Orient–Occident divide. However, unlike Western philosophers before him, or social scientists who sought to rewrite Japanese thought and culture, he remained consistent with his schematic view of the Orient. Moreover, in Japan his experience compelled him to acknowledge that he needed to deepen his understanding of the culture. However, this apparent effort to make "a history of this great divide," which he hinted at in the preface to *Folie et déraison,* remained unfulfilled. Hence the "enigma" of Japanese culture was left unraveled.

The difficulties Foucault experienced in grasping the cultures of Japan, Tunisia, or Iran during his sojourns reflect his reluctance to overcome the epistemic divide he created between the West and the Orient. He consistently stressed cultural differences using Western culture, deemed uniform, as a standard of reference. This does not necessarily mean that he was convinced of a presumed superiority of Western culture. Rather, the West was a constant frame of reference and this iterated reference, when combined with what he said about non-Western cultures, calls into question his oft-asserted opposition to the universalist claims of humanist thought. If in Japan he expressed an unmitigated estrangement, in Iran, where he traveled after he had been in Japan, he strenuously attempted to bridge the divide between East and West conceptually. In defending his interpretation of the Iranian Revolution against his critics, he defined it as a special case of past protest movements in Europe, including the French Revolution, all of which were moved by a "political spirituality." However, his idealist conception of Shi'ism excluded considerations of social class (a fact Foucault acknowledged retrospectively), social inequality, and material needs at the roots of the Iranian movement and its evolution.[21]

Foucault's forays into the Orient, near and far, may not have answered the Kantian question "What is Man?," which he had once pondered. They nevertheless led him to revisit identifiers of Western specificity, such as "revolution" and "colonization." They further enabled him to sharpen the relationship he had established between religion (whether Christianity, Islam, or Buddhism), the self, the body, and action. Paradoxically, of these identifiers, "colonization," or the absence of it, emerges as the criterion of the limit as well as the mark of Western universalism. Foucault saw Japan, for example, as having escaped colonization but having the potential of "colonizing" Western thought. Hence, colonization remains the grid through which to assess the intellectual weight of a non-Western society. He could claim, for instance, that noncolonized Japan might be the crucible of a solution to the crisis of Western philosophy. Similarly, he viewed Iran, which avoided direct colonization, as a harbinger of new "spirituality movements" in the world. Ironically, colonization, a universal feature of Western rationality, does not make the culture of a formerly colonized country any more understandable than one that escaped colonization. This ambiguous stance sheds light on Foucault's search for precolonial, purportedly well-preserved, Greek sexual practices of gay Tunisian men—a sign that Foucault was on a quest for re-experiencing Western cultural practices in a non-Western milieu. Language, an important part of Foucault's archaeological method, figures prominently in his categorization of the Orient as a "limit-experience." Foucault spoke none of the native languages in the countries he lived in or visited. In Tunisia he communicated in French with the literate public of the university, but had no knowledge of Arabic, the language of the common person outside of Tunis. He did not speak Japanese and had to rely on interpreters as well as a small number of scholars who spoke French. Yet he did not discuss the role played by his lack of knowledge of Japanese in his feeling of estrangement in Japan. This is all the more intriguing given that Foucault keenly analyzed the sense of emotional isolation he experienced in Sweden as he found himself cut off from effective verbal communication with his entourage.[22] Throughout, the language he used creates cultural unease. His frequent references to the possessive "our" (civilization or culture) and the personal pronouns "we" and "us" run as a leading thread through his work and encounters with his non-Western interlocutors. Their iteration, necessary in some circumstances, nevertheless has the effect of overburdening his discussions of (the Western) cultural difference. At times, it turns it into a symbolic bludgeon wielded against the reader, or a barrier to exploring the outer limit of the Western *ratio*.

Although it focuses on Foucault's view of the Orient, this book does not characterize him as an orientalist. Claims that Foucault was an orientalist have been made before and there are indications in Foucault's work that clearly support it.[23] Foucault's thought was contemporaneous with that of Edward Said, whose treatise on orientalism appeared the year Foucault was occupied with the Iranian Revolution.[24] However, it is a peculiar consequence of Foucault's view of cultural difference that he had no political, economic, or ideological investment in the East as defined by Edward Said.[25] Indeed, it is difficult to reconcile Foucault's stance before Tunisia's youth rebellion of 1967–1968, or Iran's upheaval with any such investment. Foucault was critical of Western culture, albeit very well ensconced in it, and ultimately unable to rise above it. Furthermore, he did not write books or essays on the "Orient." This opens up a fruitful line of inquiry into his conception of the Orient focused on the nature and consistency of his epistemology, as well as the significance of his critique of the human sciences for cross-cultural understanding. In this sense, Foucault's Orient is the other side of his definition of the Occident; it is one and the same thing. Indeed, minutely describing and analyzing the specificity of Occidental thought is a way of restricting the domain of its similarity with Oriental thought, and what's more implicitly delegitimizing what is not the Occident. This book also departs from postcolonial studies, which seek to document instances of orientalism. Instead, it focuses on the unintended consequences of an anti-humanist approach to culture.

The following chapters hew to an intellectual rather than a chronological order. Thus, the chapter on Tunisia, the first non-Western country in which Foucault lived, is placed after the chapter on Iran, the second country Foucault visited. This order of presentation is meant to highlight the atemporal character of Foucault's cultural conundrum, thereby foregrounding its epistemic constancy. The chapters trace the sources and evolution of Foucault's view of the "Orient" as articulated in his philosophical-theoretical orientation and expressed in his experiences of other cultures. The first chapter examines Foucault's first cultural challenge: the analysis of Borges's Chinese encyclopedia in the preface to *The Order of Things*. It identifies the manner in which Foucault's treatment of Chinese culture frames his experiences of the cultures of Japan, Iran, and Tunisia. The second chapter locates Foucault's philosophical understanding of difference/otherness *within* Western rationalism in his critique of René Descartes's hyperbole of madness in his *Meditations of the First Philosophy*. Did Foucault's critique of Cartesian rationalism address cultural difference of the kind he encountered in the "Orient?" The third chapter builds on the previous chapters to identify the anthropological implications of Foucault's attitude toward cultural difference as mediated by his interpretation of Kant's *Anthropology from a Pragmatic Point of View*. The fourth chapter asks whether there is an anthropology that informs Foucault's view of the Orient. It compares Foucault's critique of anthropology as mediated by the concepts of culture and race to anthropologists' views of their discipline. The fifth chapter assesses the empirical challenge of the Iranian Revolution, which Foucault's antihumanist orientation faced. It helps to determine whether Foucault had an alternative anthropology to existing empirical anthropology. It documents Foucault's awareness of the limitations of his methodological approach, as well as his decision not to rethink his conception of cultural difference. The sixth chapter, devoted to Foucault's two-year stay in Tunisia, points to Foucault's silence on colonialism while he lived in the sheltered and idyllic community of Sidi Bou Saïd. What is the significance of Foucault's search for traces of ancient Greece in Tunisia even as he witnessed a students' revolt to which he provided some support? The seventh and eighth chapters focus on the place of Japanese culture in Foucault's conception of cultural difference and the struggles he experienced in attempting to come to terms with it. Both chapters highlight the contradictions inherent in Foucault's opposition to cosmopolitan anthropology yet reliance on anthropological assumptions.

A complicating factor in addressing Foucault's view of the Orient is the existence of a trend, at times acquiring cultist features, that implicitly defines the outer limits of the discourse on Foucault, and to a large extent contains its criticism.[26] This is no doubt an effect of the remarkable expansion of Foucault's thought since he died in 1984. The exponential increase in the dissemination of Foucault's work was aided by the publication of *Dits et écrits*,[27] as well as the lectures at the Collège de France in book form. It has further benefited from translations, films, and French intellectuals' active promotion of Foucault's legacy.[28] The phenomenal currency of Foucault's ideas is testimony to their richness and insightfulness.[29] However, in the wake of this success orthodoxical practices set in, even though Foucault's thought, often contradictory, ambiguous, and elusive, resists fixing.[30] The following pages are a modest contribution to the task of examining what Foucault has left in the shadows. Their ambition is to open up a space in which a productive critical analysis of Foucault's enduring legacy can occur.

On a final note, although this book refers mostly to anthropology, it does not exclude sociology. On the contrary, many of the issues and institutions Foucault analyzed, such as the clinic, the prison, mental illness, power, or the construction of knowledge, among others, are eminently sociological. Furthermore, in many instances, his analyses of these issues are similar to those availing in sociology. Hence, the focus on anthropology in this book is an imperative dictated by the subject matter rather than a deliberate choice, as Foucault considered this discipline the foundation of the human sciences.

NOTES

1. Michel Foucault, "Les 'reportages' d'idées," in *Dits et écrits,* ed. François Ewald, Daniel Defert, and Jacques Lagrange, vol. 2 (Paris: Gallimard, Quarto, 2001), 707.
2. Michel Foucault, *Folie et déraison. Histoire de la folie à l'âge classique* (Paris: Plon, 1961).
3. Daniel Defert specifies that only the Italian translation of 1963 was based on the original book. Daniel Defert, "Chronologie," in *Dits et écrits,* by Michel Foucault, ed. François Ewald, Daniel Defert, and Jacques Lagrange, vol. 1 (Paris: Gallimard, Quarto, 2001), 33. Defert notes Foucault's disappointment with Plon, his publisher of the 1964 edition of the book, which refused to publish an unabridged version. Ibid. For a brief chronology of the various versions of the book under different titles (essentially permutations on the original title), see Ian Hacking, "Foreword," in *History of Madness,* by Michel Foucault, ed. Jean Khalfa, trans. Jonathan Murphy and Jean Khalfa (London: Routledge, 2009), ix–xii.
4. Michel Foucault, *History of Madness,* ed. Jean Khalfa, trans. Jean Khalfa and Jonathan Murphy (London: Routledge, 2009). The hardcover edition of this translation appeared in 2006.
5. Georges Canguilhem, "Mort de l'homme ou épuisement du cogito," *Critique* 242 (July 1967): 600. Canguilhem borrowed the term *espagnolisme* from Henri Brulard, and notes that for Stendhal it meant "hatred of preaching and platitudes," which he believes captures Foucault's "turn of mind." Ibid. Canguilhem's review article appears in translation as "The Death of Man or the Ex-

haustion of the Cogito," in *The Cambridge Companion to Foucault*, 2nd Edition, ed. Gary Gutting (Cambridge: Cambridge University Press, 2003), 74–94.
6. According to Macey, Foucault's interest in (modernist) literature as expressed in references he made in his work as well as comments on literary figures appears to have become less pronounced after 1966, when he wrote a homage to Blanchot. David Macey, *The Lives of Michel Foucault: A Biography* (New York: Vintage Books, 1993), 181.
7. Pierre Bourdieu, "Le plaisir du savoir," *Le Monde*, 27 June 1984. This quotation was part of a statement Bourdieu made on Foucault's death in 1984.
8. See Didier Eribon, *Michel Foucault*, trans. Betsy Wang (Cambridge, MA: Harvard University Press, 1991), 242–43. Pierre Victor became Sartre's secretary beginning in 1973, when the Gauche Prolétarienne disbanded, and had by some accounts an undue influence on Sartre in his waning years.
9. Ibid., 243.
10. Daniel Defert, Interview, Paris, 2 June 2014.
11. There is a growing literature on this point. See, for example, Daniel Zamora, ed., *Critiquer Foucault: Les années 1980 et la tentation néolibérale* (Brussels: Aden, 2014), 87–113; Michael C. Behrent, "Liberalism without Humanism: Michel Foucault and Free-Market Creed, 1976–1979," *Modern Intellectual History* 6, no. 3 (November 2009): 539–68. On Foucault and Glucksmann see Michael Scott Christofferson, *French Intellectuals against the Left: The Antitotalitarian Moment of the 1970s* (New York: Berghahn Books, 2004).
12. Axel Honneth suggests that Foucault did not replace a "monological" view of humanist philosophy with a "dialogical" view. *The Critique of Power: Reflective Stages in a Critical Social Theory* (Cambridge, MA: MIT Press, 1991), 120.
13. Immanuel Kant, *Anthropology from a Pragmatic Point of View*. With an Introduction by Manfred Kuehn, trans. Robert B. Louden (Cambridge: Cambridge University Press, 2009). Translated into French by Michel Foucault as E. Kant, introduced by D. Defert, Fr. Ewald, and F. Gros, *Anthropologie du point de vue pragmatique précédé de Michel Foucault, Introduction à l'anthropologie de Kant* (Paris: Vrin, 2009).
14. Michel Foucault, "Qui êtes-vous professeur Foucault?," in *Dits et écrits*, vol. 1, 633.
15. Michel Foucault, "Préface à l'histoire de la sexualité," in *Dits et écrits*, vol. 2, 1398–99. Translated as Michel Foucault, "Preface to the History of Sexuality, Vol. II," in *The Foucault Reader*, ed. Paul Rabinow (New York: Pantheon Books, 1984).
16. For example, the interview with Duccio Trombadori is an excellent text that clarifies Foucault's views on a number of issues he had addressed in his books and travels. See Michel Foucault, *Remarks on Marx: Conversations with Duccio Trombadori*, trans. James Goldstein and James Cascaito (New York: Semiotext(e), 1991).
17. Defert worried about researchers giving more weight to interviews at the expense of Foucault's books and lectures at the Collège de France. Defert, Interview, Paris, 2 June 2014.
18. Polak translated discussions Foucault had with bonzes at the Seionji Temple.
19. Michel Foucault, *The Order of Things: An Archaeology of the Human Sciences* (New York: Vintage Books, 1994), 318.

20. Tunisia does not escape the Orient categorization despite being strenuously presented by the media as virtually Western.
21. Michel Foucault, "L'esprit d'un monde sans esprit," in *Dits et écrits,* vol. 2, 743–55. Interview with Claire Brière and Pierre Blanchet in their book, *Iran, la révolution au nom de Dieu* (Paris: Seuil, 1979), 744.
22. See Michel Foucault, *Le beau danger: entretien avec Claude Bonnefoy* (Paris: Éditions de l'EHESS, 2011).
23. Ian Almond, *The New Orientalists: Postmodern Representations of Islam from Foucault to Baudrillard* (London: IB Tauris, 2007). Almond attributes Foucault's orientalism to his idealization of a mix of spiritual fervor and political commitment he had never witnessed before he went to Tunisia and Iran, but seemed to him to be an enduring part of Islamic history. Ibid., 35–40. See also Jon Solomon, "The Experience of Culture: Eurocentric Limits and Openings in Foucault," *Transeuropéennes* 1, 1 (2010), accessed 10 March 2015, http://www.transeuropéennes/eu/en/articles/108. Solomon perceives Foucault's reports on Iran as a "breathtaking capitulation to Orientalism," Ibid., 4. See also Hidetaka Ishida, "De l'orientalisme? Du 'Japon' comme lieu de discours sur le langage, le sens et l'art," lecture given at the University of Vincennes-Saint-Denis (26 March 1996). I thank Dr. Ishida for sharing this text with me.
24. In his diary, Said recalls meeting Foucault at his apartment in Paris in March, 1979. Edward Said, "Diary," *London Review of Books* 22, no. 11, 1 June 2000, accessed 23 April 2017 from http://www.lrb.co.uk/v22/n11/edward-said/diary.
25. Edward W. Said, *Orientalism* (New York: Vintage Books, 1978).
26. At a conference sponsored by CERI-Sciences Po, in Paris, in 13–14 January 2014, one panel decried the adulation of Foucault as well as the use of his concepts as contexts unto themselves.
27. *Dits et écrits,* edited by Daniel Defert and François Ewald with the collaboration of Jacques Lagrange, is a collection of the articles, reviews, and interviews, at home and abroad, that had been published when Foucault was still alive. In French it exists in a four-volume, or two-volume (quarto) format at Gallimard.
28. In 2012, the French government engaged in a sort of nationalization of Foucault's thought by declaring his manuscripts "national treasure." See Marie Odile Germain, "Michel Foucault de retour à la BNF," *Chroniques de la Bibliothèque Nationale de France* 70 (April–June 2014): 26–27. *Chroniques* is the Library's newsletter.
29. The acquisition in 2014 by the Bibliothèque Nationale de France of 37,000 pages of reading notes, lectures, and drafts of some of his books will further broaden interest in his work.
30. Alain Brossat's barely contained anger at critics of Foucault's "Occidentalism" is an example of this trend. Alain Brossat, "Quand Foucault dit 'nous'…," *Revue Appareil* no. 8 (2011), accessed 26 January 2011, http://revues.mshparisnord.org/appareil/index.php?id=1265.

Chapter 1

The Chinese Encyclopedia and the Challenge of Difference

> "Je rêve d'un Borges chinois qui citerait, pour amuser ses lecteurs, le programme d'une classe de philosophie en France ... Mais nous devons nous garder d'en rire."
> —Michel Foucault, "Le piège de Vincennes," in *Dits et écrits**

FOUCAULT ENCOUNTERS THE "CHINESE ENCYCLOPEDIA"

To trace Foucault's view of the "Orient" is tantamount to doing an archeology of silence. Foucault did not devote any significant space to the Orient in his work. However, his conception of an originary division between the Orient and the Occident in the Western *ratio* laid out in the 1961 preface to *Folie et déraison* (*History of Madness*) frames his general perception of non-Western cultures. His suppression of the preface hardly meant he abandoned his view, as his discussion of the "Chinese encyclopedia" in the preface to *Les mots et les choses* (*The Order of Things*) makes clear. In fact, this other preface, five years after the preceding one, provides a concrete analysis of the Orient–Occident cultural difference focused on China. It further reveals in all its starkness the radical otherness Foucault contrived out of a fictitious text *in order* to study Western rationality.

In starting with the preface to *Les mots et les choses,* instead of *Folie et déraison,* this chapter adopts a regressive method in order to examine step-by-step Foucault's construction of the Oriental cultural difference in his discussion of the Chinese encyclopedia. Contextualizing the encyclopedia, this chapter explores its history, its layered meaning, as well as its consequences for

Foucault's conception of the Orient. In the preface to *Les mots et les choses* Foucault reveals that the book "was born out of a text" in which Jorge Luis Borges cites "a certain Chinese encyclopedia' in which it is written that 'animals are divided into: (a) belonging to the Emperor; (b) embalmed; (c) tame; (d) suckling pigs; (e) sirens; (f) fabulous; (g) stray dogs; (h) included in the present classification; (i) crazed-looking; (j) innumerable; (k) drawn with a fine camel hair brush; (l) et cetera; (m) having just broken the water pitcher; (n) that from afar look like flies."[1]

Foucault laughs irrepressibly at the wondrous bizarreness of the taxonomy, but not without feeling uneasy. He ponders this laughter that shakes *us* (Western readers) up due to the unfamiliarity of the Chinese taxonomy, and unsettles *our* age-old conception of the relationship between the "Same and the Other," the ordering of similarities and differences in the world. He notes that the marvelous quaintness of the taxonomy and its "exotic charm" are insufficient reasons to accept the taxonomy on its own terms. It represents "the limit of our [thought]; the stark impossibility of thinking it."[2]

However, questioning his disbelief, Foucault attempts to understand the taxonomy as it stands. Indeed, why is it impossible, he asks, for a Western man to "think" such taxonomy? What makes thinking it impossible? After all, each category has a precise meaning, and even those that refer to "fabulous" animals are clearly distinguished as imaginary and given a separate categorical space from real animals. Hence, the taxonomy appears to have a logic of its own insofar as it does not mix together creatures that are different from one another. More important, Foucault notes that the category of the "fabulous" does not contain those phantasmagorical and monstrous cross-species creatures spewing flames, living on earth and in water, with squamous flesh and contorted faces that crowd the tales we may be familiar with. What accounts for the impossibility of "thinking" the Chinese taxonomy is "the close distance" it allows and the juxtaposition it establishes between the "fabulous" animals and "stray dogs," or animals that "from a distance look like flies."[3] This juxtaposition of the category of the imaginary with the category of the real, a real described in ways that we are not accustomed to, defies "all imagination, all possible thought." The juxtaposition takes the form of "the series a, b, c, d which links each of these categories to all the others."[4] On the one hand, Foucault is perturbed by the close proximity of "things that have no relation to one another"; on the other hand, he notes that the contents of the categories "lack a common space where [the things enumerated] could meet (l'espace commun des rencontres)."[5] In other words, there is no identifiable foundation for the establishment of the series a, b, c, d. There are no criteria for the inclusion or exclusion of some creatures in one category or another. More important, the very possibility of such a foundation "is ruined." Hence, the impossibility of thinking the Chinese classification as cited by Borges does *not* lie, as Foucault had stated earlier, in the "proximity of things" such as animals that are "i) crazed-looking, j) innumerable, h) drawn with a very fine camelhair brush."[6] Rather, what is impossible to fathom is "the very site where they could be juxtaposed." The only site where they apparently meet is the "non-space of language" as spoken by the "immaterial voice of the enumerator, or the page on which they are transcribed." From Foucault's perspective, what is lacking in the (purportedly) Chinese taxonomy that would make it comprehensible is "the operating table"[7] that supports the categories just like a regular table would support various objects regardless of their shapes, forms, or functions, such as an umbrella and a typewriter, at any or all times; and the table normally used in systems of classification to order, distinguish, and group things in terms of their differences and similarities. On this table, "time and space have always intersected."[8] Implicitly, without this table, the Chinese taxonomy has content without a container, and thus the content as enumerated is laughable in its lack of an order that "our" mind is accustomed to.

Foucault's "definite uneasiness" that nagged at him stemmed from his suspicion of a far more ominous problem than the absurdity of the Chinese categories and the *incongruity* of their classification: the disorder that would reign over a multitude of possible orders arising out of a world of heterogeneity that lends itself neither to "laws, nor to geometrical logic." The Chinese encyclopedia, with its missing table, gives an inkling of a different "order" of enumerations occurring every which way, offering no possibility of making out their common location. Such disordered enumerations belong in the domain of "heterotopias,"[9] which undermine the capacity of language to name things and relate words to things worded since heterotopias create syntactic havoc by preventing adequate naming, especially naming common names.[10] Under Borges's pen, heterotopias render language sterile and arid as grammar becomes impossible to apply, and words are locked into themselves and their relation to things disallowed. As Foucault examines in depth the linguistic implications of the taxonomy, he implicates Borges's style of thought rather than the national-cultural origin attributed to the taxonomy. He fudges the reality of the Chinese encyclopedia as he shuttles back and forth between characterizing the enumeration and addressing Borges's description of it. It is not until he examines the impact of the enumeration on language that Foucault implicitly refers to Borges as the author of the taxonomy (not just the author of the citation). By then, he had already analyzed the encyclopedia as a stand-alone text. The distortions of language and logic, and the lack of an operating table, which Foucault had identified, are clearly and explicitly stated as being Borges's. Foucault's method creates an ambiguity that enables him to subject the encyclopedia to criticism (as if it were real), and invoke Borges as paradoxically the man who reported it, and who authored it. Reality and fiction merge.

Foucault asks an important question: why did Borges choose China as the site of the impossibility of thinking the taxonomy? In answer to the question, Foucault reminds himself that China holds a specific place in the Western imagination; it is a large space, one that lends itself to mythical elaborations with its strange handwriting running vertically, its historical sense of order and hierarchy, its long walls and dams and irrigation systems, among others. Although historically selective in its appreciation,[11] Foucault's description serves his method of presentation: Borges's choice of China as the "mythic homeland"[12] offers a *cultural* example (even if fictitious) fundamentally opposite the specificity of Western thought in reading, capturing as well as constructing order in the natural and social world.

However, Foucault's view of China largely contrasts with Borges's, even though both authors use the "Orient" as a trope. Foucault emphasizes space as a defining characteristic of China, yet concludes that "the Chinese encyclopedia cited by Borges and the taxonomy that it proposes lead to a thought without space, words and categories without life or place, but which in reality rest on a solemn space ...; at the other end of the planet we inhabit, there would thus be a culture entirely devoted to the ordering of space, but which would not distribute the proliferation of beings in any one of the spaces which make it possible for us to name, speak and think."[13] Foucault's assessment leaves unexplained how Borges (to whom he addresses his comment) had transformed the existence of presumably infinite space that is central to the (Western) imagination of China into a taxonomy in which space between categories essentially shrinks and the space (read the operating table) that holds the categories together disappears.

Foucault's paradoxical analysis of Chinese space as being expansive yet bounded,[14] its reduction in the encyclopedia to "close distance" between categories of animals, or their "juxtaposition," lends itself to three interpretations: first, he understood the Chinese encyclopedia as Borges's way of upsetting the Western imagination of China of an ordered and vast space. Second, Borges simply compounded the imaginary notion of China as a space "overladen with complex figures, tangled paths, strange sites, secret passages, and unexpected connections"[15] by presenting an equally strange taxonomy with bewildering categories and relations between them. Presumably, the imagination that created China as a land of utopias could only produce in Borges's mind a heightened version of utopia as the site of the absurd taxonomy, a heterotopia. Third, Foucault may have found Borges's taxonomy attractive for epistemological reasons, and contrived to accept it even though it is, at first glance, at odds with his own interpretation of China's place in the West's ("our") imaginary. I favor the latter interpretation as it gives an inkling of the manner in which Foucault thought about the relationship between culture and order as well as the practice of ordering.

The purpose of the book *Les mots et les choses* is to analyze the "naked experience of order and of its modalities,"[16] that is to say, the level of experience that has not yet been incorporated or captured by formal categories or operating tables. And that seems to be the experience of which Borges's Chinese encyclopedia had provided a glimpse by pointing to a taxonomy that defied Western understanding of codification, which orders the proliferation of beings in the empirical world. What is at work in this taxonomy is the unfolding of an ordering activity confronted with a multiplicity of dogs, pigs, and other beings perceived not in their animal genus but in their behavioral appearances or their artistic (not rational) representation.

To reiterate, throughout his discussion of the taxonomy, Foucault alternately refers to it as "a Chinese encyclopedia,"[17] "Borges's text,"[18] "the monstrosity that Borges disseminates through his enumeration."[19] All these modes of reference except one ground the taxonomy in Borges's work. The authorship of the taxonomy floats from the generic "Chinese" to the real person of Borges, his style, his text, our "reading" of *him*.[20] To make sense of Foucault's use of the purportedly Chinese encyclopedia, his discursive fudging of its status as real or a literary device, requires examining Borges's text.

BORGES AND THE "CHINESE ENCYCLOPEDIA"

Jorge Luis Borges wrote an essay, "El idioma analítico de John Wilkins," translated as "John Wilkins's Analytical Language," which appeared in the Argentine newspaper, *La Nación,* on 8 February 1942, and was translated several times in English. Borges notes that the Fourteenth Encyclopedia Britannica did not include an entry ("an article") on John Wilkins, an unconventional and innovative thinker who wrote about issues as diverse as "theology, cryptography, music, the manufacture of transparent beehives, the course of an invisible planet, the possibility of a trip to the moon, the possibility and principles of a world language."[21] Wilkins was born in 1614 and died in 1672; in his lifetime he had held a number of positions including that of bishop of Chester, warden of Wadham College at Oxford University, and first secretary of the Royal Society of London. Borges felt that the omission of an article (not just a cryptic biographical entry that had been planned) on Wilkins was "an error" since it failed to consider Wilkins's "speculative works." Borges focuses on Wilkins's project, started about 1664, to develop a new universal language in which each word would define itself. The idea of a new universal language had already been discussed by Descartes in a 20 November 1629 letter to his friend, Marin Mersenne, who had communicated six propositions for testing such a language by a third party.[22] Descartes suggested that a universal language would have to be governed by ease of use, clarity, and order: "all the thoughts which can come into the human mind must be arranged in an order like the natural order of numbers. In a single day one can learn to name every one of the infinite series of numbers, and thus to write infinitely many different words in an unknown language. The same could be done of all the other words necessary to express all the other things which fall within the purview of the human mind."[23] If this were possible, the new language would appeal to people who would "willingly spend five or six days to make themselves understood by the whole human race."[24] Such a language would put an end to cumbersome grammar and confused meanings of words; it would also have the added advantage of bringing about social leveling by "enabling peasants to be better judges of the truth of things than philosophers do now."[25] Seeking to emphasize the importance of Wilkins's task, Borges notes that every year, in spite of its singing the praise of the Spanish language, the Royal Spanish Academy deems it necessary to edit a dictionary that defines terms. Yet, in Wilkins's universal language, "each word defines itself," which makes a yearly dictionary redundant. However, the method used by Wilkins in devising a universal language was bewildering, albeit not arbitrary.[26] It is this method that retains Borges's attention: "He divided the universe into forty categories or classes, which were subdivided into differences, and subdivided in turn into species. To each class he assigned a monosyllable of two letters; to each difference, a consonant; to each species, a vowel. For example: *de,* means element; *deb,* the first of the elements, fire; *deba,* a portion of the element of fire, a flame." Borges examines the "value" that Wilkins attached to the classes (or genera), and concludes that they are ambiguous, redundant, and deficient: "Let's consider the eighth category, stones. Wilkins divides them into common (flint, gravel, slate), moderate (marble, amber, coral), precious (pearl, opal), transparent (amethyst, sapphire) and insoluble (coal, fuller's earth and arsenic). The ninth category is almost as alarming as the eighth. It reveals that metals can be imperfect (vermillion, quick-silver), artificial (bronze, brass), recremental (filings, rust) and natural (gold, tin, copper). The whale appears in the sixteenth category; it is a viviparous oblong fish."[27] This surprising taxonomy *reminds* Borges of an equally flawed taxonomy "which Doctor Franz Kuhn[28] attributes to a certain Chinese encyclopedia entitled *The Celestial Emporium of Benevolent Knowledge.*"[29] Borges proceeds to reproduce the taxonomy, which Foucault took as his point of departure in the preface to the *Order of Things*.³⁰ He further notes that The Bibliographic Institute of Brussels creates its own taxonomic "chaos," not so different from Dr. Kuhn's purportedly Chinese encyclopedia. "[I]t has parceled the universe into 1000 subdivisions, of which number 262 corresponds to the Pope; number 282 to the Roman Catholic Church; number 263 to the Lord's Day; number 268 to Sunday schools; number 298 to Mormonism; and number 294 to Brahmanism, Buddhism, Shintoism and Taoism. Nor does it disdain the employment of heterogeneous subdivisions, for example, number 179: 'Cruelty to animals. Protection of Animals. Dueling and suicide from a moral point of view. Various vices and defects. Various virtues and qualities.'" Borges concludes that "there is no classification of the universe that is not arbitrary and speculative."³¹

Borges does not only question the arbitrariness of the conceptual system that seeks to order the universe. He attributes its heterogeneity and absence of motivated order to our lack of knowledge of what the universe is. He radically doubts the very existence of a universe as such that is amenable to ordering: "we suspect that there is no universe in the organic, unifying sense of that ambitious word. If there is, we must speculate on its purpose; we must speculate on the words, definitions, etymologies, and synonymies of God's secret dictionary."³² Nevertheless, Borges returns to Wilkins's analytical language and finds that even though its categories are contradictory and "vague," it still is admirable, for "the artifice using *letters* [emphasis added] of the words to indicate divisions and subdivisions is undoubtedly ingenious. The word *salmon* tells us nothing; *zana,* the corresponding word, defines (for the person versed in the forty categories and the classes) a scaly river fish with reddish flesh. (Theoretically, a language in which the name of each thing says all the details of its destiny, past and future, is not inconceivable)."³³

Borges's conclusion, which I have quoted at length, reveals his nuanced understanding of attempts at making sense of the world, of an intractable and ultimately unknowable universe whose origin, existence, and purpose elude humans' grasp. Setting aside Borges's invocation of a divine design behind the complexity of the universe, his discussion points to a number of important aspects of classification schemes, regardless of the culture or nationality of their authors: they are ambiguous; arbitrary; assume a knowable world whose purpose can be ascertained; and may be ingenious. Classifications should make us think about the shortcomings of existing languages and of the possibility of a *new language* in which words would explain themselves, and do not impoverish their referents. Furthermore, it is noteworthy that Borges does not mention the word "order" in identifying the shortcomings of classification schemes. Perhaps even more important for this chapter, Borges unambiguously leaves open the possibility that Dr. Kuhn's "Chinese encyclopedia," may not be real (which it was not). He specifies that it is "unknown (or apocryphal)." Indeed, it may be the product of Dr. Kuhn's imagination and thus would be one more (Western) arbitrary and chaotic enumeration of the universe on a par with that of the Bibliographic Institute of Brussels and John Wilkins. In this, Dr. Kuhn, a real man, is the bearer of Borges's encyclopedic myth.

FOUCAULT'S OWN CHINESE ENCYCLOPEDIA

Borges is known for his invention of facts, which he treated in a scholarly form, with quotation marks and references so as to look authentic. That Foucault knew of Borges's literary devices and forms needs not be doubted. Besides, Foucault wrote about the significance of Borges's innovative thought on several occasions. However, Foucault's selection of this taxonomy and not that of Wilkins or The Bibliographic Institute of Brussels as an entry point into *Les mots et les choses* requires elucidation, as does the manner in which he evaluates the encyclopedia. Foucault's silence on Wilkins prompted Sidonie Clauss in an article on John Wilkins to argue that this omission was not accidental. She points out that Foucault's concern for language alone would have made it necessary for him to at least mention Wilkins's linguistic work. Besides, as indicated, Descartes, whom Foucault grappled with, had toyed with the idea of a universal language, the subject of Wilkins' book—another reason for Foucault to mention Wilkins. Clauss suggests that the omission of Wilkins's work on language casts doubt on the validity of Foucault's conclusion that the Classical Age witnessed a "tightly knit unity of language" in which "resemblance" emerges.[34] Indeed, Wilkins's *Essay* was a significant (albeit frequently ignored) attempt to confront the "limits of language."[35] Clauss intimates that Foucault's conception of language had uncanny similarities with Wilkins's, yet Foucault ignored Wilkins but turned to eighteenth-century authors such as Adam Smith or Rousseau for support for his partial construction of the seventeenth-century quandary about language.[36]

I cannot engage in the controversy simmering in Clauss's article no matter how legitimate. Nevertheless, Foucault's selection of the Chinese encyclopedia taxonomy at the exclusion of other equally problematic Western encyclopedic attempts is intriguing. What is more, as I pointed out above, Foucault neither identifies the specific location of the taxonomy he cites, nor the original source, Dr. Kuhn, of the purportedly Chinese encyclopedia. Yet, the validity of his (as it were comparative) perspective regarding the specificity of Western taxonomy, the heart of *The Order of Things*, rested on the identification. Hence Foucault gives no indication that the reality of the encyclopedia mattered. His attitude raises at least one serious question: what consideration, epistemic or scientific, motivated Foucault's selection of the Chinese encyclopedia?

To return to Wilkins's taxonomy, why would flint, gravel, and slate be classified as "common" while diamonds are excluded from the category of precious stones? Why would coral (produced in water), amber (resin produced by trees), and marble (found in quarries in the earth) be placed in the same category? Isn't the juxtaposition of heterogeneous stones as befuddling as that of dogs in the Chinese encyclopedia? Similarly, why would the Bibliographic Institute divide the universe into, among others, the Pope, Sunday schools, cruelty to animals, or the moral implications of dueling and suicide? What is the logic that ties all these categories together? Where is the "operating table," which Foucault looked for when analyzing the Chinese taxonomy? In this context would the Chinese encyclopedia still offer a more fertile ground for absurdity? Isn't there a greater variation within Western thought of unsettling taxonomies than there is between the Chinese encyclopedia and the taxonomies Foucault studies as the mark of Western rationality?

Foucault's silence on the classification of the Bibliographic Institute of Brussels is less intriguing than his silence on Wilkins's *Essay*. Admittedly, the division of the world into one thousand categories designated by numbers elaborated by the Institute grappled with the application of a (rational) decimal system of categorization in the nineteenth century, not in the Classical Age, the focus of Foucault's analysis in *Les mots et le choses*.[37] Arguably, Paul Otlet, one of the two founders of the Institute, was engaged in the classification of all *knowledge* of the world (whether emanating from the natural or social sciences) rather than the classification of beings and things in the world. Therefore, there was no apparently compelling reason for Foucault to focus on the Institute's classification. But then again, it is germane to Foucault's endeavor to uncover the process of construction of the natural sciences as they intersect with the social sciences. Categorizing knowledge is intimately linked to categorizing the universe.

All three taxonomies described by Borges lack coherence.[38] Yet, one was produced by a seventeenth-century Englishman, not a (dubious) Chinese encyclopedist of an unspecified imperial era. At first glance, it is Wilkins's taxonomy that would have been more appropriate for Foucault to discuss, for two reasons: Foucault's analysis of the construction of the method of representing order in the world starts with the sixteenth century, and thus includes the seventeenth. The inclusion of both Wilkins's as well as the purportedly Chinese taxonomy in Foucault's discussion would have explained how heterogeneous "Western" attempts at creating order shed light not only on the discontinuities in rational/scientific thought, but also on their similarities across cultures and history. It is noteworthy that Foucault went to great lengths to explain why Borges focused on China, but remained oblivious to the context within which Borges did so.

Supposing that Foucault's omission of Wilkins meant that he wished to focus primarily on French figures of the Classical Age, his selection of Rabelais's fiction poses a problem. Foucault counterposes a bizarre enumeration made by Rabelais's character Eusthènes, a companion of Pantagruel, the hero of *Gargantua et Pantagruel*, known for his outlandish behavior and language. In the enumeration, worms, snakes, spiders, putrefied and viscous creatures, as well as hemorrhoids, swarm in contiguity to one another.[39] Foucault acknowledges the bizarreness of the enumeration, which is comparable to the Chinese encyclopedia, but finds that Eusthènes's heterogeneous beings have a "common" location (that is missing in the Chinese taxonomy): the mouth of the enumerator, the saliva of Eusthènes. To be accepted, this explanation requires a leap of logic. It is unclear why the mouth of a fictitious enumerator would be any more logical than the language of the enumeration in the Chinese encyclopedia, which Foucault had presented as a dubious location of the things enumerated. By bringing up another bizarre enumeration to enhance the strangeness of Chinese taxonomy, Foucault duplicates Borges's method of describing several taxonomies for comparative purposes. However, while Borges invokes nonfictional taxonomies (with the exception of the Chinese taxonomy, the reality of which he tells the reader is doubtful), Foucault chooses a fictional character from a book that had little to do with taxonomies. Foucault's comparison of the strangeness ("monstrosity"[40]) of the Chinese taxonomy to the equally strange enumeration of the fictional character of Eusthènes, deemed more logical, clears the ground for presenting his book as an examination of the process of classifying the world in Western culture as rational even in its fictional representation.

Foucault's suspension of disbelief dispenses with an exploration of an authentic Chinese encyclopedia. He takes (or plays at taking) the Chinese encyclopedia as *typical* of China, a sort of prototype of massive cultural difference and otherness. Chinese culture is irremediably different at a basic level of thinking about the world, at a primary, "naked" level, shorn of all theoretical or philosophical reflections. Yet, it is useful, and it is so in a double sense as a counterpoint to the "West," and as an insight into the process through which culture informs various *orders* of classification. However, Foucault reminds the reader that he does not intend to trace a scientific progression in the development of an orderly classification since the sixteenth century. Rather, he intends to analyze the conditions of possibility of scientific knowledge through a regressive method[41] that proceeds back to the "naked experience" of classification in order to find out "in what way language as it was spoken, natural beings as they were perceived and grouped together, and exchanges as they were practiced, in *our* culture [emphasis added] it was revealed that there existed order ... and what modalities of order have been recognized, posited, linked to time and space in order to form the positive foundation of [various kinds of] knowledge as they unfold in grammar and philology, in natural history and biology, in the study of wealth and political economy."[42]

Culture emerges as Foucault's focus and challenge. His method, his approach, and his orientation in the first part of his book center on the power of culture to inflect scientific thought and beyond. Hence the focus on China, even at the cost of a dubious encyclopedia, with no source, no origin, no real identity.

There are three assumptions at the root of Foucault's project in *Les mots et les choses*: first, Western classifications grappled with and discovered an order from their inception; second, their order is rational; and third, it is common to the natural sciences as well as the humanities and social sciences.

As Foucault put it, "When we establish a reasoned classification, when we say that the cat and the dog resemble each other less than two hounds do, even if they each have been tamed or embalmed, even if they both run as if they were crazy, or even if they have just broken the jar, on what ground can we rest this classification in all certainty? On what 'table,' according to what space of identities, similitudes, analogies have we been accustomed to distribute so many things that are different and similar?"[43] This assessment makes it clear that even if a Western encyclopedist had adopted the enumeration of the Chinese categories, he would have nevertheless come up with a different way of ordering them—which, grounded as it is in the "fundamental codes" of his culture, provides him with a primary grid, which in turn reflects in one way or another an order that is inherent in the empirical world. For "order is at once that which is given in things as their inner law, the secret network according to which they face one another and that which only exists in the grid applied by a gaze, a reflection, a language; and it is only in the blank spaces of this grid that order manifests itself in depth as having been already there, waiting in silence for the moment of its enunciation."[44]

At first glance, Foucault examines the role of culture in classifications in a general manner using terms such as "a culture," or "any culture." However, he had previously discussed the Chinese taxonomy as being contingent on a language that "does not reproduce in horizontal lines the receding flight of voice; it draws up in columns the image of a stationary and still recognizable picture of things themselves."[45] In spite of the general character of the subsequent discussion of culture, the implication is strong that some cultures, especially the Western, may be better equipped to express the fundamental, uncoded order that exists in things than others, regardless of the arbitrariness of the coding grid. Furthermore, such cultures are also intrinsically able to question, evaluate, and refine spontaneous codifications. In other words, Western culture has depth and allows for self-reflexivity in comparison with Chinese culture, which has space and secret passages. One allows for an archeology of knowledge, whereas the other excites and bewilders the imagination. What is at once fascinating and intriguing in Foucault's comparison is its counterposing the myth of China as it presumably exists in the Western imagination to the reality of French-qua-Western culture as it is perceived by one French person. A Chinese person might say that the terms of the comparison represent two myths, one (the myth of China as it exists in the Western imagination) that Foucault acknowledges but leaves unquestioned; the other (Foucault's assertion of "our" inherently rational taxonomy) that from a Chinese perspective could be the product of a French person's imagination of his culture. Indeed, is the coexistence of hemorrhoids, spiders, and snakes any more rational than that of crazed dogs, stray dogs, and dogs drawn with a fine camelhair brush? After all, a great part of the purportedly Chinese taxonomy deals with the phenomenal forms and representations of dog-ness, and as such displays a certain logic albeit a clumsy one as Foucault momentarily fathoms. Besides, a Chinese critic steeped in the purportedly Chinese encyclopedia might find it rather strange that Foucault would relate what on the surface is unrelatable, as, for example, "the classification of plants and the theory of coinage," or the "notion of generic character and the analysis of trade."[46]

From the start, Foucault does not envisage a meta-language of classification, translatable in various cultural idioms. Yet this would have been a logical step to take after reading Borges's "John Wilkins' Analytical Language." Where Borges took the position that all classifications are arbitrary because no one knows what the nature of the universe is except perhaps God, Foucault presumes that some classifications may be arbitrary, or strange, or absurd, but they capture an order inherent in the universe, which serves as a sort of baseline against which to refine taxonomic attempts at unearthing it. Where Borges left open the possibility of creating a universal language (as Wilkins tried to do), Foucault seeks to capture the uniqueness of scientific knowledge as it emerged in Western culture and was expressed in the commonality of rules of object selection, concept formation, and theorizing used, largely unconsciously, by researchers in biology, linguistics, political economy, as well as philosophy.[47] There is to be sure nothing amiss with identifying the specific features of Western rationality. The analysis is jeopardized when it assumes a homogeneity of its constitutive elements as *contrasted* with a fictitious alternate cultural modality of ordering.

BORGES AND THE UNIVERSALITY OF CULTURAL RELATIVISM

Foucault has invoked the Chinese encyclopedia as an illustration of how Western rationality could not comprehend a taxonomic order so radically different from itself. Although such an order could exist, Foucault assigned it to an exterior of Western rationality and left it at that. Yet Borges, Foucault's inspiration, established a commonality between forms of representations. A brief analysis of his conception of cultural difference will help to understand the role played by the Chinese encyclopedia in constructing "Oriental" otherness. Borges's assessment of taxonomies (which Foucault ignores) must be read in the context of his cross-cultural descriptions of mythical animals. In *The Book of Imaginary Beings*,[48] Borges detailed in a relatively nonjudgmental manner the characteristics and functions attributed to the dragon, the unicorn, and the Phoenix in Chinese and Western lore. For example, the Chinese defined the dragon as a deity. It arose out of the Yellow River to reveal to the emperor, among other things, "the famous circular diagram that symbolizes the reciprocal play of Yin and Yang." It was the symbol of the Emperor whose throne was called the Dragon Throne. Although a dragon could be used by an occasional king for riding, or even for meat, the animal represented beneficial elements such as clouds and rain. It also represented wisdom. The Chinese pictured the dragon as having horns, claws, scales, and a saw-toothed ridge on its back; it wears a white pearl, the symbol of the sun, and the seat of its power, on its neck.[49] By contrast, the Western dragon is a fearsome and forbidding animal: it looks like a tall serpent with claws and wings; it spews fire and smoke. It craves the cold blood of the elephant and dies in the process of satisfying its lust as it also kills its victim. There are, however, benefits from a dead dragon. Its eyes when processed properly can yield protection from "specters of the night," the fat around his heart may "ensure success in lawsuits," and its teeth when worn as an amulet can mollify a potentate. Christianity associated the dragon with evil and Satan. Some saints are reputed for having slain dragons, as St. Michael purportedly did.[50]

Borges intends to describe differences in representations of mythical animals between China and the West. At times, the differences are less pronounced, as is the case with the Unicorn (although in Chinese lore this animal is not aggressive as it is in the West), or the Phoenix. Implicitly, Borges's comparison of mythical animals highlights cultural assessments and representations. By and large, Chinese lore endows animals such as the dragon with less destructive qualities than its Western counterpart. And while perhaps psychoanalysis would have a lot to say about the psychic meaning of such representations (as Jung did in his interpretation of the Western dragon arguing that it symbolized air and earth),[51] Borges refrains from drawing similar conclusions except to say that "[t]he Dragon of the Western world is terrifying in the best of cases, ridiculous in the worst."[52] Borges's understanding of cultural differences is further enhanced by his comparison of the fauna of China and the United States. In China, animals display human as well as features of other animal species in combination. For example, "the Chiang-liang has the head of a tiger, the face of a man, four hooves, long extremities, and a snake between its teeth." The Hsiao looks like a hawk, "but it has the head of a man, the body of a monkey, the tail of a dog."[53] These animals, cobbled up from various species, often presage droughts, and thus are signs of natural events that are essential to the survival of the human community. Their meaning must be deciphered, and although it is unclear whether their cross species or their very existence accounts for their portentous meanings, their fantastic appearance connotes a notion that the animal world, which includes human beings, may be one. In the mythology of Wisconsin and Minnesota, fauna is represented differently. For example, the *Roperite* is an "[a]nimal the size of a pony, has a ropelike beak that it ropes the swiftest rabbit with."

Some representations seem contradictory; others strike by their immateriality. The *Upland trout,* for instance, "builds its nests in trees, flies pretty well, and is afraid of water." The *Hide-behind* "is always hiding behind something. Whichever way a man turns, it's always behind him, which is why nobody has ever satisfactorily described one, though it has killed and eaten many a lumberjack." Some of these creatures walk, swim, or fly backward by choice as is the case with the *Goofus Bird,* "which builds its nest upside down and flies backward."[54] The mythological fauna of one part of the United States appears to be less elaborate than the Chinese, does not combine features from different species, and is not endowed with meaning. It is perhaps more in line with superstition than with mythology. Unlike the Chinese fauna, the theme of death hangs over the lumberjack who may never know when he will be eaten by the invisible *Hide-behind*.

Borges's description of Chinese and Western mythological beings highlights the differences in attitudes toward different cultural representations, East and West, evinced by Borges and Foucault. Borges's incursions into the human imagination paints a broad fresco of fantasy as it relates to everyday concerns such as power, fear, anxiety, death, drought, luck, etc. Borges evinced curiosity and wonderment at the diverse forms that human imagination can take in different cultures. There may be a slight inclination on the part of Borges to ridicule some of the Western imaginings of the characteristics or the destructive powers attributed to fantastic creatures. Borges's vast erudition about the treasures of the human imagination run amok wouldn't allow him to set up Western culture over the Chinese. Foucault, by comparison, hinted at that. Yet, his method is similar to Borges's. He started out with a discussion of the fantastic character of the purportedly Chinese encyclopedia, and proceeded to look for an equally fantastic description of animals and human parts provided by the fictional Rabelaisian character, Eusthènes. His conclusion is, however, diametrically opposed to Borges's: the French fantasy is still less absurd (insofar as it allegedly connotes an *order*) than the "monstrosity" of the Chinese encyclopedia. To reiterate, where Foucault strenuously strove for the discovery of an order, Borges demonstrated the lack of an intrinsic order, an arbitrarily imposed order that had all the features of disorder.

The question remains why Foucault, the relentless critic of Western culture, would feel obligated to use a rather primitive representation of another culture as the epistemic opening of his book. There are a number of possible reasons, one of which, I suggest, lies in his philosophical rejection of universalism. Borges emphasized cultural variation as well as a universal incapacity of human language in any culture to capture an essential order in the universe. Foucault passes under silence Borges's radical universalism (albeit in a new key), and interprets the Chinese encyclopedia outside of Borges's or any other context, except the Western *ratio*. Yet Borges, the author of the encyclopedia, was operating within the Western *ratio* to probe its fundamental limitations.

CHINA'S APHASIA AND THE CHALLENGE OF UNIVERSALISM

Engaging Borges on the issue of universalism would have meant that Foucault would not have selected the Chinese encyclopedia as a text against which to define the purpose of his book. Ignoring a crucial part of Borges's essay on John Wilkins, Foucault retreated into a position that allowed him to blur the line between fiction and reality. A blind spot, a sort of amnesia that needs to be brought out, informs his attitude.

Foucault charges Borges with having "removed the table of operation" from the Chinese taxonomy even though he had not ascertained what the original (authentic) taxonomy was like. Furthermore, he argues that Borges gave a semblance of orderliness to the Chinese taxonomy by using the "series of our alphabetical enumeration as a guiding thread." This is a Borgesian "futile trick" that "masks or rather points" to his removal of the operating table.[55] Furthermore, Foucault locates the flaws of the Chinese taxonomy in Borges's heterotopias that destroy the capacity of language to produce meaning, to relate words to things. In a move that contradicts Foucault's own objection to using the language of pathology to refer to phenomena that appear to resist rational constructions (such as madness), he compares the linguistic effect of the Chinese taxonomy to that experienced by people afflicted by aphasia, the inability to make out the common ground of place and name.[56] Unexpectedly, Foucault claims that nevertheless, Borges's "text" cannot be properly assimilated to the language of aphasiacs. Indeed, Borges "gave China as the mythical homeland" the distorted classification that resists (logical) thought. In other words, Borges *created* a "monstrous," absurd heterotopia that he attributed to China. In shifting the ground of his discussion from the brute fact of the Chinese enumeration to Borges's style of thought and method of presentation of the enumeration, Foucault creates a space in which to argue: "The fundamental codes of a culture—those that govern its language, its perceptual schemas, its techniques, its *values,* its hierarchical practices—fix from the start for every man the empirical orders with which he will be dealing and in which he will be at home."[57] Since the Chinese language is quite different from anyone of the Western languages, Foucault stacks the deck against Chinese culture as being unable to produce order of the kind Western reason finds familiar.

The constantly shifting ground of Foucault's discussion makes the epistemic function of the encyclopedia contrived. It excludes real domains of Chinese culture such as biology or medical science, subjects that Foucault takes up in *Les mots et les choses.*

Noteworthy is Foucault's attempt at creating a fundamental and culturally irredeemable difference between Western and Chinese cultures as a condition for opening up a space in which to develop his thesis. The gain from this method may be appreciable only if its terms are uncritically accepted. However, considering that Foucault's method is also based on an interpretation of a text that essentially truncates Borges's essay, it becomes clear that Foucault's ultimate purpose is to reveal from the outset that he rejects any leveling of cultural differences, any notion that when confronted with the universe, no language is intrinsically more capable of capturing its "order." Consequently, in order to override Borges's elevation of cultural relativism to a universal principle that hails similarities between cultures, Foucault defines the logic of the Chinese encyclopedia as akin to the pathological condition of aphasia. In other words, the very thought of a culturally different order threatens Western reason, which must exclude it as a form of pathology in a manner similar to Descartes's exclusion of madness from the certainty of reason. Oddly, in rejecting Borges's view that human languages construct taxonomies that are essentially and equally arbitrary, Foucault's view of (Western) cultural difference ends up espousing a universalism of its own by identifying it as a more rational reason, which time and again he characterized as universal in his conceptions of revolution, colonialism, and political spirituality, as will be discussed in later chapters.

BORGES AND THE UBIQUITOUS THEME OF ENCYCLOPEDIA

Foucault was keenly aware of the recurring theme of the notion of encyclopedia in Borges's work by which this author conveyed the futility of human beings' efforts to know every nook and cranny of the universe by producing knowledge that claims to be universal and indubitably certain. He questions both the universality and certainty of encyclopedic knowledge while pointing to its reflexivity, for in the end, it reflects back on people's fantasy and wishes for a different universe that would be as valid as the one that the encyclopedia purports to encapsulate in its enumerations, definitions, and classifications. In "Tlön, Uqbar and Orbis Tertius," Borges remarks that the act of naming "implies a falsification" of the thing named,[58] whether it be a state of mind or the state of the universe. The arbitrariness, which Borges highlights in his discussions of classifications, is best illustrated by his conception of time in the mythical land of Tlön where one century is equal to our 140 years.[59] Why not? A characterization of the metaphysicians of Tlön appears to be singularly applicable to Foucault's treatment of the Chinese: "They [Tlön metaphysicians] are not looking for the truth or an approximation of it; they are after a kind of amazement," the kind similar to Foucault's astonishment and marvel at the quaintness of the Chinese encyclopedia and the culture that sustains it. In the mythical "Garden of Forking Paths," Borges's character, a Chinese man, Dr. Yu Tsun, who turns out to be a spy for Germany, finds in his host's library "some large volume bound in yellow silk-manuscripts of the Lost Encyclopedia which was edited by the Third Emperor of the Luminous Dynasty. They had never been printed."[60] Needless to say that there was no such emperor just as there was no such encyclopedia. Nevertheless, the themes of encyclopedias, libraries, and novels constructed as labyrinths reveal the complex nature of the human quest for meaning and order in a universe that is disordered and meaningless.

To return to Foucault, his assumption that there is an order in the universe that some cultures are more equipped to decipher, or capture, albeit in tentative steps, forecloses debates over the indeterminacy, fluidity, and uncertainty that make attempts at fixing the character of the universe problematic. For Foucault, the problem is not in fixing the character of the world, but in capturing it and constructing it in a rational manner.

FOUCAULT AS BORGES'S DOUBLE

A brief digression is in order to shed light on Foucault's choice of the Chinese encyclopedia as the marker of Western reason's self-definition. Foucault had a complex relation to Borges's work. In some of his literary studies, he focuses on the figure of the "encyclopedia" in seeking to trace changes in conceptions of writing and the notion of the book. In "Un [sic] fantastique de bibliothèque" (One fantastic library),[61] an essay on the imaginary in Gustave Flaubert's books, especially *La Tentation de St. Antoine* (St Anthony's temptation), Foucault uses the same method as Borges. He argues, for example, that the book stands for "the fiction of book," the locus of temptation. In the end, Foucault adopts a Borgesian theme of the destruction of the library by concluding that "La biliothèque est en feu" (The library is on fire).[62] Like Borges, Foucault evokes the role played by "encyclopedia" in the literary quest for meaning. He sees in Flaubert's *Bouvard et Pécuchet*, "l'encyclopédie érudite d' une culture,"[63] ("the erudite encyclopedia of a culture"). Coincidentally, Borges also wrote two essays on Flaubert, one, "A Defense of Bouvard et Pécuchet," the other, "Flaubert and his Exemplary Destiny."[64]

In a clear style, Borges foregrounds the significance of the "idiots," Bouvard and Pécuchet, as representations of Flaubert's' "final doubts and fears." Noting that the book had been written in the final six years of the author's life, Borges lauds the book for its aesthetic value and hails Flaubert for shattering the realist novel, which he had pioneered, and for harking back instead to the "parables of Voltaire and Swift and the Orientals, and forward to Kafka."[65] From Borges's perspective, Flaubert used the "death of the novel" (a theme that Foucault also revisits) to "mock humanity's yearnings"—a task that Borges had also assigned himself.[66] In the end, Borges felt that Flaubert's books are about Flaubert, and Flaubert was "the Adam of a new species."[67] Borges focused on Flaubert, the author, the man, and the symbolic significance of the characters of Bouvard and Pécuchet, without evoking the themes of encyclopedia or libraries. However, he could not avoid making allusion to language, but noted Flaubert's austere search for the *mot juste*. In examining the meaning of writing a book (another of Foucault's concerns), Borges does so by way of Mallarmé's epigram that "[e]verything in the world exists to end up in a book."[68] Nevertheless, the Borgesian themes and concepts that Foucault uses denote his appreciation of Borges's contribution to a new understanding of literature, a new form of writing, and a unique relation of language to death as well as to knowledge.[69] There appears to be no evidence of any communication between Borges and Foucault. A Borges expert whom I consulted, Professor Evelyn Fishburn, does not believe there has been any.[70]

Foucault's examination of the Chinese encyclopedia was a different foray into Borges's thought than Flaubert's literary work. The encyclopedia presented Foucault with a non-Western culture, the significance of which he took in a different direction from Borges's. At any rate, given Foucault's appreciation of Borges's literary contributions and his shared interest in Flaubert, it is intriguing that he did not take into consideration the full measure of Borges's unique method of writing that weaves the real and the fictitious in ways such that the reader does not always know whether she is reading about factual or fictitious characters and events as was the case with the Chinese encyclopedia. Is it Foucault's appreciation of Borges's novelty in Western letters that somehow predisposed him to overlooking Borges's blurred lines between facts and fiction? Foucault also does not address Borges's philosophical orientation as he did for example with Descartes, Derrida, and Claude Lévi-Strauss, among others.

Returning to the Chinese encyclopedia, its selection denotes a tacit understanding that Foucault finds Borges important to his own work, but is indifferent to the epistemic significance as well as relevance of Borges's approach to his own orientation in *Les mots et les choses*. In the preface, Foucault writes past Borges, although evoking his name and his encyclopedia, but avoids coming to terms with the ideas expressed in "The Universal Language of John Wilkins" that frames the Chinese encyclopedia.

NORMALIZING THE CHINESE ENCYCLOPEDIA

Foucault's reference to the Chinese encyclopedia is frequently cited by his commentators, as well as readers struck by its oddity. It is often quoted to buttress one point or another that is alien to Foucault's writing. Some, however, invoke his citation in support of their views about culture without considering the meaning that Foucault imparted to the Chinese classification. With an occasional exception, Foucault's interpretation of Borges's Chinese encyclopedia is (mis)read in a positive manner. Implied in this interpretation is that Foucault had said all there was to be said about the strangeness of the Chinese encyclopedia in comparison with Western systems of classification, and that his reaction to it is proper. In commenting on a paper given by a Chinese professor and expert in Confucian philosophy, Tu Weiming, at a congress held in Berlin in 1981, the late anthropologist Clifford Geertz pointed out that this paper had the same effect on him as the Chinese encyclopedia had had on Foucault. He opined that "Tu has provided us with such a Chinese encyclopedia," and proceeded to quote one sentence from the preface to *Les mots et les choses* to indicate that Foucault found the encyclopedia a welcome and even liberating alternative to Western modes of classification. Misconstruing Foucault's analysis, Geertz wrote "Tu's paper can serve, I think, such a liberating function for us if we but let it, allow it to grant its otherness, and the otherness it records, rather than bringing it too quickly back within the range of our own conceptual categories."[71] It is as if Geertz failed to read what came after the one sentence in which Foucault asserted the "exotic charm of another system of thought," which represents not only the "limitation of our own," but also "the stark impossibility [for us] of thinking that." Foucault did not mention experiencing a liberating effect upon reading the encyclopedia. On the contrary, to fathom the possibility that such a system of thought could exist at all filled him with uneasiness. Admittedly, Geertz's call for allowing Chinese thought to grant its otherness might reveal awareness of Foucault's ultimate dismissal of the Chinese encyclopedia, but his positive misreading is at odds with Foucault's stated view.

Similarly, the insight that Bruno Bosteels provides in his essay on the topography of epistemology as represented by the concept of the "nonplace" draws its inspiration from a noncritical understanding of Foucault's treatment of the Chinese encyclopedia. He argues that "Borges's Chinese encyclopedia and the laughter it provokes in Foucault, by rendering the anthropological reference null and void, give us a glimpse of what might lie beyond the threshold of the modern. In this sense, the non place of language, with its monstrous arbitrariness not only marks the birthplace of *Les mots et les choses* but also gives Foucault indispensable leverage throughout all of his so-called archaeological works, to awaken 'us moderns' from our 'anthropological sleep'"[72] Yet, Foucault's discussion of the representation of China in the French-qua-Western imaginary, which he does not question, functions as an anthropological referent to a society and culture deemed impossible to understand on its own terms. Such a referent is neither null nor void. Rather, it is full with a cultural presence and a language the anthropological significance of which is presumed to be antithetical to Western comprehension. The language that Foucault qualifies as a nonplace that holds the classification together could easily be interpreted as that of Borges, who had written in Spanish about an encyclopedia he had invented and attributed to the Chinese; Foucault read it in French translation and retranslated it from fiction into reality expressed in the French cultural idiom. Given this layered narrative in several languages, it is hard to imagine Bosteels's acceptance of language in general as being a nonplace, when the context of its discussion in *Les mots et les choses* is China, its language and culture mediated by Borges's own conception of the arbitrariness of language. It is worth noting that Foucault did not discuss the arbitrariness of language in his analysis of the Chinese encyclopedia. Rather, he pointed to the limitations of the

Chinese language as a reflection of a massive cultural difference. The slippage in meaning between Foucault's intent and Bosteels's interpretation is a reminder that as concepts and ideas from *Les mots et les choses* become assimilated, "the distinctive features of the ideas being assimilated disappear."⁷³

Ignoring the fictitious character of the Chinese encyclopedia, Jean Zoungrana sees it as an example of Foucault's adaptation of Claude Lévi-Strauss's structural ethnological method. Foucault, he argues, refrained from attributing the oddity of the Chinese encyclopedia to some prelogical mentality as anthropologists such as Lévy-Bruhl might have done.⁷⁴ Rather, he wondered about the conditions of possibility of the heterogeneity of the Chinese taxonomy, thus pointing to the system of knowledge that it denotes.⁷⁵ However, the focus of *Les mots et les choses* is not the study of the unthinkable character of the Chinese encyclopedia but how Western culture constructs order. Bearing in mind Foucault's critique of anthropology, Daniel Defert suggests Foucault intended to point to the existence of multiple orders prior to the ordering work of the anthropologist.⁷⁶ By the same token, Foucault wished to foreground the impossibility of contemporary Western thought thinking the Chinese taxonomy or a similar one occurring at a different period of time in the West. Again, the fictitious character of the encyclopedia (analyzed as if it were real) eludes this interpretation. A similar interpretation stresses Foucault's tacit agreement with Borges that there are multiple ways of ordering the world but from "our" historical a priori, these strike us as impossible. Consequently, "we" realize the limits of our own rationality. Such an interpretation seeks to avert a possible construal of Foucault's view of Western rationality as somehow superior to "Oriental" rationality. However, from the perspective of this book, Foucault does not have to explicitly state Western superiority. Rather, the point is that Foucault clearly asserts that the "Orient" falls outside the Western *ratio* and as such remains an unmediated other. Furthermore, the exclusion of the "Orient" from the Western ratio obviates the inner exclusions such as the bizarre taxonomies of John Wilkins or the Bibliographical Institutes. Foucault's erection of the barrier of cultural difference cuts both ways, externally as well as internally just as he had explained in the 1961 preface to the *History of Madness*.

Departing from previous commentators, Béatrice Han focuses on the philosophical implications of Foucault's critique of the Chinese encyclopedia, although not without noting that its description is "flamboyant."⁷⁷ She seeks to demonstrate that the nature of Foucault's critique, couched in such terms as "operating table, "the table," "the grid," or the "gaze," attests to Foucault's Kantian influence although he sought to distance himself from Kant's conception of knowledge.⁷⁸ Han rightly distinguishes between the Chinese encyclopedia and this other dramatic incident with which Foucault opens *Discipline and Punish,* which describes the public execution of Damiens, an eighteenth-century man who attempted to stab Louis XV to death. Nevertheless, Han failed to note that Damiens was a real character whereas the Chinese encyclopedia was fictitious. To be sure, Foucault invokes the fictional character of Don Quixote, but in the context of illustrating arguments central to his book. By contrast, the Chinese encyclopedia is not part of a novel; rather, it is a technical device contrived by Borges. In passing Han notices the encyclopedia's "exoticism of form"[79] which enlivens the preface to *Les mots et les choses,* but does not question its implication for Foucault's conception of otherness in spite of her discussion of the notion and field of anthropology. A biographer of Foucault, David Macey, also did not fail to mention the Chinese encyclopedia, but mentioned it merely to note that its effect is similar to that provoked by passages of History of Madness, namely, a "pleasing bewilderment."[80] Yet, Macey implicitly points to a possible connection between the Chinese encyclopedia and Foucault's conception of madness, a connection Foucault does not make, and thus remains silent. Macey's insight is valuable in that it burdens Foucault's attitude with an additional question: why did Foucault analyze the Chinese encyclopedia from the perspective he had sought to debunk in his work on madness—the excluded other of reason?

CHINESE SCHOLARS ON FOUCAULT'S CHINESE ENCYCLOPEDIA

The reaction of Chinese scholars to Foucault's uncritical acceptance of the Chinese encyclopedia as being virtually the real thing reveals at once frustration and rejection of the contents of the fictitious encyclopedia. Chinese scholars began formulating critiques of images of China constructed by Western writers as early as 1941.[81] However, specific Chinese critiques of Foucault's acceptance of the reality of the Chinese encyclopedia are more recent. Perhaps the most comprehensive was by Zhang Longxi, who addressed the many facets of negative as well as positive Western prejudice against the Chinese language, culture, and political systems. Longxi agrees (with Foucault) that the Chinese encyclopedia was "hilarious," just as he rightly points out that Borges did not intend it as an indictment of Chinese culture. He also emphatically states that the encyclopedia was fictitious. However, unexpectedly, he concludes that "it seems that we have argued, ironically, not against Foucault but for him completely. All we have shown is precisely the validity of his proposition that it is hardly possible to get out of the confinement of the historical a priori, the epistemes or fundamental codes of cultural systems."[82] In other words, oblivious of Foucault's philosophical and theoretical orientation that seeks to cast doubt on Western representation of difference (as between the mad and the sane for instance), Longxi validates Foucault's use of Chinese culture as a counterpoint to Western culture and as introduction to *Les mots et les choses*. If indeed it is impossible, as Longxi claims, to transcend culture as an epistemic obstacle, what is the point of denouncing distortions of Chinese culture? Out of Longxi's text, Foucault emerges unscathed but paradoxically diminished since he is excused for being unable to overcome stereotypical thinking. Longxi's conclusion leaves unexplained appreciations of Chinese culture, some of which he acknowledges but also dismisses as a mere trope for Western scholars' self-understanding (through the device of cross-cultural comparison) rather than for reaching a genuine understanding of China.

Zhengguo Kang, Professor of Chinese at Yale University, pointed out to me that there exists a real Chinese encyclopedia–like text, the *leishu*.[83] Although displaying some characteristics of encyclopedias common in the West, such as concordances, *leishu* is a reference book in several volumes organized according to subjects derived from the canon of Chinese literature. For example, "Vol. 90-92 is devoted to Bird; Vol. 93-95 to Beast; Vol. 96-97 to Aquatic animals and insects; Vol. 98 to Animals that are auspicious signs." Kang notes that *leishu* was a handbook for writing poems or essays. The intellectual class in medieval China was required to reference or quote from classical works in their poems or essays. Kang compares *leishu* to "a google.com." However, he cautions against assimilating it to the notion of an encyclopedia, which would be misleading. Indeed, such an attempt would not only obscure the historicity of the *leishu* but also detract from, or even dismiss, its function as a repository of knowledge. When examined in light of *leishu*, the Chinese encyclopedia, although in its fictitious form, could be seen as representing concordances, references to animals as they appeared in poems, literature, and essays. Such an interpretation stacks the deck against Foucault's dismissal of the encyclopedia as laughably quaint and beyond the Western pale.

Yet, there are instances in Western societies of scholars who engaged in the same kind of classifications as appear in *leishu*. One of these was the Roman author, Priscus, who embarked on a "maniacal project, to preserve classical learning by assembling excerpts from all the great works of antiquity."[84] Priscus proceeded in a manner not so different from the *leishu*'s authors. He organized a vast body of excerpts into categories with titles such as "*Excerpts concerning Victories; Excerpts concerning Nations; Excerpts concerning Embassies*," which were in turn subdivided into "*Embassies from the Romans to Foreigners*" and "*Embassies from Foreigners to the Romans*."[85] Furthermore, paleontologist Stephen Jay Gould notes with amazement the "wonderfully weird" classification of fifteenth-century natural historian Konrad Gesner (1516–1565). The first volume of his *Historia animalium,* published in 1551, was organized in a manner similar to the *leishu*. Under the mammals caption it displayed chapters on animals ranging from elks and wolves "with each entry structured as a compendium of everything ever recorded about the species at hand, with pride of place, and maximum length of treatment, granted to the claims of classical authors."[86] Gesner also included mythic animals such as the unicorn and satyrs among his classification of real mammals. Gould explains that Gesner did not necessarily believe in the existence of unicorns and satyrs, but that the unreality of these animals mattered less than the human attitudes toward all four-footed animals, real or imaginary, which was his goal. In another echo of the *leishu*, as well as the Chinese encyclopedia, one of Gesner's chapters, "De sue (On pigs)," lists "pigs as emblems and metaphors in literature, and a list of all recorded proverbs about pigs."[87] Given that *Les mots et les choses* focuses on the Renaissance, Foucault must have been familiar with the manner in which natural historians, such as Gesner, constructed classifications of the animal world.

Kang's clarification opens up new directions in which the apocryphal Chinese encyclopedia could be taken. At the very least, it leads to a different appreciation of Borges's fiction, which, in one sense, may very well not have been too far off the mark. Nevertheless, he was as guilty as Foucault for not distinguishing concordances from taxonomies. It would be all too easy to see in Foucault's dismissal of the Chinese encyclopedia a lack of discernment. In light of the extant sixteenth-century European taxonomies that strongly resembled the Chinese encyclopedia, Foucault's attitude may have stemmed from an unexamined desire to think of Chinese culture as producing fundamentally flawed taxonomies in comparison with Western culture.

RETURNING TO CHINA AND ITS OTHERNESS: BAUDELAIRE

To reiterate, for Foucault, China's cultural difference as expressed in the encyclopedia was at once an epistemic obstacle and a literary device. Yet, China was potentially an opportunity to redefine the manner in which Western culture represents itself to itself. Baudelaire, whom Foucault praised for his definition of modernity,[88] took such an opportunity. A brief discussion of Baudelaire's view of Chinese art underscores the particularity of Foucault's stance before the Chinese encyclopedia.

In 1855 Baudelaire wrote an essay on the Paris World's Fair (L' Exposition Universelle) expressing an alternative mode of approaching cultural difference. Baudelaire asks "what I say, would a modern Wickelmann do at the sight of a Chinese product, a strange product, weird, contorted in shape, intense in color and sometimes delicate to the point of fading away?"[89] Would such a man "*see* [emphasis added] this object as one of universal beauty?" Or would he, using "the academic eye that judges see it as offensive," thereby transforming "the other into a "barbarian?"[90] Baudelaire, it must be noted, argues for a "modern" experiencing of cultural difference, an attitude that strips what is unfamiliar of its strangeness. Such an experiencing is similar to the transformation that a lone traveler who is open to his new environment undergoes. The traveler makes an "effort" to contemplate and study otherness, "use[s] his will power as well as imagination to develop a keen empathy [sympathy in French] and bring in himself a transformation through new harmonies and ideas." Baudelaire sees the overcoming of what at first glance appears disconcertingly strange, even "barbaric," about non-Western art forms, as an active process involving willingness to change the manner in which one *sees*. Learning to see differently requires a suspension of dismissive judgment, a removal of the "scholastic veil," "the academic paradox," and "pedagogic utopia." The last term felicitously captures Foucault's analytical exercise in abstractly unraveling a mythic taxonomy in order to better define his own book project. From Baudelaire's perspective, anyone can overcome such obstacles and bring about in himself a transformation in his way of seeing and experiencing the "divine grace of cosmopolitanism."[91] Undoubtedly, this is contingent on his willpower and imagination, and an effort to experience life as it is lived in other societies. Imagination, which Foucault also identified as important to Baudelaire's conception of modernity,[92] plays a role in distinguishing the man who is unmoved by cultural otherness from the modern man who allows himself, by working on himself, to be transformed by it.[93]

In invoking Baudelaire's entreaty, I do not suggest that the Chinese encyclopedia could be assimilated to a work of art. When read against the background of Baudelaire's critique of parochialism in appreciation of Chinese art, Foucault's treatment of the Chinese taxonomy bears similarities to the work of the "pedagogue." Admittedly, Foucault is simply stating a fact about the differentness of the Chinese encyclopedia. Yet the judgment is there, behind each word and behind the very idea of using the Chinese encyclopedia as an entry point to a book on the specificity of Western production of scientific thought.

Borges also drew attention to the transformation that takes place within the person who immerses himself in a culture alien to his own. In "The Anthropologist," a graduate student, Fred Murdock, in the course of his fieldwork on a reservation in the Southwest among Native Americans, discovers a new way of life under the guidance of the medicine man whose "secret" he has been sent to crack.[94] Upon his return to his university after two years of life as a native, speaking the natives' tongue, eating their food, partaking in their rituals, and dreaming like them, Murdock refused to divulge the secret he had uncovered. To his adviser, who threatened to report him to the university board, he said: "no, maybe I won't go back to the reservation. What I learned there I can apply any place on earth and under any circumstances."[95] The suggestion is not that Foucault should have gone to China or lived among a Chinese community in order to question the Chinese encyclopedia, or French imagination of China. Rather, his unwillingness to confront otherness in fact or fiction needs elucidation. Fred Murdock (a fictitious character) stayed in the United States, did the things that people do in marrying and divorcing, "and is now a librarian at Yale."[96] In *Les mots et les choses*, Foucault, the archivist, has yet to cross path with Borges's librarian. This Borges story could just as well have been used as a prelude to Foucault's conception of madness.

In sum, Foucault's attention to the Chinese encyclopedia, oblivious to its layered history and implications, frames and structures his view of the Orient, as well as his experiences of Japan, Tunisia, and Iran. Excised from Borges's original essay, and presented as a limit to Western thought, the encyclopedia epitomizes a conception of unmediated cultural difference.

There is an element of theatricality in Foucault's approach: the décor is set up in a way calculated to achieve estrangement in the audience but the actors perform in familiar costumes. Thus, the strange and the familiar create a momentary ambiguity and perhaps even unease before the lines are said and relief takes place in the form of laughter. China, its language, and its presumed opaqueness and inscrutably absurd logic set the stage for the study of a (Western) system of thought that may be imperfect but has the advantage of being rational and thus comprehensible. Foucault's purpose then appears to be a veiled critique of Borges's assertion of the arbitrary nature of *all* cultural attempts at developing a universal language of classifications. By contrasting Chinese with Western culture, Foucault makes the latter a referent point even though he does not specifically claim its superiority. Ultimately, Foucault's stance is paradoxical. On the one hand, he ignores the implied cultural relativism in Borges's critique of a universal language of classification. But, although he does not mention Borges's discussion of a universal language (the context within which Borges developed the Chinese encyclopedia) his dismissal of a Chinese order of things indicates that. On the one hand, he rejected the notion of the universality of taxonomic arbitrariness, which Borges upholds. On the other hand, Foucault claims that the focus of his book is to demonstrate how Western culture produced, albeit by fits and starts, a unique method of reflecting as well as constructing order in the natural world and in social life. The advantage that Western culture affords in searching for and creating a rational order in the world is predicated on the lack of such capacity as epitomized by Chinese culture. Hence, he sets up a de facto universal Western cultural rational standard ("the table") that relegates the non-West to a "limit experience," a bit like madness or death.

I wish to stress the epistemic impossibility that Foucault implies for understanding cultures and people bearing the mark of difference. The lack of a discussion that would complicate his use of a fictitious encyclopedia as an exemplar of a limit-experience is not fortuitous. As if to correct this glaring gap, Foucault points out that *The Order of Things* was a precursor to the *History of Madness*. While the latter is the history of the Other, the mad, the former is the history of the Same. If the *Order of Things* is the history of the Same, it is perplexing that it required the evocation of a fictitious massive cultural difference? Foucault's stance signals a fundamental uncertainty about whether cultural difference can be integrated in the epistemology he formulates as an alternative to the humanist epistemology. It also calls into question the translatability of his conception of (social) difference as exemplified by madness, homosexuality, or the treatment of prisoners into the language of cultural difference.

Herein lies Foucault's cultural conundrum: how to articulate an epistemology that broadens the concept of the "other" but does not get swallowed up in the epistemology of the Other as the flip side of the self Same. Or, to put it differently, how to acknowledge cultural otherness outside of a cosmopolitan anthropology.

NOTES

*Epigraph translation: "I dream of a Chinese Borges who would cite, for his readers' amusement, the program of a philosophy class in France...However, we should refrain from laughing at it."

1. Michel Foucault, *Les mots et les choses: une archéologie des sciences humaines* (Paris: Gallimard, 1966), 7. Translation mine. The English edition is *The Order of Things*, xv. The English translation (xv) uses "fable" for "apologue," which in French is a narration or story. *Récit* can mean a fable or an allegory, etc.
2. Foucault, *Les mots et les choses*, 8; *The Order of Things*, xv.
3. Foucault, *Les mots et les choses*, 8; *The Order of Things*, xvi.
4. Foucault, *Les mots et les choses*, 8.
5. Ibid.
6. Ibid.
7. Ibid., 9.
8. Ibid.
9. Ibid.

10. Ibid.; *The Order of Things*, xviii.
11. For a description of European views of China, including the French, as interpreted by a Chinese scholar, see Longxi Zhang, "The Myth of the Other: China in the Eyes of the West," *Critical Inquiry* 15, no. 1 (1988), especially 116–26. See also, among others, Jamie Morgan, "Distinguishing Truth, Knowledge, and Belief: A Philosophical Contribution to the Problem of Images of China," *Modern China* 30, no. 3 (July 2004): 398–427.
12. Foucault, *Les mots et les choses*, 10; *The Order of Things*, xix.
13. Foucault, *Les mots et les choses*, 10; *The Order of Things*, xix.
14. In discussing the Western imagination of China, Foucault uses the pronouns "we" and "our," in which he presumably includes himself. See Foucault, *Les mots et les choses*, 10; *The Order of Things*, xix.
15. Foucault, *Les mots et les choses*, 11; *The Order of Things*, xix.
16. Foucault, *Les mots et les choses*, 13; *The Order of Things*, xxi. The English version translates "nue" (which means "naked") as "pure," which may be more sophisticated, but loses the connotations that the word "nue" evokes when placed within the context of the discussion of the differences that Foucault drew between the Chinese manner of ordering and the West's prior to defining the purpose of his book.
17. *Les mots et les choses*, 9; *The Order of Things*, xvi.
18. *Les mots et les choses*, 10; *The Order of Things*, xvii.
19. *Les mots et les choses*, 8; *The Order of Things*, xvi.
20. *Les mots et les choses*, 10; *The Order of Things*, xviii.
21. Jorge Luis Borges, "John Wilkins' Analytical Language," in *Selected Non-Fictions*, ed. Eliot Weinberger, trans. Eliot Weinberger, Esther Allen, and Suzanne Jill Levine (New York: Penguin Books, 2000), 229. John Wilkins (1614–1672) had written *An Essay towards a Real Character, and a Philosophical Language* (Menston: Scolar Press, 1968).
22. René Descartes, "To Mersenne," in *The Philosophical Writings of Descartes*, trans. John Cottingham et al., vol. 3 (Cambridge: Cambridge University Press, 1991), 10. The editors-translators note in footnote 1, p. 10, that Descartes may have been commenting on a proposal by his friend, Claude Hardy, a mathematician, who was said to know thirty-six Oriental languages.
23. Ibid., 12.
24. Ibid., 13.
25. Ibid., 3. Borges gives a slightly different version of Descartes's view by stating that Descartes suggested modeling the new language on the language "of ciphers," that could learn all the numbers up to infinity "by using the decimal system of enumeration." Borges, "John Wilkins," 230.
26. A commentator, Mauthner, cited by Borges, suggested that Wilkins's universal language was meant to serve as "a secret encyclopedia." Borges compares the symbolic significance Wilkins attributed to each letter in his new language to the kabbalists' reading of the "Holy Scriptures." Borges, "John Wilkins," 230.
27. Ibid., 230–31.
28. Franz Kuhn (1884–1961) was a German lawyer and interpreter. He translated

classical Chinese literary works into German. There is no evidence that he translated any Chinese encyclopedia. Encyclopedia is a ubiquitous theme in Borges's work of demystification of classifications. For example, in the "Garden of Forking Paths," a Chinese character, Dr. Yu Tsun, finds a "Lost Encyclopedia." Jorge Luis Borges in *Ficciones,* trans. Alastair Reid (New York: Grove Press, 1962), 95.

29. Borges, "John Wilkins," 231.
30. There are several translations of the "Chinese encyclopedia," all of which differ from one another. For example, Eliot Weinberger translates *al jarrón* as "flower vase." In the translation used by Foucault, the source of which he does not identify, this term appears as "water pitcher." For a translation that also reproduces the Spanish text see "The Analytical Language of John Wilkins," accessed 8 December 2016, http://www.crockford.com/wrrrld/wilkins.html.
31. Borges, "John Wilkins," 231.
32. Ibid.
33. Ibid., 232.
34. Foucault, *The Order of Things,* 120.
35. Sidonie Clauss, "John Wilkins' Essay Toward a Real Character: Its Place in the Seventeenth-Century Episteme," *Journal of the History of Ideas* 43, no. 4 (1 October 1982): 552. Foucault's citation of Borges also appears in Clauss's essay.
36. Ibid., 551.
37. This Institute was not a figment of Borges's imagination but was founded in 1895 by two lawyers, Paul Otlet and Henri La Fontaine, the latter of whom was also a member of the Belgian parliament, to study issues of bibliographic organization and classification. Both men asked for, and received, permission from Melvil Dewey to translate and use his decimal system of classification in their work at the Institute. However, Otlet modified the Dewey decimal system, which Dewey found objectionable. Some of his modifications lent credence to Borges's notion that the search of a universal language of classification (Otlet and La Fontaine's goal) is arbitrary. For example, Otlet proposed regarding the decimal point in the Dewey system as "a mark of punctuation" and placing between parentheses "different categories of indices borrowed from corresponding classification numbers." The result was a cumbersome system of numbers that were assigned branches of knowledge. Number 913 was given physical geography "so that number 911 was free for use as a chronological subdivision and 912 for indications of aspects of physical geography. The common 91 indicating geography could be suppressed and the 1 and 2 would appear in parentheses to indicate time and place respectively with another number for further specification." In defending his system Dewey pointed out that it had been built "from the standpoint of a scientific specialist and not a librarian collecting and classifying a great quantity of books, pamphlets, clippings and notes. Our advice has been chiefly from university professors in the various subjects, and other specialists working from distinctly practical ends." See W. Boyd Rayward, *The Universe of Information: The Work of Paul Otlet for Documentation and International Organisation* (Moscow: All-Union Institute for Scientific and Technical Information (VINITI), 1975), 90, 100. See also W. Boyd Rayward, "The International

Federation for Information and Documentation (FID)," in *Encyclopedia of Library History*, ed. Wayne A. Wiegand and Donald G. Davis (New York: Garland, 1994), 290–94. A good source of Otlet's contribution to modern information science, including his intriguing conception of the book as an organic machine, is Trudi Bellardo Hahn and Michael Keeble Buckland, eds., *Historical Studies in Information Science* (Medford, NJ: Published for the American Society for Information Science by Information Today, 1998), especially Ron Day, "Paul Otlet's Book and the Writing of Social Space," 43–50. Note must be taken of the work of the Indian mathematician turned librarian, S.R. Ranganathan, who developed a different classification system, the analytico-synthetic, based on the categories of "personality, matter, energy, space and time," assumed to reflect the characteristics (or "facets") of objects of classification. Ranganathan is credited with reversing the method of classification by starting with the characteristics of books instead of the classification system. See Mike Steckel, "Ranganathan for IAs," 7 October 2002, accessed 8 December 2016, http://www.boxesandarrows.com/ranganathan_for_ias. I am grateful to Hal Grossman, reference librarian at Hunter College, for information about Ranganathan. My thanks go to Clay Williams, librarian at Hunter College, for bringing Ranganathan's work to my attention, and to Jean-Jacques Strayer for his bibliographical support to this chapter.
38. In his article Borges also refers to the method used in 1850 by a Letellier to create a new language, which resembled Wilkins's.
39. Foucault, *Les mots et les choses*, 8; *The Order of Things*, xvi.
40. Foucault, *Les mots et les choses*, 8.
41. Foucault uses the expression "en remontant, comme à contre-courant," which is reminiscent of Jean-Paul Sartre's "progressive-regressive method," as formulated in *Search for a Method*, trans. Hazel E. Barnes (New York: Vintage Books, 1968).
42. Foucault, *Les mots et les choses*, 13; *The Order of Things*, xxi.
43. Foucault, *Les mots et les choses*, 11; *The Order of Things*, xix.
44. Foucault, *Les mots et les choses*, 10; *The Order of Things*, xx.
45. Foucault, *Les mots et les choses*, 12; *The Order of Things*, xix.
46. Foucault, *The Order of Things*, xi.
47. Michel Foucault, "Préface à l'édition anglaise," in *Dits et écrits*, vol. 1, 878; Foucault, *The Order of Things*, xi (Foucault's preface to the English edition of *Les mots et les choses*).
48. Jorge Luis Borges and Margarita Guerrero, *The Book of Imaginary Beings*, trans. Andrew Hurley (New York: Penguin, 2006). It is important to note that this book was not a work of fiction, although it dealt with fictitious, fantastic creatures. The translator, Andrew Hurley, went to great lengths to document the sources from which Borges quoted. See Translator's Note, 211–18.
49. Ibid., 66–68.
50. Ibid., 68–71.
51. Ibid., 71.
52. Ibid., 66.
53. Ibid., 81.
54. Ibid., 83.

55. Foucault, *Les mots et les choses*, 9; *The Order of Things*, xvii.
56. Foucault, *Les mots et les choses*, 10; *The Order of Things*, xix.
57. Foucault, *Les mots et les choses*, 10; *The Order of Things*, xx.
58. Borges, "Tlön, Uqbar, Orbis Tertius," in *Ficciones*, 23.
59. Ibid., 25.
60. Borges, "The Garden of Forking Path," 95.
61. Michel Foucault, "Sans titre," in *Dits et écrits*, vol. 1, 321–53. This essay was published under the title of "Un [*sic*] fantastique de bibliothèque," *Cahiers de la Compagnie Madeleine Renaud-Jean-Louis Barrrault* 59 (March 1967): 7–30. Another revised version was published as "La bibliothèque fantastique" by Raymonde Debray Genette, ed., in *Flaubert—Miroir de la critique* (Paris: Firmin-Didot, M. Didier, 1970), 171–90.
62. Foucault, "Sans titre," 326.
63. Ibid., 337.
64. Jorge Luis Borges, "A Defense of *Bouvard et Pécuchet*," in *Selected Non-Fictions*, 386–88, 390–93. There is a discrepancy in the date of publication of these essays: the original essay on *Bouvard et Pécuchet*, "Vindicación de Bouvard y Pécuchet," as well as the second one, "Flaubert y su Destino Ejemplar," appeared in *Discusión* in 1932. There were several reprints thereafter. See Jorge Luis Borges, *Discusión* (Madrid: Alianza Editorial, 2008), 181–87. In *Selected Non-Fictions*, Eliot Weinberger, who translated the essays, grouped them under the period 1946–1955, and identified them as dating back to 1954.
65. Borges, "A Defense of *Bouvard et Pécuchet*," 389.
66. Ibid.
67. Borges, "Flaubert and his Exemplary Destiny," in *Selected Non-Fictions*, 390.
68. Ibid., 393.
69. For language and death see Michel Foucault, "Le langage à l'infini," in *Dits et écrits*, vol. 1, 280, 288. In this essay, Foucault refers to Borges's *Library of Babel*.
70. Evelyn Fishburn is Professor Emeritus, London Metropolitan University and Honorary Senior Research Fellow, University College London. I communicated with her on 24 August 2010. I am grateful to her for taking the time to answer my questions.
71. Clifford Geertz, "Comment on Professor Tu's Paper," *Philosophy East and West* 31, no. 3 (July 1981): 269.
72. Bruno Bosteels, "Nonplace: An Anecdoted Topography of Contemporary French Theory," *Diacritics* 33, no. 3–4 (Autumn–Winter 2003): 121.
73. See Allan Megill, "The Reception of Foucault by Historians," *Journal of the History of Ideas* 48, no. 1 (January–March 1987): 131.
74. Jean Zoungrana, *Michel Foucault: un parcours croisé: Lévi-Strauss, Heidegger* (Paris: L'Harmattan, 1998), 126. See also ibid., 101–2.
75. Ibid., 130.
76. Daniel Defert, Interview, Paris, 2 June 2014.
77. Béatrice Han, *Foucault's Critical Project: Between the Transcendental and the Historical*, trans. Edward Pile (Stanford: Stanford University Press, 2002), 149.
78. Ibid., 38–44.

79. Ibid., 39.
80. Macey, *The Lives of Michel Foucault*: A Biography (New York: Vintage Boos, 1993), 96.
81. See for example Qian Zhongshu, "China in the English Literature of the Seventeenth Century," *Quarterly Bulletin of Chinese Bibliography* 1 (December 1941): 113–52.
82. Zhang, "The Myth of the Other: China in the Eyes of the West," 127. Longxi belongs to a trend among Chinese scholars, including Tu Weiming, who have been attracted to poststructuralism/postmodernism. Hence the apparent contradiction in his critique of Foucault's use of the Chinese encyclopedia.
83. I am grateful to Professor Kang for sharing his knowledge and insights with me in a written communication.
84. Peter Heather, *The Fall of the Roman Empire: A New History of Rome and the Barbarians* (New York: Oxford University Press, 2006), 305. I am grateful to Ramsi A. Woodcock for bringing this source to my attention.
85. Ibid., 305–6.
86. Stephen Jay Gould, *The Hedgehog, the Fox, and the Magister's Pox: Mending the Gap Between Science and the Humanities* (New York: Harmony Books, 2003), 37.
87. Ibid., 37–38.
88. See Michel Foucault, "Qu'est-ce-que les Lumières?," in *Dits et écrits*, vol. 2, 1976–1988, especially 1387–90. For the English translation, see Michel Foucault, "What Is Enlightenment?," in *The Foucault Reader,* ed. Paul Rabinow (New York: Pantheon Books, 1984), 32–50. The discussion of Baudelaire was later added to the French version. Foucault asserted that Baudelaire best understood what modernity is, but that the meaning of the concept was lost after him. See Michel Foucault, "Structuralisme et poststructuralisme," in *Dits et écrits,* vol. 2, 1265. In another context, Foucault considered Baudelaire an example of the nineteenth-century poets who were mad, or experimented with a sort of madness through drugs—an experience that helped them to escape the limitations of the literary institutional frameworks of their time. Michel Foucault, "La folie et la société," in *Dits et écrits,* vol. 1, 490.
89. Charles Baudelaire, "The Universal Exhibition of 1855: The Fine Arts," in *Selected Writings on Art and Artists,* trans. P. F. Charvet (Harmondsworth: Penguin Books, 1972), 116. Johan Joachim Winckelmann was an eighteenth-century German art historian who had a lasting influence on the art of antiquity, especially Greece, as well as architecture.
90. Ibid.
91. Ibid.
92. Foucault, "Qu'est-ce-que les Lumières?," 1389.
93. Baudelaire, "The Universal Exhibition of 1855: The Fine Arts," 116.
94. Jorge Luis Borges, "The Anthropologist," in *In Praise of Darkness*, trans. Norman Thomas Di Giovanni (New York: Dutton, 1974), 47.
95. Ibid., 51.
96. Ibid.

Chapter 2

Madness and Cultural Difference

> The wise man laughs only with fear and trembling.
> —Charles-Pierre Baudelaire, "Of the Essence of Laughter"

In an essay, Baudelaire briefly explored the relationship between laughter and madness.[1] On close examination, there is a similar relationship between Foucault's laughter at the strangeness of the Chinese taxonomy and his skepticism about the role of madness in Descartes's First Meditation on radical doubt. Foucault formulated his notion of the cultural divide between Orient and Occident in the context of his critique of Descartes's originary exclusion of madness as unreason from Western rationality. Foucault described the effects the Chinese encyclopedia had on him as a loss of sense, a disturbance of common understanding of taxonomic construction, and a realization of reaching the limit to thought. This chapter explores the paradox of Foucault's radical conception of cultural difference: on the one hand, he critiqued as well as historicized the Cartesian conception of madness, thus opening up a potential new path to an inclusive conception of cultural otherness. On the other hand, he excluded the "Orient" from Western rationality, even though he was a student of forms of rationality. In other words, Foucault did with the Orient what Descartes did with madness.

FOUCAULT'S CRITIQUE OF MADNESS IN THE COGITO

An exploration of how Foucault constructed his critique of Descartes's rationalism will help to understand the continuity as well as the inner contradiction of his conception of non-Western rationality as a "limit-experience." In

Histoire de la Folie à l'Age Classique, Foucault ponders step-by-step Descartes's method of establishing proof that he is indubitably the doubting subject. He rightly notes that madness played a different role in Descartes's demonstration than dreams or errors derived from sense perception. From Descartes's perspective, dreams, no matter how fantastic they may be, are fundamentally different from madness because in them we recognize some simple and general objects as belonging to our state of wakefulness rather than to sleep.[2] Consequently, "whether I am awake or dreaming, it remains true that two and three make five, and that a square has but four sides."[3] Although sleep and dreams are sources of illusions, I, as "a man," can still make out the difference between my state of wakefulness and my state of sleep. I cannot "deny that I possess this hand and this body."[4]

By contrast, Descartes dismisses the possibility that he might be mad, which would have caused him to hallucinate about his doubt, because thinking like a madman would be as "extravagant" as being mad. A madman's "brains are disordered and clouded," and may make him assert that he is a king when he is a pauper, he is clothed when he is naked, or that he has a "head of clay, a body of glass," or even that he is a gourd.[5] From Descartes's perspective, as Foucault rightly points out, it is possible to imagine one's self sleeping or dreaming, but it is impossible to imagine one's self insane. Indeed, "truth appears as the condition of possibility of dreaming," but "madness is precisely the condition of impossibility of thinking."[6] Foucault adds: "madness is excluded by the thinking subject, just as it will soon be excluded that he cannot think, or that he cannot exist."[7] In other words, madness constitutes for Descartes a form of otherness that is not comprehensible because it is not reproducible in one's self. Descartes could feign to sleep and to dream but he could not feign to be insane.

Foucault notes that Descartes disposed of the possibility of his madness as a source of his doubt before he evoked sleep and dreams. Nevertheless, Descartes still alluded to madness again as a possible source of some of the illusions he experienced *in his sleep*. While the madman thinks (he does think) extravagant things *in his waking hours,* the subject of doubt thinks them in his sleep.[8] As Foucault suggests, sleep can be re-experienced, recalled, or feigned by the meditating subject, whereas madness cannot. Hence sleep is crucial as a test of the sanity of the meditating subject; it is proof that he cannot be mad inasmuch as he is aware that what he experiences in his sleep are mere illusions since he can wake up. He can recall the illusions, no matter how fantastic, from his sleep, but try as he may, he cannot re-experience in thought the illusions that a madman experiences, just as he cannot feign madness. There is no possibility for the doubting subject to double up as an insane man. In other words, madness is on the outer edge of the domain of sleep, of what is familiar to the meditating subject. The madman cannot be understood empathically; he can only be evoked as an enclosed and impenetrable being. Madness is not in the same class as perceptual error; it is in a class by itself. Yet, what is noteworthy is Descartes's recognition that a madman is a man *who thinks,* but whose mind is "disordered" due to a physiological condition (e.g., "dark bilious vapors"). The madman is a man who thinks thoughts that are so extravagant that it would be equally extravagant to think them in a meditation on doubt. Yet, it might be objected that it is just as easy to act like a madman as it is to act like a dreamer. The question is whether Descartes's refusal (for it is a refusal) to subject his search for certainty to the test of madness was motivated by his rejection of previous forms of doing philosophy (how could a philosopher entertain the notion of his own madness?), philosophical decorum, or a concern to locate his meditation in an indubitably sound mind.[9] For Descartes, even though madness alters the perception of self, it is not a source of error that can be overcome meditatively. It would not make sense from his perspective to subject his doubt to the test of an illness.

Descartes's exclusion of madness as a test of the certainty of doubt is on a par with his evocation of "a malignant demon" who too might disturb his senses. Like madness, demonic disturbance is beyond the meditating subject's control; it is an external force. Descartes did not see a demonic hand in the disruption of the madman's perception of himself admittedly because this would imply that God—a source of good—willed the madness of the madman. Descartes disposes of the powerful and deceitful demonic force in a manner that contrasts with that of the exclusion of madness from his meditation. He entertains the possibility that a demon might cause him to doubt the existence of the natural world around him as well as his perceptions of sound and color, among others. Such a condition may not be so different from the madman's assertion that his body does not exist in the shape in which a sane man sees it. Yet, Descartes likens the illusions forced on him by the demon, no matter how extravagant, to dreams rather than madness. Prior to conjuring up the figure of the malignant demon, Descartes wondered whether God could will him to be a creature of deception and thus make him implicitly unable to reach truth or think him undeserving of it. However, Descartes extricates himself from a theological bind by simply reminding his reader that a Being that is good and stands for goodness could not will him to be deceived.[10] (God is therefore the upper limit of the radical doubt.)

From Descartes's perspective, madness, a physiological condition, is qualitatively different from demonic deception. Madness is not willed; it just is, whereas demonic deception is the result of a malevolent power. Descartes's dismissal of madness as an unlikely source of uncertainty and error is based on his implicit distinction between pathology (insanity) and health (sanity, reason). A sane person can be deceived but he is aware of his capacity to be deceived even by himself; he can even wish to retain his comforting illusions so as not to undergo a doubt that undermines all certainty in his mind. By contrast, a madman has no awareness of being insane, nor can he have an inkling of what it is to be sane.

A most insightful component of Foucault's critique is his characterization of the Cartesian doubt as "a voluntary exercise, controlled, mastered and carried out from beginning to end by a meditating subject who never allows himself to be surprised."[11] Thus the exclusion of the other is an act of the will; it could have been avoided. Indeed, Descartes engaged in a choreographed staging of doubt involving the doubting subject and the meditating subject. On this stage, the madman does not make an appearance but is alluded to briefly. The actor lacks sufficient empathy for his character to give a convincing performance. Finally, and forsaking the stage analogy, Descartes, according to Foucault, foreclosed all possibility that madness could be one pathway to truth (as had existed in previous centuries).[12] Foucault's critique portends a break from Descartes's sundered rationalism, which even a spirited defense such as Derrida's will not shake.

DERRIDA'S DEFENSE OF CARTESIAN RATIONALISM

In the second chapter of *L'Ecriture et la différence* (*Writing and Difference*), entitled "Cogito and the history of madness," Jacques Derrida took issue with Foucault's critique of Descartes's conception of doubt as well as his treatment of madness in *History of Madness*. Examination of this exchange sheds light on differing interpretations of the foundation of Cartesian rationalism as well as how two dominant French philosophers have approached the epistemology of difference. The exchange brings up not only philosophical issues such as humanism and the role of the subject in theorizing it, but also the place of science in anti-humanism. Derrida questions Foucault's method of interpretation on two main principles: generalization and intentionality. He faults Foucault for relating Descartes's "few allusive and enigmatic pages,"[13] on madness to the (historical) totality of the Cartesian project. In other words, from Derrida's perspective, in historicizing the Cartesian Cogito as the originary point of a history of madness-as-unreason that led to the confinement of the sane to separate spaces throughout the Classical Age, Foucault made an unwarranted leap establishing a "semantic relationship"[14] between one statement (the hyperbole of madness) and the historic discourse of rationalism. In so doing, according to Derrida, Foucault had violated a sine qua non principle of hermeneutics, namely, to distinguish between the sign and the signified, between what Descartes said or intended to say from what the analyst thinks he said.

Derrida points to evidence of conceptions of certainty that defined madness as the opposite of reason in ancient Greece and notes that "classical reason and before it medieval reason were related to Greek reason."[15] What's more, Derrida claims that Foucault (who had rejected Hegelian philosophy) remains Hegelian insofar as in doing a critique of the Classical Age's exclusion of unreason from the rational discourse he used the very structure of rational discourse. Consequently, Foucault's anti-rationalist discourse takes place within the parameters of the Logos—a history of madness is unthinkable without the history of reason and can only be written with reference to reason in the language of reason.[16] In spite of his customary play on words, Derrida rightly draws attention to Foucault's challenge of finding a space from which to mount a critique of rationalist philosophy without relinquishing a methodology steeped in it—a point to which I will return later.

Derrida's defense of the Cogito rests on an acknowledgment of the problematic character of the Cartesian hyperbole of the madman, which it also attempts to explain away. From the outset, Derrida halfheartedly concedes that madness and its various characterizations (such as "extravagance, dementia, insanity *appear,* I do say *appear,* to be excluded from the dignified philosophical circle."[17] The "I do say appear" emphasizes the importance of madness (as otherness) to the Cogito, but in a way that Foucault had not apparently appreciated. Derrida admits, however, that the meditation proceeds in a "discontinuous" manner that implicitly opens it up to questioning.

Derrida resymbolizes the hypothesis of the malignant demon.[18] He argues that while sleep and dreams are "natural" states, which enabled Descartes to gradually build his case, madness is implicitly less "natural," or less experiential to the reader he needs to convince. Indeed, how could the doubting subject expect his reader to follow him on this path to demonstrating the certainty of the Cogito if he assumed that his doubt was caused by madness? Besides, unlike sleep and dreams, madness only partially affects "certain regions of sensory perception,"[19] whereas sleep and dreams affect all of them. Consequently, the hypothesis of madness was not a good "pedagogical" device for Descartes to use. It could only be evoked for "rhetorical"[20] purposes. Furthermore, madness was not a "theme" for Descartes, but something akin to an "index" of a possible illusory state that could not be believable since the doubting subject is not mad.[21] Hence, madness was not central to the Cogito (as Foucault had intimated). Derrida's interpretation begs the question why the hypothesis of madness was invoked in the first place, if it did not add any value to the convincing power of the demonstration or to the strength of the sought-after certainty. Derrida avoids the question in two ways: first by characterizing the hypothesis of the dream as the "hyperbolic enhancement (*exaspération*) of the hypothesis of madness,"[22] thus assimilating the illusions derived from ordinary dreams to the intensity of those that affect the madman; second, by folding the hypothesis of the madman into the hypothesis of the malignant demon, which is given preeminence. From this standpoint, the hyperbole of the malignant demon constitutes "the absolute hyperbolic moment."[23] At times, wandering outside the Meditations and calling on the *Discourse on Method*, Derrida describes the hyperbole of the malignant demon as a "total" disarray of the senses, a "total madness" beyond the control of the doubting subject.[24] At the heart of the Cogito, Derrida finds a form of madness madder than the illusions suffered by the madman whose "brains were clouded by dark bilious vapors." Yet, "the act of the Cogito is valid even if I am mad through and through."[25] Consequently, Derrida finds that madness is not the opposite of reason, as Foucault had claimed. Rather, it is located at the heart of the Cogito, enfolded in it, as a component of the self-same, doubling up the self into its own other. I am the same even if I am mad. In concrete terms, difference was not essential to the wholeness of the Cogito.

The validity of Derrida's interpretation principally relies on the doubting subject's comparing the state of perceptual disarray into which the malignant demon could throw him to that of the madman.[26] The demon is not a person; he is an entirely different entity. Consequently, the malignant demon is not the doubter's other, he belongs to another realm altogether, which the doubter cannot truly understand as he might understand a madman (but chooses not to). Nevertheless, Derrida's analysis is insightful: it points to another aspect of Cartesian rationalism: its capacity to theoretically subsume under its domain forms of resistance such as madness. Where Foucault saw the exclusion of real, historical forms of madness, Derrida saw a formal inclusion of otherness in the construction of self-certainty.

BORGES'S MULTIPLE OTHER

As a counterpoint to these three authors, it is instructive to note how Borges (who inspired Foucault in *Les mots et les choses*) recounts a story ("The Other") in which he met another man as he sat on a bench by the Charles River in Cambridge, Massachusetts. What followed was a surreal experience in which dream and reality mingled. The Other looked like a younger Borges and happened to have lived Borges's life and even remembered details about it with greater accuracy. The symbolic significance of the encounter was enhanced by the depiction of the Other as holding a copy of Dostoevsky's *The Possessed* in his hands and mentioning that he had also read *The Double*, books that Borges had read. During a back-and-forth discussion Borges and the Other wondered if their encounter was a dream. Borges concludes: "The encounter was real, but the other man spoke to me in a dream, which was why he could forget me; I spoke to him while I was awake, and so I am still tormented by the memory."[27] Borges was not conducting a test of reality and certainty in writing this story. Rather, he highlighted the indeterminacy of self-identity, its sundered nature, as he foregrounds the doubling up of the author with his other who wishes to reach out to his others by writing a book that would be "a hymn to the brotherhood of all mankind."[28]

This story weaves dream and reality (as Descartes did), but opens up the space in which the Other is conjured up. It orients the discourse of the Other differently from all three authors: Borges, acting his own character in the story, is affected by the encounter ("I am still tormented"). He could do so by blurring the boundary between dream and wakefulness. Borges goes one step further in opening the self to other cultural modalities. In the poem "The Keeper of the Books," he doubles up as a Chinese by the name of Hsiang. Thus, the Chinese Other slips into the space left open by Borges in his previous musings about encountering his other-himself on a bench by the Charles River. In explaining "The Keeper of the Books," passage by passage, Borges tells his interviewer, "There I was trying to do my best to be Chinese ... I was trying to be as Chinese as a good student of Arthur Waley should be.[29] "I got the name [Hsiang] from Chuang Tzu, but I have no idea how it's pronounced."[30] Apart from the symbolism of the story that the poem narrates, a story of "civilization going to pot,"[31] the poem points to the author's attempt at doubling up as yet another, which required him to enter a different cultural realm albeit, as he carefully notes, through the medium of "translation."[32] Language (Spanish, Chinese, Spanish translated into English, Chinese translated into Spanish or English, etc.) takes Borges through the journey to penetrate his otherness. In a passage from the poem, Borges reflects that "I am going back disguised as a Chinese to my first poem [June 1968]."[33] (In this latter poem, Borges depicts his happiness in spite of his blindness.) Language provides the means to play at being the other, a disguise intended to be beside oneself while staying with oneself. It can also be a means to be outside of oneself while looking into oneself as in a mirror. However, disguises are usually temporary and taken off once the acting is completed. Is there a trace left in the self after the disguise is taken off? Baudelaire had felt that a transformation takes place (or should take place) in the world view of whoever is willing to enter the culture of the

Chinese artist. Borges, writing fiction, experiments with playing at being Chinese. That the puppeteer in the fiction writer may be taken in by his own staged game is not impossible.

Unlike Descartes's search for certainty in construction of identity, however, Borges points to uncertainty as a characteristic of self-identity. Japanese or Iranian cultures, for example, give us glimpses of what we could be rather than how irremediably different we are from the Japanese or the Iranians. By introducing language as crucial to understanding how uncertainty defines self-identity, Borges gives a glimpse of the possibility of writing a dialogical philosophy in which cultural otherness is conceptualized as a necessary path to truth. By the same token, language raises the issue of translation literally and figuratively: translation of terms and cultural translation, as in how to be at home in other cultures.

To return to the exchange between Foucault and Derrida regarding the historical significance of the hyperbole of the madman, neither author perceives the exclusion of madness as symbolizing a possible exclusion of the cultural other, such as the Japanese or the Iranian. However, from the perspective of this book, Foucault's critique of Descartes's treatment of madness as unreason, fruitful as it is, leaves unexplored other avenues, such as those evoked in Borges's identity games. Foucault considers madness the quintessential representation of concrete otherness. His historicizing the consequences of Descartes's conception of madness for the treatment of mad people in the Classical Age allows for a critique of Western rationalism for its exclusion of non-Western forms of rationality. However, by not taking this path, Foucault foreclosed a reflection on the relationship between Western and non-Western forms of rationality. Concretely, Foucault was well aware that actual madness was a universal institution, perceived differently in different cultures. He spoke about madness when in Japan, and had difficulty discussing its representation in the traditional Japanese theater. Nevertheless, his historicizing the role of madness in the Cogito is important: he drew attention to the relationship between knowledge and power—the power to exclude. But, he fell short of drawing the necessary conclusion from this insight, that the Western *ratio* as defined by Descartes was but a *region* of *human* reason.[34] His denunciation of the exclusion of madness from the Cartesian Cogito held the promise of a different understanding of otherness. Yet his analysis of the Chinese encyclopedia situates him squarely inside the rationalist discourse, which he had questioned. In other words, Foucault's critique of the Cogito was grounded in his familiarity with the "common space of culture"[35] he shared with Descartes and in which he remained. It was an inner critique framed by and confined to a specific culture.

MODERNIZING THE COGITO: FOUCAULT'S CRITICAL RETREAT

Interestingly, Foucault's perspective did not change but it received a different inflection in his analysis of the "modern" Cogito. In chapter 9 of *Les mots et les choses,* Foucault revisits the Cartesian Cogito in the context of his discussion of the function of language in the Classical Age. In the seventeenth century, language functioned as representation in which relationships between words and the objects they named was transparent; it needed no deciphering, and it did not leave room for ambiguity. In this phase of European history, the notion of "Man" as an object of study in his capacity as a living, working, and communicating subject could not be countenanced. It is the advent of the language of the "sciences of man"[36] that would make it possible to consider Man in his ambiguity, his complexity, his problematic relation to nature (including his own), his history, and his knowledge. In the seventeenth century, human nature was part of nature insofar as it was the object of a *discourse* that ordered, classified, isolated, and combined the plurality of beings that constitute the world.[37] The Classical Age could not conceive of the human being as the originator of knowledge as well as its object, as a being shot through with ambiguity, or uncertainty, and whose purpose eludes the transparency of language as representation. As Foucault put it: "The passage from 'I think' to 'I am,' took place in the glare of proof (*sous la lumière de l'évidence*), within a discourse whose entire domain and functioning was to superimpose the articulation of what is thought and what is."[38] To object that "being in general is not contained in thought or that this singular being as it is designated by the 'I think' has been neither interrogated nor analyzed in itself" is hardly relevant.[39] Objections of this sort can only arise out of a "discourse that is profoundly different and whose raison d'être is not the linkage between representation and being."[40] Does this revision of the Cogito mean Foucault is backing away from his earlier critique as it appeared in *History of Madness* in 1961 and 1972? If the Cartesian Cogito could not have been expressed differently and if questioning it is intelligible only after a new episteme had emerged, how is it possible to claim that it inflected the history of madness from the seventeenth century onward? Isn't Foucault in the end undermining his critique by justifying the role Descartes assigned madness as unreason? There is a difference between unearthing the philosophical underpinning of unreason, and justifying its modality.

To recall, in concluding his disagreement with Derrida over the Cartesian Cogito, Foucault charged Derrida with "reducing discursive practices to textual traces," which led to a "failure to examine the modes of implication of the subject in discourses."[41] In other words, Derrida failed to question the embededness of the Cogito in an act of philosophical reflection that sought to build the foundation of certainty and truth by excluding from the doubt, as a matter of choice, inconvenient things, such as madness, naming them instead as resistant to thought. But in *Les mots et les choses,* Foucault appears to sidestep the implication of the subject of the Cogito in his exclusion of madness from his search for certainty.[42] This may be one of the many inconsistencies that Foucault's work displays. However, the subject matter, unreason-as-otherness, is far too important a part of Foucault's view of the Orient to be dismissed. It begs the question whether the emergence of the "sciences of man" have constructed an epistemology that departs from the Cartesian search for certainty. Foucault may have had this question on his mind as he pointed to the scope of the epistemological shift from the seventeenth century to the nineteenth, which made unavoidable the revival of "the theme of the Cogito." This is a fourfold shift "from truth to being, from nature to man, from the possibility of knowledge to that of a primary lack of recognition (*méconnaissance*), from the ungrounded philosophical theories in relation to science, to a clear philosophical consciousness that assumes all this field of ungrounded experiences in which man does not recognize himself."[43] A "modern Cogito" would not seek, as Descartes did, to bring out "thought in its most general form [that encompasses] such thoughts as illusion and error in order to reveal their danger ... and to provide the method to guard against them."[44] It would, on the contrary, avoid reducing being to thought and focus instead on the "distance that at once separates and links present thought to the self," and constantly and incessantly address all that is unthought.[45] In practical terms, does this mean that the focus on the self obviates the significance of the cultural other for knowledge of the self—a main goal of anthropology?

The modern Cogito can no longer lead to the certainty of being; rather, it destabilizes it. (With the advent of psychoanalysis, certainty in thought is all but dubious.) As Foucault suggests, it is no longer possible to affirm "I think, therefore I am." In reality, "I could easily affirm that I think, therefore I am not all that [defines me as a living being]."[46] This re-examination of the Cartesian Cogito may signify Foucault's abiding concern with its significance in French letters, although he also refers to its integration in Husserlian phenomenology alongside Immanuel Kant's transcendentalism.[47] After all, there were other philosophers outside France who had defined rationalism differently from Descartes. It may also mean Foucault's commitment to the necessity of maintaining the validity of the Cogito, albeit redefining it in a new key. The revision of the Cogito in *Les mots et les choses* no longer mentions madness or otherness; it evokes the "unthought" and emphasizes the complexity as well as indeterminacy of being, which eludes the confines of thought. Admittedly, difference and otherness are subsumed under the unthought.[48] However, to accept this assumption would mean that cultural otherness—when expressed as the existence of a different way of thinking, or of a being that is not necessarily unthought but willfully ignored, explained away, dismissed, or redefined as insufficiently human—cannot be grasped in its own.

At any rate, Foucault trusts that the modern Cogito's function is to reveal that at the heart of self-reflection lies man's inability to capture himself with transparency, untrammeled by the exteriority constituted by his living body, his labor, and his language, all of which largely escape his total grasp. Not even phenomenology, at least as Husserl defined it, managed to break away from the empirical studies of man, although it remains, according to Foucault, an "ontology of the untought"[49] with its eidetic bracketing of the Cogito.[50] However, this skepticism about empirical knowledge of the self overlooks the fact that the existence of the unconscious permits the study of man as he reaches the limit of his reflection upon himself reflecting. The unthought—whether as the unconscious, alienation as analyzed by Marx, the passage of the in-itself to the for-itself, or the "implicit" in Husserl's phenomenology—is the "double" of man.[51] For Foucault, the unthought, the shadow of man, is the Other, a "fraternal and twin Other, … born out of a duality without recourse … the blind spot from which it is possible to know him."[52] It is easy to conclude that this is the beginning of an expansive conception of otherness. But Foucault points out that the emergence of the unthought as a challenge to knowledge is "intimately linked to our modernity." It is so because "thought … must be at once knowledge and modification of what it knows, a reflection and transformation of the mode of being of what it reflects upon."[53] In this process, thought cannot reveal the unthought without "bringing it closer to itself,—or perhaps even pushing it away without … effectively causing the being of man to be altered."[54] The question is, can this man so conceived know other men outside of his cultural space if he cannot know himself fully? Or, does his knowledge of himself require excluding others from his world?

An obscure passage from *Les mots et les choses* reveals a contorted view of otherness that cannot be contained in the bounds in which Foucault maintained it: "for it [the analytic of finitude], it is a question of showing how the Other (*l'Autre*) and the Distant (*le Lointain*) is also the 'Near and the Same.'"[55] (Foucault revisits this notion as "proximity" and "distance" in Tokyo.) The opposite pair, *le Proche* and *le Même* is meant to be what lies behind or underneath the "Near and the Same." In other words, what appears to be distant and different is in reality near and not so different at all; it is the self-same. This process of revealing the truth of the other unfolds within what might be called the circle of modernity. Modern thought is a constant "revealing of the Same."[56] The circle is drawn around the self-same; it is the outer limit of the endless search of the Same at the same time that it is the world in which the dialectic of identity plays itself out in a movement of discovery and repetition. Foucault calls this "a dialectical game."[57] When he was in Japan, in the midst of modernity, Foucault drew the circle around himself closer, as he experienced a strong sense of estrangement; he did not see in the Japanese modalities of himself, of the Same.

The lexical register of the game is appealing to one who is placed in "modernity" by accident and may not identify with its history as are those who were colonized or whose history was inflected by it, as was China. *L'Autre et le Lointain* captures the empirical otherness of these people well enough, and the pair *le Proche* and *le Même* may illustrate their yearning for a full recognition of their common humanity. But the circle of modernity that Foucault draws around "man" militates against this reading. The circle may seem unbounded to this figure, ever receding. However, it remains a circle, which means that it excludes the variegated modalities of empirical otherness that have eluded modernity, were bypassed by it while living in its heart, were slighted by it, resisted its Western modality, or are still clamoring for it, depending, naturally, on what is meant by it.[58]

At any rate, the last line of the passage entitled "The Cogito and the Unthought," in chapter 9 of *Les mots et les choses,* suggesting that "more profoundly, modern thought is moving towards that direction where the Other of man must become the Same as himself"[59] sounds a hopeful note. One could imagine Foucault moving cross the "Oriental" divide he proffered and recognizing himself in the cultural other. In spite of its generality, the configuration (*Lointain/Proche*; *L'Autre/le Même*) holds the possibility of a conception of the empirical cultural other as a modality of the self-same. It may also imply, but only imply, that the reconciliation of the self-same with its unthought other can occur only if the self-same recognizes that it, itself, is no more than one of the modalities of the empirical cultural other as intuited by Baudelaire's call for cosmopolitanism. This would stretch Marx's conception of alienation (to which Foucault refers) to include the alienation of the human from other humans, not simply from himself.

It is unclear why Foucault returns to the Cogito at all given his serious misgivings about it. As Georges Canguilhem suggests in his review of *Les mots et les choses,* there are attempts at elaborating non-Cartesian as well as non-Kantian epistemologies in the modern era, such as those made by Gaston Bachelard. Canguilhem does not specifically wonder why Foucault did not address Bachelard's work, but leaves open the possibility that he might have been following in Bachelard's "footsteps."[60] Would including Bachelard's views have changed the tenor of Foucault's discussion of the

"Cogito and the Unthought" or its necessity? The question may not be important since it would require a critique of the selection of the Cartesian Cogito as a key to understanding *History of Madness*. In addition to Bachelard, Canguilhem also notes Foucault's near silence on the overlap between his work and that of Auguste Comte who sought to overcome Kant's metaphysics while dismissing the Cartesian Cogito.[61]

In sum, the revival of the theme of the Cogito in the modern era builds on a Cartesian kernel that Foucault identifies as the unthought, and which in his estimation Descartes had prefigured. In *Les mots et les choses*, Foucault no longer problematizes the exclusion of madness; his concern shifts from the significance of the exclusion of difference to identifying the role of the untought in knowledge of man from the eighteenth century onward. Rather than signifying a coming to terms with cultural otherness (such as that of the Japanese or the Iranian), the shift normalizes its exclusion from the Western *ratio*. The focus is on the self and its constant struggle to know itself. What is noteworthy is Foucault's definition of the Other as the twin of the self-same, which brings him close to Borges. But, where Borges expands his other to embrace the real, empirical other, Foucault remains in the cultural domain of the West, and points to a "destin occidental" (Western destiny).[62] Borges reminds the reader of the tradition of the double, the döppelgänger, in German, Jewish, as well as Scottish superstitions whereby "if you meet yourself you meet your real self, and this other will come to fetch you."[63] He also notes that the self-double dynamics may signal that "the door of suicide is open."[64] Coincidentally, in *Les mots et les choses*, Foucault comes figuratively close to the theme of suicide at the end of the process of searching for the double, as he claims that the emergence of the "sciences of man" ushered in the "death of man."

I take as a weakness of the modern Cogito its inability to think of the unthought as nothing more than a mere, albeit complex, revelation to the Same of itself thus enclosing it upon itself in a constant shuttle from itself to itself. Unwittingly, in a moment of insightful candor, and in a different context, Foucault gave this condition a name: narcissism.[65]

To reiterate, the question is, how does this elusive unthought/self permit an understanding of the empirical other, the China or Japan other, for example? The "man" of the social sciences such as sociology or anthropology may not be the same "man" as that of philosophy. Yet, the social sciences as empirical sciences at least theoretically hold the promise of bringing modalities of empirical men closer together. Foucault had serious misgivings about anthropology, as one of the "sciences of man." To examine the role that Foucault attributed to anthropology in the undoing of man sheds light on his conception of the Orient as a limit-experience.

NOTES

1. Charles-Pierre Baudelaire, "Of the Essence of Laughter, and Generally of the Comic in the Plastic Arts," in *Baudelaire: Selected Writings on Arts and Artists,* trans. P.E Charvet (Harmondsworth: Penguin, 1972), 143.
2. These objects are "extension, the figure of extended things, their quantity or magnitude, and their number, as also the place in, and the time during which they exist ..." René Descartes, *The Meditations and Selections from the Principles of René Descartes,* trans. John Veitch (La Salle, Ill.: Open Court, 1966), 25.
3. Ibid.
4. Ibid., 23.
5. Ibid.
6. Foucault, *History of Madness,* ed. Jean Khalfa, trans. Jonathan Murphy and Jean Khalfa (London: Routledge, 2009), 57. Foucault elaborated on his critique of Descartes in an essay, "Mon corps, ce papier, ce feu," which initially appeared in the Japanese review *Paideia* under the title "Réponse à Derrida." Michel Foucault, "Réponse à Derrida," *Paideia,* no. 11 (1 February 1972): 131–47. An English translation appears in *The Essential Works of Michel Foucault, 1954-1984,* ed. Paul Rabinow, vol. 2, Aesthetics, Method, and Epistemology, ed. James B. Faubion, trans. Robert Hurley and others (New York: The New Press, 1998): 393–417. The editors of *Dits et écrits* and Rabinow note that the French text was published as Appendix II in *Histoire de la folie á l'âge classique* in 1972. However, the paperback edition of this book published the same year does not contain Appendix II. Gallimard's "collection Tel quel" points out that it gathers together works "as they have been published in their original edition." See end of book. Both of the essays "My Body" and "Reply to Derrida" were also published in *History of Madness.*
7. Descartes, *The Meditations.*
8. Ibid., 23. Descartes writes on p. 23: "I am in the habit of sleeping and representing to myself in dreams those same dreams ... which the insane think are presented to them in their waking moments."
9. Jacques Derrida, in his critique of Foucault's interpretation of Descartes's doubt, alludes to a "philosophical circle of dignity" as a possible reason for Descartes's "seeming" exclusion of madness from his doubt. Jacques Derrida, *L'Écriture et la différence* (Paris: Éditions du Seuil, 1967), 52. Translated as *Writing and Difference,* trans. Alan Bass (Chicago: Chicago University Press, 1978), 31.
10. Descartes, *The Meditations,* 26.
11. Foucault, *History of Madness,* 571.
12. Ibid., 566.
13. Derrida, *L'Écriture et la différence,* 52; *Writing and Difference,* 31.
14. Derrida, *L'Écriture et la différence,* 53; *Writing and Difference,* 32.
15. Derrida, *L'Écriture et la différence,* 66; *Writing and Difference,* 41.
16. Derrida's critique is riddled with references to Hegel. *L'Écriture et la différence,* 59 (Hegel is mentioned twice on this page), 62, 68.

17. Ibid., 52; *Writing and Difference*, 32.
18. Derrida sets up a stage (the same device Foucault adopted in "My Body, This Paper," in *History of Madness*, 556) on which the Cartesian doubt unfolds between three protagonists: the doubting subject, his "non-philosopher" reader, and "us" (*nous*), presumably the philosophically enlightened readers. The doubting subject moves from one scene (hyperbolic doubt) to the next, making sure that he keeps his readers on board.
19. Derrida, *L'Écriture et la différence*, 79.
20. Derrida redefines Foucault's use of "demonstration" and "exercise" as moments of the hyperbolic doubt as "pedagogy and rhetoric."
21. Derrida, *L'Écriture et la différence*, 79n1; *Writing and Difference*, 308n15.
22. Derrida, *L'Écriture et la différence*, 79n1.
23. Ibid., 81; *Writing and Difference*, 52.
24. Derrida, *L'Écriture et la différence*, 81.
25. Ibid., 85; *Writing and Difference*, 55.
26. However, comparing the illusions that the malignant demon might cause is different from actually exploring madness, reducing it through depth analysis in order to expose that "kernel" of certainty, which Derrida admitted was missing at least prior to Descartes's invocation of the hypothesis of the malignant demon.
27. Jorge Luis Borges, "The Other," in *Book of Sand and Shakespeare's Memory*, trans. Andrew Hurley (New York: Viking Penguin, 1998), 11.
28. Ibid., 7.
29. Jorge Luis Borges, "The Keeper of the Books," in *Borges on Writing*, ed. Norman Thomas Di Giovanni, Daniel Halpern, and Frank MacShane (New York: Dutton, 1973), 86. Arthur David Waley (1889–1966) was a translator of Chinese poetry and prose.
30. Borges, "The Keeper of the Books," 90.
31. Ibid.
32. Ibid., 86. In his discussion of a passage in the poem referring to the "conduct of the Emperor," Borges explains, "[t]hat's cribbed from Confucius—in translation of course." Ibid.
33. Ibid., 87.
34. I am grateful to Professor Yasuo Kobayashi for making it possible for me to glimpse this point in the course of a discussion. Interview, Tokyo, 25 July 2014.
35. Foucault, *L'Archéologie du Savoir*, Bibliothèque Nationale de France, Richelieu site, NAF 2028 (1), Box XLVIII, 34. (This draft is identified in the inventory as "intermédiaire," suggesting that it is not the first one, p. 7.)
36. Foucault, *Les mots et les choses*, 322; *The Order of Things*, 311.
37. Foucault, *Les mots et les choses*, 322.
38. Ibid. Literally, "sous la lumière de l'évidence" means "under the light of evidence"; it refers to the demonstration that Descartes provided of the certainty of his being. In his essay, "This body, this paper, this fire," Foucault uses the term *épreuve*, a test, a concept that is close to "evidence."

39. *Les mots et les choses*, 323; *The Order of Things*, 312.
40. Ibid.
41. Foucault, *History of Madness*, 573.
42. It must be noted in this regard that Robert D'Amico, who directly addressed the Derrida–Foucault exchange, argues that the focus of the exchange is "the literary effects and symptoms of the text, not the traditional issues of sound philosophical argument." Robert D'Amico, "Text and Context: Derrida and Foucault on Descartes," in *The Structural Allegory: Reconstructive Encounters with the New French Thought*, ed. John Fekete (Manchester: Manchester University Press, 1984), 180. See also, Robert D'Amico, "Sed Amentes Sunt Isti: Against Michel Foucault's Account of Cartesian Skepticism and Madness," *Philosophical Forum* 26, no. 1 (Autumn 1994): 33–48. It may very well be that in the end D'Amico's interpretation is borne out by Foucault's stance in *The Order of Things*, which D'Amico does not mention in the cited essay.
43. Foucault, *Les mots et les choses*, 334; *The Order of Things*, 323. The French word *méconnaissance* is translated in the English text as "misunderstanding," which does not capture the nuanced meaning of the term. There is the notion of a lack of recognition as well as a notion of inadequate knowledge that is lost in the translation. *Méconnaissance* should be read together with Foucault's use of the concept of *non-connu* or "not-known," which derives from the same verb *connaître*, meaning "to know." Perhaps a neologism such as "mis-knowledge" would be more appropriate. It is not that man is the object of misunderstanding (although that can happen) but that he is not sufficiently or adequately grasped or acknowledged in his complexity, in his paradox (of being knower and object of knowledge), or in his exterior determinations.
44. Foucault, *Les mots et les choses*, 335; *The Order of Things*, 324.
45. Foucault, *Les mots et les choses*, 335.
46. Ibid.
47. Ibid., 336; *The Order of Things*, 325.
48. Besides its psychoanalytic meaning, the unthought may be interpreted as encompassing the cultural other.
49. Foucault, *Les mots et les choses*, 337; *The Order of Things*, 326.
50. Foucault, *Les mots et les choses*, 336–37; *The Order of Things*, 325–26.
51. Foucault, *Les mots et les choses*, 338; *The Order of Things*, 327.
52. Foucault, *Les mots et les choses*, 337; *The Order of Things*, 326.
53. Foucault, *Les mots et les choses*, 338; *The Order of Things*, 327.
54. Foucault, *Les mots et les choses*, 338.
55. Ibid., 350; *The Order of Things*, 339.
56. Foucault, *Les mots et les choses*, 351; *The Order of Things*, 340.
57. Foucault, *Les mots et les choses*, 351.
58. Foucault defines it in his comments on Kant's "What Is Enlightenment" as "an attitude."
59. Foucault, *Les mots et les choses*, 339; *The Order of Things*, 328.

60. Canguilhem, "Mort de l'homme ou épuisement du cogito," *Critique* 242 (July 1967) : 617.
61. Ibid., 615. Canguilhem notes that Foucault mentions Comte only once.
62. Foucault, *Les mots et les choses,* 338; *The Order of Things,* 328.
63. Borges, *Borges on Writing,* 97–98.
64. Ibid., 98.
65. In discussing his visit to Hungary in 1965, Foucault commented on the French ignorance of literary events abroad, which he attributed to "the monoglot narcissism of the French." Cited in Macey, *The Lives of Michel Foucault,* 180. Macey further documents Foucault's amazement at his lack of knowledge of a trend of thought in England called the "new psychiatry," which began about the time that *History of Madness* was written. Macey, 212, suspicious of Foucault's admission of his "ignorance," seeks to explain why Foucault could not have known of the existence of the trend.

Chapter 3

Foucault and Kant's Cosmopolitan Anthropology

Immanuel Kant's *Anthropology from a Pragmatic Point of View* (hereafter *Anthropology*) is crucial to understanding Foucault's positioning toward the Orient as cultural otherness. If Foucault's reading of Descartes informed his philosophical conception of the Western *ratio,* his critique of Kant's *Anthropology* framed his struggles with understanding cultural difference. Foucault had translated the *Anthropology* into French with an Introduction (hereafter *Introduction*) as his second dissertation in fulfillment of the requirements for his doctorate degree. His examiners, Jean Hyppolite and Maurice de Gandillac, suggested that he separate his *Introduction* from the translation, and consider publishing it as a book in its own right. He followed their advice and thus *Les mots et les choses* came to be. This meant that the book could be read as an elaboration on the *Introduction* to Kant's *Anthropology,* which Foucault understood as playing a foundational role in the contemporary "human sciences." The groundwork for both texts is one of the courses Foucault gave at the Ecole Normale Supérieure in 1953–1955 on anthropology.[1]

This chapter concerns itself solely with how Foucault read the *Anthropology* and how his reading shaped his critique of the human sciences, especially anthropology, whose subject has traditionally been non-Western cultures. For about twenty-three years, Kant taught a course on anthropology at the Albertina University of Königsberg alongside other courses, which included geography, theology, and the natural sciences. Initially part of the physical geography lectures which Kant started teaching in 1756, the anthropology course was taught separately and alternated with geography from 1772–1773 until 1796.[2] Traditionally courses at the university were taught as commentaries in German on a Latin textbook. However, the anthropology course was Kant's innovation and had no textbook.³ To satisfy the teaching requirement, Kant used Alexander Gottlieb Baumgarten's *Metaphysics* as text, principally the section devoted to empirical psychology.⁴ Kant never wrote a textbook for his anthropology. His students usually took notes, which they copied and circulated over the years from one cohort to the next.⁵ The lectures were very popular, attracting an average of forty-two students per year, who paid four Reichstaler each.⁶ Kant did not publish the lectures as a book until 1798, six years before his death.⁷

Alternately characterized as " marginal," "transitional," or "a crucible" for Kant's major ideas, the *Anthropology* has not received the attention it deserves among English-speaking scholars until recently.⁸ Debates over the status of the *Anthropology* in Kant's thought generally focus on the relationships between the *Anthropology,* critical philosophy, and Kant's historical-political writings.⁹ Considering that the anthropology lectures were given regularly throughout Kant's life as a parallel to his other academic activities, interpreters often find it difficult to assess it as an autonomous work. The *Anthropology*'s unusual situation of being contemporaneous with Kant's written works prompted Caygill to suggest the tantalizing idea that Kant's lectures offered him a space in which he felt free to explore ideas and pursue arguments he could not have otherwise. To be sure, there were constraints concerning the organizational form in which philosophical ideas had to be presented, in addition to the requirement of using a textbook, which framed and thus limited the nature of debates raised by the lectures. Being new to the curriculum, and having no real textbook to ground them in, the anthropology lectures allowed Kant a degree of freedom in determining their contents and structure. In this sense, the lectures were the "crucible" for some ideas, which Kant developed later in a more elaborate form in his other works.¹⁰ Caygill's suggestion raises the provocative idea that Kant may have treasured the space that the lectures offered him to explore lines of inquiry in his conception of anthropology that were different from or at odds with his philosophy.¹¹ Kant had specifically wanted his anthropology to teach his students to learn "how to philosophize," not to learn philosophy.¹² He had been critical of the prevailing scholastic pedagogical method, which caused students to become adept at juggling decontextualized, abstract concepts devoid of relevance to the real world. He noticed at the inception of his career that students "learned early to reason, without possessing sufficient historical knowledge which could take the place of [lack of] experience."¹³ Hence he intended to use his physical geography as well as anthropology lectures to prepare them for the world, as he valued relevant and applied knowledge. At any rate, the opportunity that the anthropology lectures afforded Kant is a significant intellectual event that needs to be studied in its own right, as potentially an author's intentional and strategic carving out of a space into which to escape from a rigid academic setting. It also implies that the *Anthropology* may gain by being assessed on its own merit.[14]

KANT'S ANTHROPOLOGY FROM A PRAGMATIC POINT OF VIEW

Pragmatics

A brief description of how Kant defined his *Anthropology* is necessary to understand how Foucault read it. Kant started his new course at a time when Germany was undergoing socioeconomic change under the impulse of industrialization that had already swept through other European societies. This was a time of intellectual effervescence as the German Enlightenment movement entered a new phase in which various groups competed for its contents and direction.[15] Anthropology, as an emerging area of inquiry, provided Kant and his academic contemporaries with the opportunity to escape the confines of the ascendant theological mode of academic discourse by developing new methods for how to write and speak about human beings.[16] Grafted onto this goal was interest in exploring the social purpose and meaning of science as well as the role of the intellectual in bringing about cultural change in the midst of a fraying social order. Kant intended to provide an alternative to Ernst Platner's *Anthropology for Physicians and Philosophers,* published in 1772, which studied human behavior with the method of natural history, resulting in what Kant criticized as "futile inquiries as to the manner in which bodily organs are connected with thought."[17] However, although Kant focused on Platner, there were competing anthropological views, most notably from his former student, Johann Gottfried Herder (1744–1803). Herder advocated a conception of human beings that stressed the role of language, affect, and spirituality in shaping cultures.[18]

At first glance, with its two parts titled, "Didactics" and "Characteristics," the *Anthropology* is a disconcerting book given our understanding of anthropology today.[19] It is a disquisition on a number of subjects related to human character and behavior. It strikes as much by its clarity as by some unexamined (and prejudicial) notions such as those concerning women or the character of non-Europeans, which Kant shared with his contemporaries.[20] Kant intended to make anthropology "a proper academic discipline."[21] From the outset he approached it as "[a] doctrine of knowledge of the human being,"[22] to which he intended to define a purpose and construct an epistemology. He distinguished anthropological knowledge from physiology—

the study of the organic constitution of the individual, as for example his nervous system. Unlike physiology, anthropological knowledge is knowledge of the human being carried out "from a pragmatic point of view." It is the "investigation of what *he* as a free-acting being makes of himself, or can and should make of himself."[23] In other words, pragmatic anthropology does not focus on human beings in their physiological nature because such knowledge is "the result of the play of nature," and can only count as "its theoretical knowledge."[24] A brief section of the *Anthropology* is nevertheless devoted to " the character of the races" (a subject Kant treated problematically elsewhere) in which he refers the reader to the questionable work of Christoph Girtanner.[25]

Kant's definition of the object of anthropology denotes the singularity of this type of knowledge (it is pragmatic), its assumption (a free being implicitly endowed with reason), and its moral purpose (what he should make of himself). Although intended to be academic, pragmatic anthropology is avowedly engaged in a way that seeks to understand the human being's involvement in the environment in which he lives. Anthropological knowledge is "*knowledge of the world,*" acquired after formal *schooling*. However, to qualify as pragmatic, knowledge of the world must "contain knowledge of the human being as *a citizen of the world.*"[26] A clarification of "pragmatic"[27] is required before I turn to what Kant meant by "citizen of the world."

Pragmatic knowledge includes three related ideas:[28] first, anthropological knowledge is not scholastic, not a "science for the school" (which is what Kant felt Platner's anthropology was); it is not abstract or removed from people's everyday concerns, or "common life,"[29] but oriented toward human beings acting freely in a "cosmopolitan society"[30] and a world to which they are "destined by nature."[31] Second, anthropological knowledge relies on concrete examples drawn from ordinary people's everyday life to be accessible and useful to human beings; it is "popular" as it deals with the world of experience.[32] As Kant put it, "our anthropology can be read by everyone, even by ladies getting dressed."[33] Third, anthropological knowledge aims for being prudential by giving human beings the skills necessary to use others in the pursuit of their own ends.[34] Kant defines prudential as the "inclination toward the capacity of having influence in general over other human beings." The skillful use of others for one's purposes is also a source of "well-being"[35] and "the capability of choosing the best means to happiness."[36] Anthropological knowledge is also pragmatic in another sense as Holly L. Wilson suggests, in that it concerns itself with the human beings' predispositions to cultivate and moralize themselves.[37] The popular character of anthropological knowledge obscures its significant function as a method of understanding how human beings use their capacity of judgment in acting the way they do. In this sense, it sheds light on human *nature* above and beyond its situational manifestations.

The World

Pragmatic anthropology depends on its object as "a citizen of the world." This notion connotes an individual actively engaged in a system of reciprocal rights and duties toward himself and others. It also points to Kant's conception of the ultimate purposiveness of anthropological knowledge: the human species, the world as cosmopolis.[38] In making himself, the human being distinguishes himself from nonhuman animals at the same time that he tends toward his human potential, which he shares with the human species. General knowledge is knowledge of species man, acquired through information collected on culturally situated human beings.

The human being has three functions in the *Anthropology*, all centering on the world: (a) he is an object (of the world of beings) endowed with the capacity to reason; (b) he acquires knowledge of the world; (c) he applies knowledge of the world and makes it "useful" to himself and others. Consequently, the *world* is a crucial concept in pragmatic anthropology. It indicates that anthropology has no borders; its raison d'être is to go beyond the confines of one place or one culture. Furthermore, it denotes an anthropology concerned with the complexity of human existence and relations in a world whose geography is at once physical, political, and moral.[39] Hence, knowledge of the world is also knowledge of the human being "even though he constitutes only one part of the creatures of the world."[40] Kant wishes to stress that although the world is vast and includes both humans and nonhumans, anthropological knowledge is knowledge of the human being as a being oriented toward cultural progress through knowledge of himself and others. A human being who merely focuses on knowing the world only seeks to understand it. He is only a "spectator"; the point is to be "in the game,"[41] to make use of the world through knowledge and for cultural progress. This human-in-the-game has the capacity to know himself, which begins when, as a child, he makes the transition from feeling and speaking of himself in the third person, to thinking. After discovering the "I," he begins to think himself.[42] Such an individual is oriented toward moral improvement, and even though he is inclined to do wrong, his capacity to reason inflects his behavior toward the good and thus "renders him worthy of humanity."[43] The notion of the world and the place of (anthropological) man in it is crucial to understanding the goal Kant imparted to pragmatic anthropological knowledge.

The Second Eye of Science

From Kant's perspective, anthropological knowledge must be scientific (albeit not in a positivist sense) in spite of the difficulties to make it so, considering the peculiar nature of human beings. Kant specifically describes the obstacles that stand in the way of studying human beings. For example, humans tend to conceal their motivations from others and from themselves, or fail to examine them objectively; they alter their behavior when observed by others; and they do not know how to judge themselves and perceive others due to the power of habit and limited contact with others different from themselves.[44] In the end, the task of the anthropologist is an arduous one as it is entwined with understanding the "nature" that underlies the manifestations of the complex behavior of humans interacting with one another. In spite of this, or perhaps because of it, anthropological knowledge must be guided by "general knowledge [which] always precedes *local* knowledge here *if the latter is to be ordered and directed through philosophy.*"[45] Kant worried that in the absence of general knowledge the citizen would remain "locked in very tight limits,"[46] and anthropology would "yield nothing more than fragmentary groping around and no science."[47] However, the end of the sentence mentioning general knowledge (frequently omitted by commentators), which I placed in italics, speaks to Kant's concern for making anthropology a scientific academic discipline by organizing it according to presumably rigorous and systematic philosophical categories. This also means that the anthropologist must have some conception of human beings and their nature that would help her to make sense of her observations in a coherent manner. A pragmatic anthropology, which combines a systematic design and a popular orientation would, in Kant's view, result in "the growth of science for the common good."[48]

The notion of system, an important part of any scientific enterprise, needs emphasizing. Kant defines it clearly in his *Physical Geography*: "Moreover, we must also know the objects of our experience in a general form so that our knowledge forms a system rather than an aggregate; for in a system the whole prevails over its parts while in aggregate the parts overshadow the whole." In the same manner that building a house requires a plan drawn by an architect, "we are preparing here an architectural concept, i.e. concept by which means diversity may be reconciled with totality."[49] Kant perceives the totality as "the earth." In the *Anthropology*, it is the "world."[50] Anthropological knowledge is scientific in seeking to arrive at a total (general) knowledge of human nature as it arises out of its multiple cultural modalities. This is the challenge of anthropology for Kant, as he will need to show that he is consistent with the methodological requirement (of reconciling diversity with totality) when he writes about different peoples. Because it is a science dealing with human beings, anthropology is uniquely equipped to understand the shortcomings of the abstract or natural sciences. It can act as their conscience, or a sort of science of the sciences (an echo of which is found in Auguste Comte's conception of positive sociology) in the sense that it corrects the structural problems inherent in the other sciences (such as geometry, law, medicine, or theology). The autonomy of these sciences causes their practitioners, as experts, to experience overconfidence, a sense of specialness resulting in egoism, and power that they wield in and outside of their fields. Consequently, the scientists lose a sense of purpose, and in spite of the good their knowledge contributes to society, have only a partial vision of their subject matter. Lacking reflexivity, they do not question their power or have "self-knowledge of the understanding of reason." They are "cyclops" who have lost sight of themselves and of "the humanity of the sciences." Hence, they need anthropological knowledge to give them a "second eye."[51]

Besides being systematic, pragmatic anthropological knowledge relies on observation where possible, as well as interaction of the anthropologist with her fellow citizens in big cities and seaports (like Königsberg) where commerce brings people with different experiences in contact with one another.[52] Since German cities and seaports are only a small part of the world, observation must be supplemented with travel, or reading travel accounts and chronicles,[53] as well as "world history, biographies, even plays and novels."[54] Although novels deal with fiction, their characters "have been taken from the observation of real human beings: for while they are exaggerated in degree, they must nevertheless correspond to human nature in kind."[55] Novels also provide information about the feelings of their authors—another anthropological datum. A genuinely empirical anthropology would conceivably recommend that knowledge be gathered from various locations before being systematized into general knowledge of human beings. Kant makes it theoretically possible to argue against grounding general knowledge of human beings in local knowledge that does not perceive itself as such: he shied away from "characterizing beings of a given species," because this would require grouping them with others we already know, under the same concept. However, this cannot be done because, for example, were we to define ourselves as "terrestrial rational beings," we would presume that we know "rational non-terrestrial beings," which we do not.[56] However, his intent is not to argue that we cannot know nonterrestrial beings, only that we need some comparable beings to be able to understand what they are.[57]

At first glance, there is ambiguity in Kant's attempt to make anthropological knowledge scientific, as he must uphold the notion of a general human nature at the same time that he stresses the concreteness of the experiences of human beings who actualize or diverge from their nature as active knowers and users of the knowledge they acquire about the world and about one another.[58] Comparing people inhabiting different societies is possible but it requires knowing one's self and one's own society in its diversity (from cities, ports, countryside, etc.). For Kant, knowledge of human beings is general insofar as it assumes that there are human attributes inherent in say Germans, or any other group of humans, that are universal but that need to be specified in their various "local" modalities. In this sense, the acquisition of empirical knowledge in one form or another is a necessity. Can the universal as the "ought" be achieved through empirical observation? To answer this moral question requires re-placing Kant's anthropology in the context of his political writings concerning ways to achieve peace and a global civil society. Progress toward a better world appears achievable through political and legal action. From this perspective, pragmatic anthropological knowledge does not rest on "a priori cognition" but targeted action.[59]

Relevance

When read as setting up a research agenda that includes a specific domain, the world; a clear objective (no matter how broadly defined), knowledge of humanity; a methodology, observation and secondary sources; a purpose, reaching one's potential as a member of the species; and a selection of social and social-psychological themes, the *Anthropology* appears as an important text that has relevance for the social sciences today, particularly anthropology and sociology.[60] First, Kant's emphasis on empirical anthropological knowledge is shared by contemporary anthropology and sociology. Parenthetically, the fieldwork that anthropologists were traditionally required to carry out by living with preliterate human groups theoretically constituted a manner of experiencing a different modality of being human. And the ultimate purpose for studying these groups was to shed light on the nature of the human condition, notwithstanding the vagaries of attempts made in pursuing this goal.[61] Second, Kant's emphasis on *culture* as the product of human activity, a socializing force, and an impediment to acquiring a cosmopolitan approach to knowledge resonates with our concerns about ethnocentrism as well as other forms of cultural self-centeredness that privilege the study of differences between cultures at the expense of their similarities. Third, Kant's objective to make anthropological knowledge useful to humanity prefigures the trend toward "public" social science (and even philosophy). Fourth, and related to the preceding, Kant's focus on people's ordinary lives in order to get at the logic underlying their judgment[62] prefigured the "sociology of everyday life" as well as attempts made by some sociologists, such as Harold Garfinkel, to focus on everyday routines in order to uncover the principles that give them meaning, of which human beings are unaware.[63] Fifth, a central question in sociological theory focuses on the relationship between the individual and society. If life in society requires socialization in the prevailing value and normative systems, how is agency possible? Kant offers an answer by positing a collective *human* purpose, which human beings tend toward, above and beyond their sociocultural trappings. He understood that this purpose, which is not achievable at once or even understood by every human being, is grounded in history and can be made out in situations of crisis.[64]

This cursory review of the relevance of the *Anthropology* to contemporary anthropology and sociology does not mean that it is without reproach. One significant methodological drawback concerns the use of travels, and travel books, which Kant recommends as one source of anthropological information. He ignored the pitfalls of using these books as a reliable source of information as they usually express the prejudices of their authors who may experience culture shocks at the sight of people different from themselves, or customs they do not understand, let alone appreciate. Even though in his *Physical Geography* Kant warned that travels "must be reliably recorded, and as such, experiences recorded are preferable to those passed along by word of mouth,"[65] he adopted, uncritically, some travel information in his writings on race as will be discussed in the next chapter.[66] The very notion of travel as a source of ("scientific") anthropological knowledge is dubious. On the one hand, Kant, who had never left his country, knew of the importance of travel in broadening one's horizons, and thus felt a need to include travel as one of the methods of acquiring anthropological information. It is difficult to fathom an anthropology without practitioners leaving their familiar surrounds. On the other hand, Kant was aware that travel must not be simply touristic, and that the traveler must "not merely observe the world as the object of sense perception.[67] Rather, travel must be undertaken with a purpose and knowledge preparation. Kant's emphasis on travel reflected the spirit of the time. The eighteenth century was heir to the Age of Discovery as Europe was gradually expanding its reach in the world. In this context, anthropological knowledge was a means of making sense of an expanding universe through travel, which makes the systematic observation of other peoples and cultures possible.

Kant's elision of power and the role it plays in impeding understanding of human beings presents another drawback.[68] Given the pragmatic character of the *Anthropology*, Kant does not explain what its benefits would be for the diverse peoples as objects of observation. For travel is understood or implied to be from Europe to the "world." However, there is no reason why travel should not be from the other direction too. Theoretically, considering his focus on the cosmopolitan nature of pragmatic anthropology, Kant leaves open the possibility that different peoples could also benefit from observing "us." Nevertheless, this is a mere conjecture as there is no compelling reason why Kant did not address the reflexivity of observation. Said in passing, Baudelaire's "cosmopolitan" traveler (discussed in chapter 1) nudges Kant's traveler to decenter himself and embrace a universal sense of self by shedding his local culture's blinders in order to be at home in other cultures, a process Kant left unspecified. Finally, Kant's use of the concept of culture as referring to activities in the arts and sciences that advance civilization leaves out the notion of culture as a mode of adaptation, and appears to detract from the significance of the epistemic question he raised concerning the integration of diversity and totality, the situational and the universal.[69]

The fact that the *Anthropology* was written by a philosopher but extolled a social science method lends itself to commentaries and interpretations that read it back into Kant's critical philosophy and thus frequently neglect to examine it on its own merits.[70] A point of contention among philosophical commentaries (which would also extend to social scientists who define scientific research narrowly) has been the *Anthropology*'s moral/ethical orientation. Kant advocates knowledge for an overarching purpose: improvement of humanity.[71] Concern for humanity means concern for the human being and his nature. Disciplines other than anthropology also deal with human beings. How is anthropology related to them?

Pragmatic Anthropology and the Human Sciences

A question that forms a significant component of Foucault's interpretation of the *Anthropology* arises: did Kant intend his anthropology to be the foundation of all knowledge of human beings? A passage from a letter he wrote to his friend, Marcus Herz, in 1773 is frequently quoted to indicate this was the case: "The intention that I have [for the lecture course on anthropology] is to make known the sources of all sciences: of morality, of skill, of social intercourse, of the methods of educating and ruling human beings, and with that everything practical. Thus I seek phenomena and their causes, rather than the ultimate conditions of possibility of the modification of human nature in general."[72] The concept "sources" makes the statement ambiguous, as a discipline cannot be the "sources" (in the plural) of other types of knowledge. Furthermore, the rubrics Kant selects hardly refer to constituted human sciences as we know them today. They relate instead to areas of investigation, some of which fall under the purview of sociology ("social intercourse"; "methods of educating") and political science ("methods of ruling"). Looking into the manner in which Kant defined the role of his physical geography course out of which the anthropology lectures emerged would shed some light on the statement. Kant intended the course to be "the ground [Grund] of all possible geographies."[73] In his letter to Herz, Kant may have meant that the pragmatic approach to anthropology would reveal an aspect of the various areas (such as education, politics, etc.) that would be unique or new. It is true that Kant's statement concerning physical geography deals with already existing geographies, which he intends to incorporate in some new framework. This was not the case for anthropology, a new discipline. Kant had already rejected Platner's physical anthropology. It is reasonable to interpret Kant's letter to Herz as meaning that Kant wished to highlight a new method of pragmatic knowledge, rather than make anthropology into the foundation of *all* the human sciences, which had yet to be established.[74] However, Kant's statement to Herz played a significant role in Foucault's reading of the *Anthropology*.

HOW FOUCAULT READ KANT'S *ANTHROPOLOGY*[75]

Foucault's reading of the *Anthropology* was guided by a concern to characterize its nature, which he later used as a foundation for a critique of the human sciences. Hence, his method of reading needs scrutiny as it has consequences for the conclusion he reached. It also helps to understand how he forecloses the as yet unfinished task of contemporary scholars engaged in tracing shifts in meanings and themes across the time span of Kant's lectures, as well as in the notes taken by Kant's students in the *Anthropology* classes.[76]

Foucault's *Introduction* is not a dissertation focused on explicating the significance of Kant's *Anthropology* for anthropology as a field of study. Nor is it the usual presentation of the place of a book in its author's oeuvre. Foucault's *Introduction* (often referred to by French analysts as "commentary") is its own genre. He adopted a "genetic perspective and a structural method,"[77] although he felt that this method would be difficult to apply given the time frame of the *Anthropology*. Kant's lectures were contemporaneous with the precritical as well as critical periods of his works, but the book came out at the close of his career. Foucault saw his task as one of either historical reconstruction (*genèse*) of the "entire critical enterprise," or the identification (if it were possible) of "the structure of the anthropological-critical relationship."[78] Consequently, his analysis unfolds on two levels: one philosophical, the other historical and interpretative. He frequently collapses one level into the other, or simply abandons them altogether for a different strategic reading.[79] The first level seeks to tease out the philosophical from the empirical; the other intends to re-interpret the meaning of Kant's *Anthropology* in a way that changes Kant's text. Throughout Foucault appears to use the *Anthropology* as an opportunity to define for himself what anthropology, used synonymously with general anthropology, written with lower case "a," really is. The *Introduction* seldom follows the original text. Instead, it picks and chooses categories and concepts from the original, which it freely relates to questions that had been addressed or left unanswered in Kant's philosophical work.

The Transcendental and the Empirical

Foucault seeks to situate the *Anthropology* in Kant's critical philosophy, assess its claim to "empiricity," and specify the (negative) epistemic knot that presumably ties it to the human sciences.[80] Foucault's fundamental question is whether *Anthropology* is a purely empirical discipline. Throughout he intends to prove that the *Anthropology* is philosophical. Succinctly, philosophical anthropology focuses on human nature or essence whereas empirical anthropology studies human beings as they act in their sociocultural milieu. Foucault argues that Kant's *Anthropology* can (and perhaps should) be read as "the examination of a field in which the practical and the theoretical intermingle and overlap entirely; it repeats in the same place and language the a-priori of knowledge and the moral imperative."[81] In other words, he reads it as "transcendental philosophy," which constitutes "the function and texture (*trame*) of its [the *Anthropology's*] empiricity."[82] His unraveling of the perceived comingling of the philosophical and the empirical does not appear to be dictated by a preoccupation with delimiting the proper sphere of anthropology. Rather, he seeks to assess what would happen to transcendental philosophy when it is "released" from anthropology.[83]

To prove his claim, Foucault identifies the linkage between the *Anthropology* in Kant's philosophical enterprise, (especially *Logic*), and *Critique*. Admittedly, since Kant had taught anthropology for decades while he published his seminal books, his conception of anthropology had been either informed by his philosophical work, or prefigured in it. Conversely, Kant's anthropology course could have inflected his philosophy. This is not an idle question for the historian of Kant's ideas.[84] However, Foucault not only raises the question, he also answers it categorically, and according to critics, without providing compelling evidence.[85] He argues that the lateness of the publication of the *Anthropology* (1798) is indicative of its author's intention to give a final meaning ("an interrogation of interrogations") to his philosophical enterprise rather than being "the ultimate empirical level of an organized philosophical knowledge." Foucault's *Introduction* was written after the publications in 1953 and 1954 respectively of his preface to Binswanger's *Rêve et existence*, and of *Maladie mentale et psychologie*. The research for *Introduction* was carried out in 1959–1960 in Hamburg.[86] Suggestions have been made that there is continuity between these three texts as is clear from Foucault's query regarding the place, if any, of psychology in the *Anthropology*. It must be remembered that Foucault had an abiding interest in psychology, a discipline in which he received a degree. Additionally, Foucault's reading of the *Anthropology* is also inflected by issues such as imagination, dreams, and mental illness—attributes of "man," conceptualized as "subject."[87] It is not clear to me how important Foucault's concern for psychology is in his reading of the *Anthropology* except that it may have influenced his assessment of its empiricity in ways that are not explicit in *Introduction*.[88]

The "World," the "Pragmatic," and the Transcendental

Foucault cites four questions, which Kant had raised in *Logic*: "What can I know?" "What should I do?" "What may I hope?" and "What is a human being?" However, he focuses on the last question, which he uses as a guide in determining the purpose of the *Anthropology*.[89] He admits that the *Anthropology* does not provide an answer to this question and, in this sense, it does not add much to Kant's critical philosophy.[90] However, the purpose of the *Anthropology* is not to answer the question, "what is man," although the answer might clarify its meaning—and the question does not figure in the book, as Kant appears to have deliberately refused answering it.[91] There is sufficient ambiguity in Foucault's recurring reference to the question that is indicative of a will to construct a critique that produces the very terms it criticizes.

Foucault's philosophical reading elides the pragmatic dimension of the *Anthropology,* qualifies Kant's emphasis on the "world," and stresses the motif of finitude (which Heidegger foregrounds in his critique of Kant).[92] First, Foucault reads the "world" as constituting the "limit" of experience, in addition to being the source of knowledge and the domain of its application.[93] The concept of "limit" restricts the field of engagement of the human being in the world, as well as his being in the game. If Foucault implies that the world limits the individual's experience because others inhabit it and their experiences limit his, it may alternatively be argued that the world constitutes an opening for the individual's experiences. For instance, does the existence of the "Orient" limit or expand the world for the non-"Oriental?"

At any rate, the idea of "limit" is at once reductive and overdetermining.[94] Foucault attempts to indirectly justify the reduction by distinguishing the "world" from the "universe." He defines the universe in terms of its function and in opposition to the world. The universe is "the unity of the possible."[95] This means that the universe is one, whereas the world, as a "system of real relations," in which "relations cannot be otherwise," is multiple.[96] The world is a space that frames as well as determines relations between objects by making them possible; their possibility is the function of the world. Foucault makes it clear that there may be several worlds in which different relations are possible. However, there is only one universe. This raises at least three major questions: (a) what accounts for the necessary character of relations that take place in one world? (b) why is it that more than one possible relation cannot coexist in one world, or that a world only encompasses one possible system of relations? (c) through what mechanism, or under what conditions, does the universe unify multiple worlds with their own necessary relations? At first glance, these questions may seem ungrounded as Foucault acknowledges that there can be only "one world" since what is possible presents itself in the experience of real relations. However, Foucault reiterates the existence of the possibility of other worlds (*d'autres mondes*), but sees "the world" (used in a generic sense that renders it synonymous with the universe) as presenting itself not only as a "source, a domain" but mostly as "a limit."[97] He concludes that the possible existence of other worlds (or the conceiving of their possibility) means that it is impossible to go beyond "the world," and that it is "compellingly necessary to accept its borders as limits."[98] Foucault's conclusion moves from Kant's definition of the object of *Anthropology*, the human being–qua–*citizen of the world*, to a redefinition of the world as a bounded *domain*. Necessarily, the move limits the scope and nature of experiences and relations. Yet this reconstruction of one term, the world, does not proceed from the *Anthropology*, but from outside of it, primarily from *Opus Postumum*, as Foucault indicates.[99] However, scholarship that looked into the history of the *Anthropology*, including notes taken by Kant's students and assembled by different people, indicates another dimension of the world. Kant wrote, "The world as an object of outer sense is nature, the world as an object of inner sense is the human being."[100]

The dismissal-elision of the pragmatic (qua empirical) dimension[101] of the *Anthropology* is an outcome of Foucault's conflation of the two levels of analysis he had adopted: the historical and the philosophical. Foucault had already defined the *Anthropology* as being neither the empirical conclusion to the *Critique* nor a clarification of it. What would then justify reading it in light of the fundamental question (namely, "what is the human being?"), and arguing (paradoxically) that the *Anthropology* nevertheless repeats the

Critique, and because it does so, its empiricity is grounded in transcendental philosophy? Within this interpretative framework, what Foucault identifies as a paradox, namely, that the *Anthropology* is at once a repetition of *Critique of Pure Reason* (at least in its organization) but is not founded on it, remains unresolved. He concludes that the "anthropological question" (e.g., what is the human being?) "has no independent content,"[102] since the *Anthropology* is a "transitional albeit necessary"[103] and "marginal" work that has inherited the serious question of the relationship between freedom and truth bequeathed to it by the *Critique*. For Kant, as Foucault points out, truth means what experience reveals as necessary, and freedom "the recognition of the particular as a universal subject."[104] In other words, Foucault does not read the *Anthropology* as anthropology, but as an attempt to give philosophy an empirical content. To reiterate, he reads it as philosophical anthropology.

The challenge for anthropology from Kant's perspective is whether the human being can indeed rise above his natural and social limitations, including his embededness in his own culture and his taken-for-granted world. The latter is exemplified by habit, or the propensity to focus on difference from others instead of similarities with them. Foucault's reading reduces pragmatic anthropology to a branch of philosophy and in so doing it discounts the significance of Kant's approach notwithstanding its peculiar format. It further obscures the purpose of the *Anthropology*, which is to seek the universal through the local by increasing knowledge of the local/particular. (The local is evidently not to be equated with one single location.) Paradoxically, although Foucault seeks to ascertain the relationship between *Critique* and the *Anthropology*, he also appears not to trust in the power of critical activity as such, preferring instead to find a ground for arguing against the possibility of empirical knowledge. To wit, "attempts were made to present *Anthropology* as *Critique*, as a critique freed from the prejudices and of the inert weight of the *a priori*" when "in reality, it can only speak the language of limit and negativity."[105] By "negativity" (a concept Foucault uses frequently along with "negation") he had in mind Kant's misgivings about human beings' shortcomings in interacting with one another. However, Kant did not see these as making the task of anthropology impossible. There is even a sense in which anthropology helps to reveal these shortcomings. For it is observation, inner or external, that identifies obstacles to the anthropological endeavor.

Reading Kant's conception of pragmatic anthropology as an instance of his philosophical work results in its inflection in a direction different from Kant's text. It is true that Kant devotes sections of his *Anthropology* to describing the faculties of human beings, including memory, imagination, and judgment. To a sociologist the description Kant provides could be verified by empirical social science research. Furthermore, since a major goal of pragmatic anthropology is to acquire knowledge of the world (personal, local, and intercultural), which citizens of the world inhabit, the modalities of the exercise of such faculties can implicitly vary from culture to culture. For example, how does an Iranian involved in the Iranian Revolution in 1978 shed light on a French student's involvement in the May '68 movement? And this is an empirical question. It is noteworthy that by eschewing a thorough discussion of the "pragmatic," Foucault failed to object to an aspect of pragmatic anthropology concerning the use of others for advancing one's goals. This raises the antinomy between Kant's assertion that the human being is an end in himself and the use of others as means toward one's ends, which Foucault obviates. Oddly, the purpose of pragmatic anthropological knowledge—to improve self-knowledge through knowledge of others—is all the more important considering that Foucault's work focuses on Western self-knowledge.

Ultimately, Foucault replaced anthropological man with philosophical man, shifted from Kant's citizen of the world to man as the object of a disquisition about a fixed human nature, and veered from the empirical to the transcendental.[106] (Perhaps his examination of the relevance of *Anthropology* for the human sciences required making a distinction between pragmatic/practical anthropology and practical philosophy.)[107]

Challenges to Foucault's Reading

The place of *Anthropology* in Kant's philosophy is a question philosophers have struggled with just as Foucault did.[108] Many have taken a position different from his. Those seeking to clarify the significance of the *Anthropology* in relation to Kant's philosophical endeavor have strongly distinguished it from metaphysics. In order to demonstrate their claim they trace the origin of Kant's interest in anthropology noting the evolution of his thinking about the *Anthropology*'s relation to physical geography, psychology, and morals. They argue that Kant clearly indicated that his *Metaphysics of Morals*, which he initially distinguished from "practical anthropology," is concerned purely with morals, whereas anthropology focuses on the empirical. Furthermore, some have also claimed that the moral relevance of the *Anthropology* decreased as Kant's thought on moral issues changed over time, implying that its "empiricity" was thereby enhanced. By the same token, they note that from Kant's perspective, practical anthropology is not part of theoretical philosophy but of practical philosophy[109]—another indication that Kant's emphasis on an empirical anthropology must be understood in its own context, not as part of philosophy. Allen W. Wood points out that the significance of Kant's ideas in the *Anthropology* is frequently obscured by interpretations that subsume it under his critical philosophy.[110] The distinction made by philosophers between the *Anthropology* and metaphysics foregrounds the importance of seriously considering what Kant, as an author, meant by a discipline he developed over the span of his teaching career rather than what the *Anthropology* might mean to the contemporary reader's narrow philosophical concerns.

Some students of the *Anthropology* also argue (in apparent agreement with Foucault) that there are "points of contact with transcendental philosophy, the aesthetics of the *Critique of Judgment*, and philosophy of law." Nevertheless, they conclude that the *Anthropology* "is also a sort of summation of the remaining themes of Kant's philosophy, even if from an empirical-pragmatic perspective. Even the final topic, the vocation of the human being, is analyzed entirely empirically and as immanent to the world."[111] Striking out in a different direction, Patrick R. Frierson demonstrates that the *Anthropology* is empirical in its method as well as in its subject matter. Methodologically, the *Anthropology* relies on observation of one's inner self, of others as well as the products of human beings' observations as revealed in history books, literature, and biographies. Its subject matter is the experience of human beings in various cultural settings as they make themselves. Although Frierson maybe overstating his case by noting that the *Anthropology* studies "empirical objects," he stays close to Kant's explicit intentions in the text.[112] In the end, Foucault's assertion that in the *Anthropology* the transcendental structures the empirical is based on philosophical criteria or concepts drawn from outside of the parameters set by Kant in the *Anthropology*. This gesture manages to turn Kant's concrete reflections on the relationship between the individual, knowledge, and the world (inhabited by people belonging to the same or to different cultures) into a priori notions.

"Local Knowledge" and the Language Turn

In addition to redefining the "world" and reading transcendental philosophy into anthropological knowledge, Foucault takes an important step: he foregrounds language as essential to the *Anthropology*. This last step permits him to further detach the *Anthropology* from its pragmatic character. Kant had brought up language as a human capacity that distinguishes man from animal; it makes it possible for the growing child to move from *feeling* himself to *thinking* himself, from speaking of himself in the third person to referring to himself in the first person as an "I."[113] The discussion of language takes place under Book one, "On the Cognitive Faculty," especially sections devoted to "On Being Conscious of One's Self," "On Egoism," and "Remark on the Formality of Egoistic Language." In all of these passages, Kant's intent is to draw attention to the difficulty of knowing one's self as mediated by the centrality of the "I" in language. The moment the human being discovered the "I," he became prone to invoking "his beloved self" in everything. In other words, the most human feature, language, that gives the human being an advantage over other species, is also an obstacle to self-knowledge and knowledge of others. This important point connotes the challenge of the new discipline: *objectivity* in knowledge not only of one's self, but also of others. Foucault interprets language in two ways, which he conflates in order to render a judgment on the ultimate meaning of the *Anthropology*: on the one hand he notes, as Kant does, the importance of language as a human capacity; on the other hand he argues that language in the *Anthropology* is neither a source of mystification nor of error. He translates Kant's warning that language is a source of self-illusion as representing linguistic reflexivity: "It is that language offers the possibility of speaking it and speaking about it, and this in the same movement."[114] Thus, Foucault's interpretation collapses two distinct levels: the philosophical and the practical. In so doing, he sacrifices Kant's nuanced approach to language, with a structural-linguistic analysis of how Kant described things in the *Anthropology*.

Foucault's interpretation hinges on Kant's goal of making the *Anthropology* "popular."[115] By this term Kant meant that even though *pragmatic* anthropology is systematic (and thus scientific) it must also be accessible to the nonexpert, the public at large, "because of reference of examples that can be checked by every reader."[116] The reader can also learn about himself through the concrete examples of human behavior that the *Anthropology* provides. Kant's provision is in keeping with his definition of pragmatic anthropology as the study of the human being for the purpose of acquiring knowledge that he can use for building culture and improving himself. (It is noteworthy in this respect that there are significant variations between Foucault's translation into French and English translations of Kant's text on the place of the "popular" and the "pragmatic" in the relevant sentence.)[117] Foucault's conclusion has implications for his claim that the *Anthropology*'s shortcomings are at the core of what is wrong with the human sciences. He argues that the *Anthropology* "will be knowledge of man, knowledge which man will be able to directly understand, recognize, and expand indefinitely because it and we are located in the same inexhaustible language."[118] "Anthropology is therefore rooted in a linguistic and experiential system that is German."[119] The emphasis on the nationality of the *Anthropology* does not flow from a critique of *Anthropology*'s universalistic claim (that its object is a "citizen of the world") but from a reading of its author's intention to make it a "popular" discipline. The pragmatic aspect of the *Anthropology* is consequently relegated to "local knowledge."[120] Foucault explains the intellectual climate within which the *Anthropology* was written. He notes that the epistemology of the *Anthropology* is different from Descartes's or Locke's.[121] By the same token he indicates, and rightly so, that it owes a great deal to German anthropological studies of the second half of the eighteenth century.[122] However, as Foucault sees it, German is the foundation of the local nature of *Anthropology*; German had displaced or became superimposed on Latin, "the language of universal science and philosophy."[123] In other words, language (in its national and intra-European sedimentation) defines the local nature of the *Anthropology* as well as the universality of its claim. Moving beyond the Germanity or Latinity of the *Anthropology*, Foucault concludes that it is ultimately "a reflection on and in a system of constituted and all-pervasive signs."[124] It is in language that he finds the common ground for both philosophy and experience.[125] He warns that the *Anthropology*'s goal to study "man as a citizen of the world" should not be taken literally. In fact, man is citizen of the world "not in the sense that he belongs to such or such social group, or social institution, but simply because he speaks. It is in linguistic exchange that he achieves the concrete universal and accomplishes it at the same time. His residence in the world is an originary sojourn in language."[126]

The language turn, which Louden thinks leads Foucault "off track,"[127] foreshadows the *Archaeology of Knowledge*; Foucault reads *Anthropology* as an incipient archaeology. Foucault's move is original although it appropriates Kant's text and reconstructs it from the perspective of the issues that occupied his own mind at the time: the psychology of existence and the epistemology of the normal and the pathological, of the mad and the sane seen as expressions of the Cartesian philosophical sundering of the rational and the a-rational. Indeed, once rewritten as a language, *Anthropology* appears as an echo of Foucault's concern for the process through which, historically, health and medical concerns (in a word, biology) emerged as distinct objects of investigation. As he put it, "Anthropology will always be the science of an animate body, completed with respect to itself, and developing according to a proper functioning. It will be the knowledge of health, which for man is synonymous with animation. In a way, it will be the science of the normal."[128] It is true that Kant discussed mental illness, including madness, as impairment of the faculty of judgment;[129] he further identified the moral qualities toward which the human being orients himself. However, Foucault's extrapolation from Kant's emphasis that pragmatic anthropology focuses on the usage that the human being makes of his knowledge of the world (and of himself) to a characterization of the anthropological being as a figure of health is questionable. Health is an inclusive concept that encompasses physical, mental, as well as social meanings. This extrapolation reduces the *Anthropology* (as well as general anthropology) to a normative discipline in an absolute sense. Foucault reaches this very conclusion, and explains that "Anthropology cannot but be at once reductive and normative; reductive because it will not accept what man knows about himself, through the 'Selbstgefühl,' but only what he can know through *Physis*."[130] Selbstgefühl refers to self-esteem or self-assurance, whereas Physis refers to the physiological nature of man, which Kant distinguished from the study of the human being as an active agent of and in the world. The normativity of the *Anthropology* resides in the pragmatic character of the *Anthropology* as defined by Kant, which Foucault reduces to an external relationship between man, language, and the world. From Foucault's perspective, Kant made the human being—a figure whose existence Foucault contests epistemically—the measure of the *Anthropology* as a science whose contours he delineated.[131]

The language turn, which Foucault took in order to arrive at the conclusion that the *Anthropology* is both reductive and normative, discounts Kant's assessment of the difficulties in reaching self-knowledge just as it transforms this assessment into an exclusion of self-knowledge from the realm of pragmatic anthropology and the *judgment* required to overcome the difficulties. Kant's anthropology is treated as a *symptomatic* discourse on what the human sciences, writ large, should include, and how they ought to conduct themselves. Foucault backs his claim by arguing that Kant had envisaged several anthropologies that would deal separately with physiology, psychology, history, and "morals or teleology."[132]

Finitude

What needs to be brought out is Foucault's secondary, yet crucial, derivation from his language turn: finitude. The focus on finitude constitutes the last component of Foucault's method of rewriting the *Anthropology*. By the same token, it ushers in the controversial theses of the "anthropological sleep" and the "death of man," both of which are taken up in detail in *Les mots et les choses*. Foucault argues that the *Anthropology* ambitiously sought to "know the possibilities as well as the limits of knowledge."[133] Yet, its critical posture and stress on empirical work did not, as a number of German anthropologists thought it did, resolve or overcome the philosophical problem of the dualism between body and soul, or subject and object. In reality, as Foucault asserts again, the *Anthropology* did not succeed in shedding its philosophical foundations as they appear in *Critique*.[134] It repeats the a priori of *Critique*.

(This assertion is questioned by Robert B. Louden; he does not see evidence of the a priori in the *Anthropology*.)[135] In other words, the empiricity of the *Anthropology* is illusory insofar as it cannot stand on its own; it needs and rests on *Critique*; it depends on it. This assessment rests on Foucault's reading "finitude" in "the general organization of Kantian thought," not in the *Anthropology*. From Foucault's perspective, even though pragmatic anthropology identifies the imperfect nature of the human being, it still entrusts him with the task of knowing. Consequently, empirical anthropology is as limited in its (truth) value as the nature of the human being is limited in time.

Foucault's emphasis on the concept of "finitude" to cast doubt on the empiricity of *Anthropology* envisions the anthropological task in a way that presents the *Anthropology* as evolving in an epistemic circle from which it cannot extirpate itself. The *Anthropology* does draw attention to death as an impediment to the human being's scientific endeavors in the sense that the work of a scientist is interrupted by his death at the point when he is about to "broaden the field," which causes a younger scientist to take over, whose work will also be interrupted by death.[136] However, the shift from "death" to "finitude" is epistemically motivated. Just as Foucault's language turn predefines the *Anthropology* as primarily concerned with the exteriority of knowledge, the introduction of "finitude" in the text works to strengthen his definition of the world as "a limit" to experience. This compounds the perceived boundedness of the anthropological endeavor. Foucault argues that since Kant, anthropologists have been laboring under the "anthropological illusion" of empiricity as they failed to identify and address the "transcendental illusion" that made it possible. By "transcendental illusion," Foucault means that the empirical in the *Anthropology* is subjected to philosophical assumptions about the nature of the human being, which in reality Kant wished to keep separate from the empirical experience of the human being. The relative autonomy of the empirical cannot, from this perspective, be sustained since the empirical is informed by the philosophical. The impossibility of uncoupling the philosophical from the anthropological is evidenced, according to Foucault, in Kant's concern for self-knowledge (*connaissance de soi*). Foucault indicates that the *Anthropology* signals a "return (in French *repli* as well as *retour*)[137] to the self—a marker of the subjective character of philosophical assumptions that, by implication, contradicts the scienticity of empirical knowledge. He uses the expression *retour à soi*, which could be counterposed to another expression *retour sur soi*. The choice of the preposition *à* over *sur* (literally "on") denotes Foucault's intention to stress the circularity of the *Anthropology*: he claims that empirical knowledge is vitiated by its own advocacy of knowledge of the self—a knowledge that is grounded in an initial philosophical reflection that transcends the world of experience. Assuming that Foucault is correct, his assessment still falls short when it is considered that the *Anthropology* recognizes the problematic nature of the empirical knowledge of the human being. Furthermore, it is unclear what makes self-reflection, or a *retour à soi*, incompatible with experience or the empirical. (This denotes a problem of consistency as Foucault's turn to language had implied that the manner in which the *Anthropology* uses language practically rendered self-knowledge unattainable.) In reality the *Anthropology* anticipates Foucault's objections by stressing the elusive "nature" of the human being. The question is: can the study of human beings dispense with any general philosophical notion of what it means to be human as one engages in interaction with others?

Because Foucault took the *Anthropology* as emblematic of general anthropology's characteristics, his objection to it has significance for his conception of the human sciences; its validity must ultimately be gauged against his own ("anthropological") method as he sought to make sense of cultures different from his own. Is Foucault simply objecting to the claim that the study of human beings (or more accurately human nature) is scientific? However, his objection would have to take into account Kant's own misgivings about knowing human nature scientifically. A number of sociologists had started to critically assess the scientific claims made by their discipline by the time Foucault wrote *Les mots et les choses*, a book in which he refined and expanded his critique of the *Anthropology*. They did so not only to object to the quantification of sociology, but also to the conflation of conceptual systems with social reality as multiple critiques of Talcott Parsons's social theory have indicated.[138]

At any rate, Foucault's critique of the *Anthropology* set the basic framework of his view of cultural difference as a limit-experience from which he was unable to depart. The preceding indicates Foucault's persistent reading of the *Anthropology* as philosophical at the risk of omissions, exaggerations, and generalizations[139] was just as significant as his misgivings about empirical anthropology. He restrictively redefined the basic terms of the anthropological enterprise. His rewriting of *Anthropology* denotes an attitude toward cultural otherness from which reflexivity and cosmopolitanism (hallmarks of Kant's view) are missing. From such an attitude, others appear impenetrable, and their world bounded. Foucault's interpretation of *Anthropology* took place twelve years before he went to Tunisia and twenty-five years before he went to Japan and Iran. His experiences in these countries brought him face to face with the empirical reality of others, the domain of empirical anthropology writ large—not that he went to these countries as an anthropologist. But he was in the situation of estrangement familiar to anthropologists.

NOTES

1. "Cours de Michel Foucault donnés à l' Ecole Normale Supérieure (1953–1955)," in notes taken and edited by Jacques Lagrange, *IMEC*, FCL, 38. In the section on Kant's anthropology Foucault traces the history of anthropology since Kant as he focuses on the evolution of the relationship between critique and anthropology. He devotes a long section to "Nietzsche's anthropology."
2. For a description of the origins of *Anthropology*, see Werner Stark, "Historical Notes and Interpretive Questions about Kant's Lectures on Anthropology," in *Essays on Kant's Anthropology*, ed. Brian Jacobs and Patrick Kain, trans. Jaimey Fisher and Patrick Kain (New York: Cambridge University Press, 2003), 15–16. See also, among others, Howard Caygill, *A Kant Dictionary* (Oxford: Blackwell, 2008), 73; Holly L. Wilson, *Kant's Pragmatic Anthropology: Its Origin, Meaning and Critical Significance* (Albany: State University of New York Press, 2007), chap. 1.
3. The physical geography course did not have a textbook either. Upon his request, Kant received an official dispensation from a textbook in 1778 from the minister of education, Karl Abraham Zedlitz. Robert B. Louden, "The Play of Nature: Human Beings in Kant's Geography," in *Kant's Human Being: Essays on His Theory of Human Nature* (Oxford: Oxford University Press, 2011), 122.
4. Stark compared the *Anthropology* to the various texts of Kant's students' notes of the lectures. It must be noted that John H. Zammito goes against the grain in arguing that the first part of the *Anthropology* was borrowed largely from Baumgarten's book "without much amendment," and had been what he had taught under "empirical psychology." Zammito, *Kant, Herder, and the Birth of Anthropology* (Chicago: University of Chicago Press, 2002), 301. It is generally understood that the *organization* of the first part of the *Anthopology* relies on Baumgarten's book, and that of the second part on Kant's *Observations on the Feeling of the Beautiful and Sublime.*
5. Stark, "Historical Notes," 16–19.
6. Ibid., 16.
7. A second edition, revised for style, appeared in 1800. Philosophers refer to the 1798 edition as edition "A" and the 1800 as edition "B." After Kant's death, in 1831, a freelance writer, Adam Bergh, under the pseudonym, FC Starke, published Kant's earlier lectures as *Immanuel Kants oder Philosophische Anthropologie*, usually referred to as the *Menschenkunde.* Zammito, *Kant, Herder*, 299.
8. See Guillaume Paugam, "De l'Anthropologie à l'Archéologie," *Critique* 65, no. 749 (October 2009): 838; Foucault, *Introduction to Kant's Anthropology*, trans. Robert Nigro and Kate Briggs (Los Angeles: Semiotext(e), 2008), 54; and Howard Caygill, "Kant's Apology for Sensibility," in Jacobs and Kain, *Essays on Kant's Anthropology*, 164. Holly Wilson suggests that the lack of attention given the *Anthropology* or its dismissal reflects a bias among philosophers in favor of conceptual philosophy as rational philosophy and against empirical philosophies that focus on experience, *Kant's Pragmatic Anthropology*, 1.

There are three translations of the *Anthropology* in English: Robert B. Louden, *Immanuel Kant, Anthropology from a Pragmatic Point of View* (Cambridge: Cambridge University Press, 2010); Victor Lyle Dowdell, *Immanuel Kant, Anthropology from a Pragmatic Point of View* (Carbondale: The University of Illinois, 1996); and Mary J. Gregor, *Immanuel Kant, Anthropology from a Pragmatic Point of View* (The Hague: Martinus Nijhoff, 1974).

9. Howard Caygill points to "anti-foundational readings [that] stress the historical and political features of Kant's work over the strictly logical ones, which were the focus of earlier interpretations,"*A Kant Dictionary*, 73–74.
10. Caygill, "Kant's Apology," in Jacobs and Kain, *Essays on Kant's Anthropology*, 164. Caygill examines Kant's defense of his doctrine of sensibility, a doctrine that is an important part of the *Critique of Pure Reason*, in the lectures.
11. Caygill's suggestion is partially supported by Frederick Van de Pitte, who argues that Kant "intentionally withheld" producing a textbook for his new course in 1772–1773 to allow himself time to lay out its philosophical foundation in the critique. Pitte's purpose is to prove that Kant's entire oeuvre constitutes a "philosophical anthropology." Frederick Van de Pitte, "Kant as Philosophical Anthropologist," in *Proceedings of the Third International Kant Congress*, ed. Lewis White Beck (Dordrecht, Holland: D. Reidel Publishing Co., 1972), 578. Parenthetically, it is noteworthy that Foucault did not pick up on the lectures as an "event," an indication perhaps that his focus on the relationship between the *Anthropology* and critical philosophy may have obscured the role played by Kant as an author in the management of the *Anthropology*. Speculatively, the thought of Kant as having belonged to a one-time secret enlightenment society comes to mind in the context of his search for a freer expression of thought in the academy as do the various problems he experienced with the state-controlled university. Martin Schönfeld points out that between 1748 and 1770, Kant had been embroiled in a controversy over his ideas about cosmogony, which caused him to be demoted to the rank of adjunct faculty in 1755 and assistant librarian at Königsberg Castle. He was offered a chair in poetry instead of metaphysics. It was not until 1770 that he finally occupied a chair in metaphysics. Schönfeld, "From Confucius to Kant: The Question of Knowledge Transfer," *Journal of Chinese Philosophy* 33, no. 1 (March 2006): 78. Kant's tenuous position as an academic don in his precritical period prompted Zammito (*Kant, Herder*, 6) to suggest that Kant looked for "an alternative identity" that he found in his anthropology lectures.
12. Stark, "Historical Notes," 19.
13. Quoted in Wilson, *Kant's Pragmatic Anthropology*, 10–11.
14. Clearly one could say the same thing about the physical geography lectures.
15. For a brief discussion of the periodization of phases of the German Enlightenment, see Zammito, *Kant, Herder*, 9–10.
16. For a brief analysis of "modernity" as the context of Kant's anthropology, see Pheng Cheah, *Spectral Nationality: Passages of Freedom from Kant to Postcolonial Literatures of Liberation* (New York: Columbia University Press, 2003), 37–38.

17. Allen W. Wood, "Kant and the Problem of Human Nature," in Jacobs and Kain, *Essays on Kant's Anthropology*, 40. Ernst Platner (1744–1818) was a Leipzig physician and philosopher. His book had been reviewed by Kant's friend, Marcus Herz.
18. For a comparison of Kant's and Herder's anthropological ideas, see Zammito, *Kant, Herder*.
19. I am using Foucault's translation supplemented by Robert B. Louden's English translation. Foucault's translation appears as *E. Kant, Anthropologie du point de vue pragmatique, précédé de Michel Foucault, Introduction à l' Anthropologie*, introduced by D. Defert, Fr. Ewald, and F. Gros (Paris: Vrin, 2009), 83. In his introduction to Dowdell's translation, Frederick P. Van De Pitte notes with regret that "Foucault had planned a work which would relate the Anthropology to Kant's critical works," xxii. This statement, based on a footnote (n. 1) to the "notice historique" that accompanied the publication of the French translation, may very well refer to the rest of the *Introduction* of which the "Notice" constituted the first seven pages (of the Defert edition). In fact, that is what a long part of the Foucault's *Introduction* set out to do. The "Notice" first appeared in the first publication of the French translation of the *Anthropology* in 1964. It can also be found in *Dits et écrits,* vol. 1, 316–21.
20. With respect to women, Antje Lange shows that they constituted 1/46 or 0.0217 of all of Kant's correspondence. She concludes: "no further conclusions could be drawn from the results—except with regard to this particular group." Lange, "Kant's Correspondence with Women: A Contribution to a Statistical Evaluation of Kant's Correspondence," in *Proceedings of the Third International Kant Congress,* 684. Zammito (*Kant, Herder,* 120–128) provides an interpretation of Kant's conception of women that draws on his biography; he interprets it as largely stable from 1770 onward and linked to a cultural construction of the self, which sought to overcome sexual anxiety. Eduardo Mendieta establishes a relationship between Kant's conceptions of women and race, and argues that "Kant held on to a dualistic anthropology that correlated woman to geography as it correlated man to history." Mendieta, "Geography Is to History as Woman Is to Man," in *Reading Kant's Geography,* ed. Stuart Elden and Eduardo Mendieta (Albany: State University Press, 2011), 347.
21. Louden, "Anthropology From a Kantian Point of View: Towards a Cosmopolitan Conception of Human Nature," *Kant's Human Being,* 78.
22. Kant, *Anthropology,* Louden translation, 3.
23. Ibid.
24. Ibid., 4.
25. Christoph Girtanner was Kant's contemporary. He was trained as a pediatrician and wrote a book (which Kant refers to) in which he discussed "tail" people and the fanciful case of a "Negress" who mated with a monkey and gave birth to monsters. Girtanner presented his book as an explanation and elaboration of Kant's ideas on race. The story of the "tail" people was first elaborated by Francis de Castelnau, a Frenchman associated with the Société de Géographie de

Paris. He reported the purported existence of a central African tribe of people with tails, called the Nam-Nam. De Castelnau's story was further supported by Louis de Couret, who cited "eyewitnesses" in a book entitled *Voyages au pays des Nam-Nams ou hommes à queue,* published in 1854. Both authors were later exposed as charlatans. See Peter Rigby, *African Images: Racism and the End of Anthropology* (Oxford: Berg, 1996), 9. Also on Girtanner, see *Kant Anthropology,* Louden translation, 223n. 1, and Wulf D. Hund, "'It Must Be from Europe': The Racisms of Immanuel Kant," in *Racisms Made in Germany,* ed. Wulf D. Hund, Christian Koller, and Moses Zimmerman (Berlin: LIT Verlag, 2011).

26. Kant, *Anthropology,* Louden translation, 4.
27. Kant influenced the modern pragmatic movement, although his focus was on "pragmatic beliefs" as being concerned with the context and purpose of action rather than its attaining truth. Sydney Axinn, "The First Western Pragmatist: Immanuel Kant," *Journal of Chinese Philosophy* 33, no. 3 (March 2006): 83–94.
28. For a discussion of "pragmatic" anthropology, see Allen W. Wood, "Kant and the Problem of Human Nature," in Jacobs and Kain, as well as his *Kant's Ethical Thought* (Cambridge: Cambridge University Press, 1999), 202–7; Louden, "Applying Kant's Ethics: The Role of Anthropology," 67–70; "Anthropology from a Kantian Point of View: Toward a Cosmoplitan Conception of Human Nature" 81–83; and "The Play of Nature," in *Kant's Human Being,* 123. See also, among others, Jacobs and Kain, *Essays on Kant's Anthropology,* 113; Patrick R. Frierson, *Freedom and Anthropology in Kant's Moral Philosophy* (Cambridge: Cambridge University Press, 2003), chap. 3. Louden notes that Kant did not emphasize the word "pragmatic" in his early lectures. *Kant's Human Being,* 81.
29. Louden, "Anthropology from a Kantian Point of View," in *Kant's Human Being,* 81.
30. Kant, *Anthropology,* Louden translation, 236.
31. Ibid., 236.
32. When Kant started lecturing about anthropology, a "popular philosophie" school was competing with the "Schulphilosophie." The former, led by Christian Thomasius at the University of Halle, advocated knowledge free of dogma, relevant as well as accessible to the public. The latter, led by Christian Wolff, emphasized, among other things, the application of mathematical methodology to philosophy. (Thomasius, the first professor to teach in German, was actively engaged in creating a reading public through the publication of journals and weeklies.) See Zammito, *Kant, Herder,* 10.
33. Wood, "Kant and the Problem of Human Nature," n7.
34. One of the purposes pursued in the use of others is that "we do not become too difficult or offensive to them." Louden, "Applying Kant's Ethics," in *Kant's Human Being,* 68. The quotation is from the Busolt Lectures, 1788–1789.
35. Kant, *Anthropology,* Louden translation, 131. Louden points out that prudential knowledge can be used for moral as well as immoral purposes. Louden, "Applying Kant's Ethics," 69. Quoting from Kant's *Groundwork,* Louden also remarks that prudence can be "private" or "worldly," 68. Kant points out that "getting

other human beings' inclinations into one's power, so that one can direct and determine them according to one's intentions is almost the same as possessing others as mere tools of one's will." He further notes that striving for prudence can become a *"passion." Anthropology,* Louden translation, 171.
36. Quoted in Wilson, *Kant's Pragmatic Anthropology,* 30.
37. Wilson, *Kant's Pragmatic Anthropology,* 31. Kant briefly discusses "the technical, pragmatic and moral predispositions." He excludes the "predisposition to animality," which would not fall within the purview of pragmatic anthropology. Kant, *Anthropology,* Louden translation, 226–229.
38. Louden suggests that the single most important aspect of Kant's anthropology is its cosmopolitanism. "Anthropology from a Kantian Point of View," 83.
39. Although Kant removed the section on anthropology from his lectures on Physical Geography, and offered a separate course on anthropology, he nevertheless retained an abbreviated section on race, which would be difficult to understand outside of his conception of the relationship between race and physical environment discussed in his geography lectures.
40. Kant, *Anthropology,* Louden translation, 3.
41. Kant, *Anthropologie,* Foucault translation, 83. Louden and Dowdell use the term "play" instead of game. In French, *jeu* (which Foucault used) means both game and play.
42. Kant, *Anthropologie,* Foucault translation, 90. Kant's focus on the significance of the "I" in the development of awareness of the self in relation to others has an echo in a discussion of the same by George Herbert Mead, *Mind, Self and Society from the Standpoint of a Social Behaviorist,* ed. Charles W. Morris (Chicago: Chicago University Press, 1967), especially the chapter on "The I and the Me."
43. Kant, *Anthropologie,* Foucault translation, 255.
44. Kant, *Anthropology,* Louden translation, 5.
45. Ibid., 4. Emphasis added.
46. Kant, *Anthropologie,* Foucault translation, 84. Kant, *Anthropology,* Louden's translation yields "the citizen of the world remains very limited with regard to his anthropology," 4.
47. Kant, *Anthropology,* Louden translation, 4.
48. Ibid., 6.
49. Kant, *Physical Geography,* trans. and ann. Ronald L. Bolin, MA Thesis, Geography Department, University of Waterloo, 1968, 2.
50. Kant's conception of anthropology as a science is best exemplified in Max Weber's definition of sociology as "value-free," yet the selection of sociological themes is "value-relevant" to the researcher. As a "science of culture," sociology must be cognizant of its difference from the natural sciences. Max Weber, *Basic Concepts in Sociology* (New York: Kensington, 2002).
51. Wilson, *Kant's Pragmatic Anthropology,* 117–18.
52. Kant, *Anthropologie,* Foucault translation, 84n1.
53. Kant warns that knowledge of the cosmopolitan traveler is limited in time and space, therefore it is subject to change. This makes having general knowledge of

human beings before travel necessary. Louden, "Anthropology from a Kantian Point of View," 84–85.
54. Kant, *Anthropology,* Louden translation, 5. Kant cites Richardson and Molière as examples of authors who depict characters whose main features must have been drawn from real life.
55. Kant, *Anthropology,* Louden translation, 5.
56. Kant, *Anthropologie,* Foucault translation, 253; Kant, *Anthropology,* Louden translation, 225.
57. Manfred Kuehn, "Introduction" to *Anthropology,* trans. Louden. Kuehn points out that instead of being a sign of a departure from the Enlightenment, the notion that a nonhuman (e.g., a terrestrial being) could be the focus of an anthropology constitutes "the kernel of a cosmopolitan virtue theory in the Enlightenment tradition," xxix.
58. Louden refers to this as the ambiguity between the "empirical and the normative." He resolves it by interpreting pragmatic anthropological knowledge as constituting a categorical imperative in its own right. Consequently, the empirical and the normative are one and the same, "*Anthropology From a Kantian Point of View,*" 87. See also Frierson, *Freedom and Anthropology,* especially chap. 2.
59. Louden, "Anthropology From a Kantian Point of View," 86. Wilson makes a similar argument for reconciling the empirical and the universal. She points out that "empirical observations require teleological judgment for their organization," *Kant's Pragmatic Anthropology,* 21.
60. This discussion does not support Foucault's assessment of the *Anthropology* as the source of the inadequacies of the contemporary human sciences. It is important to remember that Kant's political writings have influenced contemporary political decisions such as the creation of the United Nations, among others. See Martin Schönfeld, "From Confucius to Kant," 75–76. Furthermore, political science has made ample use of Kant's notion of cosmopolitanism and his focus on the "world" as is evidenced in the growth of a trend on "cosmopolitics." See, for example, Isabelle Stengers, with Robert Bononno, *Cosmopolitics,* vol. 1 (Minneapolis: University of Minnesota Press, 2010). Studies of the "Global City" are also part of this trend that takes the "world" as a topic of investigation.
61. Jacobs and Kain, *Essays on Kant's Anthropology,* 3, argue that Kant may not have intended to lay the groundwork for a comparative anthropology.
62. Roger Sullivan, "The Influence of Kant's Anthropology on His Moral Theory," *Review of Metaphysics* 49 (September 1995): 77.
63. Harold Garfinkel, *Studies in Ethnomethodology* (Cambridge: UK: Polity Press, 1984). Ethnomethodology literally means the search for the folks' methods.
64. In *The Conflict of the Faculties,* trans. Mary J. Gregor (New York: Abaris Books, 1979), Kant seeks to answer the question, "Is the Human Race Constantly Progressing?" He points out that the French Revolution "as an event demonstrates the disposition and capacity of the human race to be the cause of its own advance toward the better." More important, this capacity may exist among the "spectators," who manifest "such a universal and disinterested sympathy for the

players on one side against the other, even at the risk that this partiality could become very disadvantageous for them if discovered," 153. He adds, "Genuine enthusiasm always moves only toward what is ideal and, indeed, to what is purely moral, such as the concept of right and it cannot be grafted onto self-interest," 155.
65. Kant, *Physical Geography*, Bolin translation, 2.
66. See Hund et al., *The Racisms of Immanuel Kant*.
67. Kant, *Physical Geography*, Bolin translation, 2.
68. Kant devotes one sentence to "high society, the estate of the nobles" which the anthropologist has difficulty understanding "because they are too close to one another, but too far from others." Kant, *Anthropology*, Louden translation, 4.
69. Otfried Höffe terms Kant's question "epistemic cosmopolitanism." Quoted in Jacques Galinier, "L'anthropologie hors des limites de la simple raison: actualité de la dispute entre Kant et Herder," *L'Homme* 179, (2006): 150.
70. Among those who have resisted this trend and provided reasons for understanding the *Anthropology* for what it offers, Allen W. Wood looms large. In a different vein, Frederick Van de Pitte argues that Kant's entire oeuvre constitutes a "philosophical anthropology." Pitte, "Kant as Philosophical Anthropologist," 574.
71. Reinhard Brandt rightly argues that Kant's concern for the purpose of knowledge strikes as "peculiar" because transformations in our conception of science have "led to academic resignation vis-à-vis questions where our activities lead and within which parameters, on the whole, we act." Brandt, "The Guiding Idea of Kant's Anthropology and the Vocation of the Human Being," in Jacobs and Kain, *Essays on Kant's Anthropology*, 90.
72. Quoted in Stark, "Historical Notes," 22.
73. Louden, "The Play of Nature," 128. The quotation is from the Rink edition of the *Physical Geography* lectures, which Kant did not publish as a book as he did with anthropology.
74. This interpretation is supported by Wilson: "knowledge of the world has to play an important role for all historical sciences, not just anthropology." *Kant's Pragmatic Anthropology*, 13.
75. For a rare and insightful analysis of Foucault's *Introduction* in English, see Louden, "Foucault's Kant," Paper presented at the American Philosophical Association, Pacific Division Meeting, Seattle, 2012. I am grateful to Prof. Louden for sharing with me a copy of his paper. The paper appears in Spanish translation as "El Foucault de Kant," *Estudios Kantianos* 1 (July 2013): 163–80.
76. Brian Jacobs, "Kantian Character and the Problem of a Science of Humanity," in Jacobs and Kain, *Essays on Kant's Anthropology*, 111. Caygill points out that the numerous marginalia Kant wrote on his lectures had a transformative effect on his thinking. See "Kant and the Age of Criticism," in Caygill, *A Kant Dictionary*, 21.
77. Michel Foucault, *Introduction to Kant's Anthropology*, trans. Robert Nigro and Kate Briggs (Los Angeles: Semiotext(e), 2008), 14. Foucault is implicitly referring

to Lucien Goldmann's "genetic structuralism," which combines the insights of Blaise Pascal's view of the wager, structural analysis, and Marx's conception of consciousness. See *The Hidden God: A Study of Tragic Vision in the Pensées of Pascal and the Tragedies of Racine* (London: Routledge and Kegan Paul), 1964. However, it is clear that Foucault simply means by the expression that he intends to trace the origin and evolution of the *Anthropology*—its "genesis" (*genèse*), as he explains in the same paragraph. In translating this paragraph, Robert Nigro and Kate Briggs use "genetic" where Foucault writes *genèse* (or genesis). Foucault, *Introduction to Kant's Anthropology*, 22–23.

78. Foucault, *Introduction to Kant's Anthropology*, 14–15. Foucault also argues that "the contemporaneity" of the *Anthropology* is present in both the "chronology of the [other] texts and in the architectronic of the work," 20. This statement indicates the difficulty of Foucault's task.
79. Daniel Defert rightly notes that Foucault's analysis departs from the genetic-structural model of analysis, except at the beginning and the end of his *Introduction*, where it veers instead into the Heideggerian method of "repetition." Heidegger read the *Anthropology* into Kant's critical philosophy. See Martin Heidegger, *Kant and the Problem of Metaphysics*, 5th ed. (Bloomington: Indiana University Press, 1997).
80. Given the recurrence of the "empiricity" motif, it is difficult to separate it from the analysis I am offering of the various dimensions of Kant's assessment.
81. Foucault, *Introduction to Kant's Anthropology*, 55. As Foucault notes, his translation is of the second edition of Kant's text published in 1800 when he was still alive. Louden's English translation is of the same edition. The English translation of Foucault's *Introduction* is published separately from his translation of *Anthropology*, as Michel Foucault, *Introduction to Kant's Anthropology*, trans. Roberto Nigro and Kate Briggs (Los Angeles: Semiotext(e), 2008).
82. Foucault, *Introduction to Kant's Anthropology*, 55.
83. This concern resonates with the notion that the *Anthropology* constitutes a "philosophical anthropology." Brandt rejects this characterization; see quote in Zammito, *Kant, Herder,* 301. In a departure from this facile characterization, Heidegger defined philosophical anthropology. Heidegger, *Kant and the Problem of Metaphysics*, 146–50.
84. Stark ("Historical Notes," 21) is in partial agreement with Foucault when he argues that "an internal, positive relationship exists between Kant's lectures on anthropology and his moral philosophy; more precisely that the notes of the lectures *indicate* some such relationship, at least for certain phases in the development of the critical philosophy (which I use as a shorthand for the period following 1781). In other words, I believe that Kant considered anthropology to be an integral part of his philosophy (including his critical philosophy), and that it is not to be reckoned as a mere appendage to the system." Although Stark raises insightful questions in this respect, his demonstration is more circumstantial than probative. Nevertheless, he indicates (p. 27) that the second part of *Anthropology*, devoted to character, is organized on the model of the *Observations on the*

Feeling of the Beautiful and the Sublime, not on that of *Critique*, which mentions the word "anthropology" three times.
85. Paugam, "De l'Anthropologie à l'Archéologie," 838. A close reading of Foucault's *Introduction* bears out Paugam's interpretation.
86. The translation was initially published in 1964 as E. Kant, *Anthropologie du point de vue pragmatique*, trad. Fr. Par M. Foucault (Paris: Vrin, 1964). See the "Presentation" of the 2008 edition by Daniel Defert, François Ewald, and Frédéric Gros, 7.
87. Maria Paola Fimiani argues that Foucault's interpretation of *Anthropology* is mediated by his conception of dreams and existence. *Foucault et Kant: Critique, Clinique, éthique*, trans. Nadine Le Lirzi (Paris: l'Harmattan, 1997), esp. 99. From the beginning, Foucault rereads the *Anthropology* from the perspective of his work on psychology. He argues that in spite of Kant's repeated reference to the world, *welt*, as the domain of anthropological knowledge, "most of his analyses unfold not in the cosmopolitan dimension of the Welt but in that of the Gemüt." This (psychological) concept commonly refers to a feeling of harmony, or a disposition. It is different from *seele*, which refers to the soul and has a religious meaning; it is also different from *geist* (mind or spirit), whose meaning can be both social and religious. However, Fimiani specifies that in *Critique of Pure Reason* Kant defined *gemüt* as "conscience," a faculty that imparts unity to the perception of the world. Foucault notes that the *gemüt* is internal knowledge, but not of a psychological nature. He claims that *Anthropology* draws its impetus from *geist*, which imparts movement to the (assumed) "passivity of the gemüt." He quickly concludes that the *Anthropology* does not allow any room for an examination of psychology. This conclusion manages to limit the parameters within which Foucault rereads the *Anthropology* while at the same time (and paradoxically) allowing him to continue to explore the text from the perspective of his own psychological work. To argue that Kant's *Anthropology* is not based on an identifiable psychology and that the *gemüt* is not synonymous with *seele* suggests that Kant did not concern himself with the nature of the human being as a psychological being (and by implication that the *Anthropology* is not a psychology), or as a being in his relation to the divine. Yet, Foucault leaves the implications of this conclusion unattended in favor of an interrogation of the *Anthropology* from the standpoint of Kant's philosophical texts, such as *Critique*. In other words, what the *Anthropology* says becomes secondary to what Foucault thinks its meaning should be when it is read as a piece of a larger philosophical whole, not as an autonomous work that nevertheless has some relation to the entire oeuvre. This is a decision that Foucault made and on which his critique of anthropology as a discipline rests. It must be noted that Louden suggests that Foucault's emphasis on both *gemüt* and *geist* is unwarranted. Louden, "Foucault's Kant," 12–13.
88. For a discussion of the relationship between empirical psychology and the *Anthropology*, see Wood, *Kant's Ethical Thought*, 198–97; Wilson, *Kant's Pragmatic Anthropology*, 20–26.

89. Foucault, *Introduction to Kant's Anthropology*, 40–47. The first three questions appear in *Critique of Pure Reason*, trans. Paul Guyer and Allen W. Wood (Cambridge: Cambridge University Press, 1998), 677. The fourth question appears (along with the other three) in Kant's *Introduction to Logic* (London: Longmans, Green and Co., 1885), 15 (original section 187), accessed 28 April 2012. https://playgoogle.com/store/books/details?id=iGMAYAAAIAAJ. Wood revisits the four questions in "Kant and the Problem of Human Nature," 38.
90. Foucault, *Introduction to Kant's Anthropology*, 52. Foucault goes one step further and asserts in a Heideggerian gesture that Kant's *Anthropology* is "a fundamental repetition of the *Critique*."
91. Brandt, "The Guiding Idea of Kant's Anthropology," 86–87. Brandt points out that "the marginalia in which the subtitle of Part two [of *Anthropology*, which deals with 'Anthropological Characteristic'] also includes the formulation 'What is a human being?'" but the published book does not, 86.
92. Foucault refers to Kant's *Opus Postumum* as a text in which a relationship is established between God, the world, and man. He also intimates that in some texts, "man gives unity to the world and to God." Foucault, *Introduction to Kant's Anthropology*, 48.
93. Ibid., 51.
94. Like Foucault, Pheng Cheah suggests that the world in Kant is "bounded." Cheah, *Spectral Nationality*, 37.
95. Ibid., 50.
96. Ibid.
97. Ibid., 51.
98. Ibid.
99. Louden cautions that *Opus Postumum* is a "perennially controversial work," implying that conclusions based on it may be hazardous, "Foucault's Kant," 17.
100. Cited in Rudolph A. Makkreel, "Kant on the Scientific Status of Psychology, Anthropology, and History," in *Kant and the Sciences*, ed. Eric Watkins (Oxford: Oxford University Press, 2001), 186. The source of the citation is the Friedländer anthropology lectures of 1775–1776, 25: 469.
101. Foucault writes that "[t]he pragmatic thus was but the useful turned universal." Foucault, *Introduction to Kant's Anthropology*, 32.
102. Ibid., 54.
103. Ibid., 66
104. Ibid., 65.
105. Ibid., 76.
106. A number of philosophers have pointed out that Kant's view of human nature is nuanced and reveals a struggle that pits reason against natural predispositions (to animality, humanity, and personality) for the achievement of the social good. Sharon Anderson-Gold notes that achievement of this goal constitutes a "moral revolution on the part of individuals." "Kant's Ethical Anthropology and the Critical Foundations of the Philosophy of History," *History of*

Philosophy Quarterly 11, no. 4 (October 1994):407. For an excellent and readable analysis of Kant's conception of human nature, see Wood's "Kant and the Problem of Human Nature," and "Unsociable Sociability," *Philosophical Topics* 19, no. 1 (Spring 1991): 325–51.
107. Wood, *Kant's Ethical Thought*, 198.
108. Various attempts have been made to uncover concepts that bridge the *Anthropology* and Kant's critical philosophy, such as for example, "character," "the doctrine of virtue," and the "doctrine of radical evil." Jacobs, "Kantian Character and the Problem of a Science of Humanity"; Stark, "Historical Notes," 28. Stark, like Jacobs, focuses on "character;" Anderson-Gold, "Kant's Ethical," 407, 409. "Subjectivity" as the core of Foucault's interpretation of Kant's *Anthropology* is the focus of Amy Allen's "Foucault and the Enlightenment: A Critical Appraisal," *Constellations* 10, no. 2 (2003): 180–98.
109. Wood, *Kant's Ethical Thought*, 194. In 1785, before Kant decided to publish his anthropology lectures, Manfred Kuehn notes that "he was convinced that metaphysics of morals and anthropology have nothing in common and should not be mixed." Kuehn further argues that *Anthropology* is not a moral anthropology either, even though it addresses moral questions. Manfred Kuehn, "Introduction" to Kant, *Anthropology*, Louden translation, xx. Kuehn concludes that the *Anthropology* may be an unfinished work, as Kant had alluded in *Critique of Pure Reason* to a "complete anthropology" that would be totally cleansed of metaphysics, xvi. This strikes me as an overreaching given the leap that one must make from the *Critique* to *Anthropology*. It would also mean falling into the same trap as Foucault, which is to establish an undemonstrated continuity in Kant's work. It is one thing to argue for the substantive distinctiveness of *Anthropology*; it is another to see it as part of a chain of ideas.
110. See among others, Wood, "Unsociable Sociability," 345–47.
111. Brandt, "The Guiding Idea of Kant's Anthropology," 92–93.
112. Frierson, *Freedom and Anthropology*, especially chap. 2. It is interesting to note that Frierson cites Foucault's *The Order of Things*, but does not refer to Foucault's *Introduction* to Kant's *Anthropology*. Frierson's approach is supported by Louden. See note 58.
113. Kant, *Anthropology*, Louden translation, 15.
114. Foucault, *Introduction to Kant's Anthropology*, 60.
115. Ibid., 59–60. Louden English translation, 5. Dowdell's version translates "popular" as "can be understood by the general public," 6.
116. Kant, *Anthropology*, Louden translation, 5.
117. For example, compare the following passages: Foucault "Une Anthropologie, systématiquement projetée, et cependant traitée, du point de vue pragmatique, sur le mode populaire (par référence à des exemples que chaque lecteur peut découvrir), a pour le public un avantage:…," 85. My translation of this passage that stays close to the text yields: "An Anthropology, systematically designed, yet approached from a pragmatic point of view, in a popular mode (through reference to examples that each reader can discover [on his own], holds an ad-

vantage for the public ..." Louden's translation, 5: "An Anthropology written from a pragmatic point of view that is systematically designed and yet popular (through reference to examples which can be found by every reader) yields an advantage for the reading public ..." Victor Lyle Dowdell's translation, 6, is close to Louden's: "A pragmatic Anthropology which has been systematically designed and which can be understood by the general reading public (because of reference to examples which can be checked by every reader), has the advantage ..." Foucault altered the meaning of "pragmatic" anthropology as well as of "popular." He divorced the pragmatic character of the *Anthropology* from its systematic method, thereby implying that the two terms, pragmatic and systematic, do not belong together, that the latter may detract from the former. The insertion of "mode" to qualify "popular" inserts an additional meaning. Hence Kant's goal of making pragmatic anthropology accessible to the reader appears to refer to the language of *Anthropology,* and may also be a yielding to fashion (in French, fashion is "mode"), as in a popular fad. Yet the word between parentheses in Foucault's text contradicts his use of the concept of "mode" since Kant was careful to indicate that it is the concrete examples that the *Anthropology* provides that make it readable, not necessarily the language in which it is couched. The variance between the French and English translations may be attributed to the objectives of the translators: translation for making the text known, and translation for the purpose of re-interpreting Kant. This raises the question of the integrity of the author's stated words and intent regardless of the postmodernist claim that a text is what one makes of it.
118. Foucault, *Introduction to Kant's Anthropology,* 60.
119. Ibid., 61
120. The use of German needs to be contextualized in the debates that took place among proponents of the German Enlightenment, some of whom wanted to enlarge the reading public to make their ideas accessible to all.
121. Foucault, *Introduction to Kant's Anthropology,* 73–74.
122. Ibid., 69.
123. Ibid., 62.
124. Ibid., 61.
125. Ibid., 64.
126. Ibid.
127. Louden, "Foucault's Kant," 20.
128. Foucault, *Introduction to Kant's Anthropology,* 73.
129. Kant, *Anthropology,* Louden translation, 106–107, 116.
130. Foucault, *Introduction to Kant's Anthropology,* 73.
131. Unlike Foucault, Alix Cohen argues that for Kant the human sciences provide an interpretative framework for understanding human agency grounded not only in anthropology, but also in biology and history. *Kant and the Human Sciences: Biology, Anthropology and History* (New York: Palgrave Macmillan, 2009).
132. Ibid.
133. Foucault, *Introduction to Kant's Anthropology,* 74.

134. Foucault frequently uses the shorthand "Critique" by which he alternately means *Critique of Pure Reason* or the three Critiques.
135. Louden, "Foucault's Kant," 14.
136. Kant, *Anthropology,* Louden translation, 230. Foucault kept the word "death" in his translation, 256.
137. *Repli* can also mean "retreat," as in an army retreating from the enemy.
138. See for example, C. Wright Mills, *The Sociological Imagination* (New York: Oxford University Press, 2000).
139. Louden, "Foucault's Kant."

Chapter 4

Foucault's Negative Anthropology

The case he made against the empirical character of the *Anthropology* grounds Foucault's critique of the human sciences as spelled out in *Les mots et les choses*.[1] The continuity between the two texts is testimonial to Foucault's abiding refusal of the possibility of an empirical anthropology for an understanding of "man," which presupposes the existence of others with whom the researcher (or the traveler) implicitly shares a common and comprehensible humanity. An examination of the terms of this denial will shed light on whether Foucault laid the groundwork for an alternative anthropology, one in which culture and race are squarely faced. It will also help to determine whether his misgivings about philosophical anthropology are shared by contemporary practitioners of anthropology.

In *Les mots et les choses,* Foucault retains his problematization of the *Anthropology*'s empirical character.[2] Generally, he integrates his interpretation of the *Anthropology*, with some modifications, in the larger structure and purpose of the book, in order to do *an* "archaeology of the human sciences."[3] If Foucault's *Introduction* established the baseline of his critique of Kantian philosophy and the practice of anthropology, *Les mots et les choses* traces the origin and vicissitudes of the epistemic status of Western human sciences. The shift suggests the conflicted aspect of Foucault's critique of Kant's conception of human nature. Against the Kantian search for the humanity of human beings, Foucault constructs a history of specific sciences dealing with the physiological nature of human beings, their work, and their language. In other words, Foucault stresses the lack of unity of the subject of Kantian anthropology in favor of an idea of man as dispersed and scattered across various branches of knowledge that have their own methodologies. As a representation of the "empirical-transcendental doublet,"[4] man is unable to locate himself in any definite place, or even less know himself. This is a being always in the process of figuring out what he really is, what his thought conceals from him, and how he could think what he does not (consciously) think. The evocation of the unconscious is a factor that ostensibly complicates the philosophical notion of self-consciousness. Unwittingly, it adds more force to Kant's misgivings about the opacity of self-consciousness, responsible for making knowledge an arduous task for anthropology.[5] In this respect, as Allen Wood points out, Kant's ideas were closer to Nietzsche's and Freud's.[6]

THE DEATH OF MAN AND THE ANTHROPOLOGICAL ILLUSION

In tracing the process through which "man" eludes the human sciences, Foucault's line of argument proceeds in three stages: first, the subject of the human sciences, "man," presumed to know the world and himself as an object in it, did not emerge as an object of study in his own right, alongside other objects, until the eighteenth century. This coincided with two events: the death of God (an expression Foucault borrowed from Nietzsche, and by which he means the displacement of the religious discourse by that of science) which opened up a space for anthropology; and a change in the relationship between language and reality in which language ceased to represent the things it names, and thus lost its transparency. Foucault takes Velazquez's painting, *Las Meninas,* as the best illustration of the age of representation. Velazquez paints himself painting a room full of people, and objects, including a mirror in which appear two figures assumed to be those of the king and queen, who presumably stood where the person viewing the painting would stand.[7] Velazquez's painting represents the representer representing himself. According to Foucault, Velazquez's painting exemplifies the irrelevance of assuming man as the center of knowledge once language lost its capacity to reflect the world. *Las Meninas* shows a void, an empty place, the place of the subject, which in earlier paintings would have been filled by a central figure or object. The painter is at once part of the picture, albeit not in the center of it, and absent from it since we do not see how he could have painted himself painting. Except for the faces in the mirror looking in, most of the figures in the painting appear frozen in gazes whose focus cannot be determined. Foucault concludes that the empty place is occupied by the king and queen reflected in a mirror. The complex play of light and images reflected from an invisible object (the royal couple) to the figures in the painting, and presence-absence of the artist is a metaphor for the emergence in the eighteenth century of the figure of man in the place left empty by the separation between words and the things they name. From Foucault's perspective, the lack of awareness of the conditions under which man emerged as an object and subject of knowledge gave rise to the "anthropological illusion" (or "anthropologism").[8] Instead of freeing knowledge of assumptions about the universalism of human nature, the "anthropological illusion" assumes the presence of a definite and definable human being amenable to empirical study.

If man is declared "dead"[9] (a correlate of the denial of empiricity) the object of knowledge shifts to what man has said or made in the past. The question is, can these elements of an anthropology lead to knowledge of human beings living and acting in societies in the *present,* or should knowledge become possible only after people have died?[10] In 1968, in a remarkably candid and self-revealing interview, Foucault shed light on this question. He explained the meaning of writing to him in relation to death: "and I would say that writing for me is linked to death, perhaps essentially the death of others.... For me, to write has to do with the death of others in so far as they are already dead. In a way I posit their death a little. I speak over the corpses of others."[11] In the interview, Foucault further reveals, with some apprehension, the "evident" relationship between death (as in the death of man) and his "experience of writing."[12] Finally, Foucault clarifies the temporal dimension of his analytical approach to culture: "for me it is always difficult to speak in the present."[13] But in Tunisia, Iran, as well as Japan he had to confront the present.

In Foucault's view, the "anthropological illusion," sustained by the *Anthropology* and perpetuated by post-Kantian anthropologists, accounts for the "anthropological sleep." This condition is manifested in three ways. First is the propensity of anthropologists in general to dwell in the unrecognized illusion that their discipline is empirical when in reality the empirical object is embedded in a philosophy that defines the discipline's contents. Thus, philosophy and anthropology support and give each other meaning. What philosophy defined as human nature serves as the material for empirical knowledge. The implication is that the empiricity of anthropology is but a manner of checking or confirming what philosophy has already identified. In other words, the empirical aim of anthropology so interpreted cannot be realized.

Second, this new object, "man," can be made intelligible only insofar as he has a body that lives, works, and speaks. Third, this man that acquires knowledge of the world of which he is a part is also the object of his own knowledge. He is an empirical object whose empiricity is predicated on the transcendental assumption that he has a nature (shared with others) under which he is subsumed. In this iteration of the *Introduction,* Foucault performs a double task: on the one hand, he rejects the assumption of a universal human nature, which also means a rejection of humanism, the other side of the coin of the Enlightenment. On the other hand, he argues for an alternative to humanistic thought located in a conception of language divorced from the speaker as a sentient human being. He hails linguistics for displacing the emphasis from a speaking subject to the spoken or written word; psychoanalysis for demonstrating the sundering of the unity of consciousness; and ethnology for aiming for the discovery of the conditions of possibility of cultural norms that escape the representation individuals have of them.[14] In this sense Foucault finds affinities between ethnology and psychoanalysis, and suggests that they both deal with the unconscious,[15] notwithstanding his misgivings about psychoanalysis.[16] What's more, Foucault considers these "counter-disciplines" as having the potential to afford a way out of the anthropological sleep.[17] Doing away with the assumption of a human, purposive consciousness, these disciplines point instead to the uncertainty of knowledge.[18]

AWAKENING FROM THE ANTHROPOLOGICAL SLEEP?

From Foucault's view only a new theoretical approach would awaken anthropology from its post-Kantian sleep. All methodologies of the human sciences, including phenomenology, historical materialism, and positivism are but illusory attempts at grappling with the conflation of the metaphysical/transcendental and the empirical inherited from Kant's *Anthropology*. Furthermore, he considered Husserl's emphasis on lived experience (*le vécu*) an ambitious attempt (that still fell short) to keep separate the two domains. Husserl's focus on "lived experience" was meant to indicate that the empiricity of man is given in experience, or to put it differently the empirical is experience-able.[19] By implication, the lived moment articulates the self-knowing individual in a given space and time. Foucault identifies space as that of the body (qua nature) and time as that of culture. However, experience still presupposes the assumption of an empirical world. Phenomenology is thus a "mixed discourse"[20] that combines elements of the "objectivity of knowledge of nature" (meaning the-body-in-the-lived-experience) with the purportedly "naïve" reduction of the transcendental to the empirical. Foucault considers historical materialism and positivism guilty of the same reduction. Positivism assumes that empirical man is knowable through the scientific discourse. From Foucault's perspective positivism effectively subsumes the transcendental under the empirical since it does not question the givenness of its empirical object. It presumes the existence of a human nature that can be grasped through scientific concepts. Thus, Foucault's critique of the thrust of positivism is also a critique of the scientific claims made by the human sciences. As for historical materialism, it makes the human being's empiricity the object of a transformative discourse holding the promise of revealing man's true being in a future communist utopia. Hence, its discourse projects its adequacy onto its object, which it seeks to form and transform through class consciousness and revolutionary praxis. Foucault uses "truth" rather than adequacy, and suggests that both philosophical-theoretical orientations are by nature "eschatological": positivism claims the empiricity of the human being as its ultimate truth (the human being is revealed through the application of the scientific method), whereas historical materialism claims its discourse as the truth of empirical man once he achieves his dis-alienated consciousness as discursively predicted.[21] I will not question this interpretation of Marx's thought in this book, but simply point to its categorical nature. It informs Foucault's interpretation of events such as the Iranian Revolution.

CULTURE, RACE, AND FOUCAULT'S SLEEP

Has Foucault's critique gone far enough? Did his denial of the empirical nature of anthropology conceal or obscure far more important areas in both Kant's *Anthopology* and general anthropology? Foucault did not interrogate culture, a concept central to the German Enlightenment as well as to Kant.[22] As Cheah suggests, culture transcends "finitude" by enabling the individual to share in and build on the heritage passed on to him.[23] When Foucault ventured to define culture in an early draft of *The Archaeology of Knowledge,* he did so with trepidation, referring to the concept as "ugly," "dangerous," and "bothersome" (in French, *déplaisant*). He identified two related approaches to culture. The first one, adopted by ethnologists, uses culture "to designate facts that are foreign to our coordinates," and that are presumed to form a totality that can be grasped externally. Foucault doubts the epistemological value of such a use of the concept. The second approach, deemed worrisome, "introduces quasi-objective distances and pseudo-units in our own backyard (in French, *voisinage*), and in the set of facts, processes, rules or systems in which we are implicated. To speak of 'medieval,' 'clanic,' 'slavic,' or 'mediterranean' culture is nothing more than allowing ourselves to give an ethnological glance at what is close to us." Foucault proposes his own conception of culture as "a mass of enunciations which men produced in world history and which occurred as events (even when minute), whether fleeting or lasting, long or brief." Foucault's difficulty was "to carve units" out of the mass of enunciations. As he put it "culture is everything I need to describe the mode of being of a group of enunciations; it is all that is sufficient to show that this group does constitute a coherent and autonomous whole for it to display its own modality of existence." All the enunciations and practices related to the object of study, such as madness for instance, form a "state of culture." His task is to see how states of culture are related to one another, thereby constituting a "space of culture." In this topographical, structural conception of culture, Foucault inserts a note of reflexivity: his own discourse, which occurs in the same space of culture he shares with his object of study, is grounded in an "a-priori of right." As for his cultural discourse about what was said about a state of culture, it is based on an "a-priori of fact." In this, Foucault signals the "inevitable common space between my discourse and the discourses I take as an object." His approach, he adds, "will reveal the insurmountable reciprocity of cultural a-prioris,"[24] which enable him to carve out units of discourse and presumably speak authoritatively about the culture he shares with others who preceded him. What happens when he makes statements about spaces and states of culture foreign to him? Is it possible to understand a culture without an a priori? What if the a priori of right no longer avails? This view of culture stresses past enunciations rather than human beings as they make themselves in the present, or as citizens of the world.

Whereas Foucault made an attempt at defining culture after he wrote the *Introduction,* he remained silent on the implications of Kant's conception of race for the *Anthropology,* its scope, and its method. In *Introduction,* Foucault indicates the overlap between the *Anthropology, Physical Geography* lectures, and Kant's *Essay on Race.* He also notes how brief the section on race is (less than one page) in the *Anthropology.* Yet, race is a crucial issue in assessing the empiricity as well as the cosmopolitanism of the *Anthropology*; it is a test of its applicability, if not its validity. Recent scholarship has struggled with the contradiction between Kant's claim to a universalistic anthropology and his downright racist views. These were based mostly on unquestioned travel accounts and an uncritical acceptance of David Hume's problematic view of Africans as incapable of achievement in the arts and science.[25] Kant established a hierarchy among the races with the "White race" predictably at the top, having achieved "perfection" and exhibiting greater "talent" than other races.[26] This is hardly the only prejudiced statement Kant made. There are others that defy rational understanding, such as: "Among the Hottentots, as Kolbe reports, many women have a natural piece of skin on their pubic bone, which partly covers their genitals, and which they are said to cut off from time to time … The people of Formosa, and in the centre of Borneo, etc., and whom Rytschov also encountered among the Turkomen in his 'Topography of Orenburg,' who have a small hint of a monkey tail, do not appear to be wholly fictitious."[27] No matter how one would seek to square Kant's prejudiced views with his ethical philosophy, what he wrote about race in more than one place is unambiguous, and cannot be explained away as a mishap.[28] As a nonphilosopher who came to appreciate Kant's thought when preparing this and the preceding chapter, I had to reassess my initial reading of the *Anthropology* in light of Kant's jarring racial views.

It is intriguing that Foucault, writing in 1953–1954 and having knowledge, or awareness, of two major sources of Kant's problematic conception of race, would not mention the relevance of race to his own critique of the *Anthropology*, especially his search for an answer to the recurring question "what is man?" By contrast, in *Introduction,* he discussed Kant's view of women's sexual role in marriage.[29] It must be remembered that Foucault had interest in the matter. In 1976 he lectured about racism at the Collège de France, under the rubric "society must defend itself," in which he did not address the past discourse of race (such as Kant's) in the emergence of racism as a component of state policy in Europe of the twentieth century. The shorter version of the lecture, published in *Dits et écrits,* does not contain a discussion of racism; it makes a passing reference to Kant in the context of a brief comment on the universalist discourse of right.[30] This is not to say that Kant's views somehow caused racial prejudice in Germany or elsewhere. It means, however, that the contemporary discourse on race must be understood in the larger history of racial discourse formations (to use Foucault's terminology) in European history at least from the seventeenth century in order to understand the variations, shifts, and permutations of the idea of race and the role it played in the construction of knowledge of self and others.

More important, an interview Foucault gave to the French Marxist geographers' journal, *Hérodote,* in 1976 reveals a puzzling degree of defensiveness about his neglect of geography in his work considering that he had written about space. His reaction needs interpreting for its concealed relation to Kant's conception of race, initially expressed in his physical geography lectures. In the interview, Foucault went to great lengths to argue that there is a place for geography in *the* archaeology of knowledge—a project he had no intention of undertaking. However, his purpose is to do "historical work that has political meaning," and involves him in "struggles" in the areas of his inquiries.[31] Furthermore, he embarked on a puzzling explanation according to which failing to include geography does not mean "one has an unconscious and therefore inaccessible knowledge of it."[32] At the close of the discussion, as if he had experienced a revelatory moment that put an end to his initial denial and defensive posture, Foucault told his interviewer that he realized now that "geography acted as the support, the condition of possibility for moving between a series of factors I tried to relate [to one another]. Where geography itself was concerned, I either left the question hanging or established a series of arbitrary connections."[33] The oddity of this comment brings up the unconscious incongruously.[34] One of the things left "hanging" is notably the role of race in both the *Anthropology* and *Physical Geography*. Foucault concludes with thoughts of a future project about the history of the military organization of knowledge, of the "fortress," "the campaign," "the colony." It goes without saying that race figures prominently as a principle of organization of knowledge (military as well as civilian) in the colonies. This remarkable interview encapsulates in a cameo-like fashion the amnesic character of Foucault's relation to Kant's problematic work on race. I do not know what to make of the interviewer's avoidance, either willed or imposed by circumstance, of the geography of race. Both interviewer and interviewee danced around the issue, as they identified a gap in knowledge the core of which remained concealed. In the end Foucault admits that there is more to geography than space. But the interview points to the role played by Foucault's own geography in structuring his views of places such as China, Tunisia, Japan, and Iran.

The implication is not that Foucault implicitly accepted Kant's racial views by remaining silent. Rather, the discourse of race, geography, anthropology, and power in the eighteenth and nineteenth centuries constituted a knowledge matrix without which Foucault's assessment of the *Anthropology* is incomplete. With respect to *Les mots et les choses,* the elision of race further raises questions about the validity of his conception of "man and his doubles" as a corrective to Kant's *Anthropology*. Without speculating about the ultimate meaning of Foucault' elision of race, it represents one dimension, the concrete unsaid, of Foucault's cultural challenge. Furthermore, Foucault eschews a discussion of a different and more concrete meaning of Kant's concept of the "world" in the context of the time when he wrote *Introduction*. In 1954, the French colonial empire was in decline: on 7 May, French troops had been defeated at Dien Bien Phu in Vietnam. On 1 November, Algeria started its war of decolonization. Between the writing of *Introduction* and *Les mots et les choses,* the war had been raging in Algeria, affecting French society. The terms "world" and "universe" acquire different meanings in this context: one world was collapsing; others were about to emerge in a rearranged political universe. This is not to say that Foucault should have addressed the political framework of his thought, only that it looked like he was unaware of his unthought—an essential aspect of "man."

THE END OF ANTHROPOLOGY

Foucault's selective interpretation of the *Anthropology* as the source of the fundamental problems that plague the human sciences took place at a time when anthropology as a discipline dealing with non-Western cultures was about to be questioned internally as well as externally. Was then Foucault's assertion of the anthropological illusion prescient? The vast literature announcing the "end" or the imminent "death" of anthropology appears at first glance to validate Foucault's contention. A synoptic reading of this literature will shed light on two related issues: (a) that anthropology is truly the source of all the human sciences so that the crisis of anthropology is echoed in the other human sciences; (b) the crisis is a consequence of a vain search for a dubious universality of human nature that the empirical method (e.g., ethnography) cannot reveal.

In frequently pronouncing their discipline on the verge of death or in need of an immediate salvage operation, anthropologists focus on different aspects of anthropology seen as symptoms of its crisis. These principally include the geographic-political field of its practice; its theories; its very domain, culture; and its ultimate purpose and usefulness in relation to other disciplines as well as to public life.[35] Calls have been made for its "modernization," "enhanced relevance," or return to its roots.[36] The earliest signs of an "end to anthropology" coincided with the end of colonial empires. This was an inevitable outcome considering that anthropologists generally studied societies under colonial rule. Having to secure authorizations and support from colonial administrators before engaging in fieldwork brought anthropologists, even those among them who were opposed to colonial ventures, in too close a proximity with colonial powers and their systems of control of native populations. The anthropological knowledge acquired in colonial societies was consequently subject to suspicion, at times grounded, at others assumed.[37] Access of formerly colonized societies to independence prompted an interrogation[38] on the validity of the discipline's "scientific" claims; the adequacy and ideological consequences of its structural-functionalist theoretical approach with its gloss over issues of inequality, power, and conflict; and the elision of race and racial prejudice.[39] Beyond the colonial constraints of their past, anthropologists have wondered about the purpose of their knowledge. Is it to help shed light on out-of-the-way cultural practices, and by the same token provide a perspective from which to question Western cultural norms as Margaret Mead had done with her study of adolescence in Samoa? Is it to increase the stock of ethnographic knowledge as in adding new pieces to the museum of cultural difference?[40]

Responding to its crisis, anthropology broadened its field to include urban centers and industrial societies; redefined its method as "participant observation;" and experimented with theories imported from other disciplines, including literary criticism, feminist studies, sociology, biology, media studies, and predictably post-colonial studies. Expanding its traditional field, method and theory, has not meant a radical restructuring of the discipline but appears to have proceeded by fits and starts, through accretions rather than integration, contributing to a sense of loss of identity and overarching purpose.[41] Hence episodic claims that anthropology is on its deathbed, or suffering from an "epistemological hypochondria."[42] The translation or importation of concepts and methods from other disciplines created problems of its own.[43] Although yielding some insights, reaching out into other fields has not caused anthropology to become a bridge discipline that would articulate a unified view of the nature of human beings. It signified instead a "rupture" in its four-field organization, which neither led to a radical transformation of the discipline's core concepts, such as culture, nor to an interrogation of its philosophical meaning of the sort that would ask not only "anthropology for what?" but also "social science for what?"

To circumvent the "crisis," two dominant trends, the interpretive and the postmodernist, resulted in implicitly bringing anthropology closer to Kant's perspective, although anthropologists have yet to make the linkage. The first trend, initiated by Clifford Geertz in the early 1970s, searches for meaning in interpreting local cultures semiotically. In a move away from generalizable anthropological knowledge as practiced by Claude Lévi-Strauss, this trend uses ethnography as a method of deciphering cultural practices, symbolically mediated through language. In this perspective, the empirical method is akin to travel in different cultural worlds.[44] The postmodernist trend, influenced by deconstruction and Foucault's conception of the relationship between power and knowledge, constructs culture as a site of a power struggle. It further writes the ethnographer out of the fieldwork she engages in. Unlike Foucault, who located himself outside of the epistemic formations he studied *historically*, postmodernist ethnographers attempt to disengage themselves from their knowledge construction by refraining from offering interpretive frameworks, confining themselves instead to descriptions. The result is the kind of fragmented knowledge Kant had warned against. This trend locks the ethnographer in an impasse that can only be exited by ending ethnographic work altogether. For, in light of the postmodernist conception of power, describing cultures, the method favored by the ethnographer, is an act of knowledge, and therefore power. In both trends, the empirical method is retained in some fashion, but serves localized and personalized interests. Neither trend gives up or could afford to give up the claim to the empirical method, although in its current state, the method resembles a "fractal empiricism,"[45] a collection of myriads of ethnographies frequently driven by themes or epistemic issues emerging from contiguous disciplines.

To return to the question of the ultimate source of anthropology's often-predicted death and resurrection, there is little evidence that anthropology's chronic malaise is related to its empirical method. For example, Geertz attributes the source of his discipline's increasingly dispersed nature to a changing global world, which complicates the study of culture. Moreover, he explains that anthropology's challenges do not stem from an "empirical inadequacy"; they are instead critics' projections of their own concerns such as "agency," or "subjectivity," on the discipline. Nor is the "crisis" of anthropology imputable to an entanglement of its method with a transcendental philosophical notion of the human being as Foucault indicated. Geertz offers some insights into the question. Having first considered a career in philosophy before embarking on anthropology, he had knowledge of Kantian philosophy, including presumably the *Anthropology*. Although acknowledging his indebtedness to Wittgenstein, Geertz mentions Kant episodically.[46] His veiled misgivings about Kant notwithstanding, he stresses the necessity of a close cooperation between anthropology and philosophy. To recall, Foucault had identified the association between the two fields as constituting an epistemic problem. Geertz points to the similarities between the two disciplines as they share a common interest in the fundamental question of the relationship between nature and culture, mind and body.[47] Geertz notes the precariousness of both disciplines, as they are "repeatedly invaded and imposed upon by interlopers."[48]

Anthropology's (unbridled) relativism sets it apart from Kant's anthropology. In his critique of anti-relativism, Geertz argues for the inevitability of relativism considering the very nature of anthropology's subject matter. It is precisely because the object of anthropology, cultural otherness, is different *relative* to the anthropologist's own culture that it accounts for the discipline's traditional play of difference in presenting its findings to itself and to others. It is instructive that Geertz, at the end of his career, called on anthropologists to rethink their conception of difference in a world awash with assertions of ethnic, religious, and political identities. To the point, Geertz acknowledges that in spite of its nomadic interests and its efforts to re-invent itself, the discipline has not relinquished a focus on "difference." Even the discipline's shift from the study of "the other" (the native) to the "same" (the inhabitant of the West) continues to be mediated by contingencies of social class, ethnicity, or power—a situation sociologists are familiar with. However, in spite of his insightful remark, Geertz fails to be sufficiently reflexive. Indeed, the assertion that cultural difference is a resilient problem may very well be due to the failure to conceptualize difference as the phenomenal expression of a fundamental similarity between cultures.[49] But for this to happen, the ethnographer must be able to accept herself as a modality of the other she studies.

Contemporary anthropology shares with Kant an empirical method and a concern for the usefulness of its knowledge. However, counterposing "cosmopolitan" (Kant's key concept) to "parochialism," Geertz concludes that it is anthropology's "cosmopolitanism" that would ultimately prove "valuable" in "a world in pieces."[50] He made this suggestion years after the publication of *Local Knowledge,* in which he extolled the primacy of the local over the general.[51] This (re)turn to Kant's purposive anthropology is one compelling feature of the *solutions* proposed by anthropologists concerned about the direction of their discipline.[52] Echoing Geertz, Catherine Besteman and Hugh Gusterson counterpose another of Kant's concepts, "pragmatic" to "postmodern"; they also unwittingly relink with the "popular" aspect of Kant's anthropology in their call for "a revitalized public anthropology on grounded research, translation of sophisticated anthropological knowledge into accessible English, and a passionate concern for the well-being of those at the sharp end of the neo-liberal globalization."[53] In other words, anthropology's embrace of postmodernist theorizing, with its emphasis on self-referentiality, reluctance to integrate facts and events into a coherent synthetic whole, as well as its rejection of universalizing interpretive schemes, is perceived as a symptom of a discipline in crisis instead of its enduring solution.[54]

Critical anthropologists advocate a return of their discipline to its fundamental principles and to "re-engage" with the Boasian tradition, combining a commitment to empirical (instead of empiricist) knowledge, a critical perspective, and an involvement in public life. Matti Bunzl nostalgically extolls the intellectual origin of this tradition, the "German *Geisteswissenschaften*" [arts], for its "attempt to produce general knowledge about *humanity* [emphasis added] despite and because of the inherent uniqueness of human action."[55] He could have just as well cited Kant's anthropology. Thus, where Foucault saw a problem for anthropology, anthropologists see hope. Furthermore, anthropologists seldom claim Kant's *Anthropology* as the groundwork for their discipline. A major history of anthropology published in 1968 does not mention Kant's *Anthropology* even though it traces the heritage of anthropology to the enlightenment.[56] Finally, an emergent trend foregrounds the use of difference (cultural as well as political-economic) as a way of decentering anthropological knowledge. Anthropological theory, from this perspective, is going south or native.[57] The late Claude Lévi-Strauss captured this revised conception of the significance of cultural difference in a reflection on his long career: "Traditionally, anthropology preferred to shed light on the past of our institutions by studying those societies deemed primitive instead of proceeding in the other direction." He concluded: "philosophy again is in the forefront of the anthropological stage. It is no longer our philosophy, which my generation asked exotic peoples to help us to jettison but, in a remarkable turn of events, it is theirs that occupies the stage."[58] Whether this leads in the long run to a genuine rethinking of difference that can be grasped without region-centered epistemic mediation, or to turning the table on Kant by having the "world" observe "us" in an intermediate phase, as a way of transforming the meaning of cosmopolitanism, remains to be seen.[59]

To conclude, on the whole what emerges from responses to the "crisis" of anthropology differs from Foucault's assessment of the "anthropological sleep" as well as the "death of man." Anthropology as a discipline has not shown signs of falling into a deep slumber; it exhibits energy in engaging in introspection as well as experimentation with ways of keeping itself alive. At no point do anthropologists critical of their discipline attribute its problems to the dissolution of "man." In fact they study culture, not human nature, and often the latter fades before debates over the meaning of cultural practices rather than what they tell us about human nature. In the thick of reflections on the state of the discipline, renewed interest in the fundamental aim of anthropological knowledge is identified as "human nature," defined as the nature of human beings above and beyond its cultural contingencies.[60] There are multiple signs that anthropologists are groping for a general conception of anthropology as Kant provided, combining a distinct method, a definite purpose, and a mission that connects its locally situated interests with an acknowledged (universal) moral vision. In the end, even if Kant's anthropology had been widely read and used by anthropologists, the problems encountered by their discipline would be imputable to factors Foucault did not raise, namely: (a) the *Anthropology*'s failure to uphold the distinction between the physiological (race) and the anthropological (culture); (b) the implications of its suspension of critical thought when confronted with travel reports about other peoples and cultures; and (c) its related failure to identify the linkages between the local and the general, the contingent and the necessary given its cosmopolitan purpose.

To return to the Chinese encyclopedia, could Foucault have approached it differently had he interpreted the *Anthropology* differently? Why did he use the "local culture" to which he belongs as a standard for interpreting Chinese culture? In other words, would a different reading of Kant's conception of "local culture" and a consideration of "cosmopolitanism" have led him to a different introduction to *Les mots et les choses,* and thus a different orientation toward cultural difference?

THE UNIVERSAL AS EUROPEAN

In 1983, Foucault lectured about Kant's "An Answer to the Question: What Is Enlightenment," published in 1784.[61] His commentary sheds light on yet another aspect of Foucault's reinterpretation of Kant's thought. Kant's essay was an answer to a question that occupied his contemporaries and was one of the many occasions he wrote as a public intellectual. Kant examined the meaning and conditions of possibility of the Enlightenment. He thought of the Enlightenment as a complex process grounded in a human being's effort to emerge from "self-incurred immaturity" to achieve "maturity." He defined maturity as the individual's capacity to act without the guidance of others, and thus to "dare to know" (*sapere aude*). From this perspective, Kant's contemporaries did not live in an enlightened age, but "in an age of enlightenment." However, although he focused on his own society under the reign of Frederick, he wrote about the Enlightenment as a "universal" event as made clear by his frequent use of the expression "human beings."

Foucault interprets this text as a "discursive practice" focused on "the *present*" (emphasis added). This reductive reading revolves on two sentences, one, a question; the other, an answer: "If it is now asked whether *we* [emphasis added] now live in an *Enlightenment* age," and "in this respect this age is the age of Enlightenment or the century of Frederick." Foucault remarks "it will no longer be the question of his [the philosopher, Kant's] belongingness to a human community in general, but that of a certain 'us', an 'us' that is related to a cultural collectivity [*ensemble culturel*] characteristic of its own actuality."[62] Furthermore, Foucault writes "Aufklärung named itself Aufklärung; it is without a doubt a very singular cultural process that became conscious of itself by naming itself and by designating the operations it must undertake within its own present."[63] Foucault leaves no doubt that Kant had retreated (or come out of hiding) from his universalistic approach by purportedly focusing solely on local-qua-European cultural concerns. Kant had thus ushered in a new practice, that of modern philosophizing. This is an attractive interpretation if one seeks to build a critique of simple-minded universalism. However, I find it discomforting, not the least because its purpose is not to poke holes in Kant's universalism—a laudable, if not necessary task—but to privatize him, or cast his thought in an avowedly culturalist-qua-regionalist mold that it presents as positively singular. It is not a critique but a celebration of the stated singularity of one's culture, an "us."

A detail in Foucault's recasting of Kant has significance: he conflates Enlightenment and modernity, leaving no room for arguing that modernity could take place without the equivalent of "enlightenment" in other "cultural collectivities," or that perhaps there are different modalities of enlightenment. To buttress his point, he traces the roots of modernity to Western classical culture. Frequently using "us" and "our thought," he concludes that it is not the Enlightenment as such that needs to be preserved.[64] Rather, what should be remembered is the local nature of its occurrence, "the question of the historicity of universal thought."[65] There is little room for a naïve interpretation of Foucault's statement of ownership of the Enlightenment. In 1983, when he wrote his essay, the Enlightenment's cultural origin needed no ascertaining. Therefore, the point of Foucault's reminder to his readers lies elsewhere than in a redundant observation about the origins of the movement. Perhaps Foucault means that what passes for universal is really what is local in Western countries. However, there is no inkling in this essay that Foucault implied a critique of universalistic thought, of the kind found in critiques of imperialism as a "civilizing mission." I take Foucault's statement as an attempt to *reveal* that Kant's universalistic thought is in reality local; it is a contrived illusion. It may very well be. However, the absence of a countervailing reference to the unseemly side of the Enlightenment undermines the critical potential of Foucault's assessment of Kant's universalistic thought. Foucault does not hint at Kant's racial thought to question his universalism. This failure leaves his comments on the Enlightenment at once limited as well as Euro-centered.

Foucault effectively took Kant's essay as a place to identify Kant's hidden thought. This move is parallel to Foucault's assertion that the empirical in Kant's *Anthropology* is just a foil that obscures its transcendental nature. In *Aufklärung* Foucault finds that, just as the *Anthropology* was not empirical, Kant's universalism was not universal; rather it is the expression of local knowledge. By implication, aiming for universalism (as Kant did) is disingenuous; there is only local culture and local knowledge; there are only variations and no common features in human beings as cultural beings. In his insistence to keep alive the cultural-national-regional origins of the Enlightenment-qua-modernity, Foucault jettisoned the universal value, no matter its cultural origins, of philosophical events that tap into aspirations of human beings wherever they live and whatever their local culture is. Parenthetically, Foucault later questioned the view that humanism, a correlate of the enlightenment, is a uniquely Western cultural development. At any rate, Foucault's regionalization of Kant's thought represents a culturalist interpretation.[66] Such an interpretation leads to a form of cultural relativism which, in reality, doubles up as a non- or post-Kantian universalism of its own. This new culturalism inverts Kant's search for features of the universal in the local by turning the local into the universal.

In the end, although written nearly three decades after *Introduction* (and seventeen years after *Les mots et les choses*) Foucault's reading of Kant's essay on the Enlightenment is in keeping with his reading of the *Anthropology* and sheds light on his selection of some of its concepts, such as the "world." If the universal is reduced to Europe, the world indeed is a "limit." Knowledge of the world in this interpretation is no longer a requirement as Kant's *Anthropology* maintained. Consequently, comparative anthropology as the study of human beings belonging to different cultures for the purpose of identifying their commonalities (and what they tell us about being human) becomes either unnecessary or the study of chance variations. However, from this perspective, variations acquire meaning as distances *from* some core element of human social organization, or from a cultural standard. A variation is not its own standard, and in the absence of humanity as a marker, variations necessarily become deviations from "the historicity of universal thought," which happens to be the West as Foucault conceives it.

Foucault's interpretation of Aufklärung obviates a significant part of German Enlightenment that spanned Gottfried Wilhelm Leibniz and Christian Wolff's writings and culminated in Kant's critical philosophy in which discussions of Chinese philosophy figured prominently.[67] Leibniz as well as Wolff was convinced that Confucius's fundamental concepts of humanity, natural law, progress, and ethics in general were similar to and in part "superior" to Western philosophy.[68] Having in mind the destructive Thirty Years' War, they intimated that the absence of a Christian god did not prevent China from evolving along the lines cherished by the Enlightenment. By contrast, Kant, writing at a time when European attitudes toward China had changed,[69] was dismissive of Chinese philosophy as well as the Chinese people.[70] For example, he characterized Chinese businessmen as "deceitful and unethical."[71] He further disparaged Confucian ideas as "prosaic," although he referred to Confucius as the "Chinese Socrates."[72] In a surprising generalization, based on inaccurate information, he concluded: "philosophy is not to be found in the Orient."[73] Nevertheless, Kant referred to China as "this amazing country," suggested that it be called by the name it chose for itself instead of "Sina," and bemoaned foreign encroachment on its territory.[74] Kant's attitude toward Chinese culture and philosophy obscures the close similarities between his and Confucius's fundamental concepts.[75]

This synoptic view of Kant's perceptions of Chinese philosophy, to which I will return in a later chapter, raises two related questions: on the one hand, by stressing the European situatedness of the Enlightenment, and conflating the local with the universal, Foucault detracts from his implicit critique of the universalism of Kant's thought. On the other hand, by ignoring the significance of China's place in Kant's perception of alterity, Foucault deprives himself of an angle from which to question the *Anthropology*'s claim to knowledge of the "world," or the meaning it imparts to the "citizen of the world" when confronted with the world of otherness. Compounding his neglect of China, Foucault ignored the role of colonial contacts with other non-European societies in the Enlightenment's definition of Western identity and modernity.[76] In other words, Foucault elided the question of comparative anthropology as well as political geography as a test of the *Anthropology*. He ignored the practical application of the *Anthropology* by its own author, and thus failed to question the meaning of the European-ness of the Enlightenment. When this is done, it is legitimate to ask with Martin Schönfeld "what Aufklärung really has to do with 'enlightenment.'"[77]

This book asks: does Foucault have an (alternative) "anthropology?" Could he dispense with an anthropology in dealing with the Tunisians, Iranians, or Japanese? His critique of empirical anthropology suggests a counter-anthropology, a negative anthropology, for lack of a better word. It is an anthropology that obviates issues of race or gender as constitutive of discourse or epistemology. It constructs knowledge of human beings through discontinuous collective discourses, not empirical work. Consequently, its aim is not to understand how people *make* themselves as they build culture, or how culture is a universal human social condition. It excludes universalistic propositions about social organization or social behavior. It also excludes the notion that such propositions might be or should be necessary. Paradoxically, it also intends to be useful; it does not aim for knowledge of the humanity of the human being but of how self-propelling language or power structure discourses that are devoid of the consciousness that produces them.

Foucault started out his journey into the *Anthropology* to identify linkages between anthropology and critical philosophy, and ended with the claim that the *Anthropology* is the source of the problematic nature of contemporary human sciences. From the *Anthropology* to *Les mots et les choses*, Foucault lays the groundwork for a perspective on cultural knowledge that evades the paramount question of how to understand different cultures and cultural practices (including those concerned with the self and the body) if as scholars we wish to understand *ourselves* and who we are. Foucault's interpretation is a retreat (as in *repli*) from the cosmopolitanism, which Kant stressed in the *Anthropology*.[78]

The two texts, *Introduction* and *Les mots et les choses*, more than foretell Foucault's cultural conundrum. By the time he went to Tunisia in 1966, Foucault's attitude toward cultural difference had already been enframed by his philosophical orientation.

NOTES

1. Amy Allen also reads Foucault's *Introduction* together with *The Order of Things* as well as "What is Aufklärung?" Amy Allen, "Foucault and Enlightenment: A Critical Appraisal." *Constellations* 10, no. 2 (2003).
2. Guillaume Paugam, "De l'anthropologie à l'archéologie," *Critique* 65, no. 749 (October 2009), 842, argues that *Les mots et les choses* still does not justify Foucault's rereading of Kant's *Anthropology*. However, he suggests that there is a difference between *Introduction* and *Les mots et les choses*: in the former, "the Kantian moment," *Anthropology* is presented as a work in progress, whereas in *Les mots* it is located as standing midway between the Classical Age and modernity, "which it ushers in but on which it does not depend."
3. See Foucault's interview with the French Marxist geographers' journal *Hérodote*, "Questions on Geography," in Colin Gordon, ed., *Power/Knowledge: Selected Interviews and Other Writings 1972-1977, by Michel Foucault* (New York: Pantheon Books, 1980), 65. (The interview also appears as "Questions à Michel Foucault sur la géographie," in *Dits et écrits,* vol. 2, 28-40).
4. Foucault, *Les mots et les choses,* 333; *The Order of Things,* 322.
5. Kant wrote: "We often play with obscure representations," thereby indicating that we tend to deny the "power of imagination and enjoy walking in the dark," especially in sexual matters. *Anthropology,* Louden translation, 25. See also Wood, *Kant's Ethical Thought,* 202. Wood specifies that "to see human nature as it truly is, we would have to observe behavior that is unselfconscious," 200.
6. Wood, *Kant's Ethical Thought,* 202. Wood includes in his discussion of Kant's *Anthropology* reference to eight manuscript versions of Kant's lectures of Anthropology dating from 1772-1773 to 1788-1789. See also the conclusion to Wood's "Unsociable Sociability," *Philosophical Topics* 19, no. 1 (Spring 1991), 345-47.
7. Foucault provides the names and/or functions of the figures in the paintings on p. 25; *The Order of Things,* 9.
8. Foucault, *Introduction à l'anthropologie de Kant,* 77.
9. According to Philippe Sabot, the thesis of the "death of man" was initially formulated by Alexandre Kojève. It influenced Bataille and other surrealists, who took it in a different direction, and in turn influenced Foucault. "De Kojève, à la mort de l'homme et la querelle de l'humanisme." "La Mort de L'homme et La Question de L'humanisme," *Archives de Philosophie* 72, no. 3 (2009): 523-40.
10. In reporting on the Iranian Revolution, Foucault claimed to be doing a "history of the present" as part of his *"reportages d'idées." Dits et écrits,* vol. 2, 706-7.
11. Michel Foucault, *Le beau danger: entretien avec Claude Bonnefoy* (Paris: Éditions de l'EHESS, 2011), 37.
12. Ibid., 65.
13. Ibid., 39.
14. Foucault, *Les mots et les choses,* 385-98; *The Order of Things,* 373-87.
15. Foucault's interpretation of ethnology as a discipline dealing with the social unconscious reflects his acceptance of Claude Lévi-Strauss's thesis in *Structural*

Anthropology, vol. 3, trans. Claire Jacobson and Brooke Grundfest Schoepf (New York: Basic Books, 1976). It must be noted that this conception is at odds with Foucault's rejection of universalism, a view central to Lévi-Strauss's thesis that cultural norms express a universal feature of human societies in which the mind puts form over content and that the reasons for such norms can be deciphered in people's unconscious.

16. Foucault provides a powerful critical evaluation of psychoanalysis in his Introduction to Binswanger, *Le rêve et l'existence.* The Introduction also appears in *Dits et écrits,* vol. 1, 1954–1975, 93–147.
17. Foucault modeled the expression "anthropological sleep" after "dogmatic sleep," an expression Kant used in *Prolegomena to Any Future Metaphysics* to refer to the influence that Hume had on him. Wood, *Kant* (Malden, MA: Blackwell, 2005), 6.
18. The concept of the "unthought" was interpreted by Philippe Sabot as referring to man's unacknowledged fact that he is the foundation of his own knowledge. This is a restrictive interpretation of Foucault's concept.
19. Already in 1954, in his Introduction to Binswanger, Foucault had announced that he would show in a later work "by following the inflection of phenomenology towards anthropology, what foundations have been given to the concrete knowledge [reflection] of man," 93. For an original assessment of Foucault's critique of "lived-experience," see Leonard Lawlor, "A Minuscule Hiatus: Foucault's Critique of the Concept of Lived-Experience (vécu)" in *Logos of Phenomenology and Phenomenology of the Logos, Book one,* ed. Anna-Teresa Tymieniecka. Analecta Husserliana, 88 (Dordrecht, The Netherlands: Springer, 2005).
20. Foucault, *Les mots et les choses,* 332, 336; *The Order of Things,* 321, 325.
21. Foucault, *Les mots et les choses,* 331; *The Order of Things,* 320.
22. Moses Mendelssohn, a friend of Kant's, captured the hesitations and efforts made to anchor the meaning of the concept of culture in thinking through the newly discovered and multifaceted notion of enlightenment at the time he and Kant were writing. Noting that "culture" was distinguished from both the "enlightenment" and "education," he suggests that languages had yet "to establish their borders. Education, culture and enlightenment are modifications of social life, effects of the hard work and efforts of human beings to improve their social condition." The notion of "modification" is important to stress as it reflects Kant's view that the building of culture is part of what the human being makes of himself—the subject of anthropology. Moses Mendelssohn, *Philosophical Writings,* ed. Daniel O. Dalstrom (New York: Cambridge University Press, 1997), 313. The entire quotation also appears in Pheng Cheah, *Spectral Nationality,* 39.
23. Pheng Cheah, *Spectral Nationality,* 75.
24. Foucault, manuscript of *The Archaeology of Knowledge,* Bibliothèque Nationale de France, Richelieu site, NAF 2828 (1).
25. Kant quotes Hume's assessment of Black peoples in *Observations on the Feeling of the Beautiful and Sublime,* 110–11.
26. I am grateful to Professor Robert B. Louden for sharing with me a draft of the English translation of the text, which contains a key problematic paragraph in

which Kant refers to the superiority of the white race: "Concerning Human Beings," (Vom Menchen), First Section, paragraph 4, Second Part of *Physical Geography,* trans. Olaf Reinhardt with assistance from David Oldroyd. This document helped me to read the quotation in context. The quotation also appears in Werner Stark, "Historical and Philological References on the Question of a Possible Hierarchy of Human 'Races,' 'People's,' or 'Populations' in Immanuel Kant—A Supplement," in *Reading Kant's Geography,* ed. Elden and Mendieta, 87. The full translation of *Physical Geography* is in Immanuel Kant, *Natural Science,* ed. Eric Watkins (Cambridge: Cambridge University Press, 2012).

27. Ibid. Kant made many such statements in his *Physical Geography* lectures as well as in other essays, especially "Of the Different Races of Human Beings," in "Announcement of the Physical Geography Lectures in Summer Semester 1775." Ronald Bolin's translation of Kant's *Physical Geography* appends a brief statement regarding the general organization of the course, which Kant had appended to this essay, but not the essay itself (Appendix 4).

28. Werner Stark casts doubt on the oft-quoted paragraph above in which Kant establishes a hierarchy of races; he conjectures that it must have been an annotation made by a student to the Holstein Physical Geography manuscript, one of the earlier manuscripts, of which there are twenty-seven. In dissecting the paragraph, second-guessing Kant about what he might have meant by "perfection" and the role of "talent" in assessing others, he concludes that "we can neither presume nor insinuate pejorative intention." He further checks Kant's problematic comments on the Tierra del Fuegans against those made by some French travelers to explain that Kant was merely making a statement of fact shared by others. (Kant had called the Fuegans "stupid.") Yet, the text by one such traveler, Boungainville, was far more restrained than Kant's characterization of the Fuegans. Clearly there are different ways of writing about cultural/racial differences. The manner in which Kant did was categorical and prejudicial. And it is more jarring than that of explorers or lesser intellectuals because, among other things, his anthropology was defined in cosmopolitan terms. Nevertheless Stark raises the important question of the varied language in which the idea of race can be conveyed. Kant's statement regarding the superiority of the white race cited by Stark is from *Physical Geography,* Rink edition, 1802, [2/3]. Stark, "Historical and Philological References," esp. 87–90. More striking is Kant's acceptance of Girtanner's own acceptance of the fanciful notion of the "tail people" as alluded to above. Hund, "'It Must Be from Europe," 73. See also David Harvey, "Cosmopolitanism in the Anthropology and Geography," in *Cosmopolitanism and the Geographies of Freedom* (New York: Columbia University, 2009). Harvey calls the *Anthropology* "flawed," and the Geography "an incoherent bunch of anecdotic particulars for which the general has yet to be found," 280. Harvey, however, poses an essential question: if the *Anthropology* (as the purported foundation of the human sciences) is suspect, "on what grounds can we trust Kant's cosmopolitanism?," 282. Attempts have been made to save Kant from his uncritical racial views by a number of people (in addition to Stark),

the most notable being Pauline Kleingeld ("Kant's Second Thought on Race," *The Philosophical Quarterly* 57, no. 229 (October 2007): 573–92). She argues that Kant gradually shifted his views on race, as well as slavery and the slave trade, toward the end of his career. Robert Bernasconi ("Kant's Third Thoughts on Race," in Elden and Mendiata, *Reading Kant's Geography*, 300) offers a careful rebuttal. He demonstrates continuity in Kant's racial views as indicated, among other things, in Kant's republication of his essays on race as late as 1797 and 1799. For Marc Crépon the continuity in Kant's writings on race is too evident to be questioned. *Les géographies de l'esprit: enquête sur la caractérisation des peuples de Leibniz à Hegel* (Paris: Payot & Rivages, 1996), 156–57.

29. Foucault, *Introduction to Kant's Anthropology*, 42–44. See also Kant, *The Anthropology*, Louden translation, 204–7.
30. Michel Foucault, "Il faut défendre la société," *Dits et écrits*, vol. 2, 124–30. The index of *Dits et écrits* does not contain an entry for race.
31. Michel Foucault, "Questions on Geography," in *Power/Knowledge*, 64.
32. Ibid., 66.
33. Ibid., 77.
34. Foucault had also left hanging the seamy side of one of the naturalists he discusses in *Les mots et les choses*, Georges Louis Leclerc, count of Buffon, whose problematic views on race informed Kant's geography lectures.
35. For a summary of critiques see John Comaroff, "The End of Anthropology, Again: On the Future of an In-discipline," *American Anthropologist* 112, no. 4 (2010). Comaroff suggests that "we actually require to look disciplinary death in the face in order to survive," 525. See also a summary by Matti Bunzl, "The Quest for Anthropological Relevance: Borgesian Maps and Epistemological Pitfalls," *American Anthropologist* 110, no. 1 (March 2008): 54–56; James Clifford, *The Predicament of Culture: Twentieth Century Ethnography, Literature, and Art* (Cambridge, MA: Harvard University Press, 1988), chap. 2.
36. See, among others, Don Donham, "Thinking Temporally, or Modernizing Anthropology," *American Anthropologist* 103, no.1 (March 2001), and John Comaroff's rejoinder, "Of Fallacies and Fetishes: A Rejoinder to Donham"; Matti Bunzl, "The Quest for Anthropological Relevance"; Catherine Besteman and Hugh Gusterson, "A Response to Matti Bunzl: Public Anthropology, Pragmatism, and Pundits," *American Anthropologist* 110, no. 1 (March 2008); and Matti Bunzl's "A Reply to Besteman and Gusterson," in the same issue.
37. For a critique of the colonial factor in anthropological ethnography, see Talal Asad, *Anthropology and the Colonial Encounter* (New York: New Humanities, 1973).
38. Some of these interrogations reveal a veiled sense of personal loss among anthropologists. For example, James Clifford characterizes anthropology's endeavors as "Western *visions* and practices" whose questionings "challenge the authority and even the future identity of the 'West.'" *The Predicament of Culture*, 9.
39. For how anthropology fits in the larger history of racial prejudice in Western thought, see Rigby, *African Images*. It must be noted that Marxist anthropology has not escaped criticism of Euro-centeredness. See Peter Forster, "Empiri-

cism and Imperialism: A Review of the The New Left Critique," in Talal Asad, *Anthropology*.
40. For a discussion of the critical function of anthropology, see George E. Marcus and Michael J. Fischer, *Anthropology as Cultural Critique: An Experimental Moment in the Human Sciences* (Chicago: University of Chicago Press, 1986), chap. 6.
41. James Clifford called this problem "the ethnographic modernity predicament." *The Predicament of Culture*, 3.
42. Clifford Geertz, quoted in John Comaroff, "The End of Anthropology," 525.
43. George E. Marcus bemoans the "dilution" of the concept of culture and considers the discipline in a state of "suspension." Marcus also wonders whether the anthropologist has not become a mere, albeit good, journalist. "The Ends of Ethnography: Social/Cultural/Anthropology's Signature Form of Producing Knowledge in Transition," *Cultural Anthropology* 23, no. 1 (2008), 3–4.
44. Clifford Geertz, *The Interpretation of Cultures: Selected Essays* (New York: Basic Books, 1973), especially chaps. 1, 8. For a critique of Geertz's as well as native anthropologist's (mis)representation of Islam, see Daniel Martin Varisco, *Islam Obscured: The Rhetoric of Anthropological Representation* (New York: Palgrave Macmillan, 2005).
45. John Comaroff, "The End of Anthropology," 528.
46. Clifford Geertz, *Available Light: Anthropological Reflections on Philosophical Topics* (Princeton, NJ: Princeton University Press, 2001), xii. In his review of Foucault's *Discipline and Punish*, Geertz is skeptical about Foucault's approach. "On Foucault," in *Life Among the Anthros and Other Essays*, ed. Fred Inglis (Princeton, NJ: Princeton University Press, 2001), 29–38.
47. Geertz, *Available Light*, 203. This harks back to Kant's nuanced understanding of the point at which a physiological characteristic, such as memory or race, becomes anthropologically relevant.
48. Ibid., ix.
49. George E. Marcus and Michael J. Fischer (suggest using "the traditional arena of research abroad" for "developing a distinctive anthropological cultural critique of American society"), *Anthropology as Cultural Critique: An Experimental Moment in the Human Sciences* (Chicago: Chicago University Press, 1999), 4. The purpose of this view is not to understand cultural difference but to use it in "experimentation" with the project of rebuilding the discipline.
50. Geertz, *Available Light*, chap. 11.
51. Clifford Geertz, *Local Knowledge: Further Essays in Interpretive Anthropology* (New York: Basic Books, 2000). Geertz uses the concept of culture not only for the study of art, but also for the study of common sense. In addition, he uses ethnography as a method for doing a brief intellectual history of "modern thought" that reaches beyond anthropology. This book encapsulated some of the symptoms of the crisis in anthropology. In addressing the role of the "native's point of view" in ethnographic work, he extolls understanding cultural difference as difference, even as he prefers that it not be mediated by Western cultural experience, or subsumed under it, 5.

52. There is a similar but less explicit return to Kantian anthropology in John Comaroff's stress on the significance of the "lived world" in understanding the intercultural character of anthropology. "The End of Anthropology," 530. The French anthropologist, Jacques Galinier, also briefly notes a "second turn" to Kant, and advocates that contemporary anthropologists hold philosophical debates of the kind that took place in Germany around the ideas of Herder and Kant, affect and rationality, as well as culture and cognition, "L'anthropologie hors des limites de la simple raison: actualité de la dispute entre Kant et Herder," *L'Homme* 179 (2006), 141–42.
53. Catherine Besteman and Hugh Gusterson, "A Response to Matti Bunzl," 61.
54. Georges E. Marcus considers the postmodernist trend in anthropology as a "moment" in the evolution of the discipline. "The Ends of Ethnography," 9.
55. Matti Bunzl, "The Quest for Anthropological Relevance," 61.
56. Marvin Harris, *The Rise of Anthropological Theory: A History of Theories of Culture* (New York: Thomas Y. Crowell, 1968). However, Kant's anthropology is listed in the bibliography in German. Harris also fails to discuss Kant's conception of race in a section devoted to the topic, "Monogenesis, Environmentalism and Evolution," although he cites Kant from secondary sources as among those who "anticipated modern views of the adaptive nature of social traits," or as having pointed out "the disproportion between the total body stature and the short legs of the northernmost peoples in relation to the problem of heat conservation," 85.
57. See among others, Jean Comaroff and John L. Comaroff, *Theory from the South: Or, How Euro-America is Evolving toward Africa* (Boulder: Paradigm Publishers, 2012), and Raewyn Connell, *Southern Theory: The Global Dynamics of Knowledge in Social Science* (Cambridge: Polity, 2007), esp. chaps. 5 and 6; this book focuses on sociological theory. The debate over the role of "native anthropologist," prompted Matti Bunzl to propose a synthesis of Boas's methodology and Foucault's genealogical perspective. Matti Bunzl, "Boas, Foucault, and the 'Native Anthropologist': Notes toward a Neo-Boasian Anthropology," *American Anthropologist* 106, no. 3 (September 2004): 435–42.
58. Claude Lévi-Strauss, "Postface," *l'Homme* 154–55 (Apr.–Sept., 2000), 719, 720.
59. In a review of Kant's *Physical Geography*, which is replete with uncritical acceptance of bizarre stories about other peoples and places, Roger Pol-Droit suggests a parody in which non-Western people would describe Kant's view of Königsberg and its people in the same bizarrely prejudiced manner as Kant described them. "Kant et les Fourmis du Congo," *Le Monde*, 5 February 1999.
60. "Vital Topics Forum, On Nature and the Human," *American Anthropologist* 112, no. 4 (2010): 512–21. Tim Ingold, a contributor to this debate, poses the question of human nature in Kantian terms, 514.
61. The English translation appears, among others, in Kant, *Practical Philosophy*, trans. Mary McGregor (Cambridge: Cambridge University Press, 1996).
62. Foucault, "Qu'est-ce-que les Lumières," in *Dits et écrits,* vol. 2, 1499. The English translation appears in Paul Rabinow, ed., *The Foucault Reader* (New York: Pantheon Books, 1984), 32–50.

63. Foucault, "Qu'est-ce que les Lumières?," 1500.
64. Ibid., 1505.
65. Ibid., 1505.
66. Among French critics of Foucault, Michel Amiot provides a thorough and cogent analysis of what he termed "culturalism" in *Les mots et les Choses*. "Le relativisme culturaliste de Michel Foucault," in *Les mots et les choses de Michel Foucault: Regards critiques 1966–1968*, ed. Philippe Artières et al. (Caen: Presses Universitaires de Caen, 2009), 121. Amiot suggests that Foucault's culturalism "comes dangerously close to anecdote." Ibid.
67. The history and meaning of the changing debates over Chinese culture and philosophy in Germany have been addressed in a dedicated issue of the *Journal of Chinese Philosophy*, vol. 33, no. 1 (March 2006).
68. See, among others, Wenchao Li and Hans Poser, "Leibniz's Positive View of China," *Journal of Chinese Philosophy* 33, no. 1 (March 2006): 17–33; and Bryan W. Van Norden and Robert B. Louden, "'What Does Heaven Say': Christian Wolff and Western Interpretations of Confucius Ethics," in *Confucius and the Analects: New Essays*, ed. Bryan Van Orden (New York: Oxford University Press, 2002), 73–93.
69. The discovery of classical Chinese philosophy, mediated by Jesuit missionaries, occurred at a time when Germany was barely recovering from the devastation of the Thirty Years' War (1618–1648). However, as the Church insisted that the Chinese language did not contain a concept for God as understood by Christians, and the Chinese ancestral rites were idolatrous acts (which had to be renounced by Christian converts), images of China started to shift. The religious controversy between China and the Vatican was only one, albeit crucial, aspect of the anti-Chinese sentiment. It was reinforced by the hostile writings of French authors such as Montesquieu, the racial views of Buffon, as well as reliance on dubious sources of knowledge about China, principally travelogues. The more learned Jesuit reports, held to be sinophile, became less and less available by mid eighteenth century. See Thomas Fuchs, "The European China-Reception from Leibniz to Kant," trans. Martin Schönfeld, *Journal of Chinese Philosophy* 33, no. 1 (March 2006), especially 41–46; and Martin Schönfeld, "From Confucius to Kant: the Question of Knowledge Transfer," 67–81.
70. Kant's information about China came out of his readings of Leibniz and Wolff, undoubtedly supplemented by travelogues circulating at the time.
71. Gregory M. Reihman, "Categorically Denied: Kant's Criticism of Chinese Philosophy," *Journal of Chinese Philosophy* 33, no.1 (March 2006): 55.
72. Ibid., 58.
73. Ibid., 61. Putting a good face on Kant's apparently prejudiced comments, Reihman suggests that these stem from and are consistent with Kant's philosophical views critical of mystical practices, such as upheld by some Chinese. Kant did not distinguish classical Confucianism from neo-Confucianism, and "got much of Chinese philosophy wrong," according to Reihman, 60.

74. Immanuel Kant, *Perpetual Peace, and Other Essays on Politics, History, and Morals*, trans. Ted Humphrey (Indianapolis: Hackett, 1983), 119.
75. Jeffrey Edwards and Martin Schönfeld find "conceptual links between Kant's epistemology and the Chinese ontology of qi." "Kant's Material Dynamics and the Physical View of Reality," *Journal of Chinese Philosophy* 33, no. 1 (March 2006): 121; see also Chung-Qing Chen, "Theoretical Links between Kant and Confucianism: Preliminary Remarks," *Journal of Chinese Philosophy* 33, no. 1 (March 2006): 3–15; and Christian Helmut Wenzel, "Beauty in Kant and Confucius: A First Step," in *Journal of Chinese Philosophy* 33, no. 1 (March 2006): 95–107.
76. See David N. Livingstone and Charles WJ Withers, eds., *Geography and Enlightenment* (Chicago: University of Chicago Press, 1999), especially the Introduction.
77. Shönfeld, "From Confucius to Kant," 79. It is noteworthy that Chinese scholars' reception of Kant's critical philosophy in the aftermath of the Chinese Revolution focuses on its similarities with Confucianism in their attempt to locate Chinese cultural identity in a universal system of ideas. Martin Müller, "Aspects of the Chinese reception of Kant," *Journal of Chinese Philosophy* 33, no. 1 (March 2006): 141–57.
78. It is interesting to note that Heidegger confronts the question of the multiplicity of cultures by referring to Max Scheler's view that multiplicity complicates the task of anthropology. Heidegger saw it as a problem in the search for "a unified idea of man." *Kant and the Problem of Metaphysics*, 147.

Chapter 5

Foucault's Anthropology of the Iranian Revolution

Foucault's interpretation of the Iranian Revolution of 1978–1979 is frequently regarded as an aberration because of his support for Ayatollah Khomeini's claim to power, resulting in the establishment of an Islamic republic. In the face of withering criticism by an irate press and astonished intellectuals[1] in the aftermath of the establishment of an Islamic republic, Foucault refrained from writing or speaking about Iran from 1979 until his death in 1984. Nevertheless, critics raised a number of provocative questions about Foucault's confrontation with the Iranian Revolution: did it reflect his personal nostalgia for a bygone era when religious traditions anchored the self? Did it crystallize for him a search for an alternative to a Western culture stifled by technological and scientific development—hallmarks of a modernity gone awry? Did it simply comfort his purportedly nihilistic, Nietzsche- and Heidegger-inspired quest for limit-experiences, which the idea of martyrdom in Shi'i Islam brought to the fore?[2] Or was he simply taken in by a cultural reality with which he was essentially unfamiliar?[3] Yet evidence indicates that Foucault's assessment was first and foremost a brief attempt to re-appraise his own work, including his position regarding Kant's anthropology—a dimension that controversy obscured.

This chapter does not concern itself with the accuracy of Foucault's analysis or its predictive power.[4] It does not seek to demonstrate that Foucault's interpretation was a "grave mistake," or an error of judgment.[5] It reads Foucault's series of articles on the Iranian revolution in light of his critique of the social sciences[6] in order to identify and analyze the terms of

Foucault's understanding of cultural difference. To do this, it looks at the functions that the "*reportage d'idées*" performed in Foucault's thought.

THE REPORTAGE D'IDÉES

Would Foucault's writing about the Iranian Revolution have taken a different orientation had he not decided to report about the event in a journalistic capacity? This question cannot be answered in a definite way except to take stock of Foucault's conception of reporting as an expression of his own struggles with cultural otherness. It is tempting to argue that his reporting was but a hiatus in his intellectual journey, and thus plays only a negligible role, if any, in understanding his thought. Or correlatively, that the format of reporting inflected his thought.[7] This would be tantamount to also arguing that Foucault's numerous interviews or lectures were incidental to his work, which they could not be. From the perspective of this book, his stint in journalism was an implicit engagement in an aspect of Kant's view of cosmopolitan anthropology by seeking knowledge of the world. Prior to Iran he had engaged the world on his own terms. Distinguishing himself from Jean-Paul Sartre's involvement in all progressive causes, Foucault identified himself as a "specific intellectual." He had elected to champion, among others, the rights of prisoners, mental patients, and Polish people eager to overthrow communist rule. On occasion he also took part in demonstrations in support of the rights of immigrants, some of whom were from North Africa. He had also signed petitions circulated by Jean-Paul Sartre's committee for the defense of Iranian political prisoners.[8] He once explained in an ironic tone that he was old enough to have been in the resistance movement, or in the Algerian War, but he had not participated in either. In Iran Foucault did not seek refuge from the Parisian hubbub as he did in Tunisia. Nor did he engage in a form of academic tourism as he did in Japan where he lectured and took in a puzzling local culture. Iran got him involved in a fundamentally different way. At any rate, his stance on the Iranian Revolution marked the first and last time that he had written and taken an unambiguous position on a Muslim country. His reporting on Iran was an entirely new challenge: intellectual, cultural, and historical, considering that France's empire had extended to predominantly Muslim countries and had confronted Islam as a religion since the nineteenth century.

In 1978, Foucault received an invitation from Alberto Cavallari, the editor of the Italian *Corriere della sera,* to contribute a regular column on world events. According to Foucault's biographer, Didier Eribon, Foucault, who had been smarting from what he felt was the failure of *The Archaeology of Knowledge,* and probably seeking to turn down the invitation politely, proposed that he do "on the scene 'investigations' instead."[9] The paper happened to accept his idea, and subsequently announced a series of articles entitled "Michel Foucault investigates."[10] To undertake these assignments, Foucault assembled a group of men composed, among others, of his then-companion Thierry Voeltzel (as coordinator), as well as philosophers André Glucksmann and Alain Finkielkraut. Initially, Susan Sontag, Arpad Ajtony, Jorge Semprun and Ronald D. Laing were to contribute, respectively, reports on Vietnam, Hungary, Spain, and the mass suicide of Jim Jones's sect in Guyana. As it turned out, the team's project was short-lived since it produced only two reports, one by Finkielkraut on "Carter's America," the other Foucault's articles on Iran. In a passionate critical plea, Foucault defined his project as a *"reportage d'idées,"* a reporting on ideas generated outside of books, in the "contemporary world," which he viewed as a theater of "struggles carried on, about, for, or against ideas." Against the view touting the end or irrelevance of ideology in the contemporary world, Foucault was convinced that "ideas proliferate (*fourmillent*) today; they are born, stir, disappear and reappear, shaking people and things up not only in intellectual circles or in West-European universities, but also on a world scale, particularly among minorities or people who, historically, have been bereft of the ability to speak or make themselves heard." To capture these new voices a cooperation between experts was needed: "[i]intellectuals will work together with journalists at the point where ideas and events intersect."[11] Yet, as Macey points out, the team did not include a single professional journalist.[12] As he noted in passing, Foucault was eager to make sure that his project not be understood in the tradition of idealist philosophy, as he reminds his readers that "ideas do not rule the world."[13] Foucault's description of his project leaves no doubt that his intention was not merely to report on the ideas generated in and by the world, but also to make sense of them as they appear, or as they animate events.[14] Since the "world" is defined as the place of struggles around ideas, it takes a person with knowledge of ideas as well as the skills to trace their meanings, observe, and analyze their force in contemporary events. There is a Kantian echo in Foucault's focus on knowledge of the "world" as distinguished from knowledge from books. Unmistakably, Foucault turns toward a world composed of others, whose ideas had been muted in the past—a turn toward the empirical and the cosmopolitan as it unfolds in the struggle for ideas. With respect to Iran, Foucault's *"reportage d'idées"* was based on observation and interviews, supplemented by history books, and the experience of being in a different cultural environment. In other words, the Kantian method.

By 1978 Foucault had already made "events" an important part of his genealogical method. Iran was the closest that Foucault came to doing empirical work. In this sense the description of his reporting project was an implicit acknowledgment of one limitation of his archaeological-genealogical method, which he had used in doing historical analysis; it signals a search for the world of the empirical, of the concrete event, which opens up in real time, in all its confusion, complexity, and immediacy. This turn to the empirical is one of several reversals Foucault made in assessing his own work, but one fraught with perils as will be revealed in his analyses of the Iranian Revolution. It represents an experiment with, and a groping for, an anthropology in which local (qua European) knowledge he had carried out would either confound or be transformed by cosmopolitan knowledge. It is not that Foucault would simply apply his methodology to a different cultural reality in effervescence. Rather, his conceptual challenge was to "link" ideas ("what is thought") to events ("what happens"). The nature of this linkage and the meaning it yields will shed light on the ramifications of Foucault's own struggle with Kantian anthropology.

The magnitude of Foucault's empirical task need not be emphasized. The Iranian Revolution shook the world with its scope, ferocity, theatricality, and denouement. On one side were masses of people, largely unarmed, apparently coalescing around a frail old theologian in exile, incessantly clamoring for the downfall of their sovereign and the establishment of a new order; on the other side, a government, deemed "secular," relying on a repressive security apparatus, and the full support of a super power, the United States of America. The imbalance of forces alone elicited interest if not sympathy. But there was more that excited intellectuals' imaginations: the demonstrators' apparent lack of fear of police and soldiers; public religious rituals turning into demonstrations against the state; cemeteries doubling up as spaces where public gatherings and speeches were permitted. Life and death seemed strangely united; waves of people came out on the streets over and over again, ostensibly with no particular party or organizers leading them. This looked like a grassroots movement thoroughly engaged and determined to have its way. The mass media were awash with pictures of the unexpected and sustained fervor of the demonstrators, who all seemed to move as if they had constituted one big social organism.

Prior to going to Iran, Foucault had lived for two years in another Muslim society, Tunisia.[15] However, although he had marveled at Tunisian students' fearlessness and resolve in fighting against dictatorship, what he witnessed in Iran was different. Something was new about the Iranian demonstrations: they brought into play a mix of religion (not any religion, but Islam) and politics, a desire for change without an apparent ideological blueprint. This was much more than the May '68 movement Foucault had read about, briefly witnessed, or watched on Tunisian television. Was Iran an anomaly, or was it ushering in a new political phenomenon, a new way of struggling for change for which Western theories had no adequate concepts? Furthermore, Iran in the throes of protest contradicted Foucault's predilection for silence as "the best form of protest, a total abstention."[16]

HOW FOUCAULT APPROACHED THE IRANIAN REVOLUTION

Four factors frame Foucault's approach to the Iranian revolution: from the start, Foucault read the events unfolding before his eyes as a refutation of Marx's conception of religion. He wrote in his notes that "of all the Western ideas I heard contested, of all the phrases which, for Iranians, symbolize Europe's lack of understanding as well as its [arrogant?] narrow-mindedness, the most frequently quoted is Marx's 'religion is the opium of the people.'"[17] Time and again, he reminded interviewers and the public that religion was not "the opium of the masses." Nevertheless, he tempered his view by pointing to the historicity of Marx's conception, to nineteenth century Europe when Christianity served as an instrument to "bring the rebellious workers back to religion and make them accept their faith."[18] However, in a move reminiscent of Max Weber's, Foucault intended to provide an alternative conception of the role of religious ideas in social change. And the mantle of Shi'ism, in which the Iranian demonstrators appeared to temporarily wrap themselves, lent support to Foucault's intent.

Second, Foucault also dismissed French analysts' apparent cynical or prejudiced reading of the Iranian upheaval as a rejection of the shah's modernizing policies by a largely traditional, if not archaic, society steeped in a religion that seemed impervious to change. The focus on modernization, he argued, was "kemalism," a "hackneyed idea, that is to say a certain restructuring of Muslim, Islamic societies etc. on a model borrowed from the West and developed by Kemal Ataturk, which the Pahlevi dynasty has ceaselessly invoked."[19] Yet he also accepted the notion of unsuccessful "modernization" as fueling the protests.[20] At one level, Foucault's skepticism about the modernization interpretation was on target. And his decision to look more closely at the relationship between religious beliefs and opposition to the state was courageous in the French political climate of the time. He searched for an alternative, one informed by his interlocutors' rejection of a Western-centered perspective on their movement. In this context, Foucault was walking a fine line between two world views, as well as two interpretative schemas, East and West. His notes reveal a scholar puzzled by what he heard but convinced that what he witnessed defied the analyses provided by his contemporaries. His objective was to keep an open mind.

Third, Foucault approached the Iranian movement against yet another background. He had been disenchanted by the eighteenth century ideas that had ushered in the "first painful experience," the emergence of the "monstrosity we call the state" out of the confrontation of philosophers' ideas and bourgeois society. He had been equally disappointed and radically opposed to the "second painful experience," born out of "revolutionary socialist thinkers and the socialist states," who put in place repressive governments.[21] Foucault's opposition to socialist states singled out Vietnam[22] and Cambodia, whose unhappy experiment with socialism he attributed to Marx's ideas. His view of socialism needs discussing as it frames his understanding of the apparent distinctiveness of Iran. Although appearing to make no excuses for any state, whether European or Third World, and thus standing above the fray, Foucault was nevertheless singularly oblivious to three important factors: socialism in some Third World contexts was the flip side of colonialism, a system of domination that had deepened social and economic inequities in the colonies. Furthermore, by ignoring the issue of French colonialism (but acknowledging "American imperialism"), Foucault essentially overlooked France's role in the creation of the conditions making possible the rise of political systems that destroyed life on a grand scale in Cambodia. Finally, Foucault's lumping together of Vietnam, Cambodia, and the USSR betrays a gap in his view of "the world" from which were excluded nonsocialist yet repressive Third World countries. More important, Foucault's indiscriminate statement (with libertarian undertones) targets struggles for decolonization, specifically in Vietnam and Cambodia, for failing to create societies in which "one could recognize oneself." Implicitly he wished for a liberal democracy such as in France. But, he had criticized the "first painful experience" of Western liberal thought which brought about the very system he now counterposes to socialist Viet Nam. No doubt realizing his inconsistency, Foucault corrected himself: "I do not mean [by oneself] the Westerners, since this was not their battle, I mean a society in which the face of revolution could be recognized."[23] Yet, and this is where Foucault's understanding of the non-European world goes awry, French imperialism in Indochina or Africa was a Westerner's affair (its intellectual legacy was also his own), and continues to be so in the present as exemplified by France's geopolitical and economic interest in her former empire. By the same token, does the denunciation of the excesses of the postcolonial governments mean that revolutions should not have taken place, or should be avoided?

The choice of the countries Foucault gave as examples (which happened to have experienced secular revolutions), his apparent oblivion to French imperial dominion over them, and his conception of socialism as *the* source of their problems betrayed a reductive understanding of the "ideas" that the world was producing—ideas he went to Iran to study. There is no reason to believe that the ideas of the Vietnamese during their struggles against France as well as the United States were any less oppositional or liberating than those that Foucault would report about in Iran. Why would the ideas expressed by Khomeini be any more important or worthy than those of Ho Chi Minh? The point is not to defend the failings of socialism in Vietnam or elsewhere but to identify the double standard in Foucault's map of the "world" at the time that he was engaging in the "*reportage d'idées.*" At stake is his understanding of the significance of the Iranian Revolution. If from Foucault's perspective the Vietnamese Revolution failed to produce a society in which he could recognize himself even though it adopted ideals familiar to him as a "Western" man, on what grounds would the Iranian Revolution succeed in this task when it used ideals that are not so familiar to the contemporary West? As it turned out, Foucault looked for the "familiar" in the Iranian Revolution and found it fleetingly in the iconic sign of French demonstrations, "the barricades."[24]

Alain Touraine once argued that Foucault's views of communist and Third World revolutions were meant to do away with the contradiction that the Sartrean generation had realized between the "Western freedoms" they valued and the "communist or Third World wars of liberation" they supported. That generation had considered these struggles as another phase of the same struggle the West had engaged in for the sake of freedom.[25] However, Foucault's reference to socialism implies that in Iran, a new event was taking place that contained an alternative to other Third World revolutions such as occurred in Vietnam. If he became disillusioned with Vietnam and felt that socialism ought to be "condemned" and "discarded," he nevertheless thought that "indifference" was not possible before the Iranian movement. The impulse to break away from indifference brought Foucault close to Kant's insight that in revolutionary situations, individuals find themselves drawn to actively or passively support one side or the other. And this is because human nature yearns for the universal good.[26] But, Foucault's interpretation was guided by a concern to rethink Marx, as he understood him, and to look for "another political imagination," rather than a reflection and discovery of the springs of human action, a task Kant had set in the *Anthropology*.

Fourth, Foucault approached the Iranian Revolution from a comparative perspective, using his knowledge of European history. He was "astonished by the connections and similarities between Shi'ism and the religious movements in Europe at the end of the Middle Ages, up to the seventeenth or eighteenth century."[27] He noted how these movements had been protests against the aristocracy and later against the bourgeois state. Although such similarities may be undeniable, their interpretation is noteworthy: these religious movements, such as the Anabaptists, were in reality political movements. In other words, religion was simply the *form* that they took even as they protested against established religion. Consequently, there is a relationship between religion and politics not in the manner that Marx envisaged (as politics using religion), but as religion intervening in politics to secure both religious and political rights. This attractive interpretation, focused on religion as form, instead of substance, sets the stage for Foucault's approach to the Iranian Revolution. The problem is to determine whether he would refine it or amend it as events unfolded. Lastly, Foucault implicitly defined Shi'ism as a unified religion in its own right, largely independent from the religion to which it belongs, Islam.

FOUCAULT IN IRAN

Foucault took two trips to Iran, accompanied by Thierry Voelzel: one on 16–24 September 1978 one week after "Black Friday," a day when a large demonstration had been broken up by government forces in a particularly bloody crackdown; the other on 9–15 November 1978. He spent a total of two weeks in Iran, during which he interviewed in Qom,[28] an Ayatollah, Shariat Madari, who viewed with a jaundiced eye Khomeini's effort to use religion for political ends; striking workers in Abadan, the capital of the oil region; urban middle-class individuals, including striking airline staff in Tehran; members of the military sympathizing with the movement; university people; and by some accounts, the occasional man on the street.[29]

Before embarking on his travels, Foucault educated himself about Iran, reading some of the works of major French Islamicists, Henry Corbin (who wrote about Shi'ism) and Louis Massignon. He had also spoken to a number of Iranian expatriates living in Paris, including an anti-shah militant, Ahmed Salamatian, and Abulhasan Bani Sadr, who would become the first president of Iran after the shah's downfall. On 3 October 1978 he also visited Ayatollah Khomeini, who had just arrived in a suburb of Paris from his exile in Karbala, Iraq; he finally went to the airport to see a triumphant Khomeini leave Paris for Tehran, on 1 February 1979. Foucault's reports on Iran were written in France after he returned from his two trips to Iran, and first published in Italian. In addition, he gave interviews (such as one with the Persian Baqir Parham, quoted above), answered some articles, and wrote his own in *Le Nouvel Observateur* as well as *Le Monde*.[30] The Italian articles appeared in print in French after his death in 1984 in the collection *Dits et écrits*.

On the whole Foucault went to Iran armed with general knowledge about Iran, specific knowledge about Shi'ism as interpreted primarily by Corbin, as well as viewpoints provided by middle- to upper-class Iranian expatriates. There do not appear to be major Muslim theologians, either Sunni or Shi'i, other than Shariat Madari, among the people he interviewed either in Paris or in Iran, who might have provided a range of perspectives on the relationship between religion and politics.[31]

During his two trips Foucault witnessed events developing before his own eyes that he had not seen before in Europe. It was difficult to escape the notion that he (even if as journalist) was in the situation of the modern philosopher who, like Nietzsche, diagnoses the present.[32] However, although the present may begin in the moment of the event as it surges, it is incomprehensible without knowledge of its long history. Indeed, 1978 was the year when the Iranian movement had crescendoed into a new, hardened and more uncompromising phase after stalling.[33] The evolving events needed theories and concepts to make them intelligible if they were not to be presented as expressions of aberrant behavior purportedly typical of Middle Eastern societies. For Foucault, philosophy is necessary to diagnose the present—an acknowledgment that his interpretation of Iran's singular and unfamiliar ideational struggle will be framed in terms that will be borrowed from an external system of thought. That this was inevitable goes without saying. Nevertheless, the point is to determine whether Foucault was willing to allow the new reality to transform the concepts he had hitherto used in his work, or would force this reality into his concepts in a way that absorbs the purported uniqueness of the event into European history, either as a new incarnation of it or a deviation from it. Consequently, the analysis of Foucault's *"reportage d'idées"* may reveal the contours of Foucault's approximate anthropology as it seeks to disentangle itself from Kant's.

In 1978, Foucault was writing and speaking about an array of issues ranging from disciplinary society to psychiatry to governmentality, but very much pursuing his interest in prisons. This was also the year he published Herculine Barbin, the hermaphrodite. Most important, in March he had taken a trip to Tokyo and Kyoto where he had participated in a debate on Christianity and Zen Buddhism. In Japan, he had also lectured on issues such as sexuality, power, and politics. In other words, being in Tehran was for Foucault another experience in a foreign land. In Japan he had felt disoriented by the contrast between the country's familiar urban, industrial landscape, and a culture different from his own. In Iran, he was able to witness an insufficiently developed country with an equally intriguing cultural system, religious values, and public rituals. If he could relate to Japan at a material cultural level (Japan is as developed as France), he could not relate to Iran at any level except through the mediation of concepts and ideas he gleaned through his readings or acquired through contacts with various people. Consequently, the need to rely on his theories and methods of analyses was far greater in Iran than it was in Japan, where he only intended to present his work to Japanese intellectuals. In his various reports on Iran, Foucault frequently reminded his readers that he was an outsider looking in, as can be surmised from terms such as "we Westerners," or the "European."[34] Admittedly, Foucault's reminders were meant to draw attention to inadequate "Western" views of the reality of Iran, or preserve a measure of circumspection in assessing a complex and fast-moving event. Nevertheless, his location in doing the anthropology of the Iranian present, albeit as a special sort of journalist, sheds light on his philosophical-theoretical perspective on the Orient.

AN ANTHROPOLOGY OF THE EVENT

In a 1967 interview with the Italian P. Caruso, Foucault explained that his research aims for "an analysis of cultural facts ... something like a cultural ethnology to which we belong."[35] Foucault's task in Iran was to analyze cultural facts foreign to him. Such an analysis presented a singular peculiarity that could nevertheless be perceived as an advantage: in doing research on French-qua-European culture, Foucault had located himself "outside of the culture to which we belong, to analyze its formal conditions in order to do a critique of it, not by reducing its values, but to see how it was actually constituted."[36] This was evidently an effort at social science objectivity akin to self-induced estrangement in the urban anthropological tradition. However, in Iran, Foucault was truly an outsider, ungrounded in the local culture. At a surface level, this location as an outsider was an asset in doing a cultural ethnology largely free of distortion. It required learning the meaning that the people he observed attached to their customs and institutions, seeing their world from their perspective before translating it into the language of analysis. The ethnographic translation has been a highly debatable issue among anthropologists as indicated in the previous chapter. Ultimately, the ethnographer decides the best possible way of conveying the reality of the people he observed. Granted, Foucault was not doing the same kind of ethnography as anthropologists do; and he was in Iran for only a brief period of time. However, his articles were more than journalistic reports; they were philosophically and theoretically grounded. They were social analyses of the event as it presented itself in the moment of its observation—a sort of immediate ethnography.

Although Foucault's various reports focused on different aspects of the turmoil he observed, a common thread runs through them: his personal musings. His trips and observations constituted a sort of personal journey in which he presents himself as going through a transformative experience as events around him evolve.[37] By checking what he observed against what he was told in France, or what skeptical Western analysts had written about the Iranian movement, he ostensibly underwent a change. There are moments when Foucault does not avoid cultural clichés, but there were discernible shifts in his perception of things.

Foucault understood the mass movement that spread throughout Iran in 1978 and early 1979 as a struggle of ideas pitting a people steeped in an old culture grounded in mystical Shi'ism against an autocratic sovereign imposing misguided modernist ideas on his subjects by force. As Foucault saw it, the shah, supported by American power, wrought untold misery on his people as he put in place a simulacrum of modernization that denatured Iranian culture. He had initiated a halfhearted and ill-designed land reform, which increased the pace of migrations to urban centers; shared the spoils of oil with Western, especially American, corporations; and made it possible for speculators of all kinds to enrich themselves through widespread corruption. The artificiality of the political system in place was sustained by a dreaded secret police, the SAVAK, and a well-equipped army, which, although a symbol of modern power, was so poorly trained that it could barely patrol its borders. In a country where the sovereign and his policies are at odds with the cultural ethos and the aspirations of the people, change cannot occur through laws but through the collective will of the people united against their sovereign. Remarkably, the people, motivated by a common purpose to remove the sovereign from power and replace him with an old, frail, yet charismatic religious man, Ayatollah Khomeini, fearlessly braved machine guns and live bullets, never flagging in their commitment, chanting their way to victory or death. In the Iranian movement, Foucault saw a yearning for freedom, truth, authenticity, and more important, a willingness to die for a cause. Equally important, he saw an instance of the failure of the traditional politics of compromise and half measures to achieve its ends. Politics found its limit in the intransigent faith of the people in their power to make a fresh start. Implicitly, religious faith defeats politics-as-usual. Foucault witnessed "a movement that does not allow itself to be dispersed in political choices."[38] From his perspective, a new way of thinking through the powerful ideas produced in this non-Western part of the world was necessary. Where would one start? What concepts and method should one use?

A reconstruction of the method Foucault used in his articles reveals an analysis that proceeds from the structural to the emergent. First (but not in this order) he identified the structural framework within which the movement arose. He rejected colonialism as a possible explanatory concept. He noted that Iran had never been directly colonized, but had been under foreign influences such as those of Russia, Britain, and finally the United States of America, which had turned Iran into a "political and economic sanctuary."[39] (Foucault made an odd reference to the Algerian War, claiming that transistors helped de Gaulle crush the 21–26 April putsch, staged by rebellious colonial generals just like the cassettes had been helping Khomeini to disseminate his anti-shah messages to the people in Iran. It is true that de Gaulle had used the media, especially television, to address the French nation as well as his army.) However, implied in the comparison is Foucault's view that the Iranian movement was an heir to a series of movements of liberation that had started in the 1950s, although this one might be different from those that established socialist systems. He felt that colonialism in the region destroyed or destructured local institutions, and thus triggered change that was somehow maladapted as it bore the stamp of the West, whereas uncolonized, "precolonial," contemporary Iran kept the social and cultural institutions that enabled it to muster the collective will drawn from Islam. Implied is the notion that because Iran had not been colonized (like Indochina or Algeria had been)—a condition Foucault implicitly considered uninspiring—the analysis of the movement might stress its phenomenal form at the expense of the formal political economic structure out of which the movement arose.[40] Hence the second part of Foucault's analysis focuses on the relationship between religion and politics, which needs discussing in some detail.

Political Spirituality

Foucault has been much criticized for the use of the concept of "political spirituality," with which he intended to capture the dramatic display of an apparent religiosity in demonstrations combining ritual and political protests. He also had to make sense of the sentiment among some of the protesters to establish an Islamic government. He found in the mystical aspect of Shi'ism a key to understanding the ways in which religion infused the politics of the movement. The rejection of the shah's secularizing policies tapped into a cultural fund of religious customs. The ritual of 'Ashura, enacted in public places as well as private homes, harnessed the story of the birth of Shi'ism to symbolize the contemporary struggle against the shah's political oppression. The people rising against their sovereign were re-enacting the tragedy of Hassan and Hussein, the struggle of good against evil.[41]

The fervor motivating the movement could only be spiritual. At work in Iran was a passionate politics that expressed a different relation to political change.

Political spirituality is an alluring concept highlighting the admixture of religion and politics by which Foucault wished to represent the force of the fervor and commitment of the Iranians taking part in the movement. The concept has been interpreted in different ways. It purportedly reveals Foucault's propensity to focus on the a-rational in human affairs, or his personal (Heidegger-inspired) yearning for a return to a pre-industrial social order.[42] It is also considered a modification of Foucault's conception of power as a "bi-polar" practice, expressing an oppositional force rooted in beliefs in a mythic time of salvation rather than the will of specific groups or political institutions.[43] A more challenging view grounds political spirituality in an incipient sociology of religion, assumed to exist in bits and pieces in Foucault's work and rooted in his personal life.[44] Jeremy R. Carrette carefully traced the component parts of a Foucauldian conception of religion, especially Christianity, dispersed throughout his work. He suggests that Foucault's intellectual background predisposed him to using the concept of the spiritual in a nonreligious context. Foucault had indeed been influenced by surrealist figures such as Antonin Artaud and Georges Bataille. Typically, surrealists searched for experiences beyond the confines of the real, and were eager to experiment with supranatural, a-rational situations in an effort to find a spiritual realm yielding emotions usually associated with the sacred. Surrealists were prone to using terms borrowed from religion to describe experiences that expanded their spiritual horizons, but took place outside of a narrowly defined institutional religious domain.[45] In a similar vein, Foucault intended to disembed "spirituality" from its religious context and re-embed it in a political framework. From this perspective, "spiritual politics" was meant to destabilize the religious discourse.[46] However, in the Iranian context Foucault intended to emphasize the role of religion proper, Islam, which he clearly perceived as an oppositional force in its own right, rather than to empty it of its "spiritual" content. His analysis of the role of Shi'ism in political mobilization as well as politics in general obeyed a different set of theoretical imperatives than those prevailing in the analysis of Christianity. One of these was Foucault's definition of "experience," the most significant concept he retained from Bataille, who with Blanchot, he referred to as "my real masters."[47] Experience denotes a "rupture" in the stability of the subject desiring his "own transformation, abolition, in his relation to things, to others, to truth, to death. It is to risk not being oneself."[48]

"Political spirituality" was central to Foucault's explanation of the protesters' demand for an Islamic government. It was his answer to critics' skepticism that Iranians truly believed in a utopian political system steeped in archaic religious values, as well as their dismissal of protestors as mere "fanatics."[49] Wondering why critics "resist" taking Iranians seriously, he exclaimed: "they [Iranians] believe in it; they believed in it sufficiently to rise up by the millions."[50] It is precisely belief and dream that were at work in the movement. "In order to brave a powerful army ... you need to have something in the head and the heart. It means wanting something enormous, impossible. And this is what I wanted to understand, not Islam in its real doctrine—how could I?—not the social and economic reality of the Shi-i clergy—... but the dream as they proclaimed it.... In short the dream and the imaginary of a movement that only dreamed itself."[51] Through this phenomenological description reminiscent of his Binswanger's *Dreams and Existence*, Foucault theorized the Iranian movement from an apparent cross-cultural and historical perspective. Thus, all great upheavals from the end of the Middle Ages to the sixteenth to seventeenth centuries, whether the Ascetic movements in Flanders or the Anabaptists in England, started out as "spiritual" movements. Even the French Revolution of 1789, or other movements of the nineteenth century were also steeped in spirituality.[52]

What then is spirituality? It is "something found in religion, but also outside of religion, in Buddhism, a religion without a theology, in monotheism, but also in Greek civilization. Therefore, spirituality is not necessarily linked to religion although most religions have a spiritual dimension." Furthermore, spirituality "is, I believe, a practice by which man is displaced, transformed to the point of renouncing his individuality, his own situation as a subject. It means no longer being a subject in relation to a political power, but a subject of a knowledge, subject of an experience, subject of a belief too. It seems to me that this possibility to lift oneself up from a position of subject determined (*fixée*) by a political or religious power, a dogma, a belief, a habit, a social structure etc., is spirituality, that is to say, to become something other than oneself."[53] Becoming other than oneself means staking one's life to be other, even though the substance of this other self is not necessarily known to the subject of the uprising. To stress his point, Foucault quotes from Rabaut St. Etienne, an eighteenth-century Protestant pastor and champion for the rights of French protestants: "'We need to change man, we need to change the world, we need to change ideas, we need to change language (*les mots*), we need to change everything..., we need to destroy everything and recreate everything.'" Foucault notes that the first part of the sentence sums up spirituality, as it points to "changing oneself." The second part advocates a "philosophical revolution." As noted in passing, St Etienne paid dearly for his ideas as he was executed during the French Revolution. Nevertheless, for Foucault the French Revolution was "the first and only revolution which was unaware of its spirituality." Indeed, it believed in a philosophy that "effectively enabled people to be different from what they were by becoming the subjects of universal reason etc."[54] (Parenthetically, this is the kind of reason he eschewed when he defined the Orient–Occident divide.) This intriguing redefinition of the French Revolution made it possible for Foucault to locate his conception of the Iranian Revolution as a special case of the history of social upheavals beyond Iran. It also provides insight into what might be termed a revolutionary will that occurs at historical moments. Nevertheless, there is an inconsistency in Foucault's use of "political spirituality." If the concept refers to members wanting to be different or dreaming of being different, how could they not be aware of their wish or dream? Is this but one of the totalizing concepts that impute coherence to events viewed externally, which Foucault decried in the *Archaeology of Knowledge*? Leaving unspecified the point at which "political spirituality" manifests itself, or whether it is spontaneous, compounds the question. At any rate, the fact that Iranians may not have known exactly how a change of government might change them as subjects is less important than their assumed desire to be other than what they were, "which is at the heart of the revolutionary will."[55] Indeed, to change oneself without knowing what one will be represents a "radical will to be other," and it is this will, hardly unique to Iranians, that needs to be understood. To come to terms with it requires understanding what Iranians meant by "Islamic government."

Islamic Government

Foucault distinguished between a government that uses Islam to mobilize political life (such as Saudi Arabia), and one that imposes the Shari'a as Libya did at the time. Both types of government are different from an Islamic government whose core is the "search for something that would be a political life."[56] In the Saudi and Libyan case, "religion as well as politics are eliminated," whereas in Iran, there is an impressive "political will" aimed at "politicizing the inextricably linked social and religious structure in response to current problems."[57] An Islamic government in a "non-sunnite and non-Arab" country means to open a spiritual dimension in politics. Conversely, it means to use politics to "revive religious spirituality," which had been smothered by the state appropriation of Shi'ism as an instrument of power. In this sense, the movement was using Shi'ism against Shi'ism in order to initiate a genuine "political life," originating from society itself and not from outside of it. This political life is different from politics as usual, familiar to Western societies that Foucault felt were saturated with politics without necessarily having a "political life." In an Islamic government, "political life" would not be as it has always been an obstacle to spirituality, but its outlet, its possibility (*"occasion"*), its stimulant (*ferment*)."[58] In other words, the traditional structures of society would "play a permanent role in political life." In this sense, an Islamic government is not a remote utopian idea, but "a way of life and behavior; an ethic and an unmediated politics."[59] An Islamic government brings together "the two ends of the chain" linking Islam with its mosques and other institutions to government and politics.

Parts of the above definition of an Islamic government rely on Ali Sharī'atī's conception of the relationship between Shi'i Islam and politics.[60] There was much about this leading figure in the movement that appealed to Foucault: his personal and intellectual itinerary spanning East and West; his contacts with Third World revolutionary movements; his desire to find a culturally specific answer to the Iranian crisis; his persecution by the shah's security forces; and his suspect death. Besides, Sharī'atī's death, according to Foucault, had special resonance as it "gave the invisible Present, the ever present Absent a privileged place in Shi'ism."[61] In various drafts, Foucault dwelled on Sharī'atī's popularity stemming from what seemed an authentic voice rather than the shah's mimicry of Western modernization. Furthermore, 'Alī Sharī'atī's book, *Marxism and Other Western Fallacies*,[62] resonated with Foucault's own critique of orthodox Marxism. In addition to interpreting Marxist thought as being founded on binary categories, Sharī'atī took issue with Western humanism as an ideology that denies spiritual values, and "the mystical sense that endows man with excellence and nobility."[63] For Sharī'atī, there is a "need" and "thirst" for spirituality in a mystical sense that is stifled and violated by historical materialism and other Western systems of ideas.

It is unclear what role, if any, the thought of another Iranian intellectual, Jalāl Āl-i Ahmad, a virulent critic of Western values as well as their effects on Iranians, played in Foucault's understanding of an Islamic government. In his book, *Occidentosis: A Plague from the West*, Ahmad likened the spread of Western values to developing societies to a disease such as tuberculosis, or the "infestation of weevils."[64] Combining knowledge of Iranian history and global political economy, he formulated a theory of Third World liberation that owed as much to Fanon as to liberal critiques of technology. He referred to industrial capitalism as "the machine" that grinds everything in its passage, especially the cultures of the former colonies and dependent countries. He denounced cultural mimicry as well as the unbridled search for wealth and consumerism that further eroded Iranian values. Foucault's frequent references to the effects of Western cultural domination of Iran echo Jalāl Āl-i Ahmad's.[65]

Foucault's description of the Singer sewing machines, lined up in an Iranian bazaar, recalls Ahmad's withering critique of developing countries' acceptance and admiration for "the machine,"[66] resulting in increasing their dependency on the "West." Foucault captured the time warp in which the economics of "modernization" was ensconced: with their designs of green ivy and flower buds "grossly imitating old Persian miniatures," "[t]hese broken occidentalities bearing the sign of an archaic Orient were all stamped "Made in South Korea."[67] Foucault concluded that he understood why Iranians rejected the shah's modernizing policy: it was "in itself an archaic phenomenon (*un archaïsme*)."[68] Instead of transforming society from within it simply made available on the bazaar market recycled old technologies that symbolized Western modernity. Its sweeping judgment notwithstanding, Foucault's comment agreed with the essence of Ahmad's analysis of Third World countries' predicament. Nevertheless, and in spite of his liberatory rhetoric, Ahmad evinced a form of nationalism, as he unabashedly states: "Islam became Islam when it reached … the Tigris and Euphrates."[69] Foucault's journalistic assignment clearly did not include a critique of the religious establishment as Ahmad did. But he did note the nationalist impulse behind the movement.[70]

CORBIN AND THE INTERMEDIATE CULTURAL WORLD

If Sharī'atī helped Foucault to understand how Shi'ism could revitalize political life, Henry Corbin interpreted the essence of Shi'ism in a way consistent with his predilection for the surrealists' use of "experience." Corbin, who died in October 1978, had been a professor of Islamic Studies both at the Sorbonne and Tehran University. In *Spiritual Body and Celestial Earth,* he proposed an interpretation of Shi'ism grounded in a critique of Western empiricist and rationalist approaches to reality. From Corbin's perspective, there is a world between sense perception and cognition defined as "the intuitions and categories of the intellect." This "intermediate space," is usually left to the poet, to the exploration of the mythic and the fictitious when in reality it is a real world in its own right, "independent of socio-political and socio-economic infrastructures," a world of "active imagination."[71] The in-between world "is essentially a median and mediating power, in the same way that the universe on which it is regulated and to which it gives access, is a median and mediating universe, an intermediate world between the sensible and the intellectual (*intelligible*), an intermediate world without which articulation between sensible and intellectual (*intelligible*) is definitely blocked."[72] He found the "key" to this world in the "two ages of the spiritual world of Iran," the ancient Mazdean and the Shi'i.[73] At work in this intermediate world is an imagination Corbin calls "Active" with a capital "a," or "Agent Imagination," to highlight its creative and productive power. It is an imaginative imagination—Shi'i or Mazdean epistemology is foreign to the Western dualism of body and mind. Studying the texts of Persian and Arab spiritual leaders, some of whom, like Ibn 'Arabi, were noted Sufis, Corbin found a convergence between the Latin, "mundus imaginalis," and the Arabic, "Alam al Mithali" to refer to the specificity of the intermediate world as differentiated from the conventional usage of the word "imaginary." The "Alam al Mithali" (*monde imaginal,* an imaging world) designates a real world (not a fictitious one such as could be created by a poet) between that of the intelligible ("'Alam 'Aqli'"), and the material ("'Alam Hissi'").[74]

The first part of Corbin's book waxes lyrical. It is a fascinating attempt at entering the world of the mystics whose texts he translates while searching for a language that would neither dismiss nor reify the knowledge yielded by the texts. His passion for understanding the relationship between being and knowledge in Islam, for bridging the gap between different forms of knowledge rings with an urgency that resonates with concerns we, as social scientists, grapple with today. To wit:

> How does the cultured man of today represent to himself the spirituality of Islam? ... It is a great and formidable adventure to be the guest of a culture to the point of communicating in its language and participating in its problems. But he who remains on the shore will never foretaste the secrets of the high seas. How can he know for example, what it might be to read the Qur'an as a Bible (like the Bible from which the Qur'an partially stems) unless, like those whose Bible it is, he perceives the *spiritual meaning* that they perceive in it, and as they perceive it in the traditions which unfold it. But how can we keep company with the Sufis and Spiritual Masters of Islam if we ourselves have forgotten the language of symbols, if we are blind and deaf to the *spiritual meaning* of the ancient writings, while, on the other hand, we take such pride in showing how favorably they compare with other historical or archeological documents.[75]

To be "a guest of a culture" and to "participate in its problems" are part of the anthropological endeavor. It is easy to see why Foucault would be attracted to Corbin's approach to Shi'ism. First, he found in it a convergence with his own work in two ways: In *Les mots et les choses,* he too had identified an intermediate level of knowledge between the observable and the conceptual. He too was attracted to the marginalized, or the reality that Reason distorts. Moreover, the mad or the prisoner in Foucault finds his functional equivalent in the ill-understood Islamic spirituality, or the rethinking of imagination. Second, Foucault's own misgivings about Western culture resonated with those of Corbin, who felt that "there has been a great destruction of hope in the West, and there is no telling where it will end."[76] Corbin bemoaned the lack of religious conviction and spread of moral relativism in Western societies. In retrospect Foucault's subsequent analysis of the transformations of religious ethics in Christianity echoes Corbin's concern. There are other aspects of Corbin's thought, especially his discussion of the role of music (an art Foucault wrote about) in understanding cultural difference that undoubtedly appealed to Foucault. In addition to these considerations, Corbin followed a rigorous method of analysis, which Foucault used on many occasions.

Based on the mystical texts he examined, Corbin provided a critique of Western historicism, which he considered "irritating and sterile." As an alternative to the Western linear conception of space—a cause of the reduction of objects to the same temporal level as well as the incompleteness of explanations—Corbin points to mystics' cyclical conception in which events and beings produce their own temporality and space. From this perspective, "acts of *understanding* are so many recommencements, re-*iterations* of events still unconcluded."[77] Echoing Claude Lévi-Strauss's critique of historicism,[78] Corbin stresses that a cyclical conception of time reveals the importance of *structures* and their homologies.[79] He groped for a "mode of understanding" similar to that of a musician grasping the harmony of a symphony.[80] For example, to understand the relationship between Mazdean and Shi'i thought requires identifying the terms within each system, searching for analogous relationships between terms, and examining the functions they fulfill "in the midst of homologous wholes."[81] This, in a nutshell, is the definition of the structuralist method. The question is in what way Foucault, who for all the reasons described, could have only been in agreement with the fundamentals of Corbin's conception of knowledge,[82] was also influenced by Corbin's understanding of spirituality in Islam.

Foucault was undoubtedly familiar with the displays of formal religiosity in the public ritual of 'Ashura, which accorded with Corbin's analysis of the significance of another dimension of imagination and understanding. However, Corbin's analysis focused on texts and stressed unity of thought in Islam even though he intended to specify the features of Shi'ism. By contrast, Foucault focuses on Shi'ism as a self-contained system of beliefs. The rare references he made to "Islam" do not dispel this notion. By the same token, the methodological attraction that Corbin offered was counterbalanced by the emphasis he placed on mysticism. Yet at the time of the revolution, the younger Iranian generation had little knowledge of mystical Shi'ism of the sort Corbin interpreted.[83] Consequently, the interpretation of the Iranian movement as fueled by a Shi'i spirituality fell short of the actuality of events.

Political Spirituality and Ethnology

At one level, the concept of political spirituality is Foucault's single most important contribution to theorizing the Iranian movement. It was the outcome of a reasoned, albeit intrinsically contradictory, process. Even though he defined the French Revolution as a spirituality movement, he had hesitated to call the Iranian movement a "revolution," arguing that it "is not a revolution in the literal sense of the term, a manner of standing up and rising. It is an insurrection of men who, with bare hands, wish to lift the most formidable weight that holds all of us down...: the weight of the entire world order."[84] Noteworthy is the "us"—an eruption of Kantian universalistic moment. Foucault had expressed some misgivings about the meaning of an Islamic republic. In the workings of political spirituality Foucault glimpsed a refutation of the ideology of history as progress toward a scientific future. The Iranian movement epitomized a new form of protest outside of the failed "Marxist type, or revolutionary ideologies."[85] In support of his view, he noted the absence of the word "revolution" and the frequency of references to an Islamic government in his interlocutors' description of their objectives.[86] The spirituality that carries them through was an "effect of the rising up of subjects."[87] Furthermore, not only did he wish to give a culturally marginalized people a voice by analyzing their movement from their perspective, but he also predicted that the effect of Khomeini's rise to power would be felt throughout the region as it signaled the rise of Islam as a force in reorienting the politics of protest. Overall, he offered a phenomenological analysis to account for the psycho-cultural springs of action, which a narrow political economic interpretation would have missed. Equally important was his concern to incorporate in his analysis the role played by religion in everyday life in Iran. In this sense, his position was similar to that of Max Weber in *The Protestant Ethic and the Spirit of Capitalism*. Political spirituality was also meant to indicate the positive role that religion can play in circumstances where genuine political life is but a ritualistic game, as in bourgeois democracies, or simply absent as in Iran.

The events he witnessed in Iran convinced Foucault of the need for a creative conceptualization of the relationship between politics, culture, and faith in a developing society undergoing change. Given this framework, Foucault found in the concept of *experience* the necessary articulation between politics and culture, which permitted him to focus on religion as the factor accounting for the movement's spectacular impetus. Carried out in a foreign land, in a different culture, at a time of systemic crisis, a phenomenological analysis of this kind could easily lose sight of the role played by institutions other than religion in the movement. In other words, the fervor that carried the movement could also have been the culmination of a series of factors emanating from different sources. Hence, the danger of reducing a complex situation loomed large. Nevertheless, as defined, political spirituality still captures the singular and sustained determination the demonstrators displayed in the streets at the moment of its occurrence. It further gave a concept to Sharī'atī's view of infusing politics with the conviction usually seen among believers, albeit obscuring the unintended consequences of making room for religion in politics.

The risk of relying on "political spirituality" as an explanatory concept was nevertheless great. The concept sidelines the political economy of the revolution, of which Foucault gave a sharp analysis, just as it obscures Foucault's stated methodological tenet: to attend to the "formal conditions" when doing a "cultural ethnology." Such conditions impinge on the analysis of the role that religion plays in politics without necessarily leading to a dismissal of religion as a form of false consciousness. The task of the analyst is further compounded by the difficulty of ascertaining the relationship between material struggles (those surrounding the "formal conditions") and struggles of ideas, the purpose of the *"reportage d'idées."* In a retrospective reflection on Iran, Foucault acknowledged his neglect of class antagonisms[88] in focusing on "political spirituality," but explained his oversight by the absence of discernible dissensions among the demonstrators when he was on the ground. He did not see one class fighting against the privileges of another as in the French Revolution, for example. Nor did he see a vanguard party leading the charge against a government.[89] Contrary to what Western analysts had written, Iranians did not clamor for modernization, "they clamor for men like Khomeini, or for religious leaders, [or] Islam; they clamor for another way of living in relation to modern life; they clamor for a life specifically linked to religion."[90] However, as Khomeini was assuming power, Foucault felt that the revolution was poised to acquire a familiar outlook: "the class struggle," including the use of arms. The shift from bare hands and absence of party leadership to incipient armed vanguards, a mass organization party, and the class struggles were about to give the movement "the red seal of revolutionary authentification."[91] However, Foucault still wondered whether his prognosis was accurate. In other words, he did not give up his organic view of the movement, which rested on the concept of "political spirituality."

Compounding the elision of class differences among the protest movement, political spirituality as an explanatory concept eschews the question of ideology. The challenge in accounting for the relationship between religious beliefs and political action is not one of cause and effect. It is to determine not only the points of convergence of religious ideas and political action, but also the shifting meanings that individuals attach to their behavior in situations of crisis. For example, were the people who took part in the powerful display of 'Ashura-like rituals engaged in political spirituality, or were they performing a theatrical display they habitually act out every year, that, even though it had political connotations for the observer, was in reality purely ritualistic? Assuming that ideology functions in an autonomous manner with respect to the economy, it is possible that individuals might attempt to cause religious symbols to converge with political ideology in a way unrelated to the purported spiritual search for self-transformation—the core of the definition of political spirituality. Iran in 1978 was experiencing an economic and political crisis as Foucault was well aware. And without delving into the question of determining at what point in their diminished material lives people rebel, it was clear that Iranians wished for a radical change in the economy as well as in the political system. But Foucault's rejection of a Marxist analysis stood in the way of distinguishing between religious beliefs and political ideology.

The validity of Foucault's analysis hinges not only on the long history of the relationship between government and the opposition,[92] but also on the more immediate history of the movement prior to Foucault's arrival in Tehran. Probing accounts of the Revolution stress the complexity of a movement that put into play a variety of actors, many with different interests and agendas. It was composed of former members of the Communist Tudeh Party, intellectuals of all political orientations, secular and seminary students, blue-collar workers, and merchants in the bazaars, among others. Yet the Revolution had not drawn all Iranians into its fold. Neither rural and small village populations nor poor migrants had been active participants.[93] Furthermore, in spite of his notoriety, Khomeini had not initially been popular among all those who were swept up in the demonstrations; his rise as a consensus figure was a function of his strategy as well as mounting repression from the government.[94] More to the point, radical Islamists cultivated the notion that he was a saintly figure through tales of his supranatural gifts.[95] By 1978, radical Islamists had prevailed over more moderate ones through intimidation and other means of securing their acquiescence to demonstrations that put people in harm's way. They successfully used the network of mosques, traditionally led by moderate leaders, to spread their message and galvanize the population. There was evidence that Khomeini had instructed his followers in Iran to infuse the ritual of 'Ashura with a political meaning by combining the form of public ritual with a political demonstration against the shah. Gradually, ceremonies of mourning on the fortieth and subsequently the seventh day after the death of the fallen demonstrators were infused with a religio-political meaning, as they were strategically turned into demonstrations organized in various places in an apparent stream of endless public events. Even Ramadan was imparted with a political meaning.[96] This resymbolization of religious custom as political event culminated in Khomeini's definition of the ultimate goal of the movement as the establishment of an Islamic government.[97] Prior to 1978, Khomeini had lectured on Islamic government. From his perspective, an Islamic government "is not despotic but constitutional," and it is so in the sense that rulers are bound by the Koran and the Sunna, and by the Shari'a.[98]

Nevertheless, when observed from the outside, the demonstrations Foucault witnessed must have been a rare spectacle of an inextricable union between religion and politics. But was the fervor and passion that struck the observer's imagination a cause of the public's opposition to the shah, or an effect of the painstaking work of radical Islamists' mobilization? Admittedly, what matters is the fact that people were in the streets in large numbers regardless of their manipulation. But, this would avail if Foucault had refrained from the philosophical-political kind of interpretation he gave.

In reality, Foucault had heard discordant voices, different from those he presented as reflecting the people's general will. The most important came from Shariat Madari, with whom he spoke. He had also heard from those who felt that their support for Khomeini, "the flagman,"[99] was more strategic—a temporary alliance to get rid of the shah—than a conviction that he would be the leader Iran needed. Yet he doubted their "hasty optimism."[100] It is precisely because he went against his own misgivings about an Islamic government that his interpretation cannot be simply dismissed as an intellectual accident or lapse. Indeed, in his notes he expressed his unease with evoking the idea of an Islamic government. "I feel embarrassed to talk about an Islamic government as an idea or an ideal."[101] Furthermore, he raised important objections about the prospects of such a government: protection of religious minorities and women; risk of totalitarianism; risk of oppression by the Muslim majority; tolerance for different life styles.[102] He also took the answers he received with a grain of salt. He saw the answer to the minorities question (that the minority will be protected but that the Baha'i [religion] is so false that it cannot be tolerated) as evidence that "the Western rationalist thought of this jacobin democracy reinforces to some extent this religious fundamentalism."[103] Foucault perceived these issues as the kind of "dangers" that lurk in all movements, and of which he felt Iranians were aware. He concluded: "The problem is to find out whether they will be able to get something out of this Islam, which is their tradition, their form of national conscientiousness, their instrument of struggle, as well as the principle of their uprising, something that will avoid these dangers."[104] In this context, the apparent shortsightedness of Foucault's interpretation was not the result of naïveté, as is often argued, notwithstanding his assertion that "there is no

Khomeini party, there will not be a Khomeini government, Khomeini is the focal point of a collective will."[105] This statement too was not unmotivated. When counterposed to Foucault's phenomenological analysis of political spirituality, the statement reveals a strikingly structuralist impulse (which he used as an adjuvant to his phenomenology of the movement); it proceeds in a formal fashion by positing three terms: Khomeini, party/government, and collective will (the people). The relationship between Khomeini and a putative party/government is negative, whereas the relationship between the people, abstracted as a collective will, and Khomeini is positive. Furthermore, and oddly, in a sort of Hegelian notion of the spirit of the nation, the people lose their reality as they are subsumed under the category of the will. Foucault's analysis provides an example of the formal-voluntaristic character of structural analysis as applied to a different culture: the concepts acquire a life of their own; they become synonymous with the reality they are meant to explain.

At a philosophical level, the concept of political spirituality reflects a fundamental antinomy in Foucault's critique of Kant's anthropology. To recall, *Les mots et les choses* held that the death of God had ushered in the emergence of the figure of man as an object of study when in reality man too had ceased to exist. Thus anthropology was born under the illusion that there was a human nature to be discovered empirically. Besides, there can be no human purpose or meaning to discover, no signifying consciousness, only structures that frame actions. There is a logic to Foucault's use of "political spirituality" that goes beyond what he intended by the concept. In attempting a history of the Iranian present, he was confronted with God and man. What he witnessed appeared to be in contradistinction to his conception of the conditions of possibility of anthropology, inadequate as he thought they were. Yet in order to make sense of these conditions, he relied on an analysis, which by definition stressed meaning in human action. In other words, in Iran Foucault had to avail himself of some anthropology. The abstract category of "man" discussed in *Les mots et les choses* is inseparable from Foucault's conception of an anthropology that dispenses with God and man. In Iran, Foucault found himself assuming a nature that yearns for both God and freedom. Noteworthy is Foucault's avoidance of God in his reports, or a discussion of the ultimate status of Khomeini in the minds of those who cheered for him. Was Khomeini perceived as divine? He nevertheless points out that Khomeini appeared as though he was the much awaited and occulted twelfth Imam.

The use of the concept "political spirituality" has a surplus meaning beyond the Iranian situation. It harks back to Foucault's undefined conception of a non-Kantian anthropology, which when he interpreted the Iranain

Revolution presented him with a serious difficulty on the ground. Eschewing the notion that religious beliefs and symbols could be manipulated or that the Iranian mass movement expressed a universal human yearning for freedom, Foucault focused on the limit-experience of risking one's life. At the same time, his unpublished notes cast doubt on the meaning of this notion: "But in Islam, and especially in Shi'i Islam, people do not think much about death. ... Death in Christianity is for the sake of renewal; Islamic martyrs die for [their] right."[106] If Muslims die for the affirmation of their rights, their protest is for justice and dispenses with a political spiritual incentive. At first glance, "political spirituality" seems to contradict Foucault's interpretation of the movement as carried through by a collective will, an echo of Durkheim's "conscience collective," to account for the movement's general and unrelenting purpose to overthrow the shah. Foucault's debt to Durkheim is further evidenced by his insistence that political spirituality is a "cultural fact," a rephrasing of Durkheim's "social facts." The unexpected use of concepts derived from positivist sociology (which in Durkheim's case frequently overlapped with ethnology) recalls the "anthropological illusion" of assuming a knowable human being. In a sense, the history of the present, which Foucault was carrying out in Iran, was predicated on a positive philosophy that searched for meaning in the belief system of its objects.

The Politics of Spirituality

When Shi'ism is replaced in the context of Islam as a religion, it becomes clear that Sunni Islam too fueled a number of organized uprisings in the Middle East and North Africa prior to the Iranian movement. The opposition led by Emir Abd el Kader in 1830–1844 against the French invasion of Algeria is a case in point. Emir Abd el Kader was the leader of the powerful Sufi Order of the Qadiriya. Another order, the Senusi, also fought French troops as they expanded France's reach across the Sahara at the turn of the twentieth century. The same order fought the Italian colonization of Libya between the two world wars. Thus, the historical-political dimension of the Iranian revolution brought it in proximity with the histories of other Muslim countries in the region. In more recent times, faith-based movements in the Middle East had been contesting the policies of their governments for some time as exemplified by the tribulations of the Muslim Brotherhood in Egypt. The postindependence government of Algeria was challenged in the 1990s (after Foucault's death) by the Front of Islamic Salvation, a faith-based party.

Conversely, the upheavals that have rocked Middle Eastern and North African societies beginning in 2011 to overthrow heads of state and establish representative political systems have been rooted in a commitment to change as great as the Iranians' in 1978. Yet it did not stem from a putative political spirituality. This may seem an unfair comment on Foucault's interpretation given that Islamist groups temporarily ascended to power in the aftermath of the Tunisian and Egyptian revolutions of 2011–2012. However, such groups as these competed with "secular" parties in open elections and their success has been curtailed although events continue to evolve in a region in the throes of turbulent change. Ultimately, the challenge posed by the Iranian movement was to identify changes in the function of the relationship between Islam and politics, religion and state, given that the Iranian state was not colonial but native, although lacking legitimacy. In other words, the relevance or significance of "political spirituality" was contingent on an analysis of the variance of the political, social, and cultural structures.

As a general concept "political spirituality" obscures the relationship between different modes of symbolization of the linkage between the cultural and the political-economic. For example, women, an important component of the Iranian movement, had a complicated relation to Shi'ism. Many of them took up the veil not as a mark of piety, or as a spiritual experience, but as a symbol of the rejection of the shah's government. A transformation of religious symbols, not necessarily mystical, was taking place among competing groups with different agendas. To recall, private citizens hosted their own re-enactment of the Iranian political myths out of which Shi'ism emerged—an acknowledgment that the ritual of 'Ashura itself had a contested meaning within the culture. In the end, Foucault conflated the political-qua-structural with the spiritual-qua-individual: "there was a will to renew their entire existence by relinking with a spiritual experience, which they think they find at the heart of Islam."[107] In infusing the political with the spiritual without determining the nature of the latter and how it varies from one context to the next, he fell back on a transcendentalism of his own, which ran counter his critique of Kant's anthropology.[108] It is hardly possible, for instance, to frame the attraction that the Islamic State in the Levant holds for young men, mostly members of Muslim minorities in the West, as meaning a desire for political spirituality at the risk of death, without considering how techniques of recruitment make use of selective religious symbols tailored to their marginal or disaffected status.

THE PRESENT AND CULTURE

The idealist interpretation of the Iranian Revolution sheds light on the meaning Foucault attached to studying the present. To reiterate, he defined the role of the philosopher as one of diagnostician of the present. He had also suggested that Kant ushered in the philosophy of the present. It is tempting to view Foucault's effort to do the philosophy of the present as stumbling on the reification of cultural difference inherent in an analysis confined to an assumed specialness of local knowledge. In the "present," time and space meet. The question is to determine where culture fits in this schema. The Iranian Revolution took place in a time frame shared by other cultures; it was our contemporary. As such it could not be subsumed under past European history, nor could it be subsumed under the timelessness of the spiritual-qua-transcendental that finds expression in the political form of the present. In this context, criticism was made that Foucault was a latter-day orientalist not only in his reports on the Iranian Revolution, but also in his approach to cultures such as that of Japan. His reference to Iran's history as largely static, ensconced in a form of mysticism that no modernizing policy or monarch could shake; his reading of Shi'ism as a self-contained system of beliefs sustaining its adherents in the expectation of a returning Imam whom Khomeini seemed to embody, were some of the factors making the charge of orientalism plausible. Foucault's own statements about his generally uncritical reading of orientalist Islamicists, such as Massignon, gave more force to the criticism. Afary and Anderson add the weight of Foucault's utter neglect of women to the charge that he partook in a one-sided, male worldview embedded in a mythic time so familiar in orientalist accounts of Muslim societies.

The concept of orientalism in this case obscures the relationship between Foucault's analysis of the Iranian Revolution and his philosophical-theoretical orientation. Orientalists usually are experts in things "Oriental," for which they develop specific methodologies and theories. Foucault's work focuses on French-qua-European history and culture. Although there may be points of contact between orientalism as a discourse and archaeology-genealogy, keeping them separate in analyzing Foucault's reports on Iran has more than a heuristic value. It becomes clearer that Foucault's conundrum was similar to that which anthropologists experienced when they carried out ethnographies in different societies without a sense of overall purpose except to accumulate information on the various modes of being different. In fact, Foucault made two important theoretical moves: (a) he extrapolated from the Iranian movement to past uprisings in Europe; and (b) he reinterpreted his own work as an instance of the theoretical-empirical task he performed in Iran. The latter move centered on his treatment of madness: "What is the history of madness if not the history of the experience through which the West risked constructing its status, the status of Reason as subject in relation to madness [which it] finally made an object of knowledge."[109]

Was it the purported lack of fear of death[110] exhibited by the demonstrators, which justified the comparison with madness? Was it the demonstrators' apparent oblivion to the world around them during their re-enactment of Shi'i martyrdom? At any rate, it was the *experience* of madness as risk that Foucault referred to. Witnessing the 'Ashura-like demonstrations must have called to Foucault's mind the carnival of the mad at Munsterlingen (Switzerland) when he and his friend, Jacqueline Verdeaux, visited Dr. Roland Kuhn's hospital on the eve of Mardi Gras in 1952.[111] Either way, cultural difference proved far greater than the difference between the mad and the sane in its theoretical challenge. As with Kant, who stumbled on race, Foucault stumbled on culture.

These moves brought Foucault very close to reformulating his concepts, but he fell short as he saw in the Iranian movement a vindication of his own work. There is another element of significance in Foucault's analysis of the role of Islam in the Iranian revolution: to recall, Foucault had declared Man dead, yet his use of the concept of political spirituality unwittingly contradicts this foundational theoretical approach by re-inserting Man as a political agent moved by a spiritual impetus. In this sense, Man appears as a link between God and the world. Arguably under specific historical conditions, religious ideas and symbols can be used for strategic purposes. However, there is no room in Foucault's interpretation for understanding the militancy of Iranians as a mere strategy. Faith and spiritual commitment were privileged over a political-religious calculus. Yet many demonstrators felt buoyed by the magnitude of the event, and may have even taken part in demonstrations but without necessarily being moved by a political spirituality such that their participation meant support for an Islamic government.

In conclusion, in Iran Foucault witnessed how the non-Western world positions itself discursively and behaviorally vis-à-vis the West in a moment of political crisis. Iran offered him a singular experience at a personal and intellectual level. Through his investigative *reportage d'idées,* he was engaged in a task similar to that of anthropologists in spite of its short duration. In a way he virtually experimented with Kant's anthropology: he went to the world, to another cultural universe, and largely strove to suspend cultural presuppositions for the sake of understanding the springs of action. By the same token, the Iranian movement afforded him the opportunity to rethink Euro-centered categories of thought, which his interlocutors rejected and about which he too had misgivings.

The elaboration of the concept of political spirituality helped to capture the phenomenal aspect of the Iranian uprising as it unfolded on a grand scale in fall 1978. But did he give "the people bereft of the ability to speak or make themselves heard" a new theoretical language? He was momentarily drawn into their world view. He made a significant effort to understand their world as they explained it to him and as he observed it at the cost of withering criticism from his fellow citizens. The *reportage d'idées* held the potential of orienting Foucault toward the "world" of otherness. However, and in spite of his desire to grasp the *experience* of the protestors, it remained an intellectual exercise, a sort of skirmish over concepts and standpoints, more than an opening into the inner world of what constitutes the fundamental aspirations and characteristics of the human.

Foucault's attempt to universalize political spirituality resulted in essentializing Iranian culture. Thus, Shi'i Islam appears as the source of, as well as a possible solution to, the problems of the present. It is here that the antinomy between specificity and universality in his interpretation reveals its contradiction. The Iranian revolution has a cross-cultural liberatory character, yet its specificity is Islam. This skirts the issue of the universality of Islam. In the end, Islam is perceived as a local/regional force holding the potential of fostering indigenous, culture-specific political change in Middle Eastern societies. Thus, the analysis of the present fades into a conception of religion as unchanging, yet containing a concentrated spirituality amenable to political transmutation and individual commitment such that it canceled out the fear of corporeal death. On the one hand, religion is a demystifying factor in the murkiness of forced modernization, a revealing (in the Heideggerian sense) of Iran to itself that, once their part is done, "the mullah will now disperse in a flurry of black and white robes."[112] On the other hand, Foucault defines Islamic ethics as fundamentally different from its Western-qua-Christian counterpart. As he put it, "They [Iranians] do not have the same regime of truth as ours, which is also specific although it has become universal.... And in Iran it is fashioned in large part after a religion with an exoteric form and esoteric content." In Islam, meaning is not intrinsic to words, it constantly connotes and refers to other meanings. Consequently, ambiguity rules and truth is elusive; it calls out "another deep meaning that cannot be grasped accurately or through observation."[113] Thus, Foucault resorts to the very mode of thinking about Iran that he denounced at the outset. It is tempting to speculate that, as George Stauh claims, the Iranian Revolution posed a threat to Foucault's philosophical concerns.[114]

In the end, the very culture that Foucault sought to capture conceptually acted as a confounding factor in his ultimate attempt to transcend the Marxist conception of ideology.[115] Iran remained largely the "intermediate world" between the West and the world of cognition. In spite of his effort to account for the Iranian universality, he returned, after an apparently brief hiatus, to the epistemology of the Oriental divide. Iran, the (near) East, is a limit-experience even when looked at sympathetically.[116] Ironically, it is to

Kant, Habermas, Marx (as rethought by Habermas) as well as other Western philosophers that a new generation of Iranians has turned to theorize a liberal democracy in a new key, one that would preserve their specificity but without sacrificing the universality of the quest for freedom and liberty.[117]

In a manner reminiscent of Kant, Foucault found himself defending universal rights and political accountability to an authority higher than that of a governing body. He wrote to Mehdi Bazargan, whom Khomeini had appointed to form a government in February 1979: "No more than I, I imagine, would you accept the principle of a power that would be accountable only to itself.... Those who protested against one Iranian tortured in a Savak jail were involved in the most universal act there is."[118] Oddly, Foucault also found himself correcting his assessment of Marx's conception of religion: "We always cite Marx's [phrase that] religion is the opium of the people. But the sentence that precedes it and which we never cite says that religion is the spirit of a spiritless world."[119]

Nevertheless, Foucault's reporting on Iran represents a significant effort he made to understand a part of the Orient, which like Japan, had escaped colonization. In this Foucault may have glimpsed the difficulties and pitfalls of doing a humanist anthropology while philosophically opposing humanism. In musing about the revolution in January 1979, he exclaimed "we now know that there is no subject of history"—an odd, or perhaps fitting, statement given his idealist interpretation of the revolution.

NOTES

1. See for instance Maxime Rodinson's critical article, "Critique of Foucault on Iran," in Janet Afary and Kevin B. Anderson, *Michel Foucault and the Iranian Revolution: Gender and the Seductions of Islamism* (Chicago: University of Chicago Press, 2005), 267–77.
2. James Miller, one of Foucault's biographers, argues that Foucault had "an essentially mystical vision of politics as a 'limit experience.'" James Miller, *The Passion of Michel Foucault* (Cambridge, MA: Harvard University Press, 1993), 314.
3. A number of scholars have taken Foucault to task for getting his facts wrong about Iranian history as well as the history or contents of Shi'ism. See, among others, Afary and Anderson, *Michel Foucault and the Iranian Revolution*; and Michiel Leezenberg "Power and Political Spirituality: Michel Foucault on the Islamic Revolution in Iran," in *Michel Foucault and Theology: The Politics of Religious Experience,* ed. James William Bernauer and Jeremy R. Carrette (Burlington, VT: Ashgate, 2004).
4. Foucault remarked in an interview in October 1978, a few months before he set out for Tehran, that he shied away from prophesizing. "M. Foucault. Conversa-

tion sans complexes avec le philosophe qui analyse les 'structures du pouvoir," in *Dits et écrits,* vol. 2, 669, 671. Foucault, as a reporter of ideas, will violate this principle.
5. Joahn Beukes, "*Hamartia:* Foucault and Iran 1978-1979 (1: Introduction and Texts)," HTS Theological Studies 124, no. 65, 1 (June 2009), 1. Accessed 17 September 2015. Beukes uses the Greek expression *hamartia* to convey the idea of a tragic flaw. He also imaginatively casts Foucault as a Greek in Persia. See also the second part of the article, "*Hamartia:* Foucault and Iran 1978–1979 (2: Scholarship and Significance)," 125, no. 6, 1, (July 2009).
6. For an example of an analysis in English, which raises the first three questions, see Afary and Anderson, *Michel Foucault and the Iranian Revolution.* For one detailed critique by a French orientalist, see Maxime Rodinson, "Critique of Foucault on Iran." Ibid.
7. Beukes views the aim of reporting as generalizing whereas that of the philosophizer is to dwell on the particular. "*Hamartia:* Foucault and Iran 1978-1979 (2: Scholarship and Significance)," 6.
8. Eribon, *Michel Foucault,* 282.
9. Ibid., 281.
10. David Macey, *The Lives of Michel Foucault* (New York, 1993), 406. Unlike Eribon, who felt that Foucault hesitated, Macey reports that Foucault readily agreed to Cavallari's invitation.
11. Michel Foucault, "Les 'reportages' d'idées," in *Dits et écrits,* vol. 2, 707. This article was published in the Italian paper, *Corriere della sera,* 12 November 1978. It was an introduction to Alain Finkielkraut's report on Carter's America. Eribon, *Michel Foucault,* 282.
12. Macey, *The Lives of Michel Foucault,* 407.
13. Foucault, "Les 'reportages' d'idées," 707.
14. Thierry Voeltzel pointed out that Foucault was "a simple journalist" doing what other journalists were doing in Iran. Miller, *The Passion of Michel Foucault,* 289.
15. Foucault stated that "During May 1968, just like the time of the Algerian War, I was not in France; always a bit lagging behind, on the margin." "Entretien avec Michel Foucault," (interview by D. Trombadori), in *Dits et écrits,* vol. 2, 897. This interview was also published in book form as Michel Foucault, *Remarks on Marx: Conversations with Duccio Trombadori,* trans. R. James Goldstein and James Cascaito (New York: Semiotext(e), 1991).
16. Foucault. "Conversation sans complexes avec le philosophe qui analyse les 'structures du pouvoir'," in *Dits et écrits,* vol. 2, 670.
17. Bibliothèque Nationale de France, Richelieu site, NAF 28730, L (15). (Numbers in parentheses refer to folder in files.) The brackets around "arrogance" indicate the author's best attempt to decipher the word.
18. Foucault, "Dialogue between Michel Foucault and Baqir Parham," in Afary and Anderson, *Michel Foucault and the Iranian Revolution,* 186–187. See also Foucault's article "Téhéran: La foi contre le Shah," in *Dits et écrits,* vol. 2, 686, in which Fou-

cault refers to Marx's conception of religion as "the most scoffed at notion." An English translation is in Afary and Anderson, *Michel Foucault and the Iranian Revolution*.
19. Michel Foucault, "Entretien avec Michel Foucault," *Le Nouvel Observateur*, 3 January 1979, NAF 28730 L (12). Interview by J.P. Enthoven.
20. Foucault thought of modernization as Europeanization: he assessed the shah's policy as "an attempt to modernize Islamic societies after a European fashion." "Le Chah a cent ans de retard," in *Dits et écrits*, vol. 2, 681. This view, plausible at an abstract level, has special resonance as it is in keeping with Foucault's occasional references to people he interviewed as "Westernized." There is no intimation that modernity can take a non-European form. Yet Foucault had encountered this form of modernity in Japan.
21. Foucault, "Dialogue Between Michel Foucault and Baqir Parham," 185.
22. Foucault's Iranian interlocutors too brought up Vietnam in assessing the prospects of the United States' abandonment of the shah if they were to prevail. NAF 28730 (15).
23. Afary and Anderson, *Michel Foucault and the Iranian Revolution*, 185.
24. As he put it, "Today we are in a more familiar world: there have been barricades." Michel Foucault, "Une poudrière appelée Islam," in *Dits et écrits*, vol. 2, 759. The English translation is in Afary and Anderson, *Michel Foucault and the Iranian Revolution*.
25. Alain Touraine, *Tribune*, 12 September 1994, IMEC, Dossier 4. Touraine further notes that to escape the contradiction, Foucault embraced the notion that "there is no actor, no action, no transformation, only absolute power; and that it is possible to escape the contradictions between meaning and actions by asserting that there is no meaning and action, but only an impersonal logic of domination and inequality."
26. James Miller finds in Foucault's sympathy for the Iranian Revolution an echo of Kant's view that revolutions do not leave individuals unaffected even if they do not support them actively. Miller's comment is, however, more analogical than substantive given the nature of Foucault's analysis. Miller, *The Passion of Michel Foucault*, 310.
27. Foucault, "Dialogue between Michel Foucault and Baqir Parham," 186.
28. In his unpublished notes, Foucault referred to Qom as "Qhoum" and "Khom."
29. It is not clear how many people Foucault interviewed, and how many were individuals he approached on the street as distinguished from those whose meetings had been arranged through his Iranian contacts.
30. Afary and Anderson, *Michel Foucault and the Iranian Revolution*, 181–82.
31. Foucault's travel notes do not indicate the names of all the people he spoke to. NAF 28730, L (11).
32. Foucault, "Qui êtes-vous professeur Foucault?, in *Dits et écrits*, vol. 2," 634. Michiel Leezenberg stresses the present as an important part of Foucault's reporting about Iran. This implies that Foucault's reports can only be evaluated as a chronicle of the moment. Leezenberg, "Power and Political Spirituality," 102.

33. See the lucid and detailed chronology of the phases of the movement by Charles Kurzman, *The Unthinkable Revolution in Iran* (Cambridge, MA: Harvard University Press, 2014).
34. See for example Foucault, "Une révolte à mains nues," in *Dits et écrits,* vol. 2, 704; "Téhéran: La foi contre le chah," 684; "A quoi rêvent les Iraniens?," 694.
35. Foucault, "Qui êtes-vous, professeur Foucault?," in *Dits et écrits,* vol. 2, 633. An English translation appears in Jeremy R. Carrette, ed., *Religion and Culture: Michel Foucault* (New York: Routledge, 1999).
36. Foucault, "Qui êtes-vous, professeur Foucault?," 633.
37. Foucault's estrangement, his musings, and the controversy over his intellectual stance on Iran bring to mind to some degree Lawrence of Arabia's problematic forays into Arab culture without all the drama of the power politics of World War I.
38. Foucault, "Le chef mythique de la révolte de l' Iran," in *Dits et écrits,* vol. 2, 716. The initial title that Foucault had given this article was "La folie de l'Iran" (Iran's madness).
39. NAF 28730, L (15).
40. Coincidentally, Khomeini had rejected the notion that the revolution was caused by material factors. Kurzman, *The Unthinkable Revolution in Iran,* 79.
41. Hassan and Hussein were the sons of Caliph Ali, the spiritual leader of the Shi'a, and from the perspective of Shi'ism, the legitimate heirs to the Caliphate.
42. Afary and Anderson make both arguments.
43. George Stauth, "Revolution in Spiritless Times: An Essay on Michel Foucault's Enquiries into the Iranian Revolution," *International Sociology* 6, no. 3 (1991): 273.
44. James Bernauer suggests that Foucault's commitment to friendship and love is one of many signs of his valuation of a Christian ethic and living according to it. James Bernauer, "Michel Foucault's Philosophy of Religion: An Introduction to Non-Fascist Life" in *Michel Foucault and Theology: The Politics of Religious Experience,* ed. Bernauer and Jeremy R. Carrette (Aldershot: Ashgate, 2004), 93.
45. Jeremy R. Carrette, *Foucault and Religion: Spiritual Corporality and Political Spirituality* (New York: Routledge, 2000), chap. 3.
46. Carrette argues that in using the concept of "political spirituality," Foucault wished to convey the notion that religious practices induce and reinforce existing relations of power. However, Carrette cautions that unless it is placed in its proper context, "the problematization of government," the concept can become confusing. But, in the context of Iran, this interpretation does not help to understand Foucault's analysis of the revolution given that he perceived Shi'ism as an oppositional counter-power in its own right, not as re-inforcing existing power relations. Hence, Carrette explains Foucault's stance as an outcome of his acceptance of Corbin's notion of "spiritual corpor*ei*ty" by which he meant that under some circumstances the spirit and the body become fused. Carrette notes the similarity between this concept and Foucault's "spiritual corporality." Ibid., 139.

47. *Le Nouvel Observateur.*
48. Ibid.
49. NAF 28730, L (11)
50. NAF 28730, L (15).
51. Ibid.
52. *Le Nouvel Observateur.*
53. Ibid.
54. Ibid
55. Ibid.
56. NAF 28730, L (15).
57. Ibid.
58. Ibid.
59. Ibid.
60. It is not clear from Foucault's notes preceding his 1979 interview with *Le Nouvel Observateur* whether he was quoting what Sharī'atī and others said about a future Islamic government. Nevertheless, the interview makes it clear that whatever the case might be, he accepted the fundamentals of Sharī'atī's view.
61. NAF 28730, L (1-10, 13). This is undoubtedly a reference to the idea of the hidden imam.
62. 'Alī Sharī'atī, *Marxism and Other Western Fallacies: An Islamic Critique,* ed. Hamid Algar, trans. R. Campbell (Berkeley: Mizan Press, 1980).
63. Ibid., 91.
64. Jalāl Āl-i Aḥmad, *Occidentosis: A Plague from the West,* ed. Hamid Algar, trans. R. Campbell (Berkeley: Mizan Press, 1984), 27. Ahmad claims that he understood the meaning of "occidentosis," 136, when he started translating Albert Camus's *The Plague.*
65. In his unpublished notes Foucault wrote of the "reality of an Islamic movement" with "here resistance and opposition, there definite nationalisms with their attendant chauvinism, xenophobia, racism; everywhere a strong hostility towards the West, and a will to economic and political independence, as well as to cultural autonomy from European civilization in general." NAF 28730, L (15).
66. Foucault, "Le Chah a cent ans de retard," 680.
67. Ibid.
68. Ibid. Foucault's rejection of Iranian modernization was not necessarily a rejection of modernity as such, but that of the mimicry of Western modernization without modernity.
69. Aḥmad, *Occidentosis,* 140n25.
70. Foucault felt that, although the Pahlevi dynasty had been inspired by Kemal Ataturk's "nationalism, secularism and modernity," it had been unable to and incapable of reaching the first (as well as the second) objective, as it alternately sought the protection of Britain and later the United States, thus compromising political sovereignty. Foucault, "Le Chah a cent ans de retard," 681.
71. Henry Corbin, *Spiritual Body and Celestial Earth: From Mazdean Iran to Shī'ite Iran,*

2nd Edition, trans. Nancy Pearson (Princeton, NJ: Princeton University Press, 1989), vii.
72. Ibid., viii.
73. Ibid.
74. Ibid., ix.
75. Ibid., xxi.
76. Ibid., xxii. Emphasis in text.
77. Ibid., xxix.
78. Claude Lévi-Strauss, *Anthropologie Structurale* (Paris: Plon, 1958), Introduction, 3–33.
79. Corbin, *Spiritual Body*, xxvii.
80. Ibid., xxviii.
81. Ibid.
82. In the interview with the Iranian Bakir Parham, Foucault had said that he agreed with all the books he read about Islam in Iran. Afary and Anderson, *Michel Foucault and the Iranian Revolution*, 186.
83. I am grateful to Professor Charles Kurzman for bringing this point to my attention.
84. Foucault, "Le chef mythique de la révolte de l'Iran," 716. English translation in Afary and Anderson, *Michel Foucault and the Iranian Revolution*.
85. *Le Nouvel Observateur*.
86. NAF 28730, L (1-10, 13).
87. Ibid.
88. Leezenberg, 144, argues that in fact Foucault's philosophical work could not countenance understanding events in terms of class struggle.
89. Foucault, "L'esprit d'un monde sans esprit," in *Dits et Ecrits*, vol. 2, 744. Interview with Claire Brière and Pierre Blanchet in their book, *Iran: la révolution au nom de dieu*. In this interview, which appeared after Khomeini ascended to power, Foucault explains how the Iranian Revolution defied the categories of analysis with which revolutions are traditionally analyzed. Read closely, the interview reveals how Foucault shuttled from Islam tout court to Shi'ism, just as it sheds light on the manner in which he applied Corbin's conception of Shi'ism. The discussion with Claire Brière, who also reported on the Iranian Revolution, is a revealing document on two French analysts exchanging some problematic views on Iran and Islam. Foucault frequently gives the impression of discussing a literary text rather than a real sociopolitical event.
90. *Le Nouvel Observateur*.
91. Foucault, "Une poudrière appelée Islam," 759. English translation in Afary and Anderson, *Michel Foucault and the Iranian Revolution*.
92. Although he occasionally referred to the Iranian past, Foucault did so in a selective manner. For example, he noted that Shi'ism was instituted as a state religion in the sixteenth century. But this was done at the cost of a massacre of Sunni Iranians—a fact that already pointed to the danger of the intrusion of the political into the religious.

93. Kurzman, *The Unthinkable Revolution in Iran*, 100.
94. Ibid., 67–68
95. Ibid., 67. The mythification of Khomeini bears similarities to the Algerian Front of National Liberation (FLN) propaganda myth that the Companions of Prophet Muhammed were fighting alongside combatants, which all but ensured their victory against the French Army. Khomeini's transformation of Ramadan and Eid el Fetr as political observances also echoed the FLN prohibition against celebrating joyous events, such as weddings, with loud music and ululation since the nation was deemed to be in mourning until it recovered its sovereignty.
96. Ibid., 59–64.
97. Kurzman dates the crowd's use of the slogan of Islamic government to 7 September 1978. Ibid., 65
98. Ayatollah Khomeini, *Islamic Government* (New York: Manor Books, 1979), 31. This a series of lectures Khomeini gave on Jurisprudence in Islam in 1969–1970.
99. NAF 28730, L (15). Foucault may have heard the expression used by his interlocutors.
100. NAF 28730, L (1-10, 13).
101. NAF, 28730, L (1-10, 13).
102. NAF, 28730 L (15).
103. *Le Nouvel Observateur*. The handwritten text indicates "Mahi" but it clearly refers to the Baha'i religion, which is not recognized as such in Iran.
104. Ibid.
105. Foucault, "Le chef mythique de la révolte de l' Iran," 715.
106. NAF 28730, L (15).
107. Foucault, "L'esprit d'un monde sans esprit," 749.
108. Behrooz Ghamari-Tabrizi, in his defense of Foucault against Afary and Anderson, argues that Foucault captured the "spirit" of the revolution as well as the productive role of Islam in politics. "When Life Will No Longer Barter Itself: In Defense of Foucault on the Iranian Revolution," in *A Foucault for the 21st Century: Governmentality, Biopolitics and Discipline in the New Millennium*, ed. Sam Binkley and Jorge Capetillo Ponce (Newcastle-upon-Tyne: Cambridge Scholars Publishing, 2010), 273–92. See also his *Foucault in Iran: Islamic Revolution after the Enlightenment* (Minneapolis: University of Minnesota Press, 2016).
109. *Le Nouvel Observateur*.
110. Interviewed years after the Revolution, some of the protesters recall being afraid, and joining in only when it became clear there would be large crowds. Kurzman, *The Unthinkable Revolution in Iran*, 72–73.
111. Eribon, *Michel Foucault*, 46. Eribon reports that Dr. Kuhn's patients made costumes and masks and, along with the hospital staff and doctors, went in disguise to the village hall. The ceremony ended with all masks thrown into the fire "where the figure of Carnival was sacrificed."
112. Foucault, "Une poudrière appelée Islam," in *Dits et écrits*, vol. 2, 759.

113. Foucault, "L'esprit d'un monde sans esprit," 753.
114. Stauth, "Revolution in Spiritless Times," 262.
115. Afary and Anderson conclude that Foucault rejected the "emancipatory claims of the Enlightenment." *Foucault and the Iranian Revolution*, 15. Although this is a plausible conclusion, Foucault's reductive critique of Marx's conception of ideology was dictated by his anti-humanist impulse as well as his critique of anthropology. It should be noted that Amy Allen's claim that Foucault refined Kant's conception of anthropology by making it historically specific is not borne out by his analysis of the Iranian Revolution. The question hinges on whether the specific event, the revolution, exhausts itself in its present, or serves to enlighten the analyst on its human and thus universal significance.
116. Jon Solomon interprets the "*reportage d'idées*" as signaling Foucault's new focus starting in 1978 on "experience beyond knowledge," which involves the intellectual as the active mediator between the two terms. Solomon also sees the reportage as the best expression of Foucault's "orientalism." Jon Solomon, "The Experience of Culture: Eurocentric Limits and Openings in Foucault," in *Transeuropéennes*, 2013, 4–5.
117. See interview with the Iranian philosopher Ramin Jahanbegloo in Danny Postel, *Reading Legitimation Crisis in Tehran: Iran and the Future of Liberalism* (Chicago: Prickly Paradigm Press, 2006), chap. 4. On Habermas's reception, see Ali Paya and Mohamad Amin Ghaneirad, "Habermas and Iranian Intellectuals," *Iranian Studies* 20, no. 3 (June 2007). Foucault's work too is being read.
118. Foucault, "Lettre ouverte à Mehdi Bazargan," in *Dits et écrits*, vol. 2, 782.
119. Foucault, "L'esprit d'un monde sans esprit," 749.

Chapter 6

The Heterotopia of Tunisia

Foucault lived in Tunisia from November 1966 to October 1968.¹ Unlike Iran, Tunisia had been part of France's colonial empire, the imprint of which was still visible during Foucault's stay. In 1967 a severe political crisis erupted, comparable to the events of May '68 in France. The same year, he lectured on "Des espaces autres,"² in which he defined places such as the nudist huts³ of the island of Djerba and the village in which he lived, as heterotopias. These are spaces in which utopian elements are juxtaposed and behaviors that are prohibited elsewhere are expressed freely. In many ways, Foucault's perception and experience of Tunisia was a form of heterotopia characterized by its own temporality, history, politics, and anthropology. How did the heterotopian aspect of Foucault's presence in Tunisia encapsulate his contradictory attitude toward Kant's cosmopolitan anthropology, and how did it shed light on his stance toward colonialism?

ANCIENT GREECE IN TUNISIA

In interviews Foucault always specified that he lived in Sidi Bou Saïd, an old village within commuting distance of Tunis, perched on a hill overlooking the sea. With its whitewashed houses, Moorish-style homes and narrow streets, it lends itself to an easygoing and bohemian lifestyle much appreciated by tourists, French and European expatriates (many of whom own their homes there), and a community of artists, local and international.⁴ In Sidi Bou Saïd, a true heterotopia, life was different from in the rest of Tunisia, occurring in a sort of a bubble, where people led a dream-like life. After "the long Swedish night"⁵ he lived through in 1954–1958, Foucault could at last satisfy his "Nietzschean need for the sun."[6] He marveled at the social significance of the light and color in Sidi Bou Saïd: "That Mediterranean light can be said to enhance the perception of values. In North Africa, everyone is taken for what he is worth. Every individual asserts himself by what he says, not by what he does or by his reputation. No one jumps up at the name of Sartre."[7] (It is worth noting how Sartre's shadow followed Foucault to Sidi Bou Saïd.) Initially Foucault lived at the Dar Zarouk Hotel while looking for a place on the slope of Sidi Bou Saïd's hill, as "he wanted to have with the sea an immediate and absolute rapport without civilization."[8] He eventually moved into the refurbished stables of the former Bey of Tunis.

Tunisia, or its region, was not entirely new to Foucault. He had visited with Daniel Defert before, when Defert taught philosophy in high school in Sfax in lieu of doing his military service.[9] He had also traveled to nearby Morocco,[10] and spent Christmas 1966 camping with Defert on the High Plateau of the Tassili des Ajjers in Algeria, surrounded by camels and donkeys.[11] However, Tunisia was the first and last Third World country where Foucault lived. Prior to going to Tunisia, he had lectured and held different positions as France's cultural adviser and director of various cultural institutions sponsored by French embassies.[12] He had been ostensibly searching for personal freedoms, which did not avail in France.[13] Homosexuality was still taboo in France in the 1950s, and thus Sweden, where he first lived, held up the promise of a freer society. However, Foucault soon realized that beneath its apparent freedom, Swedish society was also restrictive in its own way.[14] Poland proved to be "a prison."[15] Nevertheless, in Sweden he learned about a well-functioning social democratic political system as opposed to Poland, where he observed a dysfunctional and stifling people's democracy; in West Germany he witnessed a country in full economic growth.[16] He had at different points in his life contemplated settling in Brazil, and even in Congo-Kinshasa[17] but these fell short of being dreams of becoming a citizen of the world in a Kantian sense. They were most likely thoughts or desires for estrangement as well as adventure than viable alternatives to living in France. They may also have been attempts to teach in places that did not cause him any prejudice while he was waiting for the right position to open up in Paris.[18]

The range of Foucault's European experiences was different from what he observed in Tunisia, a North African country, the unacknowledged Orient close to home. Time and again in interviews he recounted the "impressive" and unique political experience he had in Tunisia. Indeed, although similar to the French May '68, the turmoil of March '68 in Tunis was quite different—a sentiment shared by Tunisian intellectuals who also think of March '68 as the precursor of the French May '68.[19] Besides, being in Tunisia gave Foucault the credentials necessary to speak authoritatively about political engagement without using May '68 as a coming of age, or a personal landmark.[20] Yet, by no means was Foucault living the life of a stranger, in isolation from home. Sidi Bou Saïd was filled with French intellectual expatriates, and thus offered him the opportunity to rekindle ties or make new acquaintances. He also made frequent trips back home, was in touch with friends and colleagues, kept abreast of French news, and continued to partake in debates about his work.[21]

Aware of Tunisia's place in the European imagination, Foucault mockingly remarked: "I had come because of the myths that actually all Europeans have of Tunisia: the sun, the sea, enveloping warmth of Africa, in a word I came to look for a Thebaid without the asceticism"—or for Ancient Egypt in Tunisia.[22] But he also perceived Tunisia as "a country blessed by history, one that deserves to live for ever because it was where Hannibal and St. Augustine lived."[23] Jélila Hafsia,[24] who arranged Foucault's lectures at the Club Culturel Tahar Haddad, of which she was the director, recounts their visit one Monday morning to the Carthage ruins, guided by a young archaeologist.[25] She described the pleasure Foucault experienced during the visit. However, Tunis (and Carthage) had also been the theater of the 8th crusade, and the place where the French king, Louis IX, canonized St. Louis, had perished in 1270. Furthermore, unlike his recognition of Hannibal and St. Augustine, Foucault showed little awareness of Sidi Bou Saïd's identity. Sidi Bou Saïd Abu Khalef Ibn Yahia Ibn Ettamini El Beji, was a medieval Sufi who resisted the crusades. His eponymous village was closed to foreigners until about the French occupation of Tunisia in 1881.[26] Legend in Tunisia, retold in several versions since the nineteenth century, and reported by several French travelers, described King Louis IX as having converted to Islam after meeting a Muslim Saint who made him realize the error of his (crusader) mission. Thereupon, the saint found a dying leper to stand in for the new convert to give the illusion that the king had died. The real crusader king was canonized as St. Louis, and as if to counter the legend, a chapel was erected in his honor in 1840 on land that France compelled the Tunisian government to cede to it on a hill in Carthage. The chapel itself was incorporated in the legend by the popular imagination, which saw it as a mosque for Sidi Bou Saïd, aka St. Louis.[27] Sidi Bou Saïd was thus at the center of layered images and symbols, including those of nineteenth-century France returning as an occupying power, virtually relinking with St Louis.[28]

Admittedly, Foucault's classical education predisposed him to reading Tunisia's present into its ancient past.[29] Nevertheless, Tunisia was for Foucault a historical heterotopia from which Arab and Islamic history had evaporated. The historical prism through which he considered Tunisians was all-encompassing. He defended men against a woman who complained of Tunisian male chauvinism: "They live among men. They are men and are made for men, with the fleeting bedazzlement, the brief reward of women."[30] Yet he related his appreciation of Tunisian males' purported homocentric attitude to a long-lost *Spanish* army tradition of "groups of ten men who never left one another."[31] These and other statements form the context within which his Tunisian students could say that he was "too Western to understand Tunisia."[32] It is unfortunate, however, that the students' comment equated the apparent incomprehension of Tunisian culture with being Western. The problem they identified lay elsewhere.

From Tunisia Foucault drove with Defert to Libya along the shore to Syrte and Leptis Magna to visit Greco-Roman sites.[33] The ancient past as well as the dream-like beauty of Sidi Bou Saïd framed Foucault's perception of events occurring around him; enhanced his preoccupation with self; and sharpened his understanding of the relationship between ancient Greece and the Orient. At Sidi Bou Saïd, Foucault cultivated the care for his body in a Nietzschean attempt to "become everyday a little bit more Greek, athletic, tanned, ascetic, and begin to give his existence a new style."[34] The preoccupation with ancient Greece while in Tunisia has resonance in the course Foucault gave in 1970–1971 at the College de France on "Leçons sur la volonté de savoir."[35] In the lectures, he sought, among other things, to trace the genealogy of knowledge as defined by Aristotle. Using the works of historians, such as Jean Pierre Vernant and Marcel Detienne,[36] Foucault noted the transformations that ancient Greeks brought to the Oriental heritage to create their distinctive notion of knowledge.[37] Although the written record of the lectures is often cryptic, the orientation Foucault took clearly favors cultural differences over similarities.[38] In Tunisia he searched for the survivals of Greek customs, thereby reversing the method he used in the lectures at the College de France, upon his (and Defert's) discovery of purportedly Greek homosexual/erotic practices among Tunisian males. There ensued a search for the extent of the intriguing practices that Defert thought were exactly as described in a classic book on Greek homosexuality.[39] Underlying the search is a sort of dubious anthropology of cultural survivals in North Africa[40] that dispenses with a consideration of the full range of influences that followed the Greek period, or non-Greek traces in the Greek practices.[41]

BEING IN TUNISIA IN TROUBLE, 1967–1968

The Letter

Beyond sun and sea, Foucault discovered something else: "In fact I met Tunisian students, and then it was love at first sight. It's probably only in Brazil and Tunisia that I have found so much seriousness and so much passion, passions so serious; and what delighted me more than anything is their absolute avidity for knowledge."[42]

A former protectorate of France since 1881, Tunisia became independent in 1956 and was led with an iron fist by Habib Bourguiba for thirty years. In August 1961 he had physically eliminated his most serious opponent and challenger, Salah Ben Youssef;[43] weathered serious crises with France; and initiated a controversial agrarian cooperative plan, which he was compelled to halt in 1969.[44] In 1956, he sponsored a liberal family law (Personal Status Code) banning polygamy—a mark of his commitment to modernism—although he maintained gender inequality in matters of inheritance. He had also democratized access to higher education, albeit actively controlling students' organizations, particularly the Union Générale des Etudiants Tunisiens (U.G.E.T). In 1966, when he arrived in Tunis, Foucault had just published *Les mots et les choses,* which established him as the foremost French philosopher. Needless to say, the Tunisian government as well as intellectuals felt extremely honored by his presence in Tunis.[45] He lectured in the philosophy department[46] about Nietzsche, Descartes, and the painter Manet, among others. He also gave popular public lectures on Friday afternoons.[47] He further spoke at the Club Culturel Tahar Haddad, where he discussed topics such as "structuralism and literary analysis" and "madness and civilization," both in spring 1967.[48]

The years Foucault spent in Tunisia were marked by severe social and political turmoil.[49] In 1966, a group of students had returned from France, where they had been studying, to form the Tunisian branch of an organization they had set up in Paris in October 1963, the Groupe d'Etudes et d'Action Socialistes Tunisien (G.E.A.S.T), also known by the name of its journal, *Perspectives.* Buoyed by the anti-colonial spirit of the time as well as the excitement generated by the Chinese Cultural Revolution, the G.E.A.S.T. agitated to put an end to Tunisia's authoritarian one-party rule and bring about freedom, democracy, and solidarity with movements of decolonization.[50] Besides Bourguiba's autocratic rule, students also opposed his foreign policy, which was aligned with the United States' while maintaining close ties with France.[51]

Although it included students with various political orientations, such as Trotskyites, the G.E.A.S.T. was primarily influenced by Maoist thought and became increasingly radicalized as state repression intensified. During Foucault's stay, *Perspectivists* engaged in a series of strikes and demonstrations that shook Foucault and other French expatriates' sense of complacency. On 5 June 1967, at the inception of the Six-Day War pitting Israel against Egypt and neighboring Arab states, demonstrations broke out in Tunis to protest the war as well as the government's support of the U.S. and U.K. pro-Israel policy.[52] The demonstrations got out of hand as attacks were staged against Jewish businesses and a synagogue. Shocked, Foucault wrote a letter to Georges Canguilhem describing and decrying the mayhem as a "day (a half-day) of pogrom. It was far more serious than *Le Monde* reported: a good fifty fires, one hundred or two hundred shops—the poorest of course—ransacked; the unforgettable spectacle of gutted synagogues; rugs dragged out in the streets, trampled on and burned; people running out in the streets taking refuge in a building the crowd wants to set on fire." He applauded the government's reaction, which he judged "quick and firm, and apparently sincere. But it [the violence] was obviously organized. Everybody knows that for weeks, no doubt months, 'this' was working underground, unbeknownst to the government and against it." He laid a strong blame on leftist students. He wrote: "In any case, nationalism plus racism adds up to something ghastly. And when one also adds the fact that the students, because they are leftist, lent a hand (and more) to all that, well, it makes one deeply sad. And one wonders through what strange cunning (or stupidity) of history Marxism could have provided the occasion (and vocabulary) for that."[53]

Foucault's understandable and deeply felt outrage was shared by leftist students. However, memoirs and other books indicate that it was the government, through students affiliated with the party in power (the Parti Socialiste Destourien) and using unemployed men, who provoked the mayhem under the benevolent eye of the police.[54] Individuals I interviewed, who had been involved in the demonstration, also dispute the accuracy of Foucault's account. A well known member of the protest movement, Simone Othmani Lellouche, who is Jewish, recalls that she had just driven some members of *Perspectives* to the site of the demonstration when she saw Ahmed Othmani, a student activist who would later become her husband,[55] and others gesturing and calling out to her from the other side of the street to admonish her to keep away, worried about her being caught in what they suspected would be attacks on Jews. As a result, they formed a cordon to protect Jewish citizens. Brahim Razgallah, one of the early adherents to *Perspectives,* noted that Foucault, whom he had not met primarily because he was in medical school at the time, while Foucault taught at the Faculty of Arts and Sciences, had simply accepted the government's interpretation of the event when it had been clear that the government had throughout the years of turmoil sought to discredit the Left. He revealed that an Italian television station had shown pictures supporting the students' account of the event.[56]

Surprising is not only the swiftness with which Foucault castigated the students, but also his uncritical view of the government. Indeed, the state under Bourguiba as well as his successor, was a security state with an extensive surveillance apparatus (with which Foucault was familiar), and could not have been unaware of the planned leftist students' demonstration.

The 5 June 1967 event is still a burning issue for Tunisians and a puzzle for researchers. Daniel Defert had no knowledge of Foucault's letter, and had not participated in the preparation of Eribon's biography of Foucault in which the letter appears. He reiterates the interpretation of the "pogrom" he gave in *Dits et écrits*[57] as probably instigated by the Destour Party, eager to arrest leftist students as well as give the United States assurances that Tunisia would not join the June War on the side of Egypt.[58] Defert recalls Foucault's personal communication to him: "Soldiers were strutting down Tunis streets for three days to indicate they were ready for the War but would not go."[59] From his perspective, Foucault must have written the letter on the spur of the moment under the shock of the news he had just heard.[60] After Defert returned from a trip to Israel during the June War, Foucault gave him a different and more accurate account of the event clearly laying the blame on the Destour Party, eager to find a pretext to discredit and arrest leftists.[61]

For Simone Othmani Lellouche the event has special resonance, as she had been vilified by the government in the thick of the repression as an agent of Zionism.[62] She recalls a time when she and fellow militants strenuously opposed those who sought to cancel a seminar convened by a noted historian at the University of Tunis, featuring an Israeli scholar. Nevertheless, even a former member of the Tunisian Communist Party, Gilbert Naccache, claimed he left Tunisia for France as a result of the 5 June event. When told, Razagallah reportedly suggested to Naccache that the severe repression that followed the 5 June 1967 demonstration was most likely the reason for his departure rather the 5 June event, as a number of non-Jewish people, including Razgallah, also left. At any rate witnesses also disagree with Foucault that Marxism provided them with a "vocabulary" for anti-Semitism.

The significance of Foucault's letter to Canguilhem[63] does not lie in its inaccurate contents, but in what it reveals about Foucault's interpretative framework. It points to Foucault's insistence, as with the Iranian Revolution, on relating unusual events to a failure of Marxist thought. It further denotes a moment when Foucault's personal political views intruded on his usually acute analysis of power. Transcending his justified outrage, the complete reversal of Foucault's interpretation of a delicate event gives short shrift to the complexity of cultural difference, which Foucault did not discern. Occurring after the publication of *Les mots et les choses,* the letter is difficult to reconcile with his critique of anthropology. Indeed, if there is no assumption that can be made about humans as agents of their thoughts and actions, how is it possible to characterize students' behavior in a general way? The putative behavior of the students as described in the letter was inferred from a presumed conscious act of applying Marxist thought in order to express a will to discriminate.

Foucault and Bourguiba's Repression

State repression after 5 June 1967 was swift: a student leader, Mohammad Ben Jennet, was arrested and condemned to twenty years in hard labor. He would become the focus of international calls for his release and condemnations of Bourguiba's repressive methods. The conviction of Ben Jennet, a student of the Zitouna University (an old and respected center of Islamic learning), also active among *Perspectivists,* holds an important place in the students' movement. A committee for his liberation was formed gathering together students of all political persuasions, eager to use his case as a symbol of judicial arbitrariness. Ben Jennet was an easy scapegoat: not only was he singled out for being associated with the Zitouna, but his physical disability, lameness, made him particularly vulnerable to identification and arrest.[64] There were more demonstrations staged in January 1968 in protest of Vice President Hubert H. Humphrey's visit. At the same time, the Comité de Solidarité avec le Peuple Vietnamien, which included members of *Perspectives,* organized protests against another state visitor, Tran Van Do, the South Vietnamese minister of foreign affairs.[65]

The demonstrations protesting the presence of both Hubert H. Humphrey and Tran Van Do included members not only of *Perspectives,* but also of the Tunisian Communist Party (banned in 1963), as well as students with Ba'athist persuasions. Vietnam, to which some members of *Perspectives* felt indebted for the independence of Tunisia,[66] and the Palestinian question[67] came to symbolize the oddity of a state out of step with the anti-imperialist mood of the global students' movement at the time. The Tunisian government's foreign policy appeared to be at odds with the people's sentiments in an era of decolonization, barely six years after the creation of the Non-Aligned movement, and a decade after the anti-colonial Afro-Asian declaration of Bandoeng pledging cooperation among Third World countries.[68] Bourguiba chafed at Gamel Abdel Nasser's anti-imperialist and pan-Arab political orientation, and the leadership role Nasser was assuming in the Arab world.[69]

The January protests were followed by more and larger protests and strikes (which spread to high schools and grade schools) in March '68, calling for the release of Mohammad Ben Jennet as well as for reforms of the political system toward greater democracy and the protection of human rights. In this sense, March '68 in Tunisia was the forerunner of May '68 in France. There were mass arrests of students, some of whom were subjected to various forms of torture.[70] Sentences were particularly heavy (up to twenty years) and given in a special court, which denied the accused due process. Charges against students ranged from subversion, to foreign-aided conspiracy, to offense to a head of state. One of those arrested tortured and convicted was Ahmed Ben Othman, aka Reddaoui[71] (who will later use the name "Othmani"), a leading member of *Perspectives* and a student of Foucault's.[72] Ben Othman's heavy (twelve-year) sentence was undoubtedly in the back of Foucault's mind when he mentioned to his interviewer, D. Trombadori, that there is no comparing French students on the barricades in Paris in 1968 and Tunisian students who risked fifteen years in prison for engaging in protests (although Ben Jennet had been sentenced to twenty years).[73]

During the March 1968 movement there were exchanges between Tunisians and French students and activists, as a number of Tunisians, many of them having studied in France at the time of the founding of *Perspectives,* traveled back and forth between the two countries. Daniel Defert helped to smuggle messages, at times hiding them in his socks.[74] Furthermore, Alain Geismar, who became a leader of May '68, made a trip to Tunis at the behest of the French community of teachers in Tunisia to lend support to the striking students.[75] However, the French ambassador cautioned his compatriots against getting involved. But Foucault became involved in his own way. In fact he felt that "being French, I was in some way protected from local authorities. I was consequently able to easily do a series of actions, and at the same time, to gauge with accuracy the reactions of the French state before all of that."[76] It is noteworthy that in retrospect, as he answered questions from interviewers, he modestly avoided describing the help he gave Tunisian students. Yet he theoretically ran the risk of being arrested and tortured (as his compatriot, the agronomist Jean-Paul Chabert, had been)[77] or expelled from the country as Anglicist Jean Gattégno, or psycho-ethnologist Georges Lapassade, among others, had been. Foucault permitted students to draft and copy tracts at his Sidi Bou Saïd home; concealed leaflets in his garden; transported some leftist students, hidden in the back of his car;[78] and gave refuge to Ahmed Ben Othman when the police were searching for him.[79] Foucault was also badly beaten by unknown assailants, who may have been police officers, in what was probably a setup: he had been driving a Tunisian sexual partner back to his home upon his request when he was stopped in traffic, pulled out of his car, and severely beaten. Defert charges that Foucault had been in effect "tortured."[80] The following day, the culture minister summoned Foucault to his office to chat without commenting on the visible fresh bruises, virtually indicating that the attack was a warning.[81] This was a traumatic event in Foucault's life, which he did not wish to see publicized.[82]

However, in spite of this attack, Foucault's notoriety as a popular French philosopher afforded him some protection from the harshness with which the Bourguiba government treated all those suspected or found guilty of support for Tunisian students. There was even a time, possibly at New Year's, when Foucault received a box of dates from Bourguiba. He shared the gift with students, while teasing them about eating the dates.[83] In September '68, when the students' trial started, Foucault had made a financial contribution to the defense fund and attempted to testify at Ahmed Ben Othman's trial in vain. He had also been unable to secure the intervention of the French ambassador.[84] Feeling under surveillance and unwelcome, Foucault left for France in October 1968 to take up a position at the University of Nanterre, and thus did not serve the full term for his three-year leave of absence.[85] He did not return to Tunis until 1971 for a lecture on "Madness and Civilization."[86]

After he left Tunisia, Foucault continued to support the movement, among other things, by gathering testimony in favor of Ben Othman from his former French professors and writing a letter testifying to the good character and intellectual value of his former student.[87] Additionally, with Jean Gattégno, the poet Michel Beau, and Daniel Defert, he helped to organize long-distance courses for the prisoners of the Bordj Er Roumi jail from the University of Paris VIII (Vincennes).[88] However, there is some controversy over the extent to which Foucault participated in the March '68 political events. Georges Lapassade, an ethno-psychologist and faculty member at the university in Tunis, who frequently quarreled with Foucault, pointed out that although he had agreed not to teach during the students' strike, Foucault had lectured as usual but students did not attend. Lapassade noted that, unlike Foucault, *he* had been arrested by Tunisian authorities and deported for having disrupted classes in violation of the terms of his contract, which prohibited French personnel from meddling in Tunisian domestic affairs. Finally, Lapassade reproached Foucault for not having objected more vigorously to his deportation.[89] The relationship between the two men was complicated. Lapassade was an outspoken critic of Bourguiba, whereas Foucault took a more guarded approach.[90] According to Defert, students had asked Foucault not to leave in the manner that Lapassade did by taking a stand and risking being deported. As it turned out, even keeping quiet was not free of risks.

BETWEEN TUNIS '68 AND PARIS '68

Foucault and Students' Marxism

Foucault's lectures, safe as they were thematically, could not have taken place at a worst time, given the conjuncture of Vietnam, Palestine, leftist activism, anti-imperialist sentiments, state repression, etc. Foucault did not remain neutral, but carefully chose his action. His support of students in Tunis reflected his opposition to restrictions on individual freedoms. He had been opposed to such restrictions in Poland and in Russia. He was genuinely appalled by the harshness of the sentences meted out to students for having demonstrated against war and for democracy. However, by inclination he was also reluctant to take great risk for the sake of individual freedoms. He explained for example that "at the time of Algeria [the Algerian War], I had not been able to participate directly either, and if I had, it would not have been at the risk of my personal security."[91] Foucault's remarkable candor is laudable. His concern for his safety sheds light on a paradoxical aspect of his thought. He greatly admired Tunisian students, "these girls and boys who took formidable risks by writing a tract, passing it around or calling for a strike. This was for me a genuine political experience."[92] Undoubtedly, Foucault witnessed something new that shook him up. He had been aware of people in Algeria, some of them French, who had risked their lives like Tunisian students. Considering that it is risk taking that struck Foucault's imagination, the risk these and other men and women took was as great as that of the Tunisian students. The difference between other instances of people taking risks to bring about change and the actions of the Tunisian students lies in Foucault's seeing with his own eyes the students' protests and witnessing the severity of the sentences they received. However, the absence of a perspective on risk taking lends an exceptional character to Foucault's analysis.[93] It also gives a glimpse into Foucault's restrictive conception of political engagement. Although Tunisian students' determination and risk taking could not be uniquely non-Western/Third World, risking life or loss of freedom does not exhaust the range of possibilities of political engagement.

It is true that Foucault wished to contrast March '68 in Tunis with May '68 in Paris, which he had not experienced. He evinced a sort of pride in recounting how "one day, Marcuse asked in a reproachful tone what I had been doing at the time of the barricades in May. Well, I was in Tunisia. And I must add, it was an important experience."[94] Tunisia, which Foucault frequently noted was a "Third World country" in his allusions to his life outside of France, played a role in alleviating a symbolic guilt, not acknowledged but hovering over his interviews, with regard to his absence from France during May 1968. As he put it, "This is what Tunisia meant for me: I had to enter the political debate. It was not May '68 in France, but March '68, in a Third World country."[95] In the interview, D. Trombadori asked Foucault whether he was not intent on diminishing the significance of May '68, thereby depriving the French students of the depth of their commitment to Marxism.[96] Foucault's answer reflects his conflicted relation to Marxism as well as a categorical cultural determinism unwittingly cast as a positive event. From Foucault's perspective, whether in his students' years, in the early fifties, or during May '68, Marxism lent itself to "cold, academic discussions." Furthermore, in countries such as Poland, Marxism was taught as a sort of "catechism," and thus caused only "disgust" among students. After his return to France from Tunisia, he had been disappointed in "the endless discussions, the hyper-marxisation, the irrepressible discursivity typical of university life, especially at Vincennes in 1969."[97] In other words, Marxism in France was an intellectual exercise centered on questions of doctrine and strategy.

Naturally, Marxism did orient concrete action (although its French proponents lacked the passion seen in Tunis) but it was also divisive. In the aftermath of May '68, French Marxists had indeed split up into myriads of small groups at odds with one another in a process known as *groupusculation*. However, this process implicitly was the result of a tradition of reflection on theory, method, and practice; it was also an ideological struggle. By contrast, Tunisian students' "training in Marxist thought was neither very deep, nor did it lend itself to deepening. The real debate among them, on the choice of tactics and strategy on what they needed to choose was filtered through different interpretations of Marxism. On the one hand, the role of a political ideology or of a political perception of the world was undoubtedly indispensable to launching the struggle; but, on the other hand, the precision of the theory and its scientific character were completely secondary questions which functioned more as an illusion ('*leurre*') than a principle of conduct at once correct and just."[98]

Simone Othmani Lellouche agrees with Foucault's assessment of the G.E.A.S.T.'s knowledge of Marxism. She remembers individual members oscillating between Marxist trends (Leninist, Trotskyite, Maoist), although many had read Marx only while they were imprisoned.[99] In reminiscing about the past, leading members such as Othmani and Naccache acknowledged that their lack of theoretical grounding and their (inexperienced) youth accounted for their increasing radicalization with its doctrinaire sectarianism, intolerance of individuals with differing political outlooks, entrism, as well as lack of democracy within the organization.[100] Naccache endorses Foucault's assessment entirely and quotes a large segment of it in his book, mostly, it seems, to draw attention to the students' fearless commitment to change, rather than ideology.[101] Schooled in the Communist Party at an early age, Naccache expected a total commitment to Marxist ideology from his Tunisian fellow members, most of whom were born Muslims. He remarked that some of them felt they were "Arab before being Marxist."[102]

For Zeineb Ben Saïd Cherni, a philosopher and former student of Foucault, there was an element of "classical" Marxism in the students' lifestyle and attitudes toward sexual freedom. However, their "total engagement, their type of paradigm of liberty, was different from classical Marxism," which puts a premium on the class struggle. Although anti-imperialists, they were also focused on pursuing the unfinished work and unfulfilled promise of the independence of Tunisia from France.[103]

If surviving members of the movement agree with Foucault's assessment of their knowledge of Marxism, others thought of Foucault at the time as "right-wing," and were annoyed by his frequent references to Nietzsche, which they thought were deliberately provocative.[104] Ahmed Hasnaoui, a former student of Foucault's, but not a *Perspectivist*, confirms Foucault's penchant for provocation, frequently pressing on with his ideas and arguments to satisfy his curiosity.[105] Ironically, it was in Tunisia that Foucault read Trotsky and Rosa Luxemburg as well as the Black Power literature.[106] In the Black Panthers, Foucault found a group engaged in a struggle that "dispensed with a Marxist theory of society." A few weeks into his stay in Tunis, Foucault had been struck by the earnestness with which students approached Althusser's ideas. He wrote to Defert: "It is strange to see what is to us a purely theoretical discourse suddenly becomes here an almost immediate imperative."[107]

When Foucault came to Tunis he was already in his post-Marxist phase. Indeed, as Ahmed Hasnaoui notes, Foucault had placed Ricardo and Marx in the same episteme. Reportedly, after Hasnaoui explained to a puzzled Foucault that Marxism was for the students a reading lens through which they could "free themselves" (*se déprendre*), Foucault started paying more attention to the students' use of Marxist thought.[108] Whatever the case may be, students were not swayed by Foucault's skepticism about their Marxism. They did not invite him to their meetings, nor did they seek his advice, although according to Hasnaoui they knew he was interested.[109] Yet as repression intensified, some of them met at Foucault's house, leaving open the possibility that he took part in the discussions. Defert's own experience partially confirms Foucault's assessment of the theoretical poverty of the students' Marxism. Defert had suggested to students that they target tourism agencies (tourism being a major source of the Tunisian state's revenue) in a joint action with his militant colleagues in France to draw attention to the plight of prisoners. Students declined purportedly because they wanted a more "proletarian action." Yet tourism thrived outside of cities, not in working-class neighborhoods.

To return to Foucault's characterization of the students' Marxism, his emphasis on "science" as the standard against which to gauge the quality of the student's theoretical orientation harks back to his interpretation of the Chinese encyclopedia, which too lacked the "table" that prefigured the scientific systems of classification of nature developed in the West. Nevertheless, in focusing on science, Foucault unwittingly negates the passion, commitment, and risk taking among students that so impressed him. The label he formulated for capturing the Marxist orientation of those among the militant students who frequently met at his house, "sino-castrists," plays symbolically on several registers.[110] The juxtaposition of China with Cuba lends more force to Foucault's perception of the theoretical poverty and lack of scientific rigor of the students' Marxism. Their orientation owed less to Marx and more to Castro and China as a whole. Mao loses his specificity, as does Maoism, which played a great role in May '68 too. Yet, to reiterate, the students' movement was not monolithic and included all sorts of Marxist currents. But Foucault's characterization was hardly consistent. Simone Othmani Lellouche remembers a statement he made at the end of a philosophy lecture that had not been taped, according to which "there is a moment when we are all together for Marxism, and there are moments when the individual is alone."[111] Was this, she wonders, because Foucault was convinced that the movement had been infiltrated by the "flics" (cops)? It could also mean that Foucault had once more shifted positions in a manner reminiscent of a pendulum oscillating back and forth.[112]

In interviews about his stay in Tunisia, Foucault was selective about the political events he discussed, disregarding the June '67 protests. For example, he focused on the March '68 protests against the Vietnam War and for civil liberties at home, including the release of students who had been jailed in the June demonstrations. Years later, in explaining the students' fearlessness and risk taking, Foucault implied that the students' behavior was extraordinary and thus had to have been sustained by belief in a "myth, a spirituality."[113] It is unclear what Foucault meant by "myth." The concept does not reflect his view that Marxism gave the Tunisian students a "sort of moral energy, a thoroughly remarkable *existential* act [emphasis added],"[114] in contrast with the cold discussions that took place among French students in Paris. Was it the myth of a Marxist utopia? Was it the hope that Tunisian students could bring about change in spite of severe repression, as Iranians would in 1979? Was it that in addition to agitating for change while appealing to Marxist ideals, students also held the religious conviction that God was with them? Or, was it that the students' Marxist conviction held for them a religious meaning?

The interview with D. Trombadori took place at the end of 1978, a time when Foucault was reporting about the Iranian Revolution. First used in his reporting on Iran, the concept of "political spirituality" seems out of context in a discussion of Tunisian demonstrators. In Iran, Shi'ism played a role in mass protests. But did Islam play a role in March '68? Foucault does not discuss Islam in his analysis of the Tunisian protests. Yet, one of the jailed student leaders and cause célèbre of the June '67 protests was a graduate of the reputed theological school of El Zitouna, and only spoke Arabic. This naturally did not make Mohammad Ben Jennet an Islamist. But the Tunisian government considered such students as well as members of the banned Communist Party enemies of the state.[115] What's more, Foucault's awareness of the movement excluded its views on religion. Although secular in their outlook, many of the students were heirs to the modernist-reformist trend sweeping the Arab world at the time.[116] Nevertheless, the notion of political spirituality as the melding of religious passion with political action appears contrived in Foucault's recounting of March '68 in Tunis. The June '67 or March '68 protests had little to do with Islam as a religion or an Islamist claim to power. They were focused on international[117] and national issues, which a Marxist analysis would necessarily see as linked. However, the use of "political spirituality" speaks of a consciousness that accepts and acts out a myth, or experiences the spiritual as a motivating force. Were the Tunisian students, the most active among them members of the radical left, acting out a myth consciously or were they acted through by myth and spirituality? In light of the Tunisian Revolution of 2011, the ideals pursued by the March '68 students appear real and their search enduring.

THE COLONIAL FACTOR: RECOGNITION AND SILENCE

Limits of Recognition

Foucault's awareness of the colonial factor in Tunisia is indisputable. In a sense he could not have avoided it. Indeed, *Perspectivists* inscribed their action in the framework of national struggles for liberation. As students in Paris they had interacted with other Third World students and participated in meetings and demonstrations in the highly political university life of the time.[118] According to Hasnaoui, Foucault knew North African history well and was fascinated by the Algerian War.[119] He was also knowledgeable about Islamic civilization. Foucault once suggested to him that perhaps a good way of rekindling classical Islamic civilization would be to "turn one's back to it." Hasnaoui took the comment to mean that "a radical contestation would be a manner of renewing it [Islamic civilization]."[120] He clearly identified some instruments of the reproduction of the colonial situation in Tunisia: continued reliance on French technical staff and language. Hasnaoui recounts a "provocative remark" Foucault made to him: "It was easy to kick the French soldiers out, but what about these people [the French *coopérants*]. What's this called?"[121] Even more important, Foucault had the merit of posing language as a dimension of colonialism. As he put it: "In Tunisia, teaching was carried out in French by a French staff, thus it was the problem of colonialism and national independence that was posed. The anti-government attack was an attack against authoritarian methods, but also against the government's submission to, and dependence on foreign interests. Hence, in the Third World, the anti-authoritarian struggle is automatically inscribed in a more general political struggle thereby losing its specificity."[122] In no small measure was Foucault's awareness of language as part of the colonial factor in his brief analysis of the Tunisian situation ahead of some of the students.[123] Besides, many in France's other former colonies, such as Algeria or Morocco, have yet to fully grasp the significance of this linguistic fact as Foucault did.

On close inspection, however, Foucault's view of the colonial situation is distinctly restrictive at a theoretical level. He paradoxically sees colonialism (or neocolonialism, which he observed in action) as a *general* political struggle divorced from specific power struggles in Western countries. This division obscures the close relationship between colonialism and authoritarianism in colonizing countries. The relationship becomes clear at times of crises as was evident in the manner in which the state suppressed the May '68 movement in France. The relationship is also manifest in France's treatment of prisoners as Foucault saw in the work of the GIP (Groupe d'Information sur les Prisons). What's more, it is the experience of prejudice in France that convinced at least one leading figure of *Perspectives* to go back home and start agitating for political change.[124]

In Tunisia, Foucault became aware of abject poverty: "I had as auditors, as students people who had spent their childhood in a really illiterate milieu. Their parents did not know how to read or write; there were no books in their homes, there was not even electricity; and thus there was no way they could study at home. What does it mean to have access to knowledge for these people? We cannot imagine, we who have always been nurtured by this petty (*petit*) competitive knowledge in which, I think, we swim or almost do."[125] What Foucault describes is a major aspect of life in the colonies. His student, Ahmed Ben Othman, was born during the colonial era to a nomadic tribe, in the region of Gafsa-Sidi Bou Zid, notorious for its armed struggle for decolonization. His family gave shelter to guerillas and he recalled taking food to combatants in the mountains. As he put it "I saw up close the tanks and planes the French used in the 50's. When I was ten, soldiers nearly burned down my parents' tent to force them to give away the *fellagha* [combatants]."[126] His father, who was bigamous, learned to read and write at thirty, with his children; Othmani, himself, did not start formal schooling until he moved to

Tunis at age thirteen. Hence, what Foucault discovered among his students was a common condition among rural people in colonized Tunisia, which the postindependence government had not remedied.

Paradoxically, Foucault stressed the significance of the twilight of empire in the reshuffling of the deck among the French Left. As he put it: "Finally, we need to recall the Algerian War. For us, those who were most radically opposed to it were mostly members of the PCF [French Communist Party] or those close to it. But we did not find support in the Party, which had an ambiguous attitude towards the war. And it paid dearly for it as it progressively lost control over youth and students and ended up with the largest oppositions in 1968–1970. In fact with the Algerian War ends a long period during which the Left had naively believed that the Communist Party, struggles for justice and just causes were one and the same thing."[127] It is true that the PCF for a long time subordinated the resolution of the colonial question to the interest of the working classes in industrial countries. Not only does Foucault express his disenchantment with the PCF, but he assigns the end of colonialism a historic role in Western philosophy of freedom and revolution. In Japan he would attribute the crisis of Western thought to the end of imperialism.

Silence

Given his awareness, why was Foucault silent on the colonial factor in Tunisia? Was it because Sartre had been vocal about the issue?[128] Daniel Defert explains how delicate it was for Foucault and him to raise this touchy issue with Tunisians. From his perspective, compared to Algeria, which put an end to colonialism in a "heroic" manner, Tunisia had negotiated its gradual independence. Eager to avoid another war, the French government initiated talks with Bourguiba while he was still in prison, at the first sign of a military escalation of the struggle for decolonization.[129] Besides, Bourguiba, out of pragmatism and personal inclination, was pro-French regardless of his alliance with the United States. Nevertheless, there is something disquieting about Foucault's silence on the issue. It raises the question of his tolerance for a security state that wreaked havoc among his own students and subjected him to tight surveillance. Foucault's phone, graciously offered by Bourguiba, was tapped; his mail was opened; and his movements were watched.[130] Above and beyond personal style and attitude toward political figures, Foucault's silence connotes a tacit acquiescence to the prevailing view among Europeans that Bourguiba may have been a dictator, be he was a modernist and a friend of the West.[131]

The abstractness of life in Sidi Bou Saïd heterotopia was a contributing factor to Foucault's silence. In Sidi Bou Saïd, even discussions with students about the political events were highly "theorized,"[132] filtered by the environment, and thus seemed remote. Besides, the heterotopia itself was a feature of the neocolonial system Foucault identified. It made possible the double life he was experiencing, one in ancient Greece, the other in a version of France as Tunis university life must have seemed. The heterotopic life was undoubtedly reinforced by the language barrier, which cut Foucault off from an important part of everyday life. (Aware of the use of French, Foucault did not mention Arabic.) There is finally the shadow of Kant's cosmopolitan anthropology. Foucault was reluctant to identify the colonial factor as universal (referring to it instead as "general"), although paradoxically he acknowledged its impact on the universal character of Western thought. There is to be sure a personal political conviction that accounts for Foucault's skepticism about Third World revolutions.

Foucault and the Experience of Engagement

What was the effect that March '68 and May '68 had on Foucault as a philosopher? In the aftermath of May '68, the extreme fragmentation of French Marxism fissured the power of the party line and thus progressively created an intellectual climate such that his work on madness or psychiatry was given a second, nondoctrinaire look, as these issues were now discussed openly. He could speak out on issues such as medicine or prisons, which began to resonate with the public.[133] But March '68 also taught him how to engage the world on his own terms, with ostensibly something similar to the *existential* commitment he had witnessed among the Tunisian students: "I tried to do things that imply a personal commitment, physical as well as real, and that would pose problems in precise and concrete terms as defined inside a given situation."[134] In other words, May '68 freed Foucault from the dogmatism of the French Left, which had refused to hear him; March '68 had little identifiable theoretical import,[135] but helped to orient him toward becoming a specific intellectual, who would address *specific* issues that matter to him *personally*.

Zeineb Ben Saïd Cherni thinks that the concept of biopolitics (as well as *Discipline and Punish*) originated in Foucault's Tunisian experience. By undergoing torture and incarceration, and by staging hunger strikes, Perspectivists like herself had demonstrated that "the body and affect are forms of resistance to power, a counter-power" that incessantly reproduces itself as the struggle continued after jail, and new strategies of resistance were adopted. Besides, such forms of resistance may have had a "mnemonic effect" that was transmitted to later generations.[136] Echoing others, Cherni concludes that in the end, although Foucault provided precious support to students in Tunis as well as Paris, Tunisia benefited him more. Yet, Foucault credited both March '68 as well as May '68 with making him realize that his work before 1968 had in fact been the study of power even though he thought he had been writing the history of knowledge.[137]

The Tunisian students' protests were part of a universal yearning for freedom and coincided with other protests occurring simultaneously in West Germany, Poland, and Senegal, among other places. Foucault notes: "What was really at stake, what really made things change was of the same nature in France as well as in Tunisia."[138] Whether he had in mind the movement's tactics and strategies, Marxist engagement, or something else remains unclear. But the changes on him were the same. The connection between the Tunisian and French movements called for an exploration of the existential as well as political meaning of colonial domination and its aftermath. To a degree, and taking into consideration personal predilection and choice, Foucault's experience in Tunis illustrates his struggles with Kant's cosmopolitanism. In the midst of cultural difference, yet universal aspirations, Foucault remained centered on himself. However, he did so with a difference insofar as he claimed a change in his relation to his own environment. He met Kant halfway: he returned to Paris from Tunis a Frenchman eager to espouse French or European causes, some of which naturally involved Third World immigrants to France.[139] In this his attitude was consistent with his critique of Kant's cosmopolitan anthropology. Where Kant aimed for the universal in the local, Foucault looked for the local in the universal. The latter remained unexplored for its human aspirational content.

I do not wish to diminish the transformative effect that Tunisia may have had on Foucault. Tunisians credit Foucault's involvement in the GIP to March '68. But this claim may be exaggerated.[140] In reality, the effect of March '68 has an epistemic resonance when analyzed through the concept of experience. Foucault defined experience as "neither true nor false. It is always fictitious; it is something that makes itself (*se fabrique à soi-même*), something that did not exist before and which will exist afterwards."[141] This does not mean that he fabricated his Tunisian experience, simply that he constructed its significance in the context of events that were taking place in France as well. Foucault carefully defines the role of experience, which he believes is central to his desire to produce two effects in the reader (as well as himself). First, the reader recognizes the truthfulness of the issue discussed; second, the reader experiences sufficient detachment from the issue to perceive it as being "altered." This process of detachment and transformation summarizes, according to Foucault, a relation (albeit unconscious) to modernity, "a transformation of our relation to ourselves as well as to the world where up until then we recognized ourselves unproblematically (in a word, with our knowledge)."[142] In his *books* experience effectuates not only a transformation but also "a metamorphosis such that it acquires a certain value, a certain character that makes it accessible to and relivable by others (*faite par les autres*)."[143]

In focusing on the relationship between experience and transformation, Foucault came close to illustrating Kant's focus on the transformative effect of pragmatic anthropology from the local to the cosmopolitan. He further specifies that experience must be "linked to a collective practice, a way of thinking."[144] The personal experience (whether of madness, psychiatry, or death in medical knowledge) from which Foucault begins in order to arrive at a larger study of institutions is different from starting with the experience of Tunisian students' defying imprisonment and arriving at a personal decision to be selectively engaged politically. He shows little evidence of a self-transforming relation to cultural otherness. The process would be different had it involved starting with the observation that Tunisian students' staked their freedom and arriving at an understanding of colonialism or neocolonialism such that he, the Tunisians, and other formerly colonized people would have at once a sense of recognition of the experience of colonialism and be altered by its analysis. By observing the language dimension of colonialism Foucault made a step toward this outcome. As in Japan or Iran, Foucault remained an outsider looking in through a window. Perhaps the window in Tunis was a bit larger than in Iran or Japan because his audience spoke his language. Nevertheless, language could only be an additional barrier to a cosmopolitan anthropological view.

His preoccupation with Greek sexual practices among Tunisian males may have blotted out other, more political concerns. It made the heterotopia a space in which the ancient past came alive. Perhaps his "discovery of Arabs"[145] in Tunisia did not dispel the fantasy of the search for a live Greece transported into the present of the Orient at the door of France. The role of colonial knowledge in keeping the fantasy alive was not addressed.

Ultimately gaming was an aspect of Foucault's experience of Tunisia, as it was in Japan. Foucault did not take Tunisian students' Marxism seriously. In fact, he found it amusing.[146] His ubiquitous laugh hovers over Tunisia as it did over the Chinese encyclopedia. Macey suggests that the *Archaeology of Knowledge,* which Foucault completed while in Tunisia, contains the beginning of a shift in his thinking about "progressive politics."[147] Was this an example of how the Tunisian "experience" affected Foucault's theoretical thinking? Was this apparent shift toward a specific type of political engagement a harbinger of how Foucault interpreted the Iranian Revolution? It could be, except that Foucault's interest in Iran centered on its having escaped colonialism whereas Tunisia's colonial past left him intellectually indifferent, albeit politically sympathetic to Tunisian students. Foucault's experience of cultural difference in Japan will reveal the hiatus between progressive politics and understanding cultural difference to which his Tunisian heterotopia was a precursor.

NOTES

1. Foucault's leave from the Lycée of Clermont Ferrand, where he had been teaching, was not approved until 1 October 1966. Daniel Defert, "Chronologie," in *Dits et écrits*, vol. 1, 38.
2. Foucault did not allow the publication of this lecture until 1984. A shorter version of it appears in *Dits et écrits*, vol. 2, 1571–81. There is also a full text of a series of two radio conferences given on 7 and 11 December, 1966, on French culture on *Le corps utopique; suivi de les hétérotopies*, ed., Daniel Defert (Clamecy: Nouvelles Editions Lignes, 2009). The reference to Djerba is on p. 31.
3. The *paillotes* were individual huts set on the beach, with curtains and mattresses placed on an elevated platform, where nude tourists were served lunch.
4. At the time, young Frenchmen had the option of serving out their draft teaching or rendering some technical service to Tunisia, as *coopérants*. However, French people other than draftees could work in Tunisia on a contractual basis if they had the required skills.
5. Defert, "Chronologie," 25.
6. Ibid.
7. Michel Foucault. "Conversation sans complexes avec le philosophe qui analyse les 'structures du pouvoir,'" in *Dits et écrits*, vol. 2, 670.
8. Defert, "Chronologie," 38.
9. David Macey, *The Lives of Michel Foucault*, 148. Macey notes that Foucault and Defert traveled together in the country during the Christmas holiday in 1964–1965.
10. Ibid., 184.
11. Defert, "Chronologie," 38.
12. Foucault was director of La Maison de France in Uppsala, Sweden (1955–1958); cultural adviser and head of the university Center of French Civilization in Warsaw, Poland (1958–1959); and director of the Institut Français in Hamburg, Germany (1959–1960). Ibid., 24–28.
13. Michel Foucault, "Une interview de Michel Foucault par Stephen Riggins," trans. F. Durand-Bogaert, in *Dits et écrits*, vol. 2, 1345.
14. Ibid.
15. Defert, "Chronologie," 27. Defert quotes from a letter Foucault had sent a friend.

16. Foucault, "Entretien avec Michel Foucault," (interview by D. Trombadori), in *Dits et écrits,* vol. 2, 897.
17. Eribon, *Michel Foucault,* 143.
18. Eribon, 197, notes that in a letter to Foucault, sociologist Raymond Aron gently cautioned him about taking a position Fernand Braudel had offered him as director of studies in the sixth section of the Ecole Pratique des Hautes Etudes because the Collège de France, which Foucault was angling for (albeit with a shy circumspection), had "a low opinion" of the section. Thus, being abroad or even at Nanterre may have been less stigmatizing than accepting the position. David Macey reports that Daniel Defert thought that given the success of *Les mots et les choses,* Foucault might have wished to give his companion some space within which to develop his own work. Macey, *The Lives of Michel Foucault,* 184.
19. All interviews I had with Tunisian intellectuals who have been involved in the March '68 events agree on this point.
20. Macey suggests that after May '68, "not having taken part in the May events was a serious sin of political omission." Macey, *The Lives of Michel Foucault,* 207.
21. Macey refers to interviews Foucault gave as well as his rejoinders to critiques of his work during this period, especially Jean Paul Sartre's, as "the theoretical war." Ibid., 193.
22. The Larousse dictionary defines *Thébaïde* as an "isolated place conducive to meditation." The term refers to ancient Southern Egypt, where a number of Christian hermits lived. The conflation of ancient Egypt with contemporary Tunisia speaks to Foucault's moral geography of Tunisia-qua-Orient.
23. Eribon, *Michel Foucault,* 187.
24. Macey asserts that Hafsia "confessed to having been forlornly in love with him" [Foucault], 189. Writing before Macey, Eribon mentions Hafsia's "passions" for Foucault, 189. In an interview (Tunis, 26 March 2017) Hafsia vehemently denied this characterization. She admired Foucault for his "exceptional simplicity and generosity." He encouraged her to read his *History of Madness* and offered to help her with it against her objection that, as a self-taught woman, she was not equipped to understand it. Whenever she went to Paris, he met her and had lunch or dinner with her, often at his place, to the dismay of her friends who also knew him. She appreciated what she perceived as his supportive, if not protective, attitude toward her. Hafsia had been the wife of the chief of staff of the minister of justice (1956–58) under Bourguiba.
25. Jélila Hafsia, "Quand la passion de l'intelligence illuminait Sidi Bou Saïd," *La presse tunisienne,* 6 July 1984, 16.
26. Several dates have been put forth for when Sidid Bou Saïd village opened to foreigners (1827, 1846, 1890). Afrodesia E. McCannon, "The King's Two Lives: The Tunisian Legend of Saint Louis," *Journal of Folklore Research* 43, no. 1 (January–April 2006): 61.
27. Ibid., 64. The chapel was eventually torn down in 1950, as a cathedral (also named after St. Louis) had been built in the same area in 1884.

28. Macey, *The Lives of Michel Foucault*, 187, reports that Foucault had met not only Jean Duvignaud, Tunisia's noted sociologist, but also Jacques Berque, specialist of the Maghreb and its saints. He therefore must have known about Sidi Bou Saïd's history/legend.
29. I am grateful to Professor Ahmed Hasnaoui (Université Paris Diderot) for alerting me to this point. Interview, Paris, 20 January 2014.
30. Macey, *The Lives of Michel Foucault*, 185.
31. Ibid. (Emphasis added.)
32. Eribon, *Michel Foucault*, 189. Foucault's views also earned him the label of "representative of Gaullist technocracy." Daniel Defert interprets such comments from students as reflecting views disseminated by the French media at the time of the structuralist controversy surrounding the publication of *Les mots et les choses*. Interview, Paris, 2 June 2014.
33. It is noteworthy that Defert ("Chronologie," 43) wrote that the ride was along "the rivage des Syrtes." This is the title of Julien Gracq's 1951 novel set in a utopic fortress. It was translated as *The Opposing Shore*, trans. Richard Howard (New York: Columbia University Press, 1996).
34. Defert, "Chronologie," 38.
35. The lectures have been published in book format as Michel Foucault, *Leçons sur la volonté de savoir. Cours au Collège de France, 1970-1971, suivi de Le savoir d'Œdipe*, ed. François Ewald, Alessandro Fontana, and Daniel Defert (Paris: Gallimard/Seuil, 2011).
36. Jean Pierre Vernant was the author of several books on the culture of ancient Greece. See in particular, *Les origines de la pensée grecque* (Paris: Presses Universitaires de France, 1975), translated as *The Origins of Greek Thought* (Ithaca: Cornell, 1982). See also Marcel Detienne, *Les Maîtres de la Vérité dans la Grèce archaïque* (Paris: Maspéro, 1967), translated as *Masters of Truth in Archaïc Greece*, trans. Janet Lloyd (New York: Zone Books, 1996); and his more recent book *Les Grecs et nous: une anthropologie comparée de la Grèce antique* (Paris: Perrin, 2005), translated as *The Greeks and Us: A Comparative Anthropology of Ancient Greece*, trans. Janet Lloyd (Cambridge: Polity, 2007). In *Les Grecs et nous*, Detienne pointedly indicates that in his inaugural lecture at the Collège de France, Foucault's evocation of the "will to knowledge" and the "will to truth" was undoubtedly an allusion to his own research on truth among ancient Greeks. Detienne also notes Foucault's "ill-defined power-knowledge," 95.
37. Foucault identifies the Empires of the Euphrates States, Lydia, and the Mediterranean coast of Asia as the areas of the Orient from which Greece borrowed the practice of absolute power, the use of money and the money standard, and the idea of the complex relationship between knowledge truth and justice. *Leçons sur la volonté de savoir*, esp. 97–126.
38. Scholarship critical of the uniqueness of ancient Greek culture challenges European societies' perception of their cultures as originating in an ancient Greece purified of all other cultural influences. Detienne, among others, combines the methods of history and anthropology to decenter such perceptions. *Les Grecs et*

nous, chap. 1. See also the work of Louis Gernet, an early critic of what was considered the "Greek Miracle," of the absolute conception of Greek uniqueness: *Les Grecs sans miracle,* ed. Ricardo Di Donato (Paris: La Découverte/Maspéro, 1983). Derrida echoes this trend in his critique of Foucault's view of the uniqueness of the Greek *logos* as suffering no division or contradiction, unlike the Classical Age sundered reason. *Writing and Difference,* 39–42.

39. Kenneth James Dover, *Greek Homosexuality* (Cambridge, MA: Harvard University Press, 1978). Using vase paintings, legal case records, and Aristophanes' plays, Dover analyzed boy–man love in Ancient Greece.
40. A leading representative of this trend was the novelist and essayist Louis Bertrand, who lived in Algeria from 1891 to 1890.
41. Defert believes that these practices may have subsided or changed under the combined effects of the emergence of the feminist and Islamist movements. Private communication.
42. Gérard Fellous, "Michel Foucault," *La Presse de Tunisie,* 12 April 1967, 3. The interview is reprinted under its long title as "La philosophie structuraliste permet de diagnostiquer ce qu'est 'aujourd'hui.'" *Dits et écrits,* vol. 1, 608–12.
43. Mohsen Toumi, *La Tunisie de Bourguiba à Ben Ali* (Paris: Presses Universitaires de France, 1989), 22–23, reports that, according to a close collaborator of Ben Youssef, the United States was complicitous with Bourguiba in Ben Youssef's assassination in Frankfurt in 1961. This charge persists among critics of the Bourguiba government. Ben Youssef had favored immediate, instead of gradual, independence from France, as well as closer ties with the Arab world. He appealed to the common man as well as the peasantry.
44. The agrarian reform included destroying over 6 million olive trees deemed too old, to be replaced by new ones purportedly to increase productivity. It also included the collectivization of small plots of land. For a positive assessment of the agrarian reform. Kamel Chenoufi and Gilles Gallo, *La Tunisie en décolonisation (1957–1972): genèse des structures de développement et des structures de la République* (Le Pradet: LAU Éditions, 2004), 153. The students' Left condemned the cooperative policy, which it interpreted as facilitating the insertion of agriculture into the global capitalist economy, rather than ushering in a socialist system. They referred to it as "forced collectivization." Naccache, for example, points out that peasants preferred to kill their flocks rather than turn them over to the state. Gilbert Naccache, *Qu'as-tu fait de ta jeunesse? Itinéraire d'un opposant au régime de Bourguiba (1954-1979) suivi de Récits de prison* (Paris; Tunis: Éditions du Cerf/Mots passants, 2009), 46. In December 1970, disgruntled peasants demonstrated at El Hamaria. Fonds Othmani, SOL 28bis. For a critical account, see also Toumi, *La Tunisie de Bourguiba,* esp. chap. 1.
45. Jélila Hafsia, "Quand la passion de l'intelligence illuminait Sidi Bou Saïd," remembered that for students Foucault was "as important as Kant" in Tunis, and numerous people went to visit him in a sort of "pilgrimage."
46. Defert notes that the Tunisian government had offered Foucault the philosophy chair. This was the first time that Foucault was to teach philosophy instead of

psychology. "Chronologie," 37. It is noteworthy that during the students' rebellion, Bourguiba would consider philosophy "dangerous." Interview with Zeineb Ben Saïd Cherni, Tunis, 3 April 2017.

47. However, Jélila Hafsia remembered that on one occasion, Foucault's lecture drew few if any people as it occurred at the same time as a soccer game between L' Espérance Sportive of Tunis and L'Etoile Sportive of the Sahel. Accessed 5 September 2013, http://culture.webmanagercenter.com/article.php?aid=1617.

48. Eribon, *Michel Foucault,* 188–89. Zeineb Ben Saïd Cherni, a former student of Foucault, recalls his surprise at the students' bewildering reception of his discussion of structuralism. He wondered why they looked at him "as cows would look at a passing train." Interview, Tunis, 3 April 2017.

49. Since the "Jasmine Revolution" of 2011, Tunisians have looked on the 1967–1968 protests as the precursor of the revolution. A number of people in the Popular Front Party and the power structure had been students of Foucault's. However, Sadek Ben Mhenni, a Perspectivist who served time in jail in the mid seventies, believes that the impetus behind the Revolution was despair and economic hardship, whereas for Perspectivists it was hope. His daughter, Lina, a well-known blogger active in the Revolution, credits her father's engagement as a source of her "rebellion against the regime," but acknowledges the different circumstances out of which the 2010–11 protests emerged. Interview, Tunis, 30 March 2017. For an analysis of the cultural impact of Perspectives, see Mohammed Salah Omri, "The Movement Perspectives: Legacies and Representations," *EurOrient,* 38(2012): 149–164.

50. *Perspectives* was initially constituted in protest against the Union Générale des Etudiants Tunisiens in Paris, which operated under the control of the Government's Parti Socialiste Destourien. It is also referred to by the initials of the group that founded it, G.E.A.S.T. (Groupe d'Etudes et d'Action Socialistes Tunisien). There are a number of accounts of the formation of *Perspectives*; see, for example, Gilbert Naccache, *Qu'as-tu fait de ta jeunesse?,* 77–80; Mohamed Charfi, one of the founders of *Perspectives, Mon combat pour les lumières* (Constantine, Algeria: Editions du Champs Libre, 2011), 75–101; Burleigh Hendrickson, "May 1968: Practicing Transnational Activism from Tunis to Paris," *International Journal of Middle Eastern Studies* 44 (2012): 758; Macey, *The Lives of Michel Foucault,* 204, indicates that *Perpectives'* orientation oscillated between Trotskyism and Maoism.

51. For a lucid article on how Bourguiba manipulated international opinion by playing on a moral register, see Werner Ruf, "Le bourguibisme, doctrine de politique étrangère d'un état faible," in *Habib Bourguiba, la trace et l'héritage,* ed. Michel Camau and Vincent Geisser (Paris: Karthala, 2004), 455–61. For a Left critique of Bourguiba's maneuvers with France during the social turmoil of 1968–1972, see "La curée néo-colonialiste," *Hebdo* no. 35, 29 June 1972. Students had no illusions about their government's foreign policy. For example, they perceived Bourguiba's son, Habib Bourguiba, who was minister of foreign affairs, as a "CIA agent, lackey of imperialism." *Fonds Othmani,* SOL 28bis, *The Economist,* 21 September 1968, reports this quote from an issue of *Perspectives.*

52. During the demonstrations, the United States Information Center and Embassy as well as the British embassy were stormed. See Naccache, *Qu'as-tu fait de ta jeunesse?*, 84.
53. Eribon, *Michel Foucault*, 192–93. I modified the translation, staying closer to the French text. The letter also appears in the second French edition of the biography. See Eribon, *Michel Foucault* (Paris: Flammarion, édition revue et enrichie, 2011), 303–4. Eribon does not give a reference to the location of this letter. Macey, *The Lives of Michel Foucault*, 203–4, does not appear to have had access to the letter as he quotes from the first French edition of Eribon's book and uses his own translation.
54. See Macey, *The Lives of Michel Foucault*, 203. Gilbert Naccache, a Tunisian Jew and member of the G.E.A.S.T., says as much, *Qu'as-tu fait de ta jeunesse?*, 84.
55. See Othman Othmani, "Les premières années," in Ahmed Othmani, *Une vie militante* (Tunis: Déméter, 2012), 31.
56. Brahim Razgallah, interview, Paris, 22 January 2014. Razgallah had been arrested, tortured, and condemned to hard labor. He was released along with others and placed under house arrest as part of a qualified amnesty, but managed to escape to Paris where he joined other members of *Perspectives*-France to continue his activism. Razgallah recounted that Gilbert Naccache told him that the event was the reason that he left Tunisia for France.
57. Defert, "Chronologie," 41.
58. Interview, 2 June 2014, Paris. Naccache, 87n1, makes a similar remark. He notes that the troops Bourguiba dispatched during the June War took six days to reach the Tunisian port of Gabès, and thus never made it to the theater of war. Samuel Merlin, a cofounder of the Israeli Irgun, applauded Bourguiba's stance, although he did not rule out the United States' role in it. See his *The Search for Peace in the Middle East: The Story of President Bourguiba's Campaign for a Negotiated Peace Between Israel and the Arab States* (Cranbury, New Jersey: Thomas Yoseloff, 1968), 284.
59. Daniel Defert, Interview, 2 June 2014, Paris.
60. Defert evokes Foucault's family's staunch opposition to anti-Semitism as well as his early exposure to the Vichy France anti-Semitic policy. Interview, Paris, 2 June 2014.
61. Defert had traveled to Israel on the third or fourth day of the War with historians François Furet and Pierre Nora. On the plane he met Golda Meir, who was returning from a fundraising trip. He spoke to Foucault on 8 or 10 June 1967, after the war had ended. Interview, Paris, 2 June 2014.
62. The head of the workers' union, U.G.T.T. (Union Générale des Travailleurs Tunisiens), Habib Ben Achour, likened March '68 to May '68, naming Simone Lellouche as another Daniel Cohn-Bendit, the French students' leader, and therefore a troublemaker. See Ahmed Othmani with Sophie Bessis, *Sortir de la prison. Un combat pour réformer les systèmes carcéraux dans le monde* (Paris: La Découverte, 2002), 16. Both Lellouche and Cohn-Bendit were accused of "destructive zionism." *Fonds Othmani*, SOL 28bis, article in *L'action*, 3 February 1972. How-

ever, before expressing her view of what actually happened on 5 June 1967, Simone Othmani Lellouche initially cast doubt on the seriousness of the letter, arguing that Foucault often made provocative comments to generate debates. Therefore, the letter could have been part of this intellectual "game" Foucault played. She had been under the impression that Foucault had not been in Tunisia at the time of the demonstration. Interview, Paris, 8 January 2014.

63. Eribon did not answer my repeated emails asking to discuss the letter.
64. Ben Jennet's infirmity does not appear in the literature examined for this chapter. It was revealed to me by Simone Othmani Lellouche during a phone interview, 29 May 2013. On Simone Othmani Lellouche, see Karine Gantin, "Simone Lellouche Othmani : une tunisienne citoyenne des deux rives," *Mémoire et Horizon*," special issue (April 2007). BDIC (Bibliothèque de Documentation Internationale Contemporaine, Université de Paris, Nanterre), F pièce 8487.
65. Burleigh Hendrickson, "May 1968," 756.
66. From Mohammed Charfi's perspective, it was thanks to the Vietnamese 1954 victory at Dien Bien Phu that Pierre Mendès-France came to power, and subsequently extended to Tunisia the right to internal autonomy, a first step toward independence. See Charfi, *Mon combat pour les lumières*, 81.
67. The G.E.A.S.T. had issued a thirty-one-page position paper in the form of a brochure advocating a two-state solution, a controversial issue at the time. See Groupe d'Etudes et d'Action Socialistes Tunisien, "La question palestinienne dans ses rapports avec le développement de la lutte révolutionnaire en Tunisie," February 1968. BDIC, O pièce 43.525. In the brochure, the students affirm their commitment to Marxism-Leninism. The June War was a watershed for *Perspectivists*: they turned away from the Arab World and focused on national issues. In 1974, as Bourguiba decreed a union with Libya, the pendulum swung back to Arab unity and closer ties to the Arab world. Razgallah, Interview, Paris, 22 January 2014.
68. The Non-Aligned movement was founded in Belgrade in 1961 by a group of nations, including India, Yugoslavia, Egypt, Burma, and Ghana, all of which had socialist political orientations.
69. Defert reports an example of a direct collusion of Bourguiba with the United States clearly aimed at discrediting Nasser: Bourguiba was instructed to make public news of a secret meeting between Nasser and Israel ostensibly because the United States did not approve of a Nasser-led agreement with Israel. Bourguiba's acquiescence was in no small measure attributable to his personal competition with Nasser for leadership of the Arab world.
70. For a description of methods of torture see Ahmed Othmani *Sortir de la prison*, 17–19. Othmani also describes the technique he used to resist torture. Just as in Algeria in 1954–1962, torture was frequently carried out in farms such as those of Naâssen and Mornag. See Naccache, *Qu'as-tu fait de ta jeunesse*, 93n1. French and other European papers denounced what appeared to be a frequent use of torture. *The Observer*, 22 June 1969 reported the torture of French agronomist Jean-Paul Chabert. A Belgian student, Francis Lavaux, also described

being tortured after his arrest on 8 December 1972. See Fonds Othmani, SOL 28bis, Dossier CISDHT (Comité International pour la Sauvegarde des Droits de l'Homme en Tunisie).
71. Othmani came from a tribal rural area of Tunisia, which during the colonial era did not register children with the French Administration. Members of the same tribe went by different names; Othmani's family belonged to a fraction of the tribe bearing the name of Reddaoui (also spelled Raddaoui). After the independence of Tunisia, Bourguiba set up a commission to fix and register last names, which also enabled individuals to choose which of the names they went by should be registered. Othmani chose his grandfather's name, Ben Othmane, which he later used as Othmani. Clarification given to the author by Simone Othmani Lellouche, 8 January 2014.
72. Othmani and Foucault kept in touch and visited with each other over the years. Othmani's life's journey could only interest Foucault above and beyond his harsh treatment by Bourguiba's security forces, which gave him notoriety. Rising from modest nomadic origins, Othmani developed a keen interest in Western philosophy and enjoyed classical music.
73. "Entretien avec Michel Foucault," (interview by D. Trombadori), 899.
74. Macey, *The Lives of Michel Foucault,* 205.
75. A brochure written in August 1968 by the Parti Socialiste Destourien, "La vérité sur la subversion à l'université de Tunis," notes on p. 25 Geismar's trip as proof of foreign collusion with the Tunisian students' movement, which allegedly included not only France but also China and Syria. Fonds Othmani, SOL 28bis.
76. "Entretien avec Michel Foucault," (interview by D. Trombadori), 897.
77. Macey, *The Lives of Michel Foucault,* 204
78. Ibid., 205.
79. Ahmed Othmani acknowledged Foucault's help along with that of historian Jean-Pierre Darmon and Jean Gattégno, who too had given him refuge. See *Sortir de la prison,* 13.
80. Daniel Defert, Interview, 2 June 2014. See also Macey, *The Lives of Michel Foucault,* 205.
81. Defert, interview. Defert had had a suspicion that his and Foucault's criticism of Bourguiba in the presence of the young man was imprudent.
82. Both Simone Othmani Lellouche as well as Ahmed Hasnaoui confirm Foucault's wish to keep the incident private.
83. Simone Othmani Lellouche phone interview, 29 May 2013. She said laughingly that the dates were "delicious."
84. Macey, *The Lives of Michel Foucault,* 205. Macey notes that Foucault gave up his plan to buy a house in Sidi Bou Saïd at this time.
85. It is unclear from Defert's "Chronologie" (38, 41, 44) whether Foucault had to renew his leave every year. He had an approved three-year leave from his teaching position at Clermont-Ferrand. But in October 1967 Foucault is described as returning to Tunis from a trip to France and deciding to renew his stay in Tunis for another year because the French Ministry of Education had not yet acted

on his appointment at Nanterre. He was not apprised of the appointment until January 1968. He finally left Tunis by boat on 27 October 1968.
86. According to Jélila Hafsia, the Tunisian minister of culture invited Foucault back to Tunisia "in the early 70s as guest of the National Cultural Committee." He gave two lectures at the Club Culturel Tahar Haddad. "In one, open to the public, he spoke to us about Manet, of the conversion of space into painting, of the color-ideas and of the archaeological forms in impressionism." "Quand la passion de l'intelligence illuminait Sidi Bou Saïd," 16.
87. The handwritten letter, dated 29 August 1968, appears in Fonds Othmani, SOL 39. In the brief letter, Foucault reiterates his love of Tunisia. A note attached to the letter asks Simone Othmani Lellouche, Ben Othman's wife, whether the letter was adequate and gives Daniel Defert's telephone number as his contact in case more was needed to be done. The note also indicated that he would be returning to Tunisia within eight days. See also Burleigh Hendrickson, "May 1968," 764.
88. Interview with Simone Othmani Lellouche, Paris, 29 May 2013.
89. Macey, *The Lives of Michel Foucault*, 191. Macey reports that in 1975 Foucault happened to be near Lapassade's home in Paris and upon seeing Lapassade, he went up to him and proceeded to slap him across the face. Lapassade struck Foucault back. Lapassade had written a fictitious account of the circumstances of his deportation from Tunis, which described Foucault's comportment during the March '68 turmoil in less than honorable terms. Defert gives a different account of the encounter in which Foucault made Lapassade admit to the "lies" he wrote about him. Defert does not believe Lapassade struck Foucault back. Interview, Paris, 2 June 2014.
90. Ahmed Hasnaoui, Interview, Paris, 20 January 2014. Hasnaoui confirms Defert's view that Foucault had helped Lapassade, a somewhat isolated figure in Tunis, and had been annoyed to read "the lies" Lapassade wrote about him.
91. "Entretien avec Michel Foucault, (interview by D. Trombadori)," 898. Foucault was right to mention "girls," as there were a number of women among the students who had been arrested and convicted, including Othmani's wife, Simone Lellouche. One of the women, Aïcha Ben Abed, was sentenced to three months in prison for having married a student leader, Noureddine Ben Khader, according to Islamic customary law. As for her common law husband, he received six months for "adultery." Fonds Othmani, SOL 28bis, Dossier CISDHT, Bulletin de Liaison no. 1–4, 1969–73. Naccache, 142–43, had some stern words for Ben Khader's insistence that Aïcha was his legitimate wife. He wished him to proclaim the principle of free union. Yet, Ben Khader clearly flaunted the prohibition against polygamy.
92. Foucault, "Entretien avec Michel Foucault," (interview by D. Trombadori)," 897. The quotation ends with the sentence: "This was for me a genuine political education."
93. Razgallah rightly notes that students had not expected the ferocity of the government's response, and thus were not aware at first that they were risking their lives.

94. "Entretien avec Michel Foucault (interview by D. Trombadori)," 897.
95. Ibid., 898.
96. Ibid., 898, 899–900. Macey, *The Lives of Michel Foucault*, 207, suggests that Foucault "was often tempted to explain his non-participation by finessing potential critics with accounts of direct involvement in a struggle with much higher stakes." Macey further argues that Foucault was far more interested in May '68, had been in Paris during one march on 17 May, and was keeping abreast of events more than he let on in interviews.
97. "Entretien avec Michel Foucault," (interview by D. Trombadori)," 899.
98. Ibid.
99. Othmani, *Sortir de la prison*, 11, felt that the adoption of Maoism was "a return to the purity of Marxist thought." Nevertheless, the library gathered at Bordj Erroumi, the prison where the convicted were kept, included Foucault's *Les mots et les choses*, alongside books by Faulkner, Fanon, and Dostoevsky, among others. *Fonds Othmani*, SOL 28bis.
100. See Othmani, *Sortir de la prison*, 14; Naccache, *Qu'as-tu-fait de ta jeunesse*, 80–89. Naccache, 108, calls the G.E.A.S.T.'s Marxism a "declaration of principle."
101. Naccache, *Qu'as-tu fait de ta jeunesse*, 96.
102. Ibid., 87
103. Interview, Tunis, 3 April 2017. Cherni was arrested and mercilessly tortured in 1973 when she was 25. After her release, her passport was seized and she was barred from teaching for six years. Prior to her arrest, she had been a professor of philosophy at a lycée in the city of Kairouan. She credits Foucault's philosophy lectures (especially on Descartes) with having transformed her worldview as a young, practicing Muslim woman.
104. Eribon, *Michel Foucault*, 189. But Simone Othmani Lellouche suggests that Foucault's thought had greatly influenced Tunisian Left intellectuals.
105. Hasnaoui had met Foucault at the time when he visited his companion Defert in Sfax. After he moved to Tunis to attend the university, Hasnaoui and a group of fellow students regularly met Foucault at a café in Sidi Bou Saïd. They talked about a number of issues, including *Les mots et les choses*, Marxism and its overcoming, as well as Foucault's relation to Heidegger. When in 1969–1970 Hasnaoui attended the University of Paris, at Vincennes, he prepared an MA under Foucault's supervision on "conceptions of poverty in seventeenth-eighteenth century," a question Foucault had touched on in his history of madness. He also attended a number Foucault's lectures at the Collège de France. He recalls questioning Foucault's ideas and arguing with him to the point where Foucault felt he was not respectful to him. He fell out of touch with Foucault as of 1976. Interview, 20 January 2014, Paris.
106. Macey, *The Lives of Michel Foucault*, 190.
107. Defert, "Chronologie," 38.
108. Interview, Paris, 20 January 2014.
109. It is highly possible that students were eager to avoid giving their government tangible proof of their movement's alleged foreign inspiration and support.

110. Defert, "Chronologie," 41.
111. Simone Othmani Lellouche emphasized that as a scientist (*une scientifique*) she did not always fully grasp the philosophical points made by Foucault, but this one lecture stuck in her mind.
112. I am borrowing the image of the pendulum from the interview with Hasnaoui.
113. "Entretien avec Michel Foucault," (interview by D. Trombadori)" 898.
114. Ibid.
115. Bourguiba took pride as a modern, secularist leader. However, he turned to Islam to fight the Left, which was deemed culturally inauthentic and foreign-inspired.
116. Although a small group of students may have been atheists, most advocated a progressive Islam. Razgallah, Interview, Paris, 20 January 2014.
117. Both Othmani, *Sortir de la prison,* 14, and Naccache, *Qu'as-tu fait de ta jeunesse,* 87, emphasize the "internationalist" outlook of the G.E.A.S.T. and their actions. Naccache argues that many saw Marxism as an alternative to nationalism, 87.
118. B. Razgallah, Interview, Paris, 22 January 2014.
119. Maurice Pinguet, a friend of Foucault's from the Ecole Normale Supérieure, remembers that the Algerian War did not "move" Foucault when he tried to talk to him about it in 1956. By comparison "[May] 1968 excited him." See Maurice Pinguet, "Michel Foucault. Les années d'apprentissage," in *Maurice Pinguet. Le texte Japon introuvables et inédits,* ed. Michaël Ferrier (Paris: Éditions du Seuil, 2009), 52.
120. A. Hasnaoui, Interview, Paris, 20 January 2014.
121. Ibid.
122. "Michel Foucault: les réponses du philosophe," *Dits et écrits,* vol. 1, 1674. See also "Entretien avec Michel Foucault," (interview by D. Trombadori), 898.
123. Reflecting on language, *Perspectivists* advocated making Tunisian colloquial Arabic their country's medium of communication instead of modern Arabic, but do not appear to have questioned the continued use of French at the university, or among themselves. They had an Arabic language section for those who did not speak French, such as Ben Jennet. However, as *Perspectives* evolved into the 1970s there was a trend toward Modern Arabic and pan-Arabism.
124. Razgallah reports how a "dark-skinned" leading *Perspectivist,* Ben Khader, was once sitting on a bench in a public park after attending a general assembly meeting of *Perspectives* in Paris when a homeless Frenchman approached him and said "go home, bicot!" Ben Khader told Razgallah this experience played a catalytic role in his decision to go back to Tunisia. Interview, Paris, 22 January 2014. There was another such incident with the same effect.
125. "Radioscopie de Michel Foucault." Interview with J. Chancel, *Dits et écrits,* vol. 1, 1652–53.
126. Othmani, *Sortir de la prison,* 6–7.
127. "Entretien avec Michel Foucault," (interview by D. Trombadori)," 890.
128. See for example Sartre's introduction to Frantz Fanon's *The Wretched of the Earth* (New York: Grove Press, 1961) or to Henri Alleg's *La Question* (Paris: Edi-

tions de Minuit, 1958). At the time, Albert Memmi had written *The Colonizer and the Colonized* (Boston: Beacon Press, 1965). The original was published in 1957 as *Portrait du colonisé*.
129. Interview with Daniel Defert, Paris, 2 June 2014.
130. Ibid. See also Macey, *The Lives of Michel Foucault*, 205.
131. Razgallah too, once condemned to fourteen years in prison, allows for Bourguiba's modernism. He describes the students' movement as a "continuation of Bourguiba's modernist project" before he turned autocratic. Interview, Paris, 22 January 2014.
132. Daniel Defert, Interview, Paris, 2 June 2014. Defert was keenly aware of this side of life in Tunis.
133. Foucault, "Entretien avec Michel Foucault," (interview by D. Trombadori), 900.
134. Ibid., 898.
135. Following the lead of a number of Tunisians who think Tunisia was a watershed in Foucault's life as an intellectual, Mark LeVine argues that it inflected Foucault's conception of power. See "Tunis and the Birth of a 'Planetary Genealogy' in the Work of Michel Foucault," in *CELAAN* (Review of the Center for the Studies of the Literatures and Arts of North Africa), special issue, "Michel Foucault en Tunisie (1966-1968)," 79–100.
136. Interview, Tunis, 3 April 2017. No matter the effect of Tunisia on Foucault' thought, scholars interpreting the aftermath of the 2011 Revolution turn to Gramsci, among others, for inspiration. See Baccar Gherib, *Penser la Transition avec Gramsci. Tunisie (2011–2014)* (Tunis: Editions Diwen, 2017); Michel Camau, "Les 'printemps tunisiens' de mars 1968 et de janvier 2011," in *Le movement Perspectives Amel-Ettounsi: son histoire, ses ramifications. Actes du colloque qui célèbre le cinquantenaire de Perspectives, 18–20 décembre 2013 à la Bibliothèque nationale de Tunis* (Sfax: CAEU-Med Ali Editions, 2016), 119–133.
137. Foucault, "Entretien avec Michel Foucault," (interview by D. Trombadori), 901.
138. Ibid., 900. In a special sense, Foucault's comment resonates with Naccache's (*Qu'as-tu fait de ta jeunesse*, 93) as well as Othmani's assessment of the Tunisian student Left as being fundamentally hostage to Bourguiba's (French) modernism. As Othmani put it (*Sortir de la prison*, 13): "We had nothing to say about societal questions. Bourguiba deprived us of that struggle, but in a positive way: we were in symbiosis with him." It is the insufficiencies or drawbacks of modernity that students in Tunisia (as well as in France) had protested, not modernity itself. By the same token, implicitly, Foucault intimates a sort of community of kind between students in France and in Tunisia not simply because they were young people seeking change, but because the Tunisians were subsumed under the French since the ideas motivating them were imported from France.
139. For instance, Foucault found himself alongside Sartre in "Comité Djellali" to bring justice to the killing of an Algerian adolescent, Djellali Ben Ali, by a

Frenchman in the Goutte d'Or neighborhood, where the population was predominantly Algerian. See Abdellali Hajjat, "Alliances inattendues à la Goutte d'Or," in *68, Une histoire collective: 1962–1981,* ed. Philippe Artières and Michelle Zancarini-Fournel (Paris: La Découverte, 2008), 522.

140. Undoubtedly, Foucault had been affected by the plight of imprisoned students in Tunis, and learned a lot about repression in Tunis prisons, but Defert reports that the idea for the GIP was initiated by him in the aftermath of the ban on La Gauche Prolétarienne, of which he had been an active member. He then joined Jacques Rancière's "Organisation des Prisonniers Politiques," which fought for the status of political prisoner for jailed Maoists. The GIP was thus formed to investigate conditions in prisons. Foucault was asked to join given his notoriety and his work on madness. He accepted wholeheartedly. Interview, Paris, 2 June 2014.

141. Foucault, "Entretien avec Michel Foucault," (interview by D. Trombadori), 864.

142. Ibid., 864–65.

143. Ibid., 865.

144. Ibid.

145. I am borrowing the expression from Simone Othmani Lellouche, who said jokingly in the course of a discussion that Foucault had in a way "discovered Arabs" in Tunisia. Interview, Paris, 8 January 2014.

146. Daniel Defert, Interview, Paris, 2 June 2014.

147. Macey, *The Lives of Michel Foucault,* 195.

Chapter 7

The Enigma of Japan

> The Orient is for Europe the rear: it cannot be seen with the eyes.
>
> —Takeuchi Yoshimi, *What Is Modernity?*

Of the non-Western countries Foucault visited, Japan stands out in his perception of cultural otherness. According to one biographer, he had had a long-standing fascination with Japan, a country where, just like Nietzsche before him, he entertained the idea of settling.[1] In Paris, he received his friends in a kimono, his bed was low to the floor in the old Japanese fashion, and his distinctively shaved head looked like that of a bonze.[2] Once in Japan, however, he was at a loss, and planned to come to terms with Japanese culture, but in the end did not. There were moments when, caught off guard, he unwittingly revealed the limitations of the categories of analysis that sustain his conception of the Orient–Occident divide. This chapter traces Foucault's difficulties comprehending his *experience* of Japanese culture in light of his past struggle with anthropology as well as his construction of the Western *ratio*.

JAPAN AS A LIMIT-EXPERIENCE

In addition to *Introduction* to Kant's *Anthropology,* Foucault's poetic musing on the "Orient" in the preface to the 1961 edition of *History of Madness,* written nine years before his first trip to Japan,[3] encapsulates his attitude toward cultural otherness just as it delineates its parameters: "In the universal Western *ratio* there is this division which is the Orient: the Orient, thought of as the origin, dreamt of as the vertiginous point from which the nostalgia and promises of return are born, the Orient offered to the colonising reason of the occident, but indefinitely inaccessible, for it always remains the limit: the night of the beginning, in which the Occident was formed, but in which it traced a dividing line, the Orient is for the Occident everything that it is not, while remaining the place in which its primitive truth must be sought."[4]

In part this statement is a reminder of a long tradition in European letters (as indicated in chapter 4) of using the "Orient" in various ways, as a "utopian exemplar"[5] of perfectly functioning institutions: a vantage point from which to criticize Western cultures; glimpse solutions to personal problems; make pronouncements about fundamental cultural differences; or establish genealogies of political systems. Hegel devoted a section of his *Philosophy of History* to "The Oriental World."[6] Arthur Schopenhauer, perhaps the philosopher most invested in the "Orient," sometimes identified himself as a Buddhist,[7] and attempted a synthesis of Kantian philosophy and Buddhism. Following in Schopenhauer's footsteps, Nietzsche also looked to the Orient, especially in his critique of Christianity.[8] He found that "[a]t bottom there are in Christianity one or two subtleties which belong to the Orient"; nevertheless, it is Buddhism that represents "the close and exhaustion of civilization,"[9] and thus its ultimate truth. Heidegger had had a long-standing interest in Zen Buddhism and Japanese thought. Remarkably, to convey his view of the Orient–Occident divide, mediated by the Japanese language, he rewrote, in a fictitious form presented as genuine, a dialogue he had had with a Japanese scholar, Germanist Tezuka Tomio.[10] It is therefore no surprise that Foucault's thinking of the Orient as "the origin" would also echo Hegel's comments that "With the Empire of China History has to begin"[11] or that his formulation of the Orient as "the primitive truth" of the West would recall Nietzsche's view of the Orient as demystifying Western culture.[12] The quotation from Foucault also speaks of the projection of the Occident's fantasies onto an implicitly homogeneous *space,* yet it is a bit difficult to visualize since it is drawn as a line and a point. However, Foucault did not single out a concrete aspect of the cultures of the "Orient"; he expressed his thought philosophically.

Apart from its use of totalizing concepts, Orient and Occident, denoting questionable homogeneous cultures, what stands out in the quotation is its unambiguous character.[13] The Orient–Occident divide (*partage*) in the Western *ratio* is presumably unquestioned and unquestionable except as needing a study of its own. In other words, it does not problematize the divide; it takes it as a given. The meaning of Foucault's categorical statement lies in his definition of "limit-experience" (a concept borrowed from Bataille),[14] as well as the role he assigned the concept in his understanding of

Western identity. From his perspective, all societies function on the principle of inclusion/exclusion by keeping certain members in and rejecting others. Acts of rejection acquire a taken-for-granted, and thus unconscious, character as soon as they have been initiated. Their function is to "isolate" culture from its exterior, thereby enabling it to enhance with clarity the "positivity" of its values and choices. A culture has limits internally, creating an exterior edge within its interior, and externally with another culture. Hence, the division that traces the limit "is the originary thickness in which a culture takes place."[15] Western culture draws two fundamental limits, one within itself, between madness and reason, the other between Orient and Occident. Both are "tears" in the fabric of the Western "ratio." Around the originary internal division "gravitate" other limit-experiences, such as, for example, those concerning dreams, sexual prohibition, and desire. Foucault imagines the limit as "a knife's edge" (*lame de couteau*)[16] to signal its sharpness as well as its radicalness, as what is cut with a sharp knife is unlikely to be put back together again. The second caesura, the Orient–Occident, is as philosophically motivated as the madness–reason divide.

The concept "originary," which characterizes the cultural divide, needs clarification before the radicalness of Foucault's thought can be grasped. He used it as part of the expression "originary choice" to refer to the delimitation of knowledge inherent in any culture, which begins with a philosophical act of defining the starting point of a reflection on human behavior, activity, and thought. It is the acknowledged or taken-for-granted philosophical foundation of knowledge in a given civilizational era. Initially made by philosophers, originary choices continue to inform systems of knowledge formulated by nonphilosophers. For example, according to Foucault, Marx's historical materialism, Freud's psychoanalytical conception of sexuality, and Saussure's linguistics could only have emerged out of the Western philosophical originary choice (from Plato to Hegel).[17] As Foucault put it, "it is not only a speculative choice in the field of pure ideas. It is a choice that delimits a whole body of human knowledge, human activities, perception and sensibility."[18] In this context, the Orient–Occident limit-experience is grounded in the Western philosophical originary choice. Implicitly, it cannot be changed (internally) except if the philosophical system that grounds it changes, an unlikely possibility given that the system is taken for granted, and writers who are not philosophers reproduce its contours. This apparent aporia may be at the root of Foucault's inability to resolve the "enigma" of Japan. Why Foucault chose the Orient–Occident regional divide, and not another one, such as West/non-West, is a matter of speculation.[19] The omission of the 1961 preface from subsequent editions of the book suggests that he had occasion to think it through after he made his trips to Japan in 1970 and 1978, and perhaps found it wanting. However, the various statements he made about Japanese culture afterward do not, in their essentials, depart from the view expressed in the quotation. To a large extent, they flesh it out.

Foucault's view rests on three main notions: first, the Orient represents for the Occident a region of its *dreams,* a *nostalgia* for an origin[20] it cannot fathom, a "night of the beginning," to which it obscurely aspires to *return*.[21] This is clearly a psychological-emotional, if not ontological, condition that the Occident experiences before the idea of the Orient. Second, in spite of or because of the emotion with which the Occident charges it, the Orient is "indefinitely inaccessible," and thus "always remains the limit." The notion of dreams (which expands horizons even as it may connote their inaccessibility), is antinomic with the idea of *limit,* which draws boundaries between cultures with the sharpness of a knife's edge. Third, the Orient is subject to, "offered" to, the "colonizing reason of the Occident." It is unclear whether the Western *ratio* sees the Orient as an object of its colonizing power because it finds it emotionally and ontologically challenging, or because by establishing its dominion over it, it wishes to get rid of the idea of the Orient within itself thereby achieving a cathartic effect. It is also unclear whether the Orient's differentness invites colonization. Finally, the Orient, regardless of the dreams it evokes in the Occident, is its antithesis, "everything that it is not."

Foucault presumes his view of the Orient to be self-explanatory. Yet the quotation bore no direct relation to the object of the book (madness) in whose preface it appeared. It harks back to the incongruity of the place of the Chinese encyclopedia in the preface to *Les mots et les choses*. The passage is puzzling to Japanese scholars, who respond to it in different ways. Yasuo Kobayashi suggests that Foucault's notion of an Orient–Occident divide was a methodological imperative. "Given that Foucault intended to trace the limits of Western reason internally as well as externally, he was obligated to posit an Orient that stood outside of the Occident. However, Foucault could not (and possibly sensed that he could not) proceed with the Orient, as that which purportedly escapes Western reason, in the same manner as he did, for example, with the internal division of madness. This explains the indeterminate aspect of Foucault's characterization of the Orient. This thing that is 'everything that the Occident is not' is left vague. He glimpsed the necessity to approach this other (possible) reason differently, but did not do so."[22] Acknowledging the problematic nature of Foucault's view, Yasuyuki Shinkai, a Foucault scholar and translator, suggests that the quotation is a legacy of the phenomenological phase of Foucault's work, which started with his publications of the 1950s and lingered on in *History of Madness*. At any rate, once Foucault removed the quotation from subsequent editions of the book, Foucault never referred to it again and essentially abandoned the notion of the Orient as a limit-experience.[23] However, that Foucault refrained from referring to the divide does not necessarily mean that he abandoned the notion. Explaining away Foucault's view poses a logical problem. For instance, for Daniel Defert the very idea of "limit-experience," associated with Bataille, was not part of Foucault's regular vocabulary, suggesting that it was limited to the quotation. Yet the idea also appears in *Les mots et les choses,* published after *Histoire de la folie.* Moreover, Foucault returns to the concept and explains its significance in an interview with Duccio Trombadori. He notes that he learned in the wake of Bataille and Blanchot to conceive books as "direct experiences to 'tear' me away from myself, to prevent me from always being the same." By the same token, he reasserts the idea of "limit-experience" as pointing to "intensity" and "impossibility of living."[24] Even if the Orient–Occident division was an epistemic imperative for the purpose of demonstrating how Western reason seeks to establish limits, Foucault's conception nevertheless remains wanting for its failure to question the propensity of reason to establish limits or that the Orient should be its limit. Kobayashi adequately expressed the issue: "once you give a great deal of importance to reason, how do you manage the 'limit' to this reason? Is it possible to have a non-Western reason, that is to say a universal reason?... The limit of reason that does not know a limit to itself but always sets limits to others, is a perennial problem in which Western reason is stuck (*'coïncée'*)." It is symptomatic that Foucault eschewed a definition of the reason, which the Orient presumably exemplifies as the "limit" of the Western *ratio*.

By the same token, reference to the Orient, as a leitmotif, symbolizes Foucault's difficulty with a significant paradox: on the one hand, he stressed the "universality of the Western ratio." On the other hand, he relied on the notion of "limit-experience," which establishes a binary opposition between cultures for the purpose of enhancing Western cultural identity—which, from his perspective, does not countenance human universals. The paradox thus reveals a political conception of the West's universality that thwarts understanding cultural-qua-anthropological universals. Indeed, Foucault leaves unquestioned the "universal" character of the Western *ratio*. As Kobayashi suggests, "universal reason does not permit division." In this sense, "Foucault positioned himself within Western history (and European societies). In so doing, he left in abeyance the significance, for the presumed universality of Western reason (itself a particular or regional reason), of the limits within itself."[25] To return to the quotation, Western reason establishes its universality through "colonization," implicitly as if to compensate for the cultural division it makes and that it cannot resolve culturally. In this sense, Foucault's trips to Japan acquire special importance in understanding whether and how he *experienced* Japanese culture as a limit, and whether he truly abandoned the view expressed in the preface to the *Histoire de la folie* as a result of his experience of Japan.

GETTING TO JAPAN

The trips Foucault made to Japan[26] in September 1970 and March 1978 reveal an intellectual at times frustrated, at others perplexed, but always holding on to his cultural grounding. The first trip, which took him to Tokyo, Osaka, and Kyoto, was at the invitation of Foucault's friend, Maurice Pinguet, a fellow normalien who was at the time director of the Institut Franco-Japonais of Tokyo.[27] There is a little-known history behind this invitation:[28] Traditionally, the French government sent a French professor holding an aggrégation degree to the University of Tokyo to serve as principal professor in the French department. At the end of the 1960s and early 1970s, there appeared to be a scarcity of agrégés professors, as a result of which the French government sent a professor holding a CAPES (Certificat d'Aptitude Professionnelle à l' Enseignement Secondaire) only, the equivalent of a license to teach at the high school level. The chair of the French department, Yoishi Maeda, a Blaise Pascal scholar, insisted on a more qualified person. Maurice Pinguet proposed Foucault to Maeda. Foucault was not unknown to Maeda. Miyeko Kamiya, Maeda's sister and a psychiatrist, had translated Foucault's *Naissance de la Clinique* (1969) as well as *Maladie Mentale et Psychologie* (1970). The three of them had met in Paris in 1963–1964.[29] Professor Moriaki Watanabe, who facilitated Foucault's academic tour, notes that when Foucault arrived in Tokyo, *Les mots et les choses* had not been translated yet as it had sold out in France, and Japanese scholars were waiting for the second edition to begin a translation. However, *L'Archéologie du savoir* had just been published in what Watanabe thinks was a bad Japanese translation.[30] In June 1970, Foucault had been officially appointed to the Collège de France, and would give his inaugural lecture in December.[31]

What Foucault did not know before he embarked on this first trip was that Sartre's thought at the time had reigned supreme among Japanese intellectuals, especially the Left among them who wielded some influence over the media. Sartre had visited Japan in 1966 with Simone de Beauvoir. Following in Sartre's footsteps, his admirers perceived Foucault as the representative of a "pseudo anti-humanist bourgeoisie."[32] Their staunch opposition to structuralism was partly due to their rejection of Ferdinand de Saussure's conception of linguistics, which they had read in a "translation so below par as to be aberrant." Consequently, they made sure that Foucault's lectures would receive as little coverage as possible. As Watanabe recalls, "there was no interview with papers, no article in journals. Our only testimonial [of Foucault's passage] was the conversation ['Folie, littérature et société'] which appeared in the review *Bungei,* and Foucault's lecture on 'La folie et la société,' published in our [Toyo University's] journal.[33] The same thing happened in Kyoto where the same two lectures were published."[34]

Japan held some attraction for Foucault.[35] In 1963, he had the opportunity to become director of the Institut Franco-Japonais of Tokyo, but in the end he passed it up for personal reasons.[36] Foucault made the first trip alone, and was hosted by Maurice Pinguet, who accompanied him to his lectures, although Watanabe acted as his intellectual guide. Watanabe indicates that he managed to squeeze into a tight schedule a Nō theater performance. However, the performance (about the phantom of an old woman) was all that was available and did not feature a translation. As a result, it was an "ordeal" for Foucault, who looked visibly "bored."[37]

The 1978 trip had been arranged by Thierry de Beaucé, Cultural Adviser at the French Embassy, with the help of Christian Polak, an interpreter, as part of a "cultural mission for the French government."[38] Tokyo University was also involved as Watanabe, among others, participated in interviews as well as the translation of the lecture that had appeared in the national paper, *ASAHI.*[39] Polak, who had prepared Foucault's program,[40] claims that a book, *L'île absolue* (The total island, e.g., Japan), was in all probability the sole source of Foucault's information about Japanese culture.[41] He informed Foucault of the presumed peculiarity of the Japanese language, which "does not have concepts," and of the Japanese people's "lack of a notion of self."[42] Parenthetically, the French version of the book in its essentials bears strong similarities with Foucault's conception of the Orient–Occident, even though the book appeared eighteen years after the publication of *Histoire de la folie,* suggesting a commonality of views among Thierry de Beaucé, the author, and Foucault.[43]

On this 1978 trip Foucault also toured two prisons in the region of Fukuoka,[44] as well as a psychiatric ward; met with leading intellectuals, including the head of Japan's Socialist Party; gave talks at universities and interviews with major newspapers; and held discussions with opponents of the construction of the Narita airport.[45] He also acquainted himself with all-male nightclubs.[46] A highlight of the 1978 trip, however, was a retreat to a Zen temple in the company of Defert and Polak.[47] Under the guidance of a bonze, he learned how to position his body for meditation. He found the exercise "very hard."[48] On this second trip, Watanabe had had time to prepare for another visit to a Nō theater. The performance was well selected and featured a translation. Foucault was reportedly "moved" by it. As a person who participated in both trips, Watanabe found a marked difference in Foucault's general attitude in 1978. Foucault's bewilderment of 1970 gave way, eight years later, to more openness as well as willingness to "deepen his knowledge and curiosity about Japanese culture. He gave his audience his best and offered his interlocutors to join in further research." Watanabe attributes the change to Foucault's by-then-established status as professor at the Collège de France, which may have accounted for his relaxed demeanor, as well as Daniel Defert's presence on his side.[49] An example of Foucault's openness to Japanese culture, was Foucault's invitation of Masao Maruyama (1914–1996), Japan's foremost Marxist-leaning political theorist and cultural analyst, to lecture at the Collège de France, but Maruyama became ill, and the invitation fell through.[50]

Polak gives a different account of Foucault's second trip. He insists that the 1978 visit (he was not present at the first one) was but a "hiatus" (*parenthèse*) in Foucault's life and work. From his description, Foucault enjoyed himself tremendously, laughing so much that at times he struggled to keep his composure, even when performing the Zen meditation. Polak took pictures portraying Foucault enjoying himself at the Zen temple. To support his view, Polak notes (not without reason) that upon his return to Paris, Foucault never pursued his interest in Zen, or referred to his visit to Japan in his writings. He also did not quote any of the intellectuals he had met in Japan. Polak allows that the only way that Japan might have influenced Foucault's work would have been through his using concrete examples or suggestive metaphors to describe concepts (in the Japanese manner).[51] Polak, as well as Defert, affirm Foucault's lack of interest in Zen philosophy. Echoing this sentiment, Watanabe suggests that "everything concerning Foucault's interest in Zen, including a picture of him disguised as a bonze, was a media hype engineered by Polak." Watanabe too felt that "Foucault was enjoying himself.... He did not take it [the Zen experience] seriously, but lent himself to the game." However, Watanabe notes that Foucault's visit to the temple is a source of "misunderstanding." Foucault's interest in Zen "is not false, but exaggerated." But according to Polak, even the bonzes understood that the visitors were having fun, yet given their legendary tolerance they did not seem to mind. Nevertheless, Foucault's visits to Japan provide a window into his conception of cultural difference despite his playfulness during his 1978 trip. Part of the fun in Polak's reminiscence was finding feminine nicknames for Japanese interlocutors.[52]

COMMUNICATING IN JAPAN

As is routine, the Embassy kept a file and wrote a report to the French Ministry of Foreign Affairs under the rubric "Missions-78, Michel Foucault." The file included, among other things, a copy of a thirty-two-page essay written by Masao Maruyama on "problems of Japanese intellectuals," which Foucault undoubtedly read. It provided information on the plurality of terms used in Japan to refer to the concept "intellectual," as well as a historical analysis of the evolution of the role of intellectuals. Of note is Maruyama's acknowledgment of the effect of the "Westernization" of Japan on intellectuals as well as the introduction of "red ideas" in the aftermath of the Bolshevik revolution. These were topics Foucault had a special interest in.

Some embassy documents reveal a frustrated Foucault, unable to get his message across. In a letter to the French foreign affairs minister, Ambassador Louis Dauge noted Foucault's difficulty in establishing communication with the new head of the Socialist Party, the late Ichio Asukata, using his knowledge of Marxism. Dauge described Foucault's plan to address "the current meaning of Marxism"; "daily practices of democracy"; and "social experiment, source of contemporary thought," in his exchange with Asukata, "a man of action and reflection." The ambassador bemoans Asukata's view that the solution to the problems of the Party must be Japanese.[53] Asukata even feared that Japan might become "the Asian branch of eurocommunism." Remarkably, according to the ambassador, Foucault expressed his worry to Asukata that there could be "difficulties in communicating with intellectuals belonging to a different culture since the collapse of Marxism as a movement among international intellectuals, which at least had given them a common language." He suggested, according to the ambassador, "exchanges on [social] experimentation between party members [French and Japanese] as well as intellectuals in order to avoid leaving the monopoly of communication to the apparatuses."[54] Doing an end run around Foucault, Asukata reportedly replied that he had agreed to having Japanese socialist militants study the literature of the French Socialist Party. However, difficulties related to language, money, and distance prevented this from happening.

The ambassador added a comment that resonates with Foucault's conception of the Orient as a limit-experience for the Occident: "To Mr. Foucault's attempt to start a dialogue between intellectuals, Mr. Ichio Asukata implicitly invoked variations on the theme 'Orient-Occident'. He harbored a real inferiority complex towards French socialists as well as their intellectuals. He probably worried about being tested, all the more so that he spoke in the name of his party." Foucault autographed a copy of the *Archaeology of Knowledge,* of which Asukata had read about 100 pages, and the two men shook hands under two posters of the (then) last electoral campaign, which the French Socialist Party had sent. In the words of the ambassador, "Mr. Michel Foucault still wondered how he should have approached this political man."[55]

As a sort of politically ecumenical intellectual, Foucault went to great lengths to convince Asukata to learn from the French Socialist Party's experience. His "frustration" at his failure of "communication" only underscores the seriousness with which Foucault took his role. Asukata's awareness of the "Occident-Orient" divide (as reported by the ambassador) presented Foucault with the opportunity to address the issue directly with Asukata, explore its contours, and possibly come to terms with it. But it left Foucault in a state of cultural confusion. The experience with Asukata[56] reveals an aspect of Foucault's thought that needs to be brought out: Foucault's use of universalist/humanist Marxist ideas in order to establish a common ground with Asukata in spite of his critical attitude toward Marxism. In other words, faced with a purported Japanese nationalization of socialism, Foucault adopted a universalist (Marxist) stance. The frustration must have been all the more intense that Foucault did not speak Japanese.

THE CULTURAL ENIGMA

Zen and Mentalité

As the Asukata exchange indicates, Foucault felt estranged in Japan in a way he had not experienced in Tunisia or would experience in Iran. Yet there *was* something disconcertingly familiar in Japan: modernity. He was surrounded by modernity of the kind he had left behind in Paris. However, he did not feel in his element as he had been to some degree in Sweden, Germany, or even Poland. "To me, from the standpoint of technology and lifestyle and apparent social structure, Japan is a country extremely close to the Western world. By the same token, the people of this country appeared to me at all levels to be much more mysterious than the people of all the other countries in the world. What impressed me was this mix of proximity and distance. I could not form a more distinct impression."[57] In a way, being in Japan was akin to being in a dream in which familiar things appear strange; and dreams are the stuff out of which the traditional Occidental idea of the Orient is made of. Implicitly, Foucault's attempt to come to grips with Japan followed the terms of his definition of the Orient as a limit-experience: he gave concrete instances of Japan as a source of knowledge; focused on the nature of Buddhism as its distinguishing feature; and pondered the role of the dialectic of colonialism in mediating between the present and the future of the cultural divide.

Recalling his first trip, Foucault regretted that "I had seen nothing and understood nothing"[58] even though he had visited places. A number of the questions Foucault was asked on this trip compounded his sense of puzzlement. For example, in an interview with the paper *Yomiuri,* he was asked a question that went to the core of his misgivings about Kant's *Anthropology*: what does he think as a philosopher of people applauding a monkey for catching candy thrown at him by a visitor at a Japanese zoological garden? The question compelled Foucault to address the nature of human nature as it relates to animals. However, it also led the interviewer to bring up Europeans' treatment of human beings: "Mexicans took Europeans for gods, whereas the Europeans treated the natives as animals."[59] To deflect the question, Foucault provided an historical analysis of the notion of human nature in a manner made familiar in *Les mots et les choses.*

In 1978 a bonze asked Foucault a question that indirectly probed the foundation of his selection of the Orient as a divide in the Western ratio: "Is your interest in Japan deep or superficial?" To which Foucault gave a candid yet politically significant answer: "Honestly, Japan is not an abiding interest for me. What interests me is the history of Western rationality and its limit. On this point, Japan poses an unavoidable problem of which it is an illustration because Japan is an enigma, very difficult to understand. This does not mean that it is what is opposed to Western rationality.[60] In reality, the latter builds colonies everywhere else whereas in Japan it is far from building one; on the contrary it is rather colonized by Japan."[61] The answer sheds light on the grounds for Foucault's decision to affirm a fundamental cultural divide between Orient and Occident: colonization by the Western Logos, or resistance to Western "colonization." This begs the question of why and how Western "technology and lifestyle," which allowed Foucault to find familiarity with Japan, were not forms of "colonization" in their own right. If Japan is not what is opposed to Western rationality, why is it that its successful use of the technology (which the West has touted as its mark of (rational) superiority over the non-West) still sets it apart from the West? More important, in what way and on what grounds would Japan appear as a colonizer of the West? Such questions belong in the domain of the sociology of development and "modernization," which are beyond the scope of this book. Suffice it to say that this domain is still the object of controversy over what truly constitutes modernity and whether the path taken by Japan is an exception to the one pursued by the West.

In a Weberian manner,[62] Foucault located the specificity of Japan in Zen, which purportedly shapes a mind-set that distinguishes Japanese culture in spite of its Western-like modernity. As he put it, "I think that a mentality totally different from ours gets formed through practice and training at the Zen temple."[63] It might be remarked, as Defert does, that the concept of "mentality" does not belong to Foucault's vocabulary.[64] Indeed, in *L'Archéologie du savoir,* Foucault argues for undertaking a "negative work" that would free him of "a play of notions that multiply, each in its own right, the theme of continuity." Among these notions figure tradition, influence, evolution, mentality, or spirit.[65] He objects to the "notion" of mentality, not only because it establishes "a community of meanings" between various "phenomena" of a given period, no matter their chronological order, but also because it introduces "the sovereignty of a collective conscience as a principle of unity and explanation."[66] Foucault further calls for a questioning of "these already-made syntheses ... [and to] track down these obscure forms and forces with which we usually link together men's discourses." Indeed, "mentality" would establish a link between contemporary Japan and either preliterate societies or premodern Western historical periods. Defert warns against the accuracy of such concepts as a number of Foucault's interviews and lectures given in Japan had at first been translated into Japanese and retranslated into French for inclusion in *Dits et écrits.* The editors indicate that some of the discussions that took place at the Zen temple had been recorded by the Buddhist review *Shunjû* and translated by Christian Polak.[67] However, Polak asserts that the piece "Michel Foucault et le zen: un séjour dans un temple zen," was a "transcription" of what he had recorded, not an interpretative translation. In other words, he was not the author of the word "mentality." Polak kept the notes he took at Foucault's lectures.

Polak made it clear that "I have a very close relation to Mr. Foucault and never allowed myself to write about Michel Foucault or interpret his words. I have always been transparent with him. This is why he wanted me to be his interpreter at some very important meetings." Indeed, Polak was the only person present at a secret meeting Foucault had with Masao Maruyama in a hotel, as his interpreter, because the conversation between the two scholars was in English. Polak intervened whenever Foucault had difficulty with the language. It is noteworthy than none of the Japanese scholars who spoke fluent French were at the meeting. According to Polak, both Foucault and Maruyama gave him permission to record the meeting, but he lost the small cassette tape, although he possesses a transcription.[68] Upon rereading the relevant passage containing the word, "mentality," Polak confirmed the accuracy of his translation.

Four factors weigh in favor of accepting the concept of mentality as having been used by Foucault. First, it is a commonly used word in French conversations. Furthermore, Foucault did not use a qualifier such as "something akin to a different mentality," in the same way that he sought to qualify the Orient–Occident division. Second, Foucault generally felt estranged in

Japan on both trips, and could have found in "mentality" a useful concept to capture the idea of distance from what appears familiar. Third, in some discussions, as recounted earlier, he was at a loss answering his interlocutors, and struggled with the identification of concrete and fundamental differences between Western and Japanese cultures. This suggests that "mentality" appeared as the appropriate concept in the conversation. Writing it would perhaps have given Foucault pause. But there is no compelling reason to assume that because Foucault questioned a concept in his work, he would never use it again. This sort of consistency, if not infallibility, goes against his stated freedom to change his mind. In the Introduction of *L'archéologie du savoir*, he specifically warned: "Do not ask me who I am and do not tell me to remain the same..."[69]

The French dictionary *Littré* defines *mentalité* as "state of mind, a person's way of thinking" or "a group's totality of habits and beliefs."[70] One of the synonyms *Littré* gives is "nature." The 1885 edition of *Littré* had no entry for the word,[71] suggesting that it was introduced in the language at a later date. The term became known in anthropology and gained currency after the publication of Lucien Lévy-Bruhl's *La Mentalité Primitive*. Lévy-Bruhl noted in his preface to the book that his previous 1910 book, *Les Fonctions Mentales dans les Sociétés Inférieures* (literally, *Mental Functions among Inferior Societies*), should have been titled *La Mentalité Primitive*. However, since the concept *mentalité* (or "primitive") had not entered the common language yet he refrained from using it. Although it is applicable to all people, the concept is frequently employed when speaking of people of other cultures to draw attention to fundamental cultural differences. It thus retains a trace of anthropological condescension. The concept was also central to the Annales School of French historians, who used it in the plural (*mentalités*) and in at least two different ways. Marc Bloch understood it to mean culturally shaped collective representations, whereas Lucien Febvre intended it to stress the psychological aspect of representations.[72] The Annales School generally focused on the relationship between milieu (physical and material), language, affect, as well as the social contents of the mind that characterize the specificity of an historical era while also accounting for the role of the individual as a social being. The early Annales historians intended to capture the prevailing ambiance of an era. However, over time, the concept underwent several transformations that reinforced and expanded its heterogeneity. Consequently, the concept lost any specific referent, and became used "whenever reality is difficult to assess."[73] Nevertheless, it is noteworthy that the Annales School focused on the concept for the study of the past (such as the French sixteenth century) as well as to guard against anachronism, or reading the past in the present. Noted in passing, Foucault did not use the concept in *The Order of Things* to refer to the peculiar ways in which past centuries constructed the idea of order.

In the context of Japan, Foucault used the concept (in the collective singular) to denote the traditional (and implicitly alien to the West) forms of thinking in contemporary Japanese culture. The adjective, "different" (in *mentalité différente*), does not neutralize the latent meaning of the term; it amplifies it. It is not that Foucault harbored some unconscious prejudices against the Japanese. Rather, he selected a concept he knew had a loaded history. He understood that the concept reinforces cultural difference, which he reduced to religion; it enabled him to stress the irremediable character of the difference. Furthermore, through the concept (used in the singular) he introduces the idea of anachronism (that which the Annales School wished to avoid) by juxtaposing present-day Japanese modernity to Japanese ways of thinking deemed discordant and puzzling because they belong to another, premodern, era. Implicitly, from Foucault's perspective, Japanese modernity was incomplete since it could not get rid of the past.

It is noteworthy that of late, French scholars such as sinologist François Jullien and Thierry Marchaisse found Foucault's use of the concept of mentality puzzling. Jullien emphatically rejected it; Marchaisse called it "dated and especially tainted (*connoté*)," and "a pure product of the nineteenth century of which it retains the worst aspects: ethnocentrism, colonialism and racism..."[74] Both had in mind the common usage of *mentalité* and wondered why Foucault would resort to the concept except that he must have been at a loss, unable to get a grip on Japanese culture or find his bearing. In this, Jullien notes ungenerously, Foucault "repeats here, after so many others, beginning with the first missionaries, the same scene of disembarking on Leibniz's 'other planet'"[75]—Leibniz had compared China to "another planet." The comparison has the advantage, however, of capturing Foucault's intellectual bewilderment and the necessity to find a conceptual crutch. Why Foucault used a historically loaded concept to refer to a reality that baffled him instead of formulating a new concept is a question in need of elucidation. Approaching the dialogue between Marchaisse and Jullien from the perspective of the literature on "translation," Naoki Sakai and Jon Solomon fault both of them for spinning variations of the externality of the Orient to the Occident as Foucault did.[76] At any rate, Foucault's use of *mentalité* leaves little doubt about his full knowledge of its appropriateness: it was applied to a *collective* mental configuration deemed directly related to a *religious* practice as befit a different *culture* that cannot be understood otherwise, just as it was originally used (over half a century earlier) during the career of the concept by anthropologists and historians of culture.[77]

Zen, Christianity, and Cultural Difference

In the Hegelian geographical view that Foucault had of the Orient (which includes not only China and Japan, but also ancient Assyria, Egypt, and Judea)[78] religion is a fundamental part of culture and at times sums up culture.[79] His focus on religion obscures the cultural enigma he wished to resolve; it has the effect of reinforcing his notion of Japan as a limit-experience. Whereas in Iran Foucault felt compelled by political events to focus on Shi'i spirituality, in Japan he purposely selected Zen Buddhism as his entry point into Japanese culture. However, his referent in attempting to grasp the religious status and meanings of Zen was Christianity even though he tried to display his knowledge of Zen.[80] Foucault's discussion of Zen Buddhism with the bonzes reveals preoccupations with the transnational character of Zen, its body ritual, and the ways in which it structures specific attitudes toward the self. However, his comments were couched in binary terms to illustrate differences between Zen and Christianity. Unlike Nietzsche, who used Buddhism to demystify Christianity, Foucault counterposed Christianity to Zen in a way that turns Christianity into a quasi-neutral standard of comparison.[81] As a result, Foucault's interlocutors met his analysis of Japanese culture with skepticism. Furthermore, having to explain Christianity was a distraction of sorts from learning about Zen, as he had questions of his own in light of his then ongoing work on the *History of Sexuality*.

Foucault was asked, is Zen a form of mysticism? The answer was trite: yes, but it is different from Christian mysticism. Christian spirituality seeks individuation, whereas Zen spirituality aims for its "attenuation." Thus the aims of the two mysticisms are fundamentally different, but their meditation techniques are comparable. In Zen, the positioning of the body establishes "new possible relationships between body and mind (*l'esprit*), as well as the body and the external world."[82] Foucault wished to know whether Zen was a *universal* set of practices, divorced from Buddhism as a religion. Zen master, Omori Sogen, pointed out the relative independence of Zen from Buddhism, and interpreted Foucault's comment as a testimonial to the international and universal character of Zen: "Zen is small if one thinks of it as part of Buddhism, but we do not consider it part of Buddhism. If you could understand Zen in this sense in terms of your experience, I think you would be convinced of its universality."[83] Omori's response drew no reaction from Foucault; it was met with silence. Yet Omori addressed in one simple sentence two essential concepts: experience and universalism. The "experience" Omori referred to was ostensibly Foucault's guided meditation. However, underlying this new experience as it was is the previous one of being culturally French. In the immediacy of the gathering at the temple,

Omori meant to convey the notion that the experience of meditation had (or should have) convinced Foucault of the universality of Zen since he, an outsider, appropriately understood Zen to mean a relationship between the body, mind, and outside world. In other words, Foucault's experience in the temple, grasping the Zen as a medium in a tripartite reality, was proof of *its* universality. In a sense, Omori confronted Foucault with what Kant had identified as a goal of his anthropology, the universality of the human condition as mediated by culture. It was neither the time nor the venue for Foucault to oppose the idea of universality. He was in Japan, in a temple, in presence of a Zen master and not in a university discussing human nature and culture. It is tantalizing to see the scene with Omori at that precise moment as something akin to a psychoanalytic séance where the patient stops talking for a few minutes after the doctor has untied an emotional knot thereby revealing the (surprising) truth it concealed. But, Foucault's silence could just as well represent his disagreement with Omori's interpretation of a simple experimentation with meditation in a one-time controlled setting—the meditation did not take place with other monks[84] and was hardly a spiritual affair as cameras were clicking with every move Foucault made.[85] If, as Polak maintained, the visit to the temple was no more than a fun game, Foucault's silence did not mean much. And the staged quality of the visit lends support to Polak's characterization, just as it may have caused in Foucault a sense of uncertainty.[86]

Returning to Foucault's response concerning Zen mysticism, it reveals a loss of a vocabulary with which to explain the Japanese *difference* Foucault insisted upon. On the one hand, Foucault acknowledged he did not know enough about Zen to say whether it was a mysticism; on the other hand, he asserted it was a mysticism but not like Christian mysticism. (The word Christian comes up eight times in his answer.) Besides, he also claimed that "Zen and Christian mysticism are two things that are not comparable." Furthermore, "When I say mysticism, I am using the word in a Christian sense."[87] Reflecting on this exchange, Jullien points out how the difference, which Foucault was attempting to ascertain, was not a difference at all. In reality, without being fully aware of it, Foucault described a difference of kind, not nature, an *"in-difference,"* by which Jullien meant a common feature across different cultures, one of technique of mystical practice, not a radical difference. Hence, Foucault was "trapped"[88] by his own answer, if not the question. Omori's intervention brought Foucault's groping for an essential difference between the two cultures to a close. However, at the end of the interview, Foucault thanked his hosts "for giving me this *experience* of Zen which will be precious to me. But it's a modest *experience*. I hope to be able to come back in a year or two to acquire more *experience*"[89] (emphasis added).

The experience in question in this flat expression of gratitude is carefully qualified as that of Zen, not of universality of Zen as Omori had pointed out. Foucault's enunciation neither denies nor confirms the meaning of his initial silence; it defers it.

Zen and the West

At least one major Japanese scholar, considered the father of the new Left, Ryūmei (Takaaki) Yoshimoto (1924–2012), expressed satisfaction with Foucault's response to the bonzes, although he indirectly questioned Foucault's visit to the temple. In a long letter (written in French) he sent Foucault upon reading "Michel Foucault et le Zen" (but which does not appear to have received an answer) he praised Foucault for having "avoided the mystical side of Zen and [not accepting] its universal meaning on which the monks play as if they were promoting a merchandize. Only the material and physical conditions required by the daily practice of Zen in the meditation room interested you. You also said that after your experiences, you felt the need to reflect on new relationships between the soul and the body, and between the body and its environment through the ideal posture." Yoshimoto adds: "you did not engage (in text "look for") the monks' bias."[90]

Yoshimoto's twenty-four-page letter traces the historical background of Buddhism in Japan, foregrounds the thought of Zenji Dōgen, a twelfth-century Buddhist teacher, criticizes Japanese monks, as well as analyzes Zen functions in society. However, the letter's primary concern is the significance of Zen for Western scholars, especially Hegel, who established a division between Orient and Occident. Even though Yoshimoto, who had had a long dialogue with Foucault during his visit,[91] does not refer to Foucault's conception of the Orient–Occident division, which he had undoubtedly read. Throughout the letter, Yoshimoto strove to present the ideas of the monks as out of step with modern Japan. A careful reading of the letter reveals Yoshimoto's indictment of the West's construction of knowledge of the Orient. Although generally pleased with Foucault's attitude toward the monks, he did not fail to express his annoyance with the West's interest in Zen: "In such a circumstance, we are troubled[92] not only by the strong interest that Western knowledge has for Zen but also the celebration of the purportedly universal character of Zen on which the monks insist. The state of our 'knowledge' is at stake here because this encounter between the West and Zen is somewhat annoying to us." Carefully, but as an afterthought, excluding Foucault's attitude from the annoyance caused by the West's attraction to Zen, Yoshimoto denounces the power of "incompetent" monks who manage to "force Western knowledge to understand them and even impose their ideas [on it] like a much praised merchandize."

Yoshimoto portrays the monks as "isolated" men, whose understanding of Buddhism had been distorted by their continued reliance for the past ten centuries on the Chinese translation of the sacred books. He blamed the monks for failing to translate these texts into the current Japanese language and thus do for Buddhism what "we have done for modern European ideas." Emphasizing the lag separating the monks and intellectuals such as himself, Yoshimoto insists that "the distance that separates us from the universe of the monks, confined in their meditation room, is greater than the distance that separates them from Western knowledge. Therefore, a dialogue is possible between you and them, but impossible between them and us," given that their viewpoints are "irreconcilable [with ours]." Hence, Yoshimoto finds it problematic that Western knowledge would manage to establish a dialogue with the monks inhabiting "this far away land" to suit the monks' own interest, competences, and particular motivations.

Ultimately, Yoshimoto's letter, even though it rambles on Buddhism, indulges in an incongruous application of Foucault's conception of pastoral power. At times losing focus, he tells Foucault that the West's obsession with Buddhism, as a marker of the Orient–Occident division, shows a lack of discernment. Given the flimsy foundation on which Western knowledge of Japan rests, it is no wonder that it fails to understand Japanese culture. What's more, Yoshimoto questions the appropriateness of discussing categories such as "mysticism" or "universalism" at the temple since these need, in the first place, deconstructing within the Western knowledge that produced them. For example, the so-called Zen mysticism can be considered "a psycho-pathological phenomenon. The 'Za-zen' exercise is nothing more than an attempt at reaching a positive somnambulic state at the edge of wakefulness and sleep." Yoshimoto thus opposes Western reason and rationality to the West presumably a-rational focus on Zen-Buddhism. In the end, his letter was a polite way of reminding Foucault, the rational thinker par excellence, of his apparent suspension of rationality as expressed even in the simple act of subjecting himself to a Za-zen meditation exercise under the guidance of a well-known (and by definition anachronistic) monk. But in Foucault's defense, the monks had brought up the issue of mysticism, although it was Foucault who had asked the monks whether Zen Buddhism was "universal." Yoshimoto tried to kill two birds (Zen Buddhism and the West's obsession with it) with one stone—that of questioning Western rational knowledge. Had Yoshimoto glimpsed the playful side of Foucault's visit to the temple in the manner described by Polak, he might have given his critique a different cast.

Challenging Cultural Difference

Foucault's interview with Japanese monks[93] and scholars is a sort of cameo of cultural encounter between those who experience their culture from within, but are also versed in Western culture, and those like Foucault whose knowledge of Japan, extensive as it may be, do not have the experiential depth that matches their understanding of their own culture. A discussion with Moriaki Watanabe and C. Nemoto illustrates another instance of Foucault's cultural challenge.[94] In the interview Nemoto asked Foucault whether he had seen the 1976 Nagasi Oshima's film, *In the Realm of the Senses* (Ai No Kôrida, or the Corrida of Love),[95] which raised controversy in Japan for its scenes of explicit and violent sex. To escape censorship, the director had the film edited in France. However, when shown in Japan some scenes were censored, resulting in images being cut in half. The film was based on a 1936 sensational news item about a former prostitute, Sada Abe, working as a maid in a Tokyo hotel, who choked her lover and cut off his penis during lovemaking.[96] Foucault, who had seen the film twice, expressed fascination with the couple's relation to the penis, as "it seems to belong to each in a different way."[97] From his perspective the amputation "could never happen in a French film, or in French culture." He interpreted the final scene as representing a fundamental difference with how Frenchmen understand sex with women. "For Frenchmen, the man's organ (*sexe*) is literally man's attribute, and men identify with their organ and have an absolutely special relation to it. It is an unquestionable fact that women benefit from the male organ only if men cede to them their right to it; either they lend it to them, or impose it on them."[98] Foucault further notes that in the film "the woman takes exclusive possession of the man's organ; it belongs to her only and the man allows her to dispossess him of it."[99] He perceived the crucial scene as one of "castration" albeit "not in the ordinary sense for the man was not up to the pleasures his penis gave the woman, and I think it is better to say that his penis was detached from him."[100] Implied is the idea that the man was punished for his failure to satisfy the woman; he did not deserve to have a penis. (Questioning whether castration occurred, Kazushige Shingu emphasizes that in the film Sada did not cut her lover's penis and scrotum until after she had killed him.)[101]

Watanabe's swift response stressed the complex layering of the Japanese conception of sexuality, noting the "collective and mythic illusion the Japanese have of the male organ since ancient times"; the influence of European-inspired modernization, which grafted Protestant sexual morality onto Confucian asceticism; and the spread of the Western conception of sex as an object of endless discourse and knowledge. Using Foucault's terminology, Watanabe concludes that the *ars erotica* prevalent "before Europeanization," curiously mixes with the Western *scientia sexualis* to the point where the two become indistinguishable.[102] Implicitly, Watanabe tried to impress upon Foucault a number of ideas: Japanese culture is far too complex to be understood in terms of binary oppositions, East/West;[103] the influence of the West on Japanese culture ("colonization" in Foucault's language) is real, yet it needs to be seriously examined for the transformations it may have undergone when it inflected another culture; the Western conception of the body *as interpreted* [in *History of Sexuality*] is grounded in Christianity, and thus, by implication makes little sense for the Japanese who are not Christian. At stake in Watanabe's response is a questioning of Foucault's conception of power (implicit in Foucault's analysis of the role of the male organ in French culture) as it relates to the condition of the self. At first glance Watanabe's response appears weighty, but it draws attention to the pitfalls of interpreting other cultures when they are represented by images on topics, such as sexuality, that are familiar to "us," and thus lead us to believe "we" can understand them.

Watanabe evokes the cultural layering of meaning, which to a large extent led analysts, including Foucault, astray. The film symbolically alludes to the old Japanese cult of the sacred phallus, which is also associated with the power of the emperor as the incarnation of the divine. But, from Watanabe's perspective, the film superimposed on this cult the idea that the satisfaction of sexual pleasure finds its paroxysm in death in the manner made familiar by Bataille. Sada Abe kept the penis and scrotum in her bag as she fled the scene of the crime. The play of symbols, the blurring of the line between old beliefs and new behavior, the publicity around the event, as well as the frenzied search for Sada Abe obscured the fact that the act was committed at the request of the victim. That the man explicitly *wanted* the woman to tie his penis *at the moment of the orgasm*, as Watanabe points out, is a significant factor that threw Foucault off the mark. The film further reflects what Watanabe calls "a topique" best illustrated by Mishima's seppuku"[104] (hara-kiri). From his perspective, Foucault's focus on the removal of the penis was "absolutely logical," yet it missed the point. It failed to demystify the cinematographic representation of the cutting of the penis (which was shorn of its context of meaning). By the same token, it did not consider the man's sexual game with the woman, and his desire to have his penis tied to the point of pleasurable pain, if not death.[105] Foucault's analysis barely conceals a preoccupation with what happens to a man when he allows a woman to have access to the same pleasure he derives from using his penis with her. A Frenchman would have retained control over his penis even when he "lends it to her" because "masculine pleasure comes first and is essential."

The exchange between the two scholars thus calls into question Foucault's approach to a different culture. He displayed a marked preference for quickly seizing on a cultural item as it *appears* and embedding its understanding in a Western social context. The resulting analysis is one of Western culture, once more as a referent as well as an interpretative framework stressing difference. Admittedly, Foucault did not have sufficient knowledge of Japanese culture or the news items that formed the subject matter of the film. But this only underscores the sort of conceptual hiatus in Foucault's experience of Japan before the complexity of a film fraught with ethnographic and literary symbolism.

Curious about what Foucault had learned in Japan, Watanabe asked him whether his retreat at the Zen Buddhist temple was for the purpose of "*verifying on the spot* that the meaning of the body in Zen practice is different [from that of Christianity]"[106] (emphasis added). There is veiled irony in the question since practicing a Zen meditation for a few hours or days cannot be sufficient grounds from which to infer fundamental differences between religious cultures; make definitive statement about the singularity of the Orient with respect to the body; or extrapolate from the body to attitudes toward the self. Foucault's response was as strained as it was in the interview with the bonze. He identified the role played by the body in confession in Christianity, as the "principle of movements that influence the soul," a source of desire as exemplified in masturbation. By contrast, "Zen is a *totally different* religious exercise in which the body is grasped as a sort of instrument."[107] Clearly, the asserted difference obviates the use of the body in Christianity as an instrument (of mortification) for the attainment of a higher degree of spirituality. The insistence on the "total" aspect of difference without prior understanding of how sexual desire is managed in Zen Buddhism speaks to Foucault's continued intellectual offness. The French word *désarçonné* (literally "unhorsed," fallen from his intellectual surefootedness) best conveys his conundrum. Just as Foucault gave his answer, another Japanese participant asked an unrelated question about the surprising loss of the French Left at the general elections in March 1978. Another reprieve. Foucault is back in the saddle.

THE CRISIS OF WESTERN THOUGHT AND COLONIZATION

Foucault's 1978 participation in a meditation session led by a Zen master on the occasion of the celebration of children dead before their birth was a special event. It brought together, in a nonacademic environment, Foucault, leading intellectuals, and inquisitive monks with awareness and knowledge of political as well as philosophical issues. The monks wished to hear about Foucault's views of Marxism, Euro-communism, as well as the "crisis of Western thought." In spite of Foucault's cursory answers,[108] one participant asked: "Do you think Oriental thought could help in re-examining Occidental thought? In other words, do you think that Oriental thought will in some way enable Occidental thought to find a new path?"[109] The question connotes doubts or reservations among Foucault's hosts about the tenor of Western thought, just as it signifies a sense of pride in Japanese culture (at odds with the inferiority complex the French ambassador had attributed to Asukata). (It is worth mentioning that no such question was put to Foucault in Tunisia or Iran). Equally remarkable is Foucault's answer, which revolved one more time on the idea of colonization-empire: he explained that Western thought was already being re-examined internally through psychoanalysis, anthropology as well as historical analysis.[110] It is however, at a crossroads. "This crossroads is nothing more than the end of imperialism. The crisis of Western thought is identical to the end of imperialism."[111] It signifies the end of Western philosophy. Consequently, should a "philosophy of the future emerge, it will be born outside of Europe or as a result of encounters and shocks (*percussions*) between Europe and non-Europe."[112] Noteworthy is Foucault's use of "non-Europe" in addition to the "Orient" (in the text, *la pensée de l'Orient*). These totalizing concepts reinforce Foucault's vulnerability before Japanese culture.[113] The choice of the word *percussions* connotes ideas acquiring dominance (and therefore universality) from (a power) struggle, or a clash of cultures. Foucault wistfully noted that Marxism, as a universal Western idea, put forth "by a Jew in contact with a handful of workers," has lost its appeal. Similarly, "the idea of revolution," which he traces to the French revolution of 1789, is also in the process of disappearing.[114]

Given in a country that had not been directly colonized (and in a monastery), Foucault's answer has special resonance. On the one hand, it fails to distinguish the local from the global-qua-universal. As with his interpretation of Kant's conception of *Aufklärung*, Foucault does not distinguish ideas that express *human* aspirations from the location of their formulation. Instead he insists on the geography of knowledge—a trend common among Western philosophers such as Heidegger. Unwittingly, in pointing to Marx's nationality he diminishes the universalistic appeal of Marx's thought (even as he acknowledges its international reach). By the same token, he implicitly associated Marx's intellectual heritage with imperialism—another sign of his paradoxical conception of culture. Furthermore, Foucault reduced the adoption of ideas of freedom, which implicate all human beings regardless of their location, to an expression of Western "colonization"—a condition of domination and struggle that critical traditions within Western thought opposed.

Although pertinent, Foucault's focus on the effect of the end of imperialism on Western thought nevertheless results in reinforcing his view of the West's sense of specialness. For example, he assumes that disenchantment with the idea of "revolution," which he believes is at stake in the crisis of Western thought, is a purely Western phenomenon that could not have arisen outside of Europe.[115] Singling out the idea of revolution helps to obscure the fact that it produced the very empire, which Foucault otherwise acknowledges. The relationship he establishes between the purported decline of Western thought and the end of empire has equally (and unsuspected) radical cultural implications: the West, and its ideas, can only thrive when they establish their dominion over the non-West. One part of the world appears as the condition of the intellectual survival of the other. Colonialism appears virtually inevitable. Critical scholarship on the meaning of the "West" to itself has pointed to geographical expansion as a characteristic of Western self-definition with implications for the notion of the self. According to Takeuchi Yoshimi, imperial expansion is driven as much by material interests as by the propensity of the self to "risk the danger of losing [it]self in order to be itself."[116] That there is a relationship between imperial ventures and self-presentation is evidenced in theories of imperialism and modernization. However, this is hardly the monopoly of the "West," although it is best studied in the West, which has framed and defended its reach in concepts such as reason, progress, and value-universality deemed at once transhistorical and specific to itself.

As was the case in Tunisia, the role of the colonial/imperial factor in Foucault's awareness fluctuates between being significant and fading into oblivion. In 1972, two years after his first trip to Japan, a Japanese film critic and French literature expert, Shiguehiko Hasumi, asked Foucault how he had known of a William Adams whom he had referred to in his inaugural lecture at the Collège de France.[117] Foucault's answer brings into focus a different aspect of his conception of the Orient as a limit-experience, which it also clarifies: the Orient looks in on the Occident in a way that reveals the Occident to itself. Foucault could not remember the source of his knowledge of Adams. But according to his recollection, a Shōgun had hired Adams to teach him math. Fascinated by the beauty of mathematical knowledge, the Shōgun decided to keep *it* to himself (emphasis added).[118] From Foucault's perspective, the Shōgun had discovered something the West had forgotten, "the linkages between knowledge and power." The West separates knowledge from power; since Plato, its philosophy seeks to "show or re-inscribe knowledge in an ideal sphere so that it is never touched by the historical vicissitudes of power." While the West makes this separation-division, "from the outside, in the eyes of the Shōgun, the West appears, on the contrary, as a culture in which knowledge and power are intimately linked. This appeared to me as one of the most profound views on the West. I was stunned." Foucault denounces the separation as "a fable the West tells itself to mask its thirst and gigantic appetite for power through knowledge."[119]

The significance of Foucault's statement is twofold: on the one hand, it illustrates Foucault's understanding of the Orient, "the place in which its [the Occident's] primitive truth must be sought." On the other hand, it underlines a *methodological device* to which Foucault resorts in approaching the Orient: the use of a story (such as the Chinese encyclopedia) or character (such as that of William Adams) whose ambiguity overshadows its veracity. William Adams (1564–1620) aka Anjin Miura (or pilot of Miura) was an English navigator believed to have been the first Englishman in Japan. He became an advisor, translator, cartographer, and mathematics instructor to Shōgun Tokugawa Ieyasu, for whom he built Western-type ships. He died in Japan probably of malaria contracted on a trip to Cochinchina, and was buried in Hirado, near Nagasaki.[120] He inspired the main character in James Clavell's novel *Shōgun*, (which also became a movie and a television series). It is not clear from the story as Foucault told it to his interviewer how the Shōgun kept the mathematical knowledge to himself. However, in his inaugural lecture two years earlier, Foucault had (rightly) indicated that Adams had been detained against his will in order to share his (as it turned out self-taught) knowledge with the Shōgun. In the inaugural lecture, Foucault had used this (farfetched) example not to illustrate the power of knowledge, but to explain how discourse can be restricted.[121]

In the real story, the Shōgun, a self-proclaimed ruler who started a new dynasty, was aware of the isolation of his country and had put to work a skilled foreigner, whose ship carrying goods and weapons had washed ashore, to build replicas of English vessels; give him information on Western politics and culture, especially Christianity; as well as give him advice on Dutch and English sea merchants seeking a foothold in Japan.[122] Foucault's comment does not capture the Adams side of knowledge-power. This was a shrewd man[123] who quickly adapted to Japanese culture and parlayed his knowledge of Europeans and the Japanese into wealth, privilege, and unhindered access to Ieyasu's Court as no European had done before him.[124] His notoriety earned him the freedom to return to his native land, although he decided to remain in Japan, where he married again.[125] But Foucault infused an apparently fictionalized story with a meaning that fit his conception of Japan—an instance of the Orient—as revealing its truth to the West. In this sense, William Adams plays a role in Foucault's idea of the Orient similar to that of the Chinese encyclopedia, albeit more flattering to Japan than the encyclopedia was to China. Foucault wished to illustrate the other aspect of his conception of the Orient: the Orient uses Western knowledge (such as that obtained from Adams) to resist being colonized by the West, and turns it into an instrument with which to "colonize" the West. The real story reveals another aspect, one left unaddressed, of the continuous forays made by Western merchants as well as missionaries to penetrate the non-Western world.[126] (Willy-nilly Adams played a part in this form of soft colonization by trade in the name of King James.) This trend reached its paroxysm in 1854, with Commodore M.C. Perry's opening of Japan to diplomacy and favored nation treaty backed by a squadron of U.S. Navy ships at the ready. Is it unwittingly that Foucault did not consider the geopolitical implications of his reference to William Adams? Or is it reluctance to address the universal phenomenon of imperialism/colonialism as an intricate historical system of power relations that do not necessarily involve the actual occupation of a country?

In sum, more than Tunisia or Iran, Japan reveals Foucault's struggle with a cultural space different from his own, although he shared in its modernity. The vocabulary he used, "enigma" or *mentalité,* captures his intellectual disorientation. As in Iran, he found in religion and colonization referent points to negotiate his way in the Kantian "world" he had questioned. Will he allow his *experience* of Japan to inflect his conception of otherness in his formal pronouncements about Japanese culture?

NOTES

1. Macey, *The Lives of Michel Foucault,* 146. Nietzsche told his sister, Elisabeth, that had it not been for his poor health and his limited financial means, he would have emigrated to Japan "to attain greater serenity." Quoted in Frederico Luisetti, "Nietzsche's Oriental Biopolitics," *Biopolitica,* accessed 29 November 2016, http://www.biopolitica.cl/docs/publi_bio/luisetti_nietzsche.pdf, 1. The quotation is from Graham Parkes, Nietzsche and East Asian Influences, Impacts and Resonances," in Bernd Magnus and Kathleen M. Higgins, eds., *The Cambridge Companion to Nietzsche* (Cambridge: Cambridge University Press, 1996), 359.
2. Uta Liebmann Schaub argues that Foucault's entire work was informed by an "oriental subtext," the function of which was to provide grounds for criticizing the West while at the same time asserting its uniqueness. "Foucault's Oriental Subtext," *Modern Language Association* 104, no. 3 (May 1989): 307.
3. The quotation first appeared in the 1961 original edition, *Folie et déraison. Histoire de la folie à l'âge classique* (Paris: Plon, 1961), iv. The quotation along with the entire preface was omitted from all subsequent French and foreign language editions of the book (except the Italian). The preface appears in its entirety in the English translation: *History of Madness,* ed. Jean Khalfa, trans. Jean Khalfa and Jonathan Murphy (New York: Routledge, 2009), xxx.

4. Foucault, *History of Madness*, xxx. This quotation will hereafter be referred to as "quotation," "statement," or "passage."
5. I am borrowing the expression from Peter N. Dale, *The Myth of Japanese Uniqueness* (New York: St Martin's, 1986), 2.
6. Hegel's Orient included China, India, Persia, Assyria, Egypt, and Judea. Georg Wilhelm Friedrich Hegel, *The Philosophy of History*, trans. J. Sibree (New York: Dover Publications, 1956), part I.
7. Urs App, "Arthur Schopenhauer and China: A Sino-Platonic Love Affair," *Sino Platonic Papers* 200 (April 2010): 60.
8. Nietzsche refers to, or quotes from, Asian culture throughout his works. He drew on knowledge focusing on early Indian Buddhism, the Hinayana. Johann Figl, "Nietzsche's Early Encounter with Asian Thought," in *Nietzsche and Asian Thought*, ed. and trans. Graham Parkes (Chicago: University of Chicago Press, 1996), 51–57, carefully traces Nietzsche's exposure to Oriental thought as far back as his school, Schulpforta, where some of his teachers had written about Oriental culture; his friend Paul J. Deussen, a known India and Sanskrit expert; and Schopenhauer, among others. However, according to Mervyn Sprung, Nietzsche's knowledge of Buddhism was less extensive or elaborate than Schopenhauer's, whose interpretation Nietzsche ended up repudiating. Sprung, "Nietzsche's Trans-European Eye," in Parkes, *Nietzsche and Asian Thought*, 79.
9. Friedrich Wilhelm Nietzsche, *The Antichrist*, trans. Anthony M. Ludovici (Amherst, NY: Prometheus Books, 2000), sections 23, 22 (pages 28, 27). For a brief yet interesting view of the role of the Orient in Nietzsche's work, see Luisetti, "Nietzsche's Oriental Biopolitics," i.
10. Martin Heidegger, "A Dialogue on Language between a Japanese and an Inquirer," in *On the Way to Language*, trans. Peter D. Herz (New York: Harper & Row, 1982), 1–54. I am grateful to professor Hidetaka Ishida, University of Tokyo, Bunkyô-Ku, for bringing to my attention Heidegger's "dialogue." Tezuka Tomio translated into Japanese the original discussion he had with Heidegger in March 1954 in Freiburg as "An Hour with Heidegger," which provides an indication of the extent of Heidegger's invention of the dialogue as well as his construction of the differences between Japanese and Western thought. Reinhard May, *Heidegger's Hidden Sources: East Asian Influences on His Work*, trans. Graham Parkes (New York: Routledge, 1996). The book contains an English translation of Tezuka Tomio's "An Hour with Heidegger."
11. Hegel, *The Philosophy of History*, 116. Foucault may also have had in mind the Oriental origins of ancient Greek thought.
12. Uta Liebmann Schaub, Foucault's Oriental Subtext," 308–9, traces Foucault's interest in the Orient to the influence of Nietzsche as well as the avant-garde *Tel Quel* group, including Julia Kristeva and Philippe Sollers, with whom he had contacts when he lectured before the group and published in the journal. Ian Almond, *The New Orientalists*, 25, also emphasizes the Nietzschean influence. For Foucault's association with *Tel Quel*, see Macey, *The Lives of Michel Foucault*, 149.

13. I am grateful to Professor Yasuo Kobayashi, director of the Center for Philosophical Research University of Tokyo, Komaba, for unwittingly making me aware of this point. Interview, Tokyo, 25 July 2014.
14. See Georges Bataille, *L'expérience Interne* (Paris: Gallimard, 1954). Bataille defines experience as "a voyage of man to the end of the possible," 19.
15. Hegel, *The Philosophy of History*, xxix.
16. Michel Foucault, "La folie et la société," in *Dits et Ecrits*, ed. François Ewald, Daniel Defert, and Jacques Lagrange, vol. 2 (Paris: Gallimard, Quarto, 2001), 480.
17. Michel Foucault, "Folie, littérature, société," in *Dits et écrits*, vol. 1, 974–75.
18. Ibid., 974.
19. Uta Liebmann Schaub, "Foucault's Oriental Subtext," 308–9.
20. In evoking "origin," Foucault may have had in mind the Oriental origins of Greek thought.
21. Sandrine Cottet suggests that for Foucault the Orient represented an unreachable "promised land." She distinguishes between his "discursive silence and the withdrawal of thought or meaning" to explain the unspoken and implicit references to the Orient she believes lie behind concepts such as "thinking differently" (*penser autrement*) in *l'Usage des plaisirs (The Use of Pleasure)*, 15. She is aware, however, that her approach is speculative, "l'Ethique du Samouraï," Philosophy thesis, University of Lyons, France, 69, 66.
22. Yasuo Kobayashi, University of Tokyo (Komaba campus), interview, Tokyo, 25 July 2014.
23. Yasuyuki Shinkai is professor of literature, contemporary French philosophy, and language at Meiji Gakuin University, Tokyo. Interview, Tokyo, 23 July 2014.
24. Michel Foucault, *Remarks on Marx*, Conversations with Duccio Trombadori, trans. R. James Goldstein and James Casciato. New York: Semiotext(e), 19991, 33, 31.
25. Yasuo Kobayashi, Interview, Tokyo, 25 July 2014.
26. Foucault was hardly the first French scholar to visit Japan. The cultural ties that the French government had woven with Japan were reinforced after World War II as Japan developed a predilection for all things French, including the language, the aesthetics, the arts, as well as the cuisine. In addition to Jean Paul Sartre and Simone de Beauvoir, Roland Barthes, Jacques Lacan, Jacques Derrida, Claude Lévi-Strauss, and Bourdieu, among others, have all visited Japan.
27. Daniel Defert, "Chronologie," in *Dits et écrits*, vol. 1, 49. Macey, *The Lives of Michel Foucault*, 237, indicates that Foucault had been invited by Watanabe as well as *ASAHI Janaaru*, a weekly literary magazine, sponsored by the newspaper *ASAHI*. Macey's information is not confirmed by Defert's chronology or by Moriaki Watanabe.
28. I am grateful to Moriaki Watanabe, honorary professor at the University of Tokyo and stage director, for sharing this history with me at an interview in Tokyo, 18 July 2014. Professor Watanabe belongs to the first generation of scholars (among whom are Shigehiko Hasumi and T. Shimizu, who introduced

Foucault to Japan through their translations and teaching). Watanabe had also translated Paul Claudel and Jean Genêt. In 1978, when Foucault undertook his second trip, he had translated the first volume of Foucault's *History of Sexuality*. See his interview of Foucault, "La scène de la philosophie," in *Dits et écrits*, vol. 2, 571–595.

29. Defert, "Chronologie," 48.
30. A new translation of the book by Yasuyu Shinkai is now available.
31. Macey, *The Lives of Michel Foucault*, 23, indicates that it was during his 1970 trip that Foucault wrote a response to Derrida's critique of *History of Madness* at the suggestion of Japanese colleagues. Defert, "Chronologie," 49, explains that it was Foucault who proposed a response.
32. Moriaki Watanabe, interview, Tokyo, 18 July 2014.
33. Michel Foucault, "Folie, littérature, société, 971–96; "La Folie et la socété," 996–1003.
34. Interview, Tokyo, 18 July 2014.
35. Defert, "Chronologie," 27, indicates that in 1959, Foucault was already thinking of moving to either Berkeley, California, or Japan.
36. Macey (*The Lives of Michel Foucault*, 146–47) suggests that after a number of prevarications, Foucault turned down the position because he wished to spare Daniel Defert, his companion, an interruption of his studies for the aggregation even though Defert was willing to make the sacrifice and accompany him. Defert sheds light on this event: Foucault had wished that Defert, who had an interest in Japanese culture, would make the move to Japan with him and become a Japonologist. But Defert hesitated to give up on the aggregation, a necessary degree for scholars intending to teach. However, he ultimately made up his mind to make the move. On the day he went to apprise Foucault of his decision, Foucault had already told the Ministry of Foreign Affairs, which was pressuring him to make up his mind before President Georges Pompidou's impending trip to Japan, that he declined. Defert never told Foucault about his decision since it had become irrelevant. Interview with Daniel Defert, Paris, 2 June 2014.
37. Nevertheless, a handsome young man sitting next to Foucault, who would become a noted expert on the Nō theater, drew Foucault's constant stare. Interview, Tokyo, 18 July 2014.
38. IMEC, FCL, 4.4, *Le philosophe et le politique. Dossier: Mission de Michel Foucault au Japon 4/5*. Letter no. 589, 28 April 1978. Although this is a matter of personal choice, Foucault's acceptance of the Embassy's sponsorship is, as were other instances of his closeness to the French government, at odds with his ceaseless attempt to deconstruct the mechanisms of state power to demonstrate the insidious ways in which they structure the self. His role in his country's policy of cultural influence abroad, however, has political implications that denote his sharing, even if partially, in his country's sense of cultural power.
39. Moriaki Watanabe, Interview, Tokyo, 18 July 2014.
40. Christian Polak maintains that he drew up Foucault's program, which he submitted to Foucault on one of his trips to Paris. Foucault wanted a "light pro-

gram," which prompted Polak to make the necessary adjustments. Interview, Tokyo, 25 July 2014.

41. Thierry de Beaucé, *L'île absolue* [The total island]: *Essai sur le Japon* (Paris: Editions Olivier Orban, 1979). Beaucé was the French Embassy Cultural Adviser. The Japanese version was published under Beaucé's, Polak's, as well as Tōru Araki's names. After reading the manuscript sent to him by Polak, Foucault purportedly exclaimed, "with you, I have begun to understand Japan." Interview with Christian Polak, Tokyo, 25 July 2014. In the French edition of the book (p. 7), Beaucé profusely thanks Polak, who was at the time a doctoral student at Hitotsubashi University (Tokyo). Daniel Defert explained to me that Foucault had not done extensive reading on Japan before his trips. He had nevertheless read an introductory book on Zen Buddhism by a Japanese author writing for a Western audience. Interview, Paris, 2 June 2014.

42. Christian Polak, Interview, Tokyo, 25 July 2014.

43. The book arrays historical, geographical, economic, and political factors to account for an essential Japanese differentness. Although it reifies Japanese culture and personality, it also wonders whether Japanese otherness is not the creation of the West: "Like Sartre's Jew, hasn't it [Japan] made itself different in order to be looked at differently, or by dint of being considered different, has it become truly different?," 141. Nevertheless, the book attributes the cause of Japanese cultural differentness as constructed by the West to the Japanese themselves since they collude in their objectification. Furthermore, referring to Japan as "Madame Chrysanthemum," Beaucé asserts "In mimicking our technology, our institutions, our vocabulary as well as clothing, it escapes our colonization and our mythology," 11.

44. Foucault, "La philosophie analytique de la politique," in *Dits et écrits,* vol. 2, 534.

45. Macey, *The Lives of Michel Foucault,* 401.

46. He noted the small size of one such club with no more than six people and speculated on their functions in a society where marriage is "an obligation" for men. Michel Foucault and Jean Le Bitoux, "The Gay Science," trans. Nicolae Morar and Daniel W. Smith, *Critical Inquiry* 37, no. 3 (Spring 2011): 400. This is a 1978 interview with Jean le Bitoux that had been presumed "lost." Polak accompanied Foucault to "bars and saunas." Interview, Tokyo, 25 July 2014.

47. There is a lack of clarity in the relevant literature about which temple Foucault meditated at, or whether he visited several. Macey, *The Lives of Michel Foucault,* 400, cites Kóryú-ji Temple near Kyoto; Eribon, *Michel Foucault,* 310, as well as "Michel Foucault et le Zen," in *Dits et écrits* (vol. 2, 618) mention the Seionji Temple at Uenohara. Defert as well as Polak, who both accompanied Foucault, confirmed this second location as the correct one. (One draft schedule of visits set up by the French Embassy notes Ryutakuji Zen temple in Mishima for 22–24 April, 1978. IMEC, FCL. 4.5, *Programme de séjour de M. Michel Foucault. Dossier: Mission de M. Foucault au Japon 5/5,* 7 April 1978.)

48. Didier Eribon, *Michel Foucault,* 310.

49. Watanabe, Interview, Tokyo, 18 July 2014. Watanabe notes the difference between Foucault and, for example, Lacan, who lectured the Japanese about a

Japanese essence. Typically, Lacan drew a circle on a white sheet of paper and told his audience: "the Japanese is unanalyzable!" Watanabe rightly remarks that psychoanalysis is carried out through language. Since Lacan did not speak Japanese, it is difficult to understand how he could make such a categorical statement.

50. Moriaki Watanabe, Interview, Tokyo, 18 July 2014.
51. Polak's view is consistent with Uta Schaub, "Foucault's Oriental Subtext."
52. Maurice Pinguet also remembers Foucault's penchant for the "calembour," or *mot juste* to characterize people in fun. Maurice Pinguet, *Le texte Japon: introuvables et inédits,* ed. Michaël Ferrier (Paris: Éditions du Seuil, 2009), 51.
53. The letter notes sarcastically that the experience of other countries "is of little help to this country that has not known 'The Discourse on Method' [a reference to Descartes] any more than it has been influenced by Christian thought." IMEC, FCL 4.4, *Le philosophe.*
54. The quotations refer to what the ambassador wrote, not quotation from Foucault. *Le philosophe.*
55. *Le philosophe.*
56. According to D. Defert, Foucault did not keep a diary that might shed more light on his frustrating experience with Asukata.
57. Foucault, "Michel Foucault et le Zen: un séjour dans un temple zen," in *Dits et écrits,* ed. Daniel Defert, François Ewald, and Jacques Lagrange (Paris, 2001), 618–24.
58. Ibid.
59. IMEC, audio tape, FCL 80. 1.1, 1970. *Entretien avec le journal japonais "Yomiuri."*
60. The comment is at odds with the sentence "The Orient is for the Occident everything that it is not" in the 1961 preface to *Histoire de la folie.*
61. Foucault, "Michel Foucault et le Zen," 620.
62. Max Weber, *The Protestant Ethic and the Spirit of Capitalism* (New York: Routledge, 2005). Weber had proceeded from religious doctrine to individual strategies for carrying it out, to its ultimate transformation into an ethic required by capitalism's systematic pursuit of material gain.
63. Foucault, "Michel Foucault et le Zen," 618. The concept is also used in "Sexualité et politique," in *Dits et écrits,* vol. 2, 526.
64. Daniel Defert, Interview, Paris, 2 June 2014.
65. Michel Foucault, *L'archéologie du savoir* (Paris: Gallimard, 1969), 31–33. The English translation omits the concept. *The Archaeology of Knowledge and the Discourse on Language,* trans. AM Sheridan Smith (New York: Vintage, 2010), 22.
66. Michel Foucault, *L'archéologie du savoir,* 32; *The Archaeology of Knowledge and the Discourse on Language,* 22.
67. Foucault, "Michel Foucault et le Zen," 618.
68. Christian Polak, Interview, Tokyo, 25 July 2014.
69. Michel Foucault, *L'archéologie du savoir,* 28; *The Archaeology of Knowledge and the Discourse on Language,* 17.
70. Online edition, accessed 5 October 2013, http://littre.reverso.net/dictionnaire-francais/.

71. E. Littré, *Dictionnaire de la Langue française* (Paris: Hachette, 1885), vol. 3.
72. André Burguière, "Mentalités," *Encyclopedia Universalis,* accessed 4 December 2016, www.universalis/encyclopédie/mentalités.histoire. Burguière wonders whether the Annales did not borrow the term from Lévy-Bruhl.
    Cody Franchetti notes a similarity between Erwin Panofsky's use of the concept of *mentalité* (in *Gothic Architecture and Scholasticism*) and Foucaul's "practices." He believes that Foucault's idea of "episteme" came out of his understanding of *mentalité*. If this were the case, Foucault's use of *mentalité* in reference to Japan would be meaningless since he clearly wished to point to a different way of being rather than an ascendant episteme. Cody Franchetti, "Did Foucault Revolutionize History?" *Open Journal of Philosophy* 1, no. 2 (2001): 87.
73. Nicolas Righi, "L' héritage du fondateur? L' histoire des mentalités dans l'école des 'Annales'," accessed 31 October 2013. www.cairn.info.
74. François Jullien and Thierry Marchaisse, *Penser d'un dehors, la Chine: Entretiens d'Extrême-Orient* (Paris: Editions du Seuil, 2000), 19. This chapter had already been written when I came upon these authors' book.
75. Ibid. Jullien's criticism does not imply, however, that in his own work on China he avoided pitfalls of representation, of which there were a few in his dialogue with Marchaisse. Jullien also claims in the same book to owe an intellectual debt to Foucault. He and Marchaisse overlook debates over the expansion of *mentalités* (in the plural) to the history of science to refer to the unquestionable assumptions and concepts that characterized the scientific enterprise, although they are right to stress the incongruity of the concept in the context in which Foucault applied it. Jacques Roger, "Histoire des mentalités: les questions d'un historien des sciences," *Revue de Synthèse* 111–12 (July–December 1983): 272.
76. Naoki Sakai and Jon Solomon, "Introduction: Addressing the Multitude of Foreigners, Echoing Foucault," in *Translation, Biopolitics, Colonial Difference, Traces* 4, ed. Sakai and Solomon (Ithaca: Cornell University Press, 2006), 8.
77. Jacques Roger notes that the concept of *mentalité* initially had a "quasi-normative, because pejorative, value" before becoming "descriptive." Either way, the concept has a history it cannot escape from. "Histoire des mentalités," 269.
78. Hegel, *The Philosophy of History,* part I.
79. He noted for example that in "Hebrew society" pastoral power was the most marked before it was introduced to Europe by way of Christianity. Michel Foucault, "Sécurité, territoire et population," *Dits et écrits,* vol. 2, 719. See also "Who Are You Professor Foucault?," 1967 Interview with P. Caruso translated into English, in Michel Foucault, *Religion and Culture,* ed. Jeremy Carrette (New York: Routledge, 1999), 141. The French text is in *Dits et écrits,* vol. 1, 629–51.
80. The bonzes wished to correct Foucault's knowledge. For example, when Foucault told them Zen Buddhism originated in India, they quickly responded that China, not India, was its birthplace. Both were right with respect to their own location (historical knowledge or cultural experience), as Buddhism originated in India but was introduced to Japan through China and was transformed by its new environment.

81. Nietzsche felt that Buddhism was "a hundred times more realistic religion than Christianity," although he also saw it as a mere transitional stage in the struggle against the sense of despair that the Western individual experiences in a desacralized world. *The Antichrist,* section 20, p. 23.
82. Foucault, "Michel Foucault et le Zen," 621.
83. Ibid., 622.
84. Christian Polak, Interview, Tokyo, 25 July 2014.
85. Daniel Defert points out that from the moment Foucault arrived at the temple everything was recorded. Interview, Paris, 2 June 2014.
86. Defert felt that there were undercurrents to the visit at the temple of which he and his companions were not fully cognizant. Interview, Paris, 2 June 2014.
87. Foucault, "Michel Foucault et le Zen," 621.
88. Jullien and Marchaisse, *Penser d'un dehors, la Chine,* 20–21.
89. Foucault, "Michel Foucault et le Zen," 624.
90. IMEC, FCL 59. "Lettre de Yoshimoto Ryumei addressée à M. Michel Foucault," trans. Shiguehiko Hasumi, August 1979. There is no trace at the IMEC Archives of a response from Foucault. Mention must be made of Yoshimoto's specific reference to the discussion in the temple "as described by Mr. Polak."
91. Michel Foucault, "Méthodologie pour la connaissance du monde: Comment se débarrasser du marxisme," in *Dits et écrits,* vol. 2, 595–618. Discussion between Yoshimoto and Foucault.
92. In the French translation: "nous éprouvons un sentiment de gêne." The last word can also mean "embarrassment," "unease," or "shame."
93. In 1963 Martin Heidegger too was interviewed by a Buddhist Thai monk, Bhikkhu Maha Mani, accessed 31 December 2013, http://video-text.appspot.com/v/L8HR4RXxZw8. In the interview Heidegger calls for a "new way of thinking" of being and the world.
94. Michel Foucault, "Sexualité et politique," in *Dits et écrits,* vol. 2, 522–51.
95. I thank professor Watanabe for the translation of the Japanese title of the film.
96. Abe was arrested and condemned to six years in jail, but was pardoned and released a year early.
97. Foucault, "Sexualité et politique," 524.
98. Foucault used the verb "*s'assimilent* à leur sexe," which connotes being one with their organ. Emphasis added.
99. Foucault, "Sexualité et politique," 524.
100. Ibid., 524. A literal translation would be "the man was detached from his penis."
101. Kazushige Shingu, "Freud, Lacan and Japan," *The Letter: Perspectives on Lacanian Psychoanalysis* 34 (Summer 2005): 54.
102. Foucault, "Sexualité et politique," 524.
103. The reductive East/West dichotomy has been denounced by a number of scholars from different angles. See for example Jack Goody, "Eurasia and East-West Boundaries," *Diogenes* 50, no. 4 (2003): 115–18; Junzo Kawada, "'East versus

West': Beyond Dichotomy and Towards an Acknowledgment of Differences," *Diogenes* 50, no. 4 (2003): 95–103.
104. Mishima, the film's director, committed seppuku in 1970 after unsuccessfully attempting a coup d'état.
105. Moriaki Watanabe, interview, Tokyo, 18 July 2014.
106. Foucault, "Sexualité et politique," 527
107. Ibid.
108. I am assuming that the conversations reproduced in *Dits et écrits* were taped and translated in their entirety.
109. Foucault, "Michel Foucault et le Zen," 622.
110. François Jullien and Thierry Marchaisse claim that the outline of the program of rethinking Western thought Foucault described for the bonze was that of the Collège International de Philosophie, cofounded in 1983 by four intellectuals among whom was Jacques Derrida. Its purpose was to establish linkages between philosophy and other fields of knowledge through cooperation in teaching and research among national and international scholars. *Penser d'un Dehors, la Chine*, 30–31.
111. Ibid. Foucault also felt that events such as the Chinese Cultural Revolution had affected the French Left intellectuals who began to question the efficacy of writing as a "subversive" act. Foucault, "Folie, littérature, société," 983.
112. Foucault, "Michel Foucault et le Zen," 622–23. It is unclear how this comment squares with Foucault's statement that the West has never known a philosophy such as Confucianism that fused prescriptions for individual moral conduct with the design of the state. What would the role of Confucianism be in the future regenerative Oriental philosophy? Michel Foucault, "La philosophie analytique de la politique," 538.
113. Foucault, "Michel Foucault et le zen," 622. To make sense of their surprise at Foucault's use of conventional, totalizing concepts, Jullien and Marchaisse (*Penser d'un dehors, la Chine,* 23) implausibly explain that since Foucault did not "re-categorize" his thoughts, he could only use such concepts *because* he was outside of the West, "in the Far East" looking in on it. In fact, Foucault had already used the "uncategorized" concepts in the quotation with which this chapter begins.
114. Foucault, "Michel Foucault et le Zen", 622.
115. Foucault, "Michel Foucault et le Zen," 623. Albert Camus, in *The Rebel: An Essay on Man in Revolt,* trans. Anthony Bower (New York: Vintage, 1956), also felt that revolution is a Western phenomenon. Foucault's customary questioning of accepted concepts could also be applied to "revolution," which needs to be rethought in a more cosmopolitan framework.
116. Yoshimi Takeuchi, *What Is Modernity? Writings of Takeuchi Yoshimi,* ed. and trans, Richard Calichman (New York: Columbia University Press, 2004), 55.
117. The reference to William Adams, whom Foucault called "Will" Adams, appears in Michel Foucault, *L'ordre du Discours: leçon inaugurale au Collège de France prononcée le 2 décembre 1970.* (Paris: Gallimard, 1971), 39–41.

118. The French text is ambiguous on this point: The "it" (*le* in French) refers in the text to "mathematical knowledge." Michel Foucault, "De l'archéologie à la dynastique," in *Dits et écrits,* vol. 1, 1282.
119. Ibid.
120. For a readable story of William Adams, see Giles Milton, *Samurai William: The Englishman Who Opened Japan* (New York: Penguin, 2004). Milton is not sure of the actual place of Adams's burial, but there is a grave bearing Adams's name in Sakakata-Koen Park in Hirado, alongside his Japanese wife, according to Japan's National Tourism Organization, accessed 7 August 2013, http://www.jnto.go.jp/eng/location/regional/nagasaki/hirado.html.
121. Michel Foucault, *L'ordre du Discours,* 40.
122. Ieyasu also found the guns carried by Adams's ship, the *Liefde,* useful in putting down a revolt against his rule shortly after Adams's arrival. Milton, *Samurai William,* 105. Adams also procured Ieysau gunpowder and weapons when he was challenged again by one his vassals in 1614. Ibid., 227.
123. Milton depicts a haughty and disdainful yet essentially honest and at times generous character who quickly adapted to Japanese culture and managed to undercut the influence of the Jesuits (his sworn enemies) on Ieyasu.
124. Adams helped the East India Company merchants to secure trading rights in Japan. In 1613 he became the company's full-time employee and was paid a salary he bargained for. In spite of his disapproval of the less-than-honorable behavior of his countrymen, he ceaselessly worked to facilitate English trading with Japan at a time of stiff competition with the Dutch and the Portuguese. He was also instrumental in sparing Protestants from Ieyasu's order to expel all Christians from Japan. Milton, *Samurai William,* 182, 193, 225, 262–63.
125. Adams was married and had a daughter before embarking on his perilous trip to Japan on a Dutch merchant ship.
126. Giles Milton (chap. 4) describes in vivid details the refined and sophisticated culture of the Japanese, which shocked the bawdy and rough ship pilots and crews. He also describes the manipulation of Japanese culture by the Jesuits who, initially contemptuous of the Japanese customs, went native in order to win converts.

Chapter 8

Japan and Foucault's Anthropological Bind

MAN: DEAD OR RESURRECTED?

In Japan Foucault faced more than the empirical challenge of processing the outwardly familiar with the experientially different. He confronted the notion of the universal while insisting on the Orient as a limit-experience. In a lecture, "Madness and Society," he gave at the Liberal Arts School of the University of Tokyo in 1970, Foucault analyzed the "universal status of the madman, which is unrelated to the nature of madness, but concerns the fundamental requirements of the functioning of society."[1] He applied the structuralist "ethnological" method (borrowed from Claude Lévi-Strauss) to the history of the idea of madness—a method he considered "a little ethnological game."[2] Indeed, Lévi-Strauss's method lent itself to a simple mathematical game. He reduced the study of preliterate social structures to the "elementary structure" of kinship, assimilated to a language, and composed of three "relations" between four "terms" represented by mother, father, maternal uncle, and son. This basic "kinship atom" helps the ethnologist to understand the rules governing the social edifice by a permutation of terms and relations.[3]

Selecting the family, language, and play as the anthropological universals, Foucault defined each universal as a system of rules that marginalize or exclude some individuals from social and economic reproduction as well as allow for "the circulation of symbols and games."[4] Some of those excluded are naturally the madmen. From Foucault's perspective, the madman in the Japanese theater is portrayed as representing the sacred, whereas in sixteenth- and seventeenth-century Western theater, the madman is represented as "the carrier of truth," a sort of saint: he speaks the truth without knowing it.[5] Foucault's comparison was based on Watanabe's comment (made at Foucault's lecture) that in traditional Japanese theater the representation of madness as delirium or possession is "a site in which the sacred is revealed."[6] From Watanabe's characterization Foucault concludes there is a "significant difference between the Japanese and European cultures."[7] Yet his cursory assessment of the "sacred" role of the madman in the Japanese theater does not explain what aspect of the sacred is represented, or the role of the character of the madman in the sacred. In fact, Zeami Motokiyo, a fourteenth-century Japanese dramatist who wrote what is believed to be the first treatise on Nô, distinguishes the complexity of madness from its representation, thus leaving room for doubt about the accuracy of the representation. He views the madman as one of the many characters (some of them associated with madness), such as demons, Buddhist priests, Ashuras (lower- ranked deities of wrath and violent behavior), and Chinese people, all of which are difficult roles requiring special consideration and talent.[8] He notes that "there are many different kinds of madness, but the actor who has grasped and mastered this one Way [Nô method] should be able to portray them all." The causes of madness may be religious, folk superstitions, or emotional trauma. "Of the various kinds of spirits that possess others, there are gods, buddhas, wraiths of living persons, and spirits of the dead; and if you study the essence of such spirits, you should be able to communicate them easily."[9] Among the madmen, Zeami lists distraught people, such as "parents searching for children who have become separated from them, women abandoned by their husbands, men who have outlived their wives."[10] He warned that madness encompasses a range of mental states that militate against acting it out as "a single general insanity."[11] Grasping "the cause of madness" is essential to portraying it accurately, in a way that "interests" the audience. To be convincing, the actor must also make sure that he remains true to the public's gendered understanding of madness. For example, he should not represent women as possessed by male spirits or men by female spirits, as this would not do justice to the possessor's spirit.

For Zeami, complexity of representation of madness is such that it dispenses with a common prop, the mask. "If you do not give your face the proper air, you will not resemble a madman at all. It will be unsightly if you do not fully understand the role and change the expression on your face accordingly."[12] In other words, to represent mad people, an actor must look like he is in a state of madness. This remarkable text, written by a dramatist, reveals two important ideas: madness is a complex condition with multiple causes as well as manifestations; it is *understandable*; it can be re-enacted in its various manifestations. And even though a spirit possesses the mad person, madness is a social condition that enables the possessor to express his will in the madman. Consequently, in classic Nô theater, there is little concern for the role of the madman as *representing* the sacred, even though the sacred was one dimension of madness. The theater treatise focuses on the actor's understanding of the condition of madness, not its social role as Foucault intimated. Inferring one from the other, a step usually taken by social scientists, may be tempting but is also risky when interpreting other cultures.

Foucault's analysis was an ad hoc response. Wisely, Foucault preferred to dwell heavily on representations of madness in the *European* theater. One of his interviewers, Watanabe, who it will be recalled arranged the Nô performance Foucault attended on his 1970 and 1978 visits, preferred to ask questions about the French theater too, of which Foucault spoke authoritatively, rather than discuss Foucault's statement about the representation of madness in the Japanese theater. As Watanabe notes, it is the philosophy in which Nô is grounded that gives meaning to the performance.[13] Hence, understanding representations of madness would require locating them in their philosophical context.[14] Nevertheless, Foucault's emphasis on Western, especially French, culture is understandable. An unspoken part of his visit to Japan was to increase knowledge of French culture through discussions of his works with local scholars. But Japan held an epistemic place in Foucault's thought, and thus his selection of madness, a universal condition, as yet another marker of a divide between the Occident and the Orient reveals the degree to which being in Japan had not inflected his view of cultural difference. He continued to look for differences between the two cultures when similarities were preponderant. The difference between the madman as a saint or prophet and as representative of the sacred is not great enough to characterize it as culturally "significant."

The will to stress cultural differences when they do not appear fundamental denotes Foucault's anthropological bind expressed in his awareness of a need to make anthropological assumptions, albeit without providing an alternative to (post-)Kantian anthropology. Having allowed for the existence of cultural universals, he nevertheless understood these to be configurations of *rules* regulating reproductive, economic, and social activities. They are universal insofar as they express necessary operations of forms of exclusion rather than a common *human* propensity to adapt to the environment, a yearning for order, or any other principle that human beings anywhere in the world grapple with when they live in society. If "there is a certain universal and general status of the madman that has nothing to do with the nature of madness," on what grounds does the differential status of the madman become a *significant* marker of cultural difference? Furthermore, if the comparative status of the madman as deduced from theatrical representations is fundamentally similar, does it not indicate that the purportedly originary divide Foucault identified in Western culture is the same as in Japan? And if so, how does this first originary affect the validity of the second originary divide between the Occident and the Orient, which Foucault had established? Could the Orient be viewed as different yet its difference considered a variation of a universal human condition, something akin to the mix of closeness and distance Foucault first noted when he set foot in Japan, but which he experienced as a confounding factor?

In light of Foucault's critique of Kant's *Anthropology* and his claim of the "death of man" largely at the hands of the human sciences, Foucault's adoption of Lévi-Strauss's anthropological method in explaining the universal role played by madness cross-culturally is perplexing. Lévi-Strauss, who had a fascination with Japanese culture, had developed his method to identify, among other things, universal cultural institutions.[15] A comparison of how the two authors—one insisting on cultural universalism, the other on cultural differences, yet using the same method—will shed light on Foucault's anthropological bind.

JAPAN'S COLONIAL EXCEPTION: BETWEEN FOUCAULT AND LÉVI-STRAUSS

Lévi-Strauss had had an abiding interest in Japanese culture since his childhood.[16] He was versed in Japanese philosophy, literature, as well as anthropology, and in his later years started learning the Japanese language.[17] He made five trips to Japan, between 1977 and 1988. The series of three lectures he gave on his 1986 trip focused on the question "how does anthropology address the fundamental problems confronting humanity today"?[18] Like Foucault, he felt Western thought was in crisis stemming from the West's loss of faith in the idea of progress as a driving force in history, and its incapacity to understand itself or solve its own problems. Once confident in its scientific and technological progress, the West now "hesitates to offer [its civilization] as a model."[19] To overcome the crisis, Lévi-Strauss wonders whether the West should not "broaden its traditional frameworks [of knowledge] which have restricted its reflection on the human condition?" It might then "learn something about man in general as well as about itself in those simple (*'humble'*) and despised societies, which until relatively recently had escaped its influence."[20]

Lévi-Strauss's approach to the crisis in Western thought stresses the illusory character of the West's sense of specialness. It is the Western propensity to sideline (and despise) societies it deems beneath its modernizing power that prevented the West from realizing that in reality its culture represents only one of many modalities of being human. The West now needs to embrace those its knowledge marginalized, and learn from them what it means to be *human* again. Although seemingly agreeing with Foucault, Lévi-Strauss avoids staking his assessment of the crisis of Western thought on the end of empire as Foucault did. Rather, central to his analysis is the loss of what it means to be human, which the West's faith in the ever-increasing progress in science and technology had obscured. Furthermore, Lévi-Strauss presents his discipline as a solution to the crisis. He defines anthropology as "the most general expression, and the end point, of a moral and intellectual attitude born a few centuries ago and which we designate with the word, humanism."[21] In other words, the anthropological perspective existed before it became an academic discipline; it represents a recognition that "To know and understand one's culture, one needs to look at it from the perspective of another, somewhat like the actor in [the Theater of] Nô ... who in order to assess his acting, must learn how to see himself as if he were the spectator."[22] He named the anthropological view *le regard éloigné*.[23]

Drawing on Japanese cultural history, Lévi-Strauss perplexingly pointed to an eighteenth-century scholar, Motoori Norinaga, as exemplifying the anthropological method of the *regard éloigné*.[24] Motoori Norinaga was the leader of Japan's nativist intellectual movement. His goal was to reread ancient texts, such as the myths of the *Kojiki-den*, "seeking the pure language of antiquity, without any contamination of the Chinese style." He wished to retrieve a pure Japanese identity, "to wash off and rid oneself of these Chinese customs"[25] by re-interpreting ancient texts, focusing on their recitation in the vernacular over their writing and reading (in classical Chinese). His task involved introducing phonetic characters (of the *hiragana* system) that transcribe the sounds of the ancient Japanese language.[26] Norinaga's endeavor had the trappings of cultural nationalism, and could hardly be regarded as a genuine anthropological search for cultural understanding. Nevertheless, Lévi-Strauss understood anthropology to have expanded the geographic horizons of humanism (from the south Mediterranean to the Far East).[27] He distinguished "classical culture," which defined itself within physical boundaries, from "anthropological culture," which has no physical boundaries.[28] Unlike "classical humanism" of the Renaissance, which benefited the aristocracy, and "the exotic humanism of the nineteenth century," which benefited the bourgeoisie, anthropology ushers in a "democratic humanism that transcends all those that preceded it." Thanks to its scope and methods borrowed from all the social sciences, anthropology brings about a "generalized humanism."[29]

Lévi-Strauss's reconstruction of anthropological history rests on two factors: (a) anthropology is a reflexive attitude, a gaze that is practically inherent to the human condition; all people engage in it; (b) because anthropology was relegated to the study of the societies deemed "simple," it has not been tainted by the drawbacks of classical or bourgeois humanism. In fact, like the proletariat in Marxist thought, it can perform a universal "reconciliation of man and nature."[30] Lévi-Strauss's new definition obscures his discipline's entanglement with Western colonial ventures. Where Foucault stressed cultural colonization, Lévi-Strauss presents anthropology as having the potential of bringing different societies together in a new humanist communion. Lévi-Strauss's elision of power in the birth of anthropology as a discipline, or in the spread of Western knowledge, is hardly an oversight. Rather it speaks of a belief in the scientific character of the anthropological method.[31] Implied is the hope that, like Auguste Comte's positive sociology, which was meant to help to bring about social harmony, anthropology would provide a quasi-neutral ground on which to build a new and better humanism. However, the anthropologist's positioning is a delicate one as he is in and out of the culture he observes; he must be at home in it while keeping sufficient distance from it in order to understand it *and* also "look at his own culture from afar as if he himself belonged to a different culture."[32]

The method rests on a two-step procedure requiring four mental operations: being in and out of the culture studied, and being out of the culture the anthropologist lives in and looking in on it with different eyes. The method, however, denies the native observer the capacity to experience this heroic yet necessary double estrangement because by definition no observer can escape the "magnetic attraction" of her culture. Although natives alone have the privilege of knowing their cultures from within, they are "incapable" of achieving what outside observers can offer: "an overall view—one reduced to a few schematic outlines."[33] Outsiders are better able to discern patterns in a culture than are natives.[34] What of the Western anthropologist who studies her own (industrial) society? Can she escape the magnetic pull of her culture? Lévi-Strauss treads lightly on the issue, confining himself to identifying the purpose of studying modern societies from an anthropological perspective: "to isolate levels of authenticity."[35] For a sociologist these are the informal rules of behavior, the taken-for-granted modes of interaction, the social networks, and all the social processes that lie behind, and give meaning to, the formal rationality of modern life. The role of the non-Western observer in correcting the "unrealizable" escape from the magnetism of the culture of the Western observer remains unknown. The question is whether a staunch and persistent commitment to a humanist anthropology as Lévi-Strauss exhibits permits an understanding of Japanese culture on its own terms.

Lévi-Strauss's interpretation sheds light on Foucault's attitude toward Japanese culture. On the face of it, Foucault's oft-repeated puzzlement before Japanese culture, the feeling of closeness and distance he experienced illustrates *le regard éloigné,* the view from afar. Whether focusing on Japan's treatment of madness or its religious rituals, Foucault stressed the external aspect of Japanese culture as it differs from the West's. In examining Zen practice he believed he could infer the interior from the exterior, "mentality," from body gestures—an illustration of Lévi-Strauss's observation that the movement from exterior to interior is a characteristic of Japanese culture, as exemplified by Japanese carpenters' use of the saw in a movement that brings it toward themselves. (Lévi-Strauss had deduced from this observation a propensity among the Japanese to focus on how action brings one back to oneself.)[36]

The mix of universalism and relativism of which Lévi-Strauss has a keen consciousness contrasts with Foucault's assertion of a universalism of forms (as for example madness) and reification of contents (meaning of madness in the Japanese theater), subsumed under an implicit relativism.[37] Like Foucault, he suggests that Japan offers an example of a way out since Japan had escaped absorption by Western culture: "Contrary to so many so-called under-developed peoples, it [Japan] did not surrender to a foreign model. It momentarily strayed from its spiritual center of gravity only to better secure it by protecting its contours."[38] He finds the operation of a quasi-anthropological law behind the Japanese preservation of their identity according to which "each particular culture, as well as the totality of the cultures that make up humanity, can survive and prosper except by functioning on a double rhythm of openness and closure, at times out of phase with one another, at other times coexisting in the long run."[39] Generalizing further, Lévi-Strauss sees in the Japanese example a demonstration that "every culture must be faithful to itself at the price of a certain degree of deafness and total or partial insensitivity to values different from its own."[40] In this respect, Lévi-Strauss is convinced that Japan has a great deal to offer not only to the West, but also to *anthropology.*

The comparison between Foucault and Lévi-Strauss's conceptions of Japanese cultural exceptionalism points to three crucial facts: First, Foucault's recourse to the anthropological method, even though he rejects its humanist-universalist philosophical grounding, results in conclusions similar to Lévi-Strauss's. Second, humanist anthropology fails to remedy the view of Japan as a limit-experience. Both authors present Japanese culture as fundamentally different from the West's, but in this difference the West finds a promise of a return to its rejuvenated self. Foucault's view is all the more problematic that Nietzsche, whose influence he acknowledged time and again, had taken a different stance: Nietzsche adopted the perspective of Oriental cultures (as exemplified by Islam and Buddhism) to understand his culture and himself. Using optical metaphors such as "trans-European eye,"[41] "optics," or "different way of seeing,"[42] he consistently adopted the method of "questioning behind"[43] the familiar tradition or text, to gauge the limits of his culture as well as render visible its taken-for-granted features.[44] In retrospect, Lévi-Strauss's *regard éloigné* owes a debt to Nietzsche.

Against this background, Foucault's method appears as a sort of shell for an anthropology devoid of substantive content in which social rules operate without a consciousness (or a "mind" in Lévi-Strauss's language) that produces, selects, or puts them into play. The Japanese rules of exclusion of the mad are neither described nor explained; they are assumed to be operative in, and deducible from, the Japanese Theater. Nevertheless, Foucault's comments on Japanese culture (just like those he made about Iran) still presuppose a being that plays roles, decides how to represent his institutions to himself, etc. When faced with Japanese culture, as with Iran, Foucault does not provide an alternative to Kant's cosmopolitan anthropology. However, in spite of his puzzelement before Japanese empirical reality, he was still able to communicate with the Japanese through interpreters (notwithstanding his emphasis on their essential cultural difference from him). But, given his conviction that there can be no humanist social science after Darwin, Nietzsche and Freud, Foucault could only stress Japan's cultural difference.

Yet, Foucault's misgivings about anthropological humanism are not without merit. He inadvertently points to a profoundly problematic aspect of anthropology, which is best illustrated in Lévi-Strauss's approach. On the one hand, anthropology is expected to decenter the observer (and by extension her society) by relativizing her culture. On the other hand, the encounter with other cultures allows for comparisons between cultures that frequently (and perhaps inevitably) place the culture of the observer in a favorable position.[45] The inner difficulties of anthropology were described in chapter 4 and need not be repeated here. Suffice it to say that there is another fundamental aspect of the anthropological method of reasoning that is highly questionable: endowing cultural differences in the handling of objects (as for example how to handle a saw) with the power to explain deeper, quasi-ontological meanings.[46] Nevertheless Lévi-Strauss was keenly aware of the similarities between cultures and frequently, as in the case of Japan, sought to trace their sources.

Parenthetically, Lévi-Strauss's reiterated notion, laudable as it is, that knowledge of other cultures helps Western peoples to understand their societies and themselves better[47] virtually transforms the existence of other peoples as necessary tropes for the West; it further elides a significant question about the anthropological endeavor: do the objects of the Western anthropologist's studies understand themselves better too by being studied by cultural others? What if they do not? Preliterate people served as the objects of elaborate theories and empirical disputes without ever knowing what was written about them. The unquestioned asymmetry between the observer and the observed, somehow assumed to dissolve under the scientific method, stands in the way of achieving a "third humanism."

Nevertheless, in spite of the similarities between Foucault's and Lévi-Strauss's understanding of the purported Japanese cultural uniqueness, Foucault's formal adoption of the anthropological method is a retreat from Lévi-Strauss's effort to reset anthropology on a more cosmopolitan path, rather than the formulation of a new or different approach. Predictably, where Lévi-Strauss emphasizes "the search for the commonality of forms and the invariant properties existing behind the most varied styles of life,"[48] Foucault dwells on the unique (the West). Where Lévi-Strauss stresses anthropology's ultimate objective as the study of the "human condition" (beyond the forms of humans' cultural expression), an echo of Kant's "human nature," Foucault retreats to the first stage of the anthropological method: the identification of rules of social organization and their individual or group effects.[49]

From Foucault's perspective, cross-cultural comparisons are meant to draw sharp lines between cultures presumed to be self-operating systems of rule production in a process devoid of a purpose, other than regulating itself in a history of a perpetual present. In obviating the meanings of cultural differences for understanding the "human," including oneself, Foucault's approach must partially rely on external factors such as colonialism to mediate between the cultures of the Orient and Occident. Japan is worthy of attention because it has never been colonized by the West. Yet even though it is an industrial society, it is unfathomable because it faces "us" with a massive, if opaque, otherness. Implicitly, it is easier to understand societies that have been colonized as we recognize "our" impact on them—Foucault had been less estranged in formerly colonized Tunisia. Concealed in this view is the notion that colonialism is a system of rules of inclusion/exclusion that lead to new rules of inclusion/exclusion, elaborated in the West and thus graspable. Where colonialism is missing, cultural rules, nevertheless deemed universal, are difficult to make out due to the "mentality" of their agents. Consciousness, which Foucault had in principle ruled out from his methodology, reappears as that which is not comprehensible. Hence, to reiterate, colonialism in this interpretation is only a consequence of Foucault's larger anthropological bind, rather than a system he supported.[50]

BEHIND THE JAPANESE ENIGMA

However, neither author, in their readiness to hail Japan as a society that escaped Western colonization, appreciated how the "escape" (a term left unquestioned) occurred. Neither author fathomed the unintended consequences of Western influence on Japanese culture, or looked into the underside of Japan's apparent difference, which the concept of *mentalité* obscured. The touted "escape" from colonization was in reality as brutal in its deliberateness as it was in its effects on the daily life of the Japanese. The 1868 Meiji imperial *Charter Oath* flatly ordered that "evil customs of the past shall be abandoned, and actions shall be based on international usage,"[51] meaning Western. The definition of "evil" included religious beliefs and resulted in individuals ransacking and destroying Buddhist temples, before the state realized it needed to preserve relics of the past, at least as art. Another decree issued on 9 December 1872 imposed the adoption of the Gregorian calendar and changed the dates of festivals. The lunar calendar was abandoned because it "belongs to arbitrariness and ignorance, and impedes the achievement of knowledge." The "accuracy" of the new calendar made "debate whether or not it is convenient or unnecessary."[52] Above and beyond its obvious benefit in making exchange with the West easier, facilitating the rationalization of the incipient capitalist economy, and consolidating state power over society, the change of calendar marked Japan's entry into the Western time frame and horizon by rupturing its own historical time as well as transforming its social time.[53] Unsurprisingly, the Japanese felt disoriented; some of them wondered whether they would not "lose reality when the moon is rising at the end of the month and no longer corresponds to the word *tsugomori* [end of month] or, on the other hand, when the fifteenth night is dark?"[54] Still others lamented that "nothing is the way it should be."[55] There were riots in 1871 and 1873 not only against the new conception of time and other unpopular measures taken by the state, but also against the presence and influence of foreigners-qua-Westerners, perceived as doing their own evil.[56]

It is beyond the scope of this book to describe the seismic changes ordered from above, which the Japanese people experienced under the Meiji government, or their lasting effects. However, the radical nature of these changes puts them on a par with the structural changes imposed by colonial governments in societies that had their own calendars, belief systems, and lifestyles, as for example Algeria or Vietnam. In all these instances, a colonization of the lifeworld took place insofar as the familiar space people lived in was either penetrated by, superimposed on, or replaced by new ways of marking time, celebrating religious holidays, or even having to adopt the language of the colonizer.[57]

The strategies Japan felt compelled to use to catch up to the West bespeak more than some natural immunity to absorption by the West's Logos, or some uncanny capacity to carefully find the right dose of Western culture to inject into Japanese society, as Lévi-Strauss asserted. On the face of it, slogans such as *Wakon yôsai* (Western techniques and Japanese soul), *Fukoku kyôhei* (enrich and militarize the state) and *Datsua nyûô* (leave Asia [a call to students] to become like the West) reflected a policy of selecting out of several Western societies "elements of the *civilization* of the West but not the *culture* of one particular Western country in its entirety," as was the case in colonized countries.[58] The dubious distinction between civilization and culture obscures the identity crisis that efforts to "modernize," or bring Japan in the same time frame as the West provoked—a crisis not fundamentally different from that of formerly colonized societies, albeit more intense and resulting in a different outcome.

Reacting to change from above, Japanese scholars, many hailing from the upper class, developed a comprehensive field of knowledge, the *nihonjinron* (or "discussions of the Japanese"), which, although started in the nineteenth century, achieved momentum in the aftermath of World War II. Using Western (positivist methods) of historical analysis, scholars sought to construct a Japanese historiography that would define Japanese identity as separate from both China (whose culture had dominated Japan for centuries) as well as the West. They also wished to construct for themselves a history that would indicate a movement forward analogous to the West's conception of progress toward modernity.[59] Ironically, as they strove to distinguish themselves from the "Orient," as understood by the West, scholars felt compelled to stress their Oriental origins. They set out to construct a purified Orient from the fragment of the space called Asia. Confucianism (wrested from China's ancient *past*, deemed purer than its present) played a big role as a counterpoint to unwanted Western "modern" characteristics, of which individualism was an example. They also harnessed archaeological research to find a distinctly Japanese origin different from other Asians, especially the Chinese.[60] The effort at times backfired as archaeologist Edward Morse discovered cannibalistic groups among the earliest occupants of the Japanese archipelago.[61] The effort to secure an identity befitting Japan changing position in global politics, resulted in Japan adopting some of the West's views of the Orient when studying China.

Imagining a new identity was accompanied by the reformulation of conceptual tools. The concept of Tōyō, for instance, which initially referred to "eastern seas" or the East, was imparted with more specific meaning, such as the values and culture of the East—in other words the Orient as conceived by Japan.[62] In Foucauldian terms, in Japan's *ratio* there were three divides: between the Orient and the Occident, between Japan and Asia, and between the imagined Japan and the real Japan, inhabiting an imagined space in between (as well as above) its many pasts and its present. The exaltation of the uniqueness of the Japanese could not proceed without a search for signs of Japanese uniqueness in all fields of study, including the sciences, and of a correlation between Japanese natural history and Japanese culture.[63] *Nihonjinron* also resulted in the reification of differences between Western and Japanese people—a reverse image of the West's ethnocentric understanding of Japan.[64] Oddly, it is Westerners such as the American Edward Morse, the Englishman John Milne, and the German Edmund Naumann who, through their zoological, geological, and archeological work, brought Japan into a transhistorical morphological space that could not support any stable identity myth of Japanese-Oriental uniqueness.[65] And this makes Lévi-Strauss's acceptance of the myth all the more perplexing as he studied Japan's other (ancient) cultural myths.[66]

BEYOND THE ORIENT–OCCIDENT DIVIDE

Ironically, it is Japanese scholars trained in Western philosophy who also attempted to overcome the Orient–Occident divide so central to Foucault's thought. One of these, Keiji Nishitani (1900–1999), was a renowned Nietzsche scholar,[67] who studied for two years (1937–1939) under Heidegger when he was lecturing in Freiburg on Nietzsche, and practitioner of Zen as a way of experiencing the suspension of reason.[68] Like his mentor, Kitaro Nishida,[69] he appreciated Western philosophical thought but intended to transcend the categorical divide between East and West. He critically and trenchantly described Japanese culture as "a recent offshoot of European culture and a shadow-image of European-style thinking." Nevertheless, he felt that "[t]he spiritual basis of Europe has not become our spiritual basis."[70] He reminded his contemporaries that the Japanese had embraced Western culture "naively and uncritically," not realizing that it was already in a state of internal "decay" denounced by intellectuals from Baudelaire to Nietzsche.[71] He decried the "self-contempt" as well as "self-splitting" that set in after the passing of the (Meiji period) generation that initially fueled the Westernization of his country with "moral energy."[72] If Western societies were experiencing a crisis of nihilism, Japan needed to confront itself critically and come to terms with its own unrecognized nihilistic crisis. European nihilism "now forces our historical existence, our 'being ourselves among others.'" Nishitani, unlike Foucault or Lévi-Strauss, did not see Japan as having the potential to regenerate the West. Rather, he called for a completion of the Westernization of Japan in confronting its own spiritual crisis by returning to its own "spiritual culture"—a discovery of the creativity of the past as a way of mending the (Westernized) present. He did not fail to note that Nietszche, among other Western philosophers, had (mistakenly) looked to Buddhism[73] (perceived as representing the hallmarks of nihilism in its teaching about "emptiness" or "nothingness") as a transitional way of combating nihilism with nihilism.[74] Nishitani called for a Japanese way of continuing the struggle started by thinkers such as Nietzsche to overcome "the total void and vacuum in our spiritual ground" as a result of "Europeanization and Americanization."[75]

There is no indication that Foucault had read Nishitani, his contemporary.[76] However, Nishitani's Nietzschean analysis sets the terms of knowledge of Japanese culture quite differently from Foucault. Knowing Japan means knowing the conditions of possibility of the travel of Western ideas and their long-ranging effects. It means experiencing the very crisis of Western thought, including revisiting Western philosophers' attraction to and experimentation with Oriental thought but completing the quest for a solution to a common problem (nihilism) by re-experiencing one's past in the context of an irreversible adoption of Western ideas. In other words, Western spiritual and intellectual problems are also Japanese problems, only they must receive a Japanese solution. In Foucauldian terms, Japan is to a degree the West's double, not the carrier of an inscrutable mentality or a space that escaped the West's colonizing power. The (modern) West is at the Orient's heart; the Orient must overcome the West's problems in its heart. In so doing, the Orient does not regenerate the Occident; it recognizes the West's "decay" in itself and draws on the West's groping for answers by re-exploring a misunderstood Oriental spiritual thought. The West showed the Orient its potential in resolving what turns out to be a common crisis. That the resolution of Japanese nihilism in Nishitani's perspective may be useful to the West is not impossible. A better understanding of Buddhism might be the medium through which Orient and Occident will resolve a common crisis. The Other and the self-same are embarked on the same boat.

Critical reflection on Japanese identity did not only encompass the Nihonjinron, seen as a reverse mirror-image of the West's self-representation, but also modernity. Takeuchi Yoshimi denounced the excesses of Nihonjinron, while at the same time defining "Oriental modernity as the result of European *coercion*" (emphasis added). In a manner that radicalizes Foucault's wish for the Orient to regenerate the West, he advocates that "the Orient must re-embrace the West, it must change the West itself in order to realize the latter's outstanding cultural values on a greater scale. Such a rollback of culture or value would create universality.[77]

The Japanese effort to construct an identity underscores the importance of understanding the complexity of the Western encroachment on Japanese culture and sense of self even as Japan achieved its industrialization successfully, but has yet to be on an even keel with the West.[78] Thus the fact that it was not colonized did not enable Japan to escape the negative influence of being defined over and over again as the West's limit-experience in Foucault's terms. Japan's uniqueness is in this respect a joint creation of the West as well as Japan. The West's ambivalence toward Japan as evidenced in literary works continues to hold sway, from the opera *Madama Butterfly*[79] (which originated from Pierre Loti's 1870 novel, *Madame Chrysanthème*) to the enormous popularity of Arthur Golden's 1997 fictionalized *Memoirs of a Geisha*.[80] The opera still arouses strong feelings among Japanese intellectuals and artists.[81] In other words, neither Foucault's assertion of an Orient–Occident originary divide, nor Lévi-Strauss's idealized view of Japan's capacity to purportedly preserve its culture from Western absorption, account for the complexity and ambiguity of the relationship between Japan and the West. The fear of colonization may be just as fraught with problems as actual colonization in managing cultural differences.[82]

To conclude, Foucault's conception of the Orient as a limit-experience did not cease to inform his perception of Japanese culture during his visits. Even though Japanese culture shared modern features with the West, Foucault insisted on its fundamental differentness. His resort to the anthropological method (borrowed from Lévi-Strauss) clearly indicates that he could not do away with assumptions about human behavior and thus had not developed an alternative to anthropology.

Noting that Foucault's quandary about the Orient harked back to his ambiguous attitude toward Kant's philosophy, Yasuo Kobayashi suggests that in coming to Japan, "Foucault encountered the Orient, the Oriental, the Asian, the Japanese. But in the end he could not refine his view (perhaps due to lack of time), his methodology, and really work on the 'limit'... Japan may not even have been the Orient he was looking for."[83] What he was looking for was perhaps, in Kobayashi's view, "the body," the elusive yet tangible body in Zen as ushering in the unrealizable knowledge of the Orient. Whatever that body as heterotopia might be remains a matter of speculation.

I would argue that Foucault's dream that the Orient would bring about a regeneration of the West had already been realized. Didn't Japan effectively give the West a lease on life by installing its ways of thinking and doing things, beginning with its conception of time, in the heart of Japanese society and polity? Wouldn't the West's regeneration that Foucault sought mean Japan's giving back to the West what it took from it by achieving a successful modernity, with its good and more dubious consequences? From this perspective the concept of "limit" would mean something entirely different from what Foucault understood it to be: it would mean how far Western ideas, methodologies, and ways of doing things can travel in the world and be successful by the Western standard of "modernity." Foucault's challenge was to realize that in Japan he was in presence of another modality of himself on two grounds: the Western ideas, which he cherished even as he questioned them, were embodied in the Japanese places he visited; and the continuing struggle to grapple with the past in the form of traditions to make sure that Western culture does not thoroughly erase the Japanese past was not so different from the West's own resistance to the erasure of all of its traditions. The very persistence of the Western originary choice as he viewed it is clearly one of the many surviving traditions in the West. In Japan, Foucault stood outside of the "double" he eloquently described in *Les mots et les choses*; he missed the self-same in the Japanese Other.

NOTES

1. Michel Foucault, "La folie et la société," in *Dits et écrits*, vol. 2, 482.
2. Ibid., 480.
3. Claude Lévi-Strauss, *Anthropologie structurale*, 56–57.
4. Foucault uses exclusion from *production ludique*—exclusion from playful or recreational activities.
5. There is a confusion in the text as Foucault says: "in the case of Europe, he [the madman] resembles the prophet." The preceding sentence was already focused on Europe, and had used the comparison of the madman to a saint, not a prophet.
6. Foucault, "Folie, littérature, société," in *Dits et écrits*, vol. 1, 978.
7. Ibid., 979.
8. The list includes playing the parts of "unmasked face," women, and old men. Zeami, *The Spirit of Noh: A New Translation of the Classic Noh Treatise the Fushikaden*, trans. William Scott Wilson (Boston: Shambhala, 2013), chap. 2. Zeami felt that the part of demons is just as difficult as that of madmen.
9. Ibid., 61.
10. Ibid.
11. Ibid.
12. Ibid., 63.
13. For an insightful interpretation of the cross-cultural meaning of Nô, see Maurice Pinguet, "le nô et la scène du désir," in Michaël Ferrier ed., *Maurice Pinguet. Le texte Japon*, 165–72.
14. Interview, Tokyo, 18 July 2014.

15. Interestingly, Foucault first rejected Emile Durkheim's emphasis on cultural norms before adopting Lévi-Strauss's method. Foucault, "La folie et la société," 480.
16. A collection of his articles on Japanese culture, which includes essays in Japanese only, was published as *L 'autre face de la lune: écrits sur le Japon* (Paris: Seuil, 1982), trans. Jane Marie Todd as *The Other Face of the Moon* (Cambridge, MA: Harvard College, 2011).
17. Moriaki Watanabe marvels at Lévi-Strauss's diligence in learning Japanese, noting that he had memorized a "considerable number of Chinese characters, and read Hiragana." Interview, Tokyo, 18 July 2014.
18. The lectures were published under the title, *L'anthropologie face aux problèmes du monde moderne* (Paris: Seuil, 2011), trans. Jane Marie Todd as *Anthropology Confronts the Problems of the Modern World* (Cambridge, MA: Belknap Press of Harvard University Press, 2013).
19. Lévi-Strauss, *L'anthropologie face aux problèmes*, 16.
20. Ibid., 16–17. By "humble," Lévi-Strauss meant undeveloped, small as well as poor.
21. Ibid., 42.
22. Ibid., 44.
23. This is also the title of his book (Paris: Plon, 1983, 2001), translated by Joachim Neugroschel and Phoebe Hoss as *The View from Afar* (Chicago: University of Chicago, 1992). With the help of Japanese scholars, Lévi-Strauss found a Japanese term for *le regard éloigné*: *riken no ken*.
24. Lévi-Strauss, *L'anthropologie face aux problèmes*, 45.
25. Motoori Norinaga, *Kojiki-den*, Book I, trans. Ann Wehmeyer (Ithaca: Cornell University Press, 1997), 145. See also the preface by Naoki Sakai. Norinaga (who died in 1801) wrote forty-four volumes of the *Kojiki-den* over a thirty-four-year period (1764–1798). Ibid., 11.
26. Norinaga, *Kojiki-den*, xiii–xiv; chap. 7, 8.
27. Lévi-Strauss, *L'anthropologie face aux problèmes*, 46–47. Lévi-Strauss argues that Renaissance humanism was made possible by the discovery of Greek and Roman culture. Later, China, India, and Japan provided another opportunity for self-knowledge.
28. Ibid., 46.
29. Ibid., 49–50.
30. Ibid., 50.
31. Lévi-Strauss cautions that "objectivity" in anthropology does not dispense with experience and "individual consciousness." *L'Anthropologie face aux problèmes*, 39.
32. Ibid., 44.
33. Lévi-Strauss, *The Other Face of the Moon*, 7. By the same token, Lévi-Strauss was also aware by the end of his life of the dangers of the anthropologist's substituting herself for the natives.
34. Claude Lévi-Strauss, "Questions de parenté," *L'Homme* 154–55 (April–September 2000): 720.

35. Lévi-Strauss, *L'anthropologie face aux problèmes*, 41.
36. Ibid., 36–39. Lévi-Strauss also found in the Japanese language another manifestation of the movement toward the self. However, if this movement inward gives an inkling into the "Japanese soul" as compared with the "Western soul," Lévi-Strauss warns it is just a "working hypothesis" to understand how the two cultures "relate" to each other, 39.
37. Lévi-Strauss also cautions against unbridled cultural relativism, which obscures the domination of Western culture over others.
38. Lévi-Strauss, *L'anthropologie face aux problèmes*, 143
39. Ibid., 145.
40. Ibid., 146.
41. Mervyn Sprung, "Nietzsche's Trans-European Eye," in *Nietzsche and Asian Thought*, ed. and trans. Graham Parkes (Chicago: University of Chicago Press, 1996), 76–90. Sprung also suggests, 89, that Nietzsche's method was a way to destabilize Descartes's as well as Kant's "I."
42. Eberhard Scheiffele, "Questioning One's 'Own' from the Perspective of the Foreign," in Parkes, *Nietzsche*, 43.
43. Ibid., 33. Scheiffele suggests that Nietzsche's interest lay less in understanding other cultures than in "questioning the familiar."
44. Ibid., 44.
45. Lévi-Strauss went to great pains to explain that even though cultures lend themselves to classifications, anthropologists cannot make value judgments on cultures. Nevertheless he frequently used a language implying a value judgment in referring to the societies he studied as "exotic," "savage," or "archaic," before settling on the less value-charged "humble." *Le regard éloigné*, 243; *L'Anthropologie face aux problèmes*, 43.
46. The fact that French homes and hotels, for example, are equipped with bidets, and doors have long handles instead of the customary round handles on American doors, does not tell me much about deeper cultural differences related to the self. It tells me about different traditions of hygiene and practicality. With respect to door handles, it might tell me about manufacturers' calculations of cost, ease of storage, etc. Ironically, Lévi-Strauss had denounced this kind of reasoning among anthropologists eager to reconstruct the "history" of preliterate societies by deducing it from material objects. Lévi-Strauss, *Anthropologie structurale*, Introduction.
47. Toward the end of his life, Lévi-Strauss appeared to have modified his view on this point. He noted the necessity to go beyond anthropologists' traditional propensity "to clarify the past of our institutions with the help of those of the purportedly primitive societies instead of proceeding in the opposite direction." "Questions de Parenté," 719.
48. Lévi-Strauss, *L'anthropologie face aux problèmes*, 36.
49. Uta Schaub, "Foucault's Oriental Subtext," 309, suggests that Foucault's conception of the Orient was that of an "empty presence," which helped him to use

a methodology that dispenses with "the need for working out an anthropological theory or an ethics."
50. Foucault's conception of "colonialism" differs from Jürgen Habermas's "Colonization of the Life-World," which refers to the state encroachment on citizens' private sphere in a situation of crisis. *Legitimation Crisis* (Boston: Beacon Press, 1975), esp. part I, chap. 1.
51. Stefan Tanaka, *New Times in Modern Japan* (Princeton, NJ: Princeton University Press, 2004), 9. Tanaka uses the telling expression "rupture of time," 25. He further notes that the switch of calendars resulted in samurais and feudal lords, the daimyos, losing two months of stipends, 5.
52. Ibid., 5. Tanaka suggests that traditional Japanese astronomers knew of the theories of Copernicus, Kepler, and Newton, but elected not to use them, and kept up instead with their understanding of time as cyclical, 6.
53. Tanaka points out that the new calendar "transmuted what had been the auspicious days of the week: traditionally the old weekly calendar conveyed special meanings for each day, which reflected the seven stars and the gods linked to them," 10. The change in marking and calculating time thus resulted in the "desacralization of nature," if not life, 25 and chap. 2.
54. Quoted in Tanaka, *New Times in Modern Japan*, 7.
55. Ibid., 8.
56. Ibid., 68. The imposition of the draft was one such measure.
57. In Algeria, French replaced Arabic as the official language.
58. Kawada, "'East versus West'," 97.
59. For an insightful discussion of schools of historical thought and the vicissitudes of the construction of Japanese history, see Stefan Tanaka, "Unification of Time and the Fragmentation of Pasts in Meiji Japan," in *Breaking Up Time: Negotiating the Borders Between Present, Past and Future*, ed. Chris Lorenz and Berber Bevernage (Göttingen: Vandenhoeck & Ruprecht, 2013), 224–35.
60. Stefan Tanaka, *Japan's Orient: Rendering Pasts into History* (Berkeley: University of California Press, 1993), especially the epilogue.
61. Tanaka, *New Times in Modern Japan*, 42–45. See also Tanaka, "Unification of Time," 223.
62. Tanaka, *New Times in Modern Japan*, 4.
63. A Japanese scientist (Sagami Shōichi) contrasted "Japanese bees" to "Western bees" and found that the differences between them reflected cultural differences between Japan and the West. Dale, *The Myth of Japanese Uniqueness*, 188.
64. Similarly, the Japanese brain was distinguished from the Western brain in some of its functions. Nevertheless both brains have the same morphology. Dale, *The Myth of Japanese Uniqueness*, 189.
65. See Stefan Tanaka's excellent study of the contradictions at the heart of the Japanese "modernization," *New Times in Modern Japan*, chap. 2, 3.
66. The title of Lévi-Strauss's book, *The Other Face of the Moon*, is ironic since it seems to imply the abolition of the lunar calendar and its aftermath.

67. As early as 1898 Nietzsche's work was introduced to Japan by Raphael Von Kroeber, who wished "to stimulate Japanese Buddhism to engage in philosophical reflection upon its foundations." Parkes, *Nietzsche and Asian Thought*, 5.
68. James W. Heisig, *The Philosophers of Nothingness* (Honolulu: University of Hawai'i, 2001), 184.
69. Kitaro Nishida (1870–1945) belonged to the generation of Japanese scholars under the Meiji government who absorbed Western philosophy as they sought ways to integrate it into Japanese thought. Nishida was the founder of the Kyoto School of Philosophy. He attempted to overcome the Aristotelian and Kantian binary categories.
70. Keiji Nishitani, *The Self-Overcoming of Nihilism* (Albany: State University of New York Press, 1990), 174. Nishitani noted that Christianity was at the root of Western philosophical and ethical thought.
71. Ibid., 176.
72. Ibid., 176–77. Nishitani credits those who forced Westernization on Japan with a moral will and spirit grounded in the "high quality of traditional oriental culture." Implicitly, they were less conflicted about themselves than the generations that succeeded them. 176.
73. Sprung, "Nietzsche's Trans-European Eye," 89, also casts doubt on Nietzsche's interpretation of Indian Buddhism.
74. Nishitani, *The Self-Overcoming of Nihilism*, 179.
75. Ibid.
76. Daniel Defert says he did not. Interview, Paris, 2 June 2014.
77. Takeushi, *What Is Modernity?*, 53, 165.
78. For an insightful critical analysis of the implication for the self of the West–Japan construction of modernity, see Naoki Sakai, *Translation and Subjectivity* (Minneapolis: University of Minnesota, 1999), chap. 5.
79. Junzo Kawada considers the Italian opera, *Madame Butterfly*, first performed in Milan in 1904, and in Tokyo in 2002, with a Frenchwoman cast as the heroine, to be symbolic of the West's ambivalence and Japan's sense of being the object of stereotyping and discrimination. He notes that a modified version by a Japanese filmmaker, Kijú Yosohida, introduces the bombing of Nagasaki as the final scene of the opera, with the heroine turning mad. See Kawada, "East versus West," 101.
80. For a discussion of the popularity of the book, which was translated in thirty-two languages, see Anne Allison, "Memoirs of the Orient," *Journal of Japanese Studies* 27, no. 2 (Summer, 2001): 381–98.
81. Kawada notes that a Japanese music critique saw in the attack on Pearl Harbor a revenge for the death of the main character, Cio-Cio-San. "East versus West," 100.
82. Stefan Tanaka also thinks fear of colonization was part of the reason that the Japanese state sought to "synchronize" the archipelago with the international, capitalist economic system. *New Times in Modern Japan*, 4.
83. Interview, Tokyo, 25 July 2014.

Epilogue

> I think that a writer has no right to demand that he be understood as he had wanted to when he was writing.
> —Michel Foucault, "Michel Foucault et le Zen"

This book set itself the complex task of *understanding* as well as interpreting the challenge posed by the "Orient," as an idea and an experience, to Foucault. It is located in the *béance* or unoccluded space in which Foucault left the idea of the Oriental cultural difference. The Orient, near and far, serves strategic functions in Foucault's analysis of Western thought and culture. It provides him with a methodological device with which to buttress his view of the specificity of Western culture addressed as if unitary. Whether outlining the features of an essential division between Orient and Occident, describing the oddity of the Chinese encyclopedia, or interpreting his observations of other cultures, his purpose is to draw as sharp a portrait as possible of Western culture to stress its difference from other cultures even when the difference is negligible. Furthermore, the Orient represents Foucault's enduring though contradictory philosophical orientation to otherness. Foucault's awareness of the problematic character of his view of the Orient is not in doubt: it is demonstrated in his removal of the preface containing the passage on the Orient–Occident divide from various editions of the *History of Madness,* as well as in his cursory correction of part of the passage in his discussions with monks at the Seionji Zen temple in 1978. Yet, his scholarship engaged not only the construction of knowledge about others (such as the mad), but also its constitutive power. Hence, his abiding commitment to cultural difference cannot be explained away as simply sharing in the biases of his time.

The preceding chapters grappled with two questions: did Foucault's *experiences* in Japan, Tunisia, and Iran affect his philosophical view of the cultural divide? In making sense of his experiences in lectures or interviews, did he offer an alternative to empirical anthropology, the "science of man" that he had subjected to radical criticism in his *Introduction* to Kant's *Anthropology*? In other words, could there be in the end a Foucauldian "anthropology" (for lack of a better word) that, unlike conventional anthropology, is based on irremediable cultural differences, and thus dispenses with the Kantian assertion of a common "human nature" in a cosmopolitan world? Put differently, did Foucault get an insight into the question "what is man?" Or did his experiences in different cultural settings confirm him in the notion that truly "Man is dead"?

Admittedly, Foucault did not go to the world of otherness as an anthropologist. However, his interpretations of non-Western cultures cannot be uncoupled from his philosophical orientation. Unlike Nietzsche, who attempted to decenter the Western-centric view of cultural otherness, Foucault continuously and steadfastly held on to cultural difference as defining Western self-identity. Yet he questioned as well as historicized Descartes's rationalist thought for excluding madness from its wholeness and self-certainty. However, when faced with the cultures of the "Orient," Foucault assumed a posture similar to Descartes's. He retreated behind a reified view of an insurmountable cultural difference. His approach to cultural difference is inscribed in his critique of Kant's *Anthropology*, especially his dismissal of the empirical anthropological knowledge of others in a cosmopolitan world.

Two factors emerge in Foucault's experiences with otherness: religion and colonization. In Japan, he used Christianity as a standard against which to gauge the nature of Buddhism. In Iran, he used past European Christian movements to understand the role of Shi'ism in the Revolution. Unlike religion, the notion of colonization served as the *medium* through which he expressed his interest in a culture. Tunisia, a former French protectorate, was a genuine heterotopia in which ancient Greece blotted out Arab and Muslim culture. He found the universal appeal of students' political struggle somehow diminished by its anti-colonial orientation. Implicitly, Tunisia was an example of the triumph of the universality of the West-qua-colonizer—a fact Foucault disdained. Yet it was also the unrecognized Orient at the heart of the Occident.

In Iran, ten years later, Foucault evoked escape from colonialism as a factor in Iran's specificity. However, Iran posed the theoretical challenge of religion, Islam (in its Shi'i incarnation) as a political force. The criticism leveled at his interpretation of the potential for political resistance and liberation of Islam obscured Foucault's intent to explore a non-Western cultural specificity while wondering about its similarity with the history of the West. Nevertheless, the Iranian cultural differentness persisted in Foucault's analysis of Iranians' "political spirituality," a concept through which he groped for a new way of seeing the Oriental difference. Shuttling back and forth from the Iranian cultural present to the French past, he came close to, but recoiled from, questioning his philosophical premise, the "originary choice," that underlay his intellectual orientation.

It is in Japan, particularly on his second trip undertaken approximately five months before he first went to Iran, that the full measure of Foucault's commitment to the Orient–Occident divide appears in all its starkness. Foucault's experience of Japan failed to change his view of the Orient expressed in the 1961 edition of the *History of Madness*. Daniel Defert recounts an instance when he told Foucault that he understood the people portrayed in Yasujirō Ozu's films in spite of cultural differences.[1] Foucault disagreed, pointing out that Defert was wrong because in reality one could not understand cultural others, such as the Japanese. Implied was the conviction that it is illusory to think that culturally shaped beings could be understood at all.[2]

This book has shown that Foucault's steadfast reluctance to allow for an understanding of non-Western cultures as modalities of the human experience is fraught with inner contradictions. For example, it leaves unexplained his Japanese interlocutors' capacity to understand *his* thought, which they hoped might enlighten them about the West as well as themselves. Yasuyuki Shinkai teaches about Foucault in order to reveal the similarities between the situations depicted in *Discipline and Punish* and in Japan, in particular the entanglement of the self in the web of power relations in the school setting. Shinkai felt that reading Foucault helped him to articulate the unease he experienced when as a child he was in a school where strict discipline was demanded of all pupils. Shinkai further notes how Foucault's ideas about disciplinary power resonate with his students.[3] In the same vein, Watanabe found similarities between the history of modernity in Japan and in France. He regretted that a number of his Japanese contemporaries, having insufficient knowledge of French history, might have missed the relevance of *The Order of Things* to their history. He described the book as an insightful analysis of the changes in knowledge that took place in France during its march toward modernity. Watanabe bemoaned his Japanese contemporaries' dismissal of the first part of the book as focusing on "Western [qua French] specificity." Given Japanese scholars and students' capacity to identify with the cultural situations Foucault analyzed, his insistence on the Japanese-qua-Oriental insurmountable difference needs elucidation. For how can they understand Foucault's thought and emotionally relate to it while he found their frame of mind impenetrable, unless there is a universal human capacity to reach across cultural difference to embrace commonalities that

Foucault dismissed as unrealizable? They assumed a common and understandable humanity, whereas he assumed an insurmountable difference.

Although Foucault rejected a universal human nature, he also affirmed the universalism of Western thought and practices, which even though empirically justified, remains contradictory as well as confined to the level of appearances. On the one hand he is faithful to the Kantian notion of reason's inability to comprehend the thing in itself. On the other hand, he asserts the universality of institutions such as madness, the family, or labor, which for anthropologists and sociologists speak to the multiple ways in which human beings in different cultures organize their activities and solve their problems. Remarkably, Foucault's *experience* of non-Western cultures compelled him to momentarily acknowledge that he needed to unravel the difference he so frequently stated: "I intend to work on analyzing these questions [the coexistence of Japan's pre-modern ways of thinking and that of Europe] with Japanese experts."[4] To recall, he had in mind working with Masao Maruyama, as well as others with whom he had met on his 1978 visit. Ultimately, Foucault did not follow up on this intention. Had he done so, he might have explained why he chose the "Orient" as the limit-experience of the Western *ratio*. What Foucault said in Japan cannot be simply dismissed, in the manner described by Polak, as expressing a fundamental lack of sustained interest in Japanese thought or culture,[5] or as reflecting insufficient knowledge of Zen.

Like Bataille and Blanchot among others, Foucault strove for self-effacement through writing. He wrote in order to distance himself from himself, to disengage from himself.[6] Such an endeavor would theoretically allow for the availability of the self to embrace what is culturally different and unfamiliar, or cross the "limit" as a manner of taking risks. The experience of the Orient would normally have provided Foucault with the opportunity to disengage from himself. But this did not occur. Yet, his experimentation with the Lévi-Straussian ethnological method predisposed him to being, in Gaston Bachelard's words, "a real explorer."[7] But the exploration Bachelard referred to was one that took place in the Western past. There is a sense in which Bachelard's comment that "[s]ociologists travel very far to study foreign peoples. But you [Foucault] prove to them that we are a mixture of savages," was incomplete. When Foucault traveled near and far in the Orient, he fell short of the discovery usually associated with exploration. Did Foucault's foray into ethnology demonstrate that the method somehow applies better to the study of one's culture than to cultures different from one's own? Or is his conception of the ethnological method a reflection of his writing style as well as his relation to the act of writing? In his self-revealing conversation with Claude Bonnefoy, Foucault explains that writing for him is neither a task of interpretation nor revelation of a concealed meaning. Rather, it is "a project of a presbyopic,"[8] which consists in making visible that which is too close to be seen yet establishing a "distance between the discourse of others and my own."[9] In this sense, it seems more appropriate to see in his ethnology of Western culture a recoiling from a decentering of one's self—the goal, even if receding, of anthropology.

Foucault's approach to Western culture is at times misread as a repudiation of the West as well as a manner of valuing non-Western cultures. Regretting Foucault's questioning of the notion of progress, RM Albérès mused: "He is dethroned, the white man. Michel Foucault came at the right moment to cut him up and pull his skin back."[10] Echoing Albérès, Michel Serres claims Foucault's ethnological method ushers in the "decolonization of the settler by himself."[11] Such a claim is not only premature, it also reveals a myopic approach to decolonization. Indeed, the test of the settler's decolonization is not only his acceptance or learning from a critique of the culture that sustains imperialism to which he belongs, but also a transformation of his attitude before those he colonized. The claim further omits that the flip side of Foucault's critical analysis of Western culture is to document the exceptional character of Western culture in relation to other cultures and not its repudiation as implied in Albérès's and Serres's comment. In fact Foucault made it clear that his critical "ethnology of culture" was not meant to "reduce the values" of his culture but "to see how it has effectively been constituted."[12] However, it seems as though, unwittingly, Foucault's analyses help to uncover the fragility of (Western) cultural identity, which thrives on a sense of an all-encompassing exception that suffers no unflattering comparative analysis. It requires an undisturbed relationship between geopolitical region and knowledge.[13]

In spite of its heuristic importance, the "presbyopic" approach, when applied to different cultures having their own languages, which the observer does not understand, distances the researcher from the object of his observation in a way that prevents communication. What is culturally close is blurred against the horizon of one's own culture. Presbyopics thus creates a vision impediment requiring corrective lenses. Parenthetically, the definition of culture, that "ugly word" that Foucault gave in an early draft of the *L'Archéologie du savoir*,[14] further emphasizes the local character of his approach. He acknowledged, however, that his study of Western culture was based on a double a priori: the "a-priori of right," which locates him in a "common space of culture" with which he is familiar; and the "a-priori of fact," which locates his cultural discourse in relation to those preceding his but still occurring in a "common space of culture." This moment of reflexivity stresses Foucault's concern that "in speaking I will not be external to what I am speaking about."[15] In the countries he traveled to, he was not in a historically "common space of culture" but in a larger, universal one.

Foucault did not formulate an alternative to anthropology. Rather, he used a truncated ethnological method. To recall, his experience of non-Western cultures spanned a little over a decade (1966–1978). *The Archaeology of Knowledge* was published in 1969. It remained his signal methodology no matter the variations in the themes he focused on in the following years, which ranged from surveillance and power to the care of the self. The shift from the "archaeology" to the "will to know" (*Volonté de savoir*)[16] in the *History of Sexuality* does not obscure continuity in Foucault's thought. There is little indication that the "will" to know invalidates the "archaeology" of knowing. Hence examining what the archaeology as a method intended to do, and what other method it claimed to replace, helps to shed light on its relation to anthropology.

In part IV of *L'Archéologie du savoir*, Foucault goes to great lengths to define the uniqueness of his method. In a manner reminiscent of Descartes's description of the method of doubting, Foucault reveals that the very name of the method, archaeology, was the result of "a solemn play" on his part.[17] He admits: "I acted as if I had discovered a new field, and as if to make an inventory of it, I needed new measures and referent points."[18] The archaeology is neither another study of language, nor another history of ideas. It is different from the latter discipline because it does not concern itself with "origin, continuity, totalization."[19] The archaeology eschews interpretation (the domain of anthropology) as this brings into play representations and thoughts expressed in discourse. "It does not treat discourse as a *document*, as a sign of something else ... it deals with discourse in its own volume, as a *monument*."[20] Parenthetically, the difference between a document (the domain of written archive as well as ethnological artifacts), and monument (the realm of architecture and ruins), may not be ultimately consequential since both are traces of the past. It even appears as a strained attempt to carve out for archaeology a specific domain. Furthermore, the archaeology focuses not only on the specificity of the rules but also the irreducibility of the play of rules governing discourse. Said in passing, this perspective is at odds with the play of rules discovered by Lévi-Strauss in his study of comparative myths. Because archaeology is inimical to the notion of "oeuvre," namely, authorship or subjectivity, "it is neither psychology nor sociology nor anthropology."[21]

This categorical statement makes it unnecessary to second-guess Foucault. Archaeology is purportedly unique. What then makes ethnology, a subset of anthropology, acceptable to Foucault even after the publication of *The Archaeology of Knowledge*? Foucault answers the question in *The Order of Things*: like psychoanalysis, ethnology does not study the conscious and purposive activity of people. Rather it focuses on such activities as reflections of the unconscious mind of their agents, their unthought. However, the unconscious does not inhere in ethnology; it is assumed by the structural anthropologist acting as interpreter of the behavior of people living in preliterate societies.[22] Once again, Foucault's view divorces the method of ethnology—documenting the variations in human forms of behavior and social organization— from its purpose. And the purpose of anthropology is that which Foucault specifically rejects: "The authority (*l'instance*) of the creative subject, as the reason of being of an oeuvre as well as the principle of its unity, is alien to it [archaeology]."[23] The archaeology in this sense could not accommodate anthropology. It confines itself to "re-writing that is to say in the affirmed form of exteriority."[24]

Language is also crucial to Foucault's archeological method. It provided him with the opportunity to build a method that not only defines the role of the observer as external to the culture he studies, but also cleanses concepts and the theory underlying them of their cultural contexts of meanings.[25] Paradoxically, the observer uses it as a neutral instrument devoid of subjective content, but also as an emotional refuge. Indeed, the symbolically charged interactions between observer and observed, or the intended meaning of culturally different behaviors and attitudes, lose their potency and appear as undecipherable signs much like the characters in which they are written. The paradox is reflected in the ad hoc strategies Foucault used: in Tunisia he mapped the cultural geography of Greece onto the local culture. In Iran, he subsumed the present under the European past. In Japan, he candidly expressed his estrangement but also revived the French psychological-anthropological language of unmitigated difference captured by the concept of *mentalité*. In a way, he found himself in a situation similar to the one he experienced in Sweden when he could not communicate because his Swedish was poor and his English not good enough. He came to the realization that "the only real motherland, the only ground on which we can walk, the only house where we can take refuge is the language we learned since childhood. It then became a matter for me to revive this language, to build myself a sort of little house of language of which I would be the master and know all of its nooks and crannies."[26] Being in countries where languages appeared as meaningless signs he could not decipher (although in Tunis French was used in his entourage) and having to rely on interpreters could only have increased the sense of estrangement Foucault experienced.

Foucault was in an anthropological bind. He rejected Kant's view of a cosmopolitan anthropology in favor of the study of existing social structures as sediments of activities that have escaped the will or consciousness of human beings. However, he still had to explain cultural difference, which by necessity requires acknowledging the existence of an active human consciousness, as his experience in Japan impressed upon him. In more than one way, his very insistence on the Japanese difference conceals a notion that modern Japanese people should think and behave in all respects the way Westerners do. Hence Foucault implicitly insisted on the universality of the West at the human level, but was stymied by the existence of another way of being human. Once outside of the Western *ratio*, at the heart of the Orient, among people in the flesh, he shied away from exploring the reason behind the difference, or its relation to the Western *ratio*. Unlike Nietzsche, who wished Europeans to open up to other cultures, Foucault withdrew instead inside Western reason (which he analyzed so precisely) as if worried about discovering that it is but a part of a Reason bigger than itself. It is noteworthy that Watanabe in Tokyo and Hasnaoui in Tunis had to remind Foucault of how Western ideas can be inflected or transformed by non-Western cultures, and thus that the appearance of cultural difference can be a deceptive affair. To understand this requires accepting consciousness as an active motor of action. But Foucault privileged discourse over consciousness.

The issue is not merely to object to Foucault's constant focus on cultural differences and their use as fundamental markers of otherness. Cultural differences are real and must be understood if meaningful cross-cultural communication is to occur. However, how differences are selected and how their boundaries are set determines their role in cross-cultural understanding. Differences are meaningful only if they are understood in the larger context of the human capacity for creating culture in its diversity. Should differences become reified and used as intellectual curiosities or foundations for fixed identities, the notion of what it is to be human threatens to give way to a sense of being suprahuman, of being above "culture." Consequently, the concept of culture acquires a different meaning as it merges with a reified conception of ethnicity or race. Some people are deemed to "have" ethnicity, race, or "culture," bygone relics of a past as impediment to being; others are implicitly and paradoxically presented as having no culture or ethnicity while at the same time ranking high on both dimensions. They are at once above and beyond culture or ethnicity.

Having announced the death of Man, Foucault encountered in the far Orient the challenge of resurrecting him. It is all too easy to conclude that with time, Foucault would have come to terms with Man. Admittedly, he explicitly claimed the freedom to change his mind, and would have acknowledged that he had been wrong about the absolute character he attributed to cultural difference. This would have required accepting Kant's cosmopolitan anthropology. In this sense there was an epistemic limit to how far Foucault could go in embracing otherness. In the end, he remained well ensconced in the Western *ratio* and culture he so decried, despite experiencing moments of uncertainty. As argued in chapter 3, the ultimate validity of Foucault's critique of Kant's cosmopolitan anthropology could be gauged against a methodological alternative. But Foucault offered no alternative to humanistic anthropology.

In the end, cultural otherness reveals that the greatest system of ideas of our time has a zone of shadow. It is Foucault's Achilles' heel. Nevertheless, of all the French scholars who visited or wrote about the Orient, he remains the most culturally restrained. That, regardless of his view of the Orient, it is in the Orient—in Japan—that the totality of his work, including the collection of *Dits et écrits,* has been translated testifies to the paradox of his thought: universal in its appeal, but very much local in its orientation. Foucault's claim to truth foundered on the "limit" he set for the Occident.

NOTES

1. Ozu (1903–1963) directed films frequently focusing on Japanese family life.
2. I thank Defert for sharing this anecdote with me. Interview, Paris, 2 June 2014.
3. I am grateful to Professor Shinkai for sharing his feelings with me. Interview, Tokyo, 23 July 2014.
4. Michel Foucault, "Sexualité et politique," in *Dits et écrits,* vol. 2, 526.
5. See chapter 8.
6. For a discussion of Foucault's search for effacement as an author see Zoungrana, *Michel Foucault, un parcours croisé : Lévi-Strauss, Heidegger.* Paris: L'Harmattan. 1998, 11–18.
7. Bachelard wrote a letter to Foucault upon reading *Histoire de la Folie.* See *Michel Foucault. Une histoire de la vérité.* Conception graphique Jean-Claude Hug (Paris: Syros, 1985), 119. The handwritten letter (which is difficult to decipher) is dated 1 August 1964.
8. Michel Foucault, *Le beau danger: Entretien avec Claude Bonnefoy,"* ed. Philippe Artières (Paris: Editions EHESS, 2011), 60.
9. Ibid., 63.
10. RM Albérès, "L'homme n'est pas dans l'homme," *Nouvelles littéraires* (1 September 1966), 5 (microfilm). This is a review of *Les mots et les choses.* The quotation also appears in Zoungrana, *Michel Foucault: un parcours croisé,* 121.
11. Quoted in Zoungrana, *Michel Foucault: un parcours croisé,* 121.
12. "Qui êtes-vous professeur Foucault?," in *Dits et écrits,* vol. 1, 633.
13. See Sakai and Jon Solomon, "Introduction: Addressing the Multitude of Foreigners, Echoing Foucault," in *Traces* 4, ed. Sakai and Solomon (Ithaca: Cornell University Press 2006), 17. Sakai refers to this condition as "amphibology." An amphiboly is a grammatical term referring to ambiguity resulting from the conjoining of two opposing terms.

14. Michel Foucault, *L'Archéologie du Savoir*, draft, Bibliothèque Nationale de France, Richelieu site, NAF 2028 (1), Box XLVIII. (This draft is identified in the inventory as "intermédiaire," suggesting that it is not the first one, p. 7.)
15. *L' Archéologie du savoir*, draft, NAF 2828 4(1).
16. The French title of the first volume of *History of Sexuality* is *La volonté de savoir*. The English translation replaced the title with *An Introduction*.
17. Foucault, *L'archéologie du savoir*, 177; *The Archaeology of Knowledge*, 135.
18. Foucault, *L'archéologie du savoir*, 178; *The Archaeology of Knowledge*, 136.
19. Foucault, *L'archéologie du savoir*, 181; *The Archaeology of Knowledge*, 138.
20. Foucault, *L'archéologie du savoir*, 182; *The Archaeology of Knowledge*, 138. Emphasis in text.
21. Foucault, *L'archéologie du savoir*, 182; *The Archaeology of Knowledge*, 138.
22. It is the notion that the observer can read the unconscious mind of his subjects that led to the charge of anti-humanism leveled at Lévi-Strauss. However, Lévi-Strauss defends himself (with good reason) against the charge, as he had not relinquished the humanist purpose of anthropology.
23. Foucault, *L'archéologie du savoir*, 183. *The Archaeology of Knowledge*, 139.
24. Foucault, *L'archéologie du savoir*, 183. *The Archaeology of Knowledge*, 139. Axel Honneth calls this semiologial use of ethnology a "semiological ontology" and "a fundamental misunderstanding." He suggests that it accounts for Foucault's shift of focus to discourse "as a means of domination," *Critique of Power*, 148.
25. For an insightful analysis of the meaning of Foucault's ethnological posture as well as his archeological method, see Honneth, *Critique of Power*, especially chap. 4.
26. Foucault, *Le beau danger*, 31. It was in Sweden, in this state of communicative alienation, that Foucault discovered "the pleasure of writing" in French.

Bibliography

Afary, Janet, and Kevin B. Anderson. *Foucault and the Iranian Revolution: Gender and the Seductions of Islamism.* Chicago: University of Chicago Press. 2005.
Albérès, R.M. "L'homme n'est pas dans l'homme." *Nouvelles littéraires,* September 1, 1966.
Āl-i Aḥmad, Jalāl. *Occidentosis: A Plague from the West.* Introduction by Hamid Algar. Translated by R. Campbell. Berkeley: Mizan Press. 1983.
Allen, Amy. "Foucault and the Enlightenment: A Critical Appraisal." *Constellations* 10, no. 2 (2003).
Allison, Anne. "Memoirs of the Orient." *Journal of Japanese Studies* 27, no. 2 (Summer 2001): 381–98.
Almond, Ian. *The New Orientalists: Postmodern Representations of Islam from Foucault to Baudrillard.* London: I.B. Tauris. 2007.
Amiot, Michel. "Le relativisme culturaliste de Michel Foucault." In *Les mots et les choses de Michel Foucault: regards critiques 1966-1968,* edited by Philippe Artières, Jean-François Bert, Philippe Chevallier, Pascal Michon, Mathieu Potte-Bonneville, Judith Revel, and Jean-Claude Zancarini. Caen: Presses universitaires de Caen. 2009.
Anderson-Gold, Sharon. "Kant's Ethical Anthropology and the Critical Foundations of the Philosophy of History." *History of Philosophy Quarterly* 11, no. 4 (October 1994).
App, Urs. "Arthur Schopenhauer and China: A Sino-Platonic Love Affair." *Sino-Platonic Papers* 200 (April 2010).
Asad, Talal. *Anthropology and the Colonial Encounter.* New York: New Humanities. 1973.
Axinn, Sidney. "The First Western Pragmatist, Immanuel Kant." *Journal of Chinese Philosophy* 33, no. 1 (1 January 2006): 83–94.
Bataille. Georges. *L'expérience interne.* Paris: Gallimard. 1954.
Baudelaire, Charles. "Of the Essence of Laughter, and Generally of the Comic in the Plastic Arts." In *Selected Writings on Art and Artists,* translated by P. E. Charvet. Harmondsworth: Penguin Books. 1972.

———. "The Universal Exhibition of 1855: The Fine Arts." In *Selected Writings on Art and Artists,* translated by P. E Charvet. Harmondsworth: Penguin Books. 1972.

Beaucé, Thierry de. *Thierry de Beaucé. L'Ile absolue. Essai sur le Japon.* Paris: Editions Olivier Orban. 1979.

Behrent, Michael C. "Liberalism without Humanism: Michel Foucault and Free-Market Creed, 1976-1979." *Modern Intellectual History* 6, no. 3 (November 2009): 539–68.

Bernasconi, Robert. "Kant's Third Thoughts on Race." In *Reading Kant's Geography,* edited by Stuart Elden and Eduardo Mendieta. Albany: SUNY Press. 2011.

Bernauer, James William, and Jeremy R. Carrette, eds. *Michel Foucault and Theology: The Politics of Religious Experience.* Aldershot: Ashgate. 2004.

Bernauer, James William, and David M. Rasmussen, eds. *The Final Foucault.* Cambridge, MA: MIT Press. 1988.

Bert, Jean-François. *Introduction à Michel Foucault.* Paris: La Découverte. 2011.

Bert, Jean-François, and Jérôme Lamy, eds. *Michel Foucault. Un héritage critique.* Paris: CNRS. 2014.

Besteman, Catherine, and Hugh Gusterson. "A Response to Matti Bunzl: Public Anthropology, Pragmatism, and Pundits." *American Anthropologist* 110, no. 1 (March 2008).

Beukes, Johann. "*Hamartia*: Foucault and Iran 1978-1979 (1: Introduction and Texts)." *HTS Theological Studies* 124, no. 65, 1 (June 2009).

———. "*Hamartia*: Foucault and Iran 1978-1979 (2: Scholarship and Significance)." *HTS Theological Studies* 125, no. 65, 1 (July 2009).

Billeter, Jean-François. *Chine trois fois muette: essai sur l'histoire contemporaine et la Chine; suivi de Essai sur l'histoire chinoise, d'après Spinoza.* Paris: Éditions Allia. 2010.

Binswanger, Ludwig. *Le rêve et l'existence.* Translated by Jacqueline Verdeaux. Introduction by Michel Foucault. Paris: Desclée de Brouwer. 1954. Translated as Michel Foucault and Ludwig Binswanger, by Forrest Williams and Jacob Needleman. Edited by Keith Hoeller. Atlantic Highlands, NJ: Humanities Press. 1993.

Blanc, Guillaume le. "Michel Foucault penseur oriental." In *Michel Foucault,* edited by Philippe Artières, Jean-François Bert, Frédéric Gros, and Judith Revel. Paris: Éditions de L'Herne. 2011.

Bonnafous-Boucher, Maria. *Un libéralisme sans liberté: pour une introduction du terme de "libéralisme" dans la pensée de Michel Foucault.* Paris: L'Harmattan. 2001.

Borges, Jorge Luis. *Borges on Writing,* ed. Norman Thomas Di Giovanni, Daniel Halpern, and Frank MacShane. New York: Dutton. 1973.

———. *Discusión.* Madrid: Alianza Editorial. 2008.

———. "John Wilkins' Analytical Language." In *Selected Non-Fictions,* edited by Eliot Weinberger, translated by Eliot Weinberger, Esther Allen, and Suzanne Jill Levine. New York: Penguin Books. 2000.

———. *Selected Non-Fictions.* Edited by Eliot Weinberger. Translated by Eliot Weinberger, Esther Allen, and Suzanne Jill Levine. New York: Penguin Books. 2000.

———. "The Anthropologist." In *In Praise of Darkness,* translated by Norman Thomas Di Giovanni. New York: Dutton. 1974.

———. "The Keeper of the Books." In *Borges on Writing,* edited by Norman Thomas Di Giovanni, Daniel Halpern, and Frank MacShane. New York: Dutton. 1973.
———. "The Other." In *Book of Sand and Shakespeare's Memory,* translated by Andrew Hurley. New York: Viking Penguin. 1998.
———. "Tlön, Uqbar, Orbis Tertius." In *Ficciones,* translated by Alastair Reid. New York: Grove Press. 1962.
Borges, Jorge Luis, and Margarita Guerrero. *The Book of Imaginary Beings.* Translated by Andrew Hurley. New York: Penguin. 2006.
Bosteels, Bruno. "Nonplace: An Anecdoted Topography of Contemporary French Theory." *Diacritics* 33, no. 3–4 (Autumn–Winter 2003): 117–39.
Bourdieu, Pierre. "Le plaisir du savoir." *Le Monde,* 27 June, 1984.
Bourdin, Jean-Claude, Frédéric Chauvaud, Vincent Estellon, Bertrand Geay, and Jean-Michel Passerault, eds. *Michel Foucault: savoirs, domination et sujet.* Rennes: Presses universitaires de Rennes. 2008.
Brandt, Reinhard. "The Guiding Idea of Kant's Anthropology and the Vocation of the Human Being." In *Essays on Kant's Anthropology,* edited by Brian Jacobs and Patrick Kain, translated by Jaimey Fisher and Patrick Kain. Cambridge, UK: Cambridge University Press. 2003.
Brière, Claire and Pierre Blanchet. *Iran, la révolution au nom de Dieu.* Paris: Seuil. 1979.
Brossat, Alain. "Quand Foucault dit 'nous'..." *Revue Appareil, no.* 8 (2011).
Bunzl, Matti. "A Reply to Besteman and Gusterson." *American Anthropologist* 110, no. 1 (March 2008).
———. "Boas, Foucault, and the 'Native Anthropologist': Notes toward a Neo-Boasian Anthropology." *American Anthropologist* 106, no. 3 (September 2004): 435–42.
———. "The Quest for Anthropological Relevance: Borgesian Maps and Epistemological Pitfalls." *American Anthropologist* 110, no. 1 (March 2008).
Burguière, André. "Mentalités." *Encyclopedia Universalis [Online].* Accessed 4 December 2016. www.universalis/encyclopédie/mentalités.histoire.
Camau, Michel, and Vincent Geisser. *Habib Bourguiba, la trace et l'héritage.* Paris: Karthala. 2004.
———. "Les 'printemps tunisiens' de mars 1968 et janvier 2011." In *Le movement Perspectives Amel-Ettounsi. Son histoire et ses ramificactions.* Collectif. Actes du colloque international qui célèbre le cinquantenaire de Perspectives, 18-20 décembre 2013 à la bibilothèque nationale de Tunis. Tunis: CAEU-Med Ali Editions. 2016.
Camus, Albert. *The Rebel: An Essay on Man in Revolt.* Translated by Anthony Bower. New York: Vintage. 1956.
Canguilhem, Georges. "Mort de l'homme ou épuisement du cogito." *Critique* 242 (July 1967): 599–618.
———. "The Death of Man or the Exhaustion of the Cogito." In *The Cambridge Companion to Foucault,* edited by Gary Gutting, 2nd ed. Cambridge: Cambridge University Press. 2003.
Carrette, Jeremy R. *Foucault and Religion: Spiritual Corporality and Political Spirituality.* London; New York: Routledge. 2000.
Caygill, Howard. *A Kant Dictionary.* Oxford: Blackwell. 2008.

———. "Kant and the Age of Criticism." In *A Kant Dictionary*. Oxford: Blackwell. 2008.
———. "Kant's Apology for Sensibility." In *Essays on Kant's Anthropology*, edited by Brian Jacobs and Patrick Kain. New York: Cambridge University Press. 2003.
Charfi, Mohamed. *Mon combat pour les lumières*. Constantine, Algeria: Editions du Champs Libre. 2001.
Cheah, Pheng. *Spectral Nationality: Passages of Freedom from Kant to Postcolonial Literatures of Liberation*. New York: Columbia University Press. 2003.
Chen, Chung-Qing. "Theoretical Links Between Kant and Confucianism: Preliminary Remarks." *Journal of Chinese Philosophy* 33, no. 1 (March 2006): 3–15.
Chenoufi, Kamel, and Gilles Gallo. *La Tunisie en décolonisation (1957 - 1972): genèse des structures de développement et des structures de la République*. Le Pradet: LAU Éditions. 2004.
Chevallier, Philippe. *Michel Foucault le pouvoir et la bataille*. Paris: Presses universitaires de France. 2014.
Christofferson, Michael Scott. *French Intellectuals against the Left: The Antitotalitarian Moment of the 1970s*. New York: Berghahn Books. 2004.
Clauss, Sidonie. "John Wilkins' Essay Toward a Real Character: Its Place in the Seventeenth-Century Episteme." *Journal of the History of Ideas* 43, no. 4 (1 October 1982): 531–53.
Clifford, James. *The Predicament of Culture: Twentieth-Century Ethnography, Literature, and Art*. Cambridge, MA: Harvard University Press. 1988.
Cohen, Alix. *Kant and the Human Sciences: Biology, Anthropology and History*. New York: Palgrave Macmillan. 2009.
Comaroff, Jean, and John L. Comaroff. *Theory from the South: Or, How Euro-America Is Evolving toward Africa*. Boulder: Paradigm Publishers. 2012.
Comaroff, John. "The End of Anthropology, Again: On the Future of an In-Discipline." *American Anthropologist* 112, no. 4 (2010).
———. "Of Fallacies and Fetishes: A Rejoinder to Donham." *American Anthropologist* 103, no. 1(March 2001): 150–160.
Connell, Raewyn. *Southern Theory: The Global Dynamics of Knowledge in Social Science*. Cambridge: Polity. 2007.
Connolly, William E. "Taylor, Foucault, and Otherness." *Political Theory* 13, no. 2 (August 1985): 365-376.
Corbin, Henry. *Spiritual Body and Celestial Earth: From Mazdean Iran to Shī'ite Iran*. Translated by Nancy Pearson. 2d ed. Princeton: Princeton University Press. 1989.
Cottet, Sandrine. "L'Ethique du samouraï," Philosophy thesis. University of Lyon 3, France, 1989.
Crépon, Marc. *Les géographies de l'esprit: enquête sur la caractérisation des peuples de Leibniz à Hegel*. Paris: Payot & Rivages. 1996.
Dale, Peter N. *The Myth of Japanese Uniqueness*. New York: St. Martin's Press. 1986.
Dalissier, Michel, Nagai Shin, and Sugimura Yasuhiko, eds. *Philosophie japonaise: le néant, le monde et le corps*. Paris: Vrin. 2013.
D'Amico, Robert. "Sed Amentes Sunt Isti: Against Michel Foucault's Account of Cartesian Skepticism and Madness." *Philosophical Forum* 26, no. 1 (Autumn 1994): 33–48.

D'Amico, Robert. "Text and Context: Derrida and Foucault on Descartes." In *The Structural Allegory: Reconstructive Encounters with the New French Thought*, edited by John Fekete. Manchester: Manchester University Press. 1984.

Day, Ron. "Paul Otlet's Book and the Writing of Social Space." In *Historical Studies in Information Science*, edited by Trudi Bellardo Hahn and Michael Keeble Buckland. Medford, NJ: Published for the American Society for Information Science by Information Today. 1998.

Debray Genette, Raymonde, ed. "La bibliothèque fantastique." In *Flaubert...*, Miroir de la critique 4, 171–90. Paris: Firmin-Didot, M. Didier. 1970.

Defert, Daniel. "Chronologie." In *Dits et écrits*, by Michel Foucault, edited by François Ewald, Jacques Lagrange, and Daniel Defert, 1: 13–90. Paris: Gallimard. 2001.

Defert, Daniel, Philippe Artières, Éric Favereau, and Joséphine Gross. *Une vie politique. Entretiens avec Philippe Artières et Éric Favereau*. Paris: Ed. du Seuil. 2014.

Deleuze, Gilles. *Foucault*. Translated by Seán Hand. Minneapolis: University of Minnesota Press. 1988.

Derrida, Jacques. *L'Écriture et la différence*. Paris: Éditions du Seuil. 1967. Translated by Alan Bass as *Writing and Difference*. Chicago: Chicago University Press. 1978.

Descartes, René. *The Meditations and Selections from the Principles of René Descartes*. Translated by John Veitch. La Salle, Ill.: Open Court. 1966.

———. "To Mersenne." In *The Philosophical Writings of Descartes*, translated by John Cottingham, Robert Stoothoff, Dugald Murdoch, and Anthony Kenny, Vol. 3. Cambridge: Cambridge University Press. 1991.

Detienne, Marcel. *Les Grecs et nous: une anthropologie comparée de la Grèce ancienne*. Paris: Perrin. 2005. Translated by Janet Lloyd as *The Greeks and Us: A Comparative Anthropology of Ancient Greece*. Cambridge: Polity. 2007.

———. *Les maîtres de Vérité dans la Grèce archaïque*. Paris: Maspéro. 1967. Translated by Janet Lloyd as *Masters of Truth in Archaïc Greece*. New York: Zone Books. 1996.

Djaballah, Marc. *Kant, Foucault, and Forms of Experience*. New York: Routledge. 2011.

Donham, Don. "Thinking Temporally, or Modernizing Anthropology." *American Anthropologist* 103, no. 1 (March 2001).

Dover, Kenneth James. *Greek Homosexuality*. Cambridge, MA: Harvard University Press. 1978.

Eribon, Didier. *Michel Foucault*. Translated by Betsy Wang. Cambridge, MA: Harvard University Press. 1991.

———. *Michel Foucault*. Paris: Flammarion. 2011.

Faubion, James D., ed. *Foucault Now: Current Perspectives in Foucault Studies*, 2014.

Fellous, Gérard. "Michel Foucault." *La Presse de Tunisie*, 12 April 1967. Reprinted as "La philosophie structuraliste permet de diagnostiquer ce qu'est 'aujourd'hui.'" In *Dits et écrits*, vol. 1, 608–12

Figl, Johann. "Nietzsche's Early Encounter with Asian Thought." In *Nietzsche and Asian Thought*, edited and translated by Graham Parkes, 51–57. Chicago: University of Chicago Press. 1996.

Fimiani, Mariapaola. *Foucault et Kant: critique clinique éthique*. Translated by Nadine Le Lirzin. Paris: L'Harmattan. 1998.

Forster, Peter. "Empiricism and Imperialism: A Review of The New Left Critique." In *Anthropology and the Colonial Encounter*, edited by Talal Asad. New York: Humanities Press. 1973.

Foucault, Michel. "A quoi rêvent les Iraniens?" In *Dits et écrits*, edited by François Ewald, Daniel Defert, and Jacques Lagrange, 2:688–94. Paris: Gallimard. 2001.

———. "Bio-histoire et bio-politique." In *Dits et écrits*, edited by François Ewald, Daniel Defert, and Jacques Lagrange, 2:95–97. Paris: Gallimard. 2001.

———. *Ceci n'est pas une pipe; deux lettres et quatre dessins de René Magritte*. Montpellier: Fata Morgana. 1973.

———. "Conversation sans complexes avec le philosophe qui analyse les 'structures du pouvoir.'" In *Dits et écrits*, edited by François Ewald, Daniel Defert, and Jacques Lagrange, 2:669–78. Paris: Gallimard. 2001.

———. "De l'archéologie à la dynastique." In *Dits et écrits*, edited by François Ewald, Daniel Defert, and Jacques Lagrange, 2:1273–84. Paris: Gallimard. 2001.

———. *Dits et écrits*. Edited by François Ewald, Daniel Defert, and Jacques Lagrange. 2 vols. Paris: Gallimard. 2001.

———. "Entretien avec Michel Foucault," (interview with P. Kané). In *Dits et écrits*, edited by François Ewald, Daniel Defert, and Jacques Lagrange, 2:97–101. Paris: Gallimard. 2001.

———. "Entretien avec Michel Foucault,"(interview with D. Trombadori). In *Dits et Ecrits*, edited by François Ewald, Daniel Defert, and Jacques Lagrange, 2:860–914. Paris: Gallimard. 2001.

———. "Folie, littérature, société." In *Dits et écrits*, edited by Daniel Defert, François Ewald, and Jacques Lagrange, 1:972–96. Paris: Gallimard. 2001.

———. "Foreword." In *The Order of Things: An Archaeology of the Human Sciences*. New York: Vintage Books. 1994.

———. *Foucault Live: Interviews, 1961–1984*. Edited by Sylvère Lotringer. New York: Semiotext(e). 1996.

———. "Foucault on Geography." In *Power/Knowledge: Selected Interviews and Other Writings, 1972–1977*, edited by Colin Gordon. New York: Pantheon Books. 1980.

———. *Histoire de la folie à l'âge classique*. Paris: Gallimard. 1972.

———. *Histoire de la sexualité*. Vol. 1. *La volonté de savoir*. Paris: Gallimard. 1976.

———. *History of Madness*. Edited by Jean Khalfa. Translated by Jean Khalfa and Jonathan Murphy. London: Routledge. 2009. Originally published as *Folie et déraison. Histoire de la folie à l'âge classique*. Paris: Plon. 1961.

———. "Il faut défendre la société." In *Dits et écrits*, edited by Daniel Defert, François Ewald, and Jacques Lagrange, 2:124–130. Paris: Gallimard. 2001.

———. *Introduction to Kant's Anthropology*. Translated by Roberto Nigro and Kate Briggs. Los Angeles: Semiotext(e). 2008.

———. "La bibliothèque fantastique." In *Dits et écrits*, edited by Daniel Defert, François Ewald, and Jacques Lagrange, 1:895–97. Paris: Gallimard. 2001.

———. "La folie et la société." In *Dits et écrits*, edited by Daniel Defert, François Ewald, and Jacques Lagrange, 1:996–1003. Paris: Gallimard. 2001.

———. "La philosophie analytique de la politique. In *Dits et écrits*, edited by Daniel

Defert, François Ewald, and Jacques Lagrange, 2:534–551. Paris: Gallimard. 2001.
———. "La philosophie structuraliste permet de diagnostiquer ce qu'est 'aujourd'hui'." In *Dits et écrits,* edited by Daniel Defert, François Ewald, and Jacques Lagrange, 1:608–12. Paris: Gallimard. 2001.
———. "La scène de la philosophie." In *Dits et écrits,* edited by Daniel Defert, François Ewald, and Jacques Lagrange, 2:571–595. Paris: Gallimard. 2001
———. *Le beau danger: entretien avec Claude Bonnefoy.* Paris: Éditions de l'EHESS. 2011.
———. "Le Chah a cent ans de retard." In *Dits et écrits,* edited by François Ewald, Daniel Defert, and Jacques Lagrange, 2:679–83. Paris: Gallimard. 2001.
———. "Le chef mythique de la révolte de l'Iran." In *Dits et écrits,* edited by François Ewald, Daniel Defert, and Jacques Lagrange, 2:713–16. Paris: Gallimard. 2001.
———. *Le corps utopique; suivi de Les hétérotopies.* Edited by Daniel Defert. Clamecy: Nouvelles éditions Lignes. 2009.
———. "Le langage à l'infini." In *Dits et écrits,* edited by Daniel Defert, François Ewald, and Jacques Lagrange, 1:278–89. Paris: Gallimard. 2001.
———. "Le piège de Vincennes." In *Dits et écrits,* edited by Daniel Defert, François Ewald, and Jacques Lagrange, 1:933–41. Paris: Gallimard. 2001.
———. *Leçons sur la volonté de savoir. Cours au Collège de France, 1970-1971, suivi de Le savoir d'Œdipe.* Edited by François Ewald, Alessandro Fontana, and Daniel Defert. Paris: Gallimard: Seuil. 2011.
———. *Lectures de Michel Foucault.* Edited by Emmanuel da Silva. 3 vols. Paris: ENS Éditions. 2003.
———. *Les mots et les choses: une archéologie des sciences humaines.* Paris: Gallimard. 1966.
———. "Les 'reportages' d'idées." In *Dits et écrits,* edited by François Ewald, Daniel Defert, and Jacques Lagrange, 2:706–7. Paris: Gallimard. 2001.
———. "L'esprit d'un monde sans esprit." In *Dits et écrits,* edited by François Ewald, Daniel Defert, and Jacques Lagrange, 2:743–55. Paris: Gallimard. 2001.
———. "Lettre ouverte à Mehdi Bazargan." In *Dits et écrits,* edited by François Ewald, Daniel Defert, and Jacques Lagrange, 2:780–82. Paris: Gallimard. 2001.
———. *L'ordre du discours: leçon inaugurale au Collège de France prononcée le 2 décembre 1970.* Paris: Gallimard. 1971.
———. *Maladie mentale et psychologie.* Paris: PUF. 2010.
———. "Méthodologie pour la connaissance du monde: Comment se débarrasser du marxisme." In *Dits et écrits,* edited by François Ewald, Daniel Defert, and Jacques Lagrange, 2:595–618. Paris: Gallimard. 2001.
———. "Michel Foucault: An Interview with Stephen Riggins." *Ethos* 1, no. 2 (1983): 4–9.
———. "Michel Foucault et le Zen: un séjour dans un temple zen." In *Dits et écrits,* edited by François Ewald, Daniel Defert, and Jacques Lagrange, 2:618–24. Paris: Gallimard. 2001.
———. "Michel Foucault: les réponses du philosophe." In *Dits et écrits,* edited by Daniel Defert, François Ewald, and Jacques Lagrange, 1:1673–85. Paris: Gallimard. 2001.

———. *Michel Foucault: une histoire de la vérité*. Conception graphique Jean-Claude Hug. Paris: Syros. 1985.

———. "Mon corps, ce papier, ce feu." In *Dits et écrits*, edited by Daniel Defert, François Ewald, and Jacques Lagrange, 1:1113–1136. Paris: Gallimard. 2001. Translated as "My Body, This Paper, This Fire" by Geoffrey Bennington. In Michel Foucault, *Aesthetics, Method, and Epistemology*, edited by James A. Faubion. Vol. 2 of Essential Works of Michel Foucault 1954–1984, edited by Paul Rabinow. New York: The New Press. 1998.

———. *Naissance de la biopolitique: cours au Collège de France (1978–1979)*. Paris: Gallimard: Seuil. 2004.

———. *Politics, philosophy, culture: interviews and other writings, 1977–1984*. Edited by Lawrence D. Kritzman. New York: Routledge. 1988.

———. "Préface à l'édition anglaise." In *Dits et écrits*, edited by Daniel Defert, François Ewald, and Jacques Lagrange, 1:875–81. Paris: Gallimard. 2001.

———. "Préface à l'histoire de la sexualité." In *Dits et écrits*, edited by Daniel Defert, François Ewald, and Jacques Lagrange, 2:1398–99. Paris: Gallimard. 2001.

———. "Preface to the History of Sexuality, Vol. 2." In *The Foucault Reader*, edited by Paul Rabinow. New York: Pantheon Books. 1984.

———. "Qu'est-ce-que les Lumières?" In *Dits et écrits*, edited by Daniel Defert, François Ewald, and Jacques Lagrange, 2: 1381–97. Paris: Gallimard. 2001.

———. "Questions à Michel Foucault sur la géographie." In *Dits et écrits*, edited by François Ewald, Daniel Defert, and Jacques Lagrange, 2:28–40. Paris: Gallimard. 2001.

———. "Questions on Geography." In Michel Foucault, *Power/Knowledge*, edited by Colin Gordon, translated by Colin Gordon, Leo Marshall, John Mepham, and Kate Soper, 63–77. New York: Vintage, 1980.

———. "Qui êtes-vous professeur Foucault?" In *Dits et écrits*, edited by Daniel Defert, François Ewald, and Jacques Lagrange, 1:629–648. Paris: Gallimard. 2001.

———. "Radioscopie de Michel Foucault." In *Dits et écrits*, edited by Daniel Defert, François Ewald, and Jacques Lagrange, 1:1651–70. Paris: Gallimard. 2001.

———. *Religion and Culture*. Edited by Jeremy R. Carrette. New York: Routledge. 1999.

———. *Remarks on Marx: Conversations with Duccio Trombadori*. Translated by James Goldstein and James Cascaito. New York: Semiotext(e). 1991.

———. "Réponse à Derrida." *In Dits et écrits*, edited by Daniel Defert, François Ewald, and Jacques Lagrange, 1:1149-1163. Paris: Gallimard. 2001. Previously published in a different form in *Paideia*, no. 11 (1 February 1972): 131–47.

———. *Résumé des cours, 1970-1982*. Paris: Julliard. 1989.

———. "Sans titre." In *Dits et écrits*, edited by Daniel Defert, François Ewald, and Jacques Lagrange, 1:321–53. Paris: Gallimard. 2001.

———. *Security, Territory, Population: Lectures at the Collège de France, 1977–78*. Edited by Michel Senellart, François Ewald, and Alessandro Fontana. Translated by Graham Burchell, 2007.

———. Sexualité et politique." In *Dits et écrits*, edited by Daniel Defert, François Ewald, and Jacques Lagrange, 2:522–531. Paris: Gallimard. 2001.

———. "Sexualité et pouvoir." In *Dits et écrits,* edited by François Ewald, Daniel Defert, and Jacques Lagrange, 2:552–70. Paris: Gallimard. 2001.

———. *Society Must Be Defended: Lectures at the Collège de France, 1975–1976.* Translated by David Macey. New York: Picador. 2003.

———. "Structuralisme et poststructuralisme." In *Dits et écrits,* edited by François Ewald, Daniel Defert, and Jacques Lagrange, 2:1250–76. Paris: Gallimard. 2001.

———. "Téhéran: La foi contre le Chah." In *Dits et écrits,* edited by François Ewald, Daniel Defert, and Jacques Lagrange, 2:683–88. Paris: Gallimard. 2001.

———. *The Archaeology of Knowledge and the Discourse on Language.* Translated by A. M. Sheridan Smith. New York: Vintage Books. 2010. Originally published as *L'archéologie du savoir.* Paris: Gallimard. 1969.

———. *The Essential Works of Michel Foucault, 1954–1984.* Vol. 2. Edited by Paul Rabinow. Aesthetics. London: Penguin. 2000.

———. *The Foucault Effect: Studies in Governmentality: With Two Lectures by and an Interview with Michel Foucault.* Edited by Graham Burchell, Colin Gordon, and Peter Miller. Chicago: University of Chicago Press. 1991.

———. *The Foucault Reader.* Edited by Paul Rabinow. New York: Pantheon Books. 1984.

———. *The Hermeneutics of the Subject: Lectures at the Collège de France; 1981–1982.* Edited by Frédéric Gros. Translated by Graham Burchell. New York: Picador. 2005.

———. *The History of Sexuality.* Translated by Robert Hurley. Vol. 1. *An Introduction.* New York: Vintage Books. 1990. Originally Published as *Histoire de La Sexualité.* Vol. 1. *La Volonté de Savoir.* Paris: Gallimard. 1976.

———. *The History of Sexuality.* Translated by Robert Hurley. Vol. 2. *The Use of Pleasure.* New York: Vintage Books. 1990. Originally published as *Histoire de la sexualité.* Vol. 2. *L'usage des plaisirs.* Paris: Gallimard. 1984.

———. *The History of Sexuality.* Translated by Robert Hurley. Vol. 3. *The Care of the Self.* New York: Vintage Books. 1990. Originally published as *Histoire de la sexualité.* Vol. 3. *Le souci de soi.* Paris: Gallimard. 1984.

———. *The Order of Things: An Archaeology of the Human Sciences.* New York: Vintage Books. 1994. Originally published as *Les mots et les choses, une archéologie des sciences humaines.* Paris: Gallimard. 1966.

———. "Theatrum philosophicum." In *Dits et écrits,* edited by Daniel Defert, François Ewald, and Jacques Lagrange, 1:943–66. Paris: Gallimard. 2001.

———. "Un fantastique de bibliothèque." *Cahiers de la Compagnie Madeleine Renaud-Jean-Louis Barrrault* 59 (March 1967): 7–30.

———. "Une Interview de Michel Foucault par Stephen Riggins." Translated by F. Durand-Bogaert. In *Dits et Ecrits,* edited by François Ewald, Daniel Defert, and Jacques Lagrange, 2: 1344–57. Paris: Gallimard. 2001.

———. "Une poudrière appelée islam." In *Dits et écrits,* edited by François Ewald, Daniel Defert, and Jacques Lagrange, 2:759–61. Paris: Gallimard. 2001.

———. "Une révolte à mains nues." In *Dits et écrits,* edited by François Ewald, Daniel Defert, and Jacques Lagrange, 2:701–4. Paris: Gallimard. 2001.

———. "What Is Enlightenment?" In *The Foucault Reader,* edited by Paul Rabinow. New York: Pantheon Books. 1984.

---. "Who Are You Professor Foucault?," (interview). Translated by Jeremy Carrette, ed. *Michel Foucault. Religion and Culture.* New York: Routledge. 1999.

Foucault, Michel, and Jean Le Bitoux. "The Gay Science." Translated by Nicolae Morar and Daniel W. Smith. *Critical Inquiry* 37, no. 3 (Spring 2011): 385–403.

Franchetti, Cody. "Did Foucault Revolutionize History?" *Open Journal of Philosophy* 1, no. 2 (2001): 84-89.

Frierson, Patrick R. *Freedom and Anthropology in Kant's Moral Philosophy.* Cambridge: Cambridge University Press. 2003.

Fuchs, Thomas. "The European China-Reception from Leibniz to Kant." Translated by Martin Schönfeld. *Journal of Chinese Philosophy* 33, no. 1 (March 2006):35–49.

Galinier, Jacques. "L'anthropologie hors des limites de la simple raison: actualité de la dispute entre Kant et Herder." *L' Homme* 179 (2006):141–164.

Gantin, Karine. "Simone Lellouche Othmani: une tunisienne citoyenne des deux rives." *Mémoire et Horizon,* special issue (April 2007).

Garfinkel, Harold. *Studies in Ethnomethodology.* Cambridge: Polity Press. 1984.

Garo, Isabelle. *Foucault, Deleuze, Althusser & Marx: La politique dans la philosophie.* Paris: Demopolis. 2011.

Geertz, Clifford. *Available Light: Anthropological Reflections on Philosophical Topics.* Princeton, N.J.: Princeton University Press. 2001.

---. *Local Knowledge: Further Essays in Interpretive Anthropology.* New York: Basic Books. 2000.

---. "On Foucault." In *Life Among the Anthros and Other Essays,* edited by Fred Inglis, 29–38. Princeton, N.J.: Princeton University Press. 2001.

---. *The Interpretation of Cultures: Selected Essays.* New York: Basic Books. 1973.

Gernet, Louis. *Les Grecs sans miracle.* Edited by Riccardo Di Donato. Paris: La Découverte/Maspéro. 1983.

Ghamari-Tabrizi, Behrooz. "When Life Will No Longer Barter Itself: In Defense of Foucault on the Iranian Revolution." In *A Foucault for the 21st Century: Governmentality, Biopolitics and Discipline in the New Millennium,* edited by Sam Binkley and Jorge Capetillo Ponce, 273–92. Newcastle-upon-Tyne: Cambridge Scholars Publishing. 2009.

---. *Foucault in Iran: Islamic Revolution after the Enlightenment.* Minneapolis: University of Minnesota Press. 2016.

Ghaneirad, Mohamad Amin, and Ali Paya. "Habermas and Iranian Intellectuals." *Iranian Studies* 20, no. 3 (June 2007).

Gherib, Baccar. *Penser la transition avec Gramsci. Tunisie (2011-2014).* Tunis: Editions Diwen. 2017.

Goldmann, Lucien. "Genetic Structuralism." In *The Hidden God: A Study of Tragic Vision in the Pensées of Pascal and the Tragedies of Racine.* London: Routledge and Kegan Paul. 1964.

Goody, Jack. "Eurasia and East-West Boundaries." *Diogenes* 50(2003): 115-18.

Gould, Stephen Jay. *The Hedgehog, the Fox, and the Magister's Pox: Mending the Gap Between Science and the Humanities.* New York: Harmony Books. 2003.

Guédez, Annie. *Foucault*. Paris: Éditions universitaires. 1972.
Gutting, Gary. "Foucault's Philosophy of Experience." *Boundary 2* 29, no. 2 (2002): 69–85.
Habermas, Jürgen. "Colonization of the Life-World." In *Legitimation Crisis,* part 1, chap. 1. Boston: Beacon Press. 1975.
Hacking, Ian. "Foreword." In *History of Madness,* by Michel Foucault, edited by Jean Khalfa, translated by Jonathan Murphy and Jean Khalfa. New York: Routledge. 2009.
Hafsia, Jélila. "Quand la passion de l'intelligence illuminait Sidi Bou Saïd." *La presse tunisienne,* 6 July 1984.
Hahn, Trudi Bellardo, and Michael Keeble Buckland, eds. *Historical Studies in Information Science*. Medford, NJ: Published for the American Society for Information Science by Information Today. 1998.
Hajjat, Abdellali. "Alliances inattendues à la Goutte d'Or." In *68, une histoire collective: 1962–1981,* edited by Philippe Artières and Michelle Zancarini-Fournel. Paris: La Découverte. 2008.
Han, Béatrice. *Foucault's Critical Project: Between the Transcendental and the Historical.* Translated by Edward Pile. Stanford: Stanford University Press. 2002.
Harris, Marvin. *The Rise of Anthropological Theory; a History of Theories of Culture.* New York: Thomas Y. Crowell. 1968.
Harvey, David. "Kant's Anthropology and Geography." In David Harvey. *Cosmopolitanism and the Geographies of Freedom.* New York: Columbia University Press. 2009.
Heather, P. J. *The Fall of the Roman Empire: A New History of Rome and the Barbarians.* New York: Oxford University Press. 2006.
Hegel, Georg Wilhelm Friedrich. *The Philosophy of History.* Translated by J. Sibree. New York: Dover Publications. 1956.
Heidegger, Martin. "A Dialogue on Language between a Japanese and an Inquirer." In *On the Way to Language,* translated by Peter D. Hertz, 1–54. New York: Harper Collins, HarperOne. 1982.
———. *Kant and the Problem of Metaphysics.* 5th ed. Bloomington: Indiana University Press. 1997.
Heisig, James W. *Philosophers of Nothingness.* Honolulu: University of Hawai'i. 2001.
Hendrickson, Burleigh. "May 1968: Practicing Transnational Activism from Tunis to Paris." *International Journal of Middle Eastern Studies* 44 (2012):755–774.
Heubel, Fabien. "Des enjeux d'une critique 'transculturelle' à partir de l'oeuvre du dernier Foucault." In *Michel Foucault,* edited by Philippe Artières, Jean-François Bert, Frédéric Gros, and Judith Revel, 358–63. Paris: Éditions de l'Herne. 2011.
Honneth, Axel. *The Critique of Power: Reflective Stages in a Critical Social Theory.* Cambridge, MA.: MIT Press. 1991.
Hoy, David Couzens, ed. *Foucault: A Critical Reader.* New York: Basil Blackwell. 1986.
Hund, Wulf D. "'It Must Be from Europe:' The Racisms of Immanuel Kant." In *Racisms Made in Germany,* edited by Christian Koller, Moses Zimmerman, and Wulf D. Hund. Berlin: LIT-Verlag. 2011.

Hurley, Andrew. "Translator's Note." In *The Book of Imaginary Beings*, by Jorge Luis Borges and Margarita Guerrero, translated by Andrew Hurley. New York: Penguin. 2006.

Ishida, Hidetaka. "De l'orientalisme? Du 'Japon' comme lieu de discours sur le langage, le sens et l'art." Lecture given at the University of Vincennes-Saint-Denis. 26 March 1996.

———. "Vent d'Ouest." In *Michel Foucault*, edited by Philippe Artières, Jean-François Bert, Frédéric Gros, and Judith Revel, 232–36. Paris: Éditions de l'Herne. 2011.

Jackson, Bruce. "Things That from a Long Way Off Look Like Flies." *The Journal of American Folklore* 98, no. 388 (April–June 1985): 131–47.

Jacobs, Brian. "Kantian Character and the Problem of a Science of Humanity." In *Essays on Kant's Anthropology*, edited by Brian Jacobs and Patrick Kain. New York: Cambridge University Press. 2003.

Jambet, Christian. "Retour sur l'insurrection iranienne." In *Michel Foucault*, edited by Philippe Artières, Jean-François Bert, Frédéric Gros, and Judith Revel, 372–76. Paris: Éditions de l'Herne. 2011.

Jullien, François, and Thierry Marchaisse. *Penser d'un dehors, la Chine: entretiens d'Extrême-Occident*. Paris: Éditions du Seuil. 2000.

Kant, Immanuel. "An Answer to the Question: What is the Enlightenment." In *Immanuel Kant. Practical Philosophy*. Translated and edited by Mary McGregor. Cambridge: Cambridge University Press. 1996.

———. *Anthropology from a Pragmatic Point of View*. Edited by Hans H. Rudnick. Translated by Victor Lyle Dowdell. Carbondale: Southern Illinois University Press. 1996.

———. *Anthropology from a Pragmatic Point of View*. Translated by Mary J. Gregor. The Hague: Martinus Nijhoff. 1974.

———. *Anthropology from a Pragmatic Point of View*. With an Introduction by Manfred Kuehn. Translated by Robert B. Louden. Cambridge: Cambridge University Press. 2009. Translated into French by Michel Foucault as E. Kant, *Anthropologie du point de vue pragmatique précédé de Michel Foucault Introduction à l'anthropologie de Kant*, introduced by D. Defert, Fr. Ewald and F. Gros. Paris: Vrin. 2009.

———. *Critique of Pure Reason*. Translated by Paul Guyer and Allen W. Wood. Cambridge: Cambridge University Press. 1998.

———. *Groundwork for the Metaphysics of Morals*. Edited and translated by Allen W. Wood. New Haven: Yale University Press. 2002.

———. *Introduction to Logic*. Translated by Thomas Kingsmill Abbott, London: Longmans, Green and Co. 1885.

———. *Observations on the Feeling of the Beautiful and Sublime*. Translated by John T. Goldthwait. Berkeley: University of California Press. 2003.

———. *Perpetual Peace, and Other Essays on Politics, History, and Morals*. Translated by Ted Humphrey. Indianapolis: Hackett. 1983.

———. *Physical Geography*. Translated by Ronald L. Bolin. MA Thesis, Geography Department, University of Waterloo, 1968.

———. *Physical Geography*. Translated by Olaf Reinhardt. In *Kant's Natural Science*. Edited by Eric Watkins. The Cambridge Edition of the Works of Immanuel Kant. Cambridge: Cambridge University Press. 2012.

———. *The Conflict of the Faculties*. Translated by Mary J. Gregor. New York: Abaris. 1979.

Kawada, Junzo. "'East versus West': Beyond Dichotomy and Towards an Acknowledgment of Differences." *Diogenes* 50, no. 4 (2003): 95–103.

Khomeini, Ayatollah. *Islamic Government*. New York: Manor Books, 1979.

Kleingeld, Pauline. "Kant's Second Thought on Race." *The Philosophical Quarterly* 57, no. 229 (October 2007): 573–92.

Kurzman, Charles. *The Unthinkable Revolution in Iran* (Cambridge, MA: Harvard Univeristy Press, 2014).

La Gasnerie, Geoffroy de. "Le néolibéralisme, théorie politique et pensée critique." *Raisons politiques: Revue de théorie politique* 52 (November 2013): 63–75.

Lange, Antje. "Kant's Correspondence with Women: A Contribution to a Statistical Evaluation of Kant's Correspondence." In *Proceedings of the Third International Kant Congress Held at the University of Rochester, March 30–April 4, 1970*, edited by International Kant Congress and Lewis White Beck. Dordrecht: Reidel. 1972.

Lawlor, Leonard. "A Minuscule Hiatus: Foucault's Critique of the Concept of Lived-Experience (Vécu)." In *Logos of Phenomenology and Phenomenology of the Logos. Book One.*, edited by Anna-Teresa Tymieniecka. Analecta Husserliana, LXXXVIII. Dordrecht: Springer. 2005.

Leenberg, Michiel. "Power and Political Spirituality: Michel Foucault on the Islamic Revolution in Iran." In *Michel Foucault and Theology: The Politics of Religious Experience*, edited by James William Bernauer and Jeremy R. Carrette. Burlington, VT: Ashgate. 2004.

LeVine, Mark. "Tunis and the Birth of a 'Planetary Genealogy' in the Work of Michel Foucault." In "Michel Foucault en Tunisie (1966–1968)," special issue, *CELAAN (Review of the Center for the Studies of the Literatures and Arts of North Africa)* (n.d.): 79–100.

Lévi-Strauss, Claude. *L'anthropologie face aux problèmes du monde moderne*. Paris: Seuil. 2011. Translated by Jane Marie Todd as *Anthropology Confronts the Problems of the Modern World*. Cambridge, MA: Belknap Press of Harvard University Press. 2013

Lévi-Strauss, Claude. *L'autre face de la lune: écrits sur le Japon*. Paris: Seuil. 2011. Translated by Jane Marie Todd as *The Other Face of the Moon*. Cambridge: Harvard College. 2011.

———. Le regard éloigné. Paris: Plon. 2001. Translated by Joachim Neugroschel and Phoebe Hoss as *The View from Afar*. Chicago: University of Chicago. 1992.

———. "Postface." *L'Homme* 154–155 (April–September 2000).

———. "Questions de parenté." *L'Homme* 154–155 (April–September 2000).

———. *Structural Anthropology*. Translated by Claire Jacobson and Brooke Grundfest Schoepf. Vol. 3. New York: Basic Books. 1976. Originally Published as *Anthropologie Structurale*. Paris: Plon. 1958.

Li, Wenchao, and Hans Poser. "Leibniz's Positive View of China." *Journal of Chinese Philosophy* 33, no. 1 (March 2006): 17–33.

Littré, E. *Dictionnaire de la langue française*. Vol. 3. Paris: Hachette. 1885.

Livingstone, David N., and Charles W.J. Withers, eds. *Geography and Enlightenment*. Chicago: University of Chicago Press. 1999.

Lorenz, Chris, and Berber Bevernage, eds. *Breaking up Time: Negotiating the Borders Between Present, Past and Future*. Göttingen: Vandenhoeck & Ruprecht. 2013.

Louden, Robert B. *Kant's Human Being: Essays on His Theory of Human Nature*. Oxford: Oxford University Press. 2011.

———. "Foucault's Kant." Paper Presented at the American Philosophical Association, Pacific Division Meeting. Seattle. 2012. Translated into Spanish as "El Foucault de Kant." Estudios *Kantinos,* no. 1 (July 2015).

Luisetti, Federico. "Nietzsche's Oriental Biopolitics." *Biopolitica*. Accessed November 29, 2016. http://www.biopolitica.unsw.edu.au/sites/all/files/publication_related_files/luisetti_nietzsche.pdf.

Macey, David. *The Lives of Michel Foucault: A Biography*. New York: Vintage Books. 1993.

Makkreel, Rudolph A. "Kant on the Scientific Status of Psychology, Anthropology, and History." In *Kant and the Sciences,* edited by Eric Watkins. Oxford: Oxford University Press. 2001.

Marcus, George E. "The Ends of Ethnography: Social/Cultural Anthropology's Signature Form of Producing Knowledge in Transition." *Cultural Anthropology* 23, no. 1 (2008).

Marcus, George E, and Michael M.J. Fischer. *Anthropology as Cultural Critique: An Experimental Moment in the Human Sciences*. Chicago: University of Chicago Press. 1999.

Marx, Karl. *Marx on Religion*. Edited by John C. Raines. Philadelphia: Temple University Press. 2002.

May, Reinhard. *Heidegger's Hidden Sources: East Asian Influences on His Work*. Translated by Graham Parkes. New York: Routledge. 1996.

McCannon, Afrodesia E. "The King's Two Lives: The Tunisian Legend of Saint Louis." *Journal of Folklore Research* 43, no. 1 (January–April 2006).

Mead, George Herbert. *Mind, Self, and Society; from the Standpoint of a Social Behaviorist*. Edited by Charles William Morris. Chicago: University of Chicago Press. 1967.

Megill, Allan. "The Reception of Foucault by Historians." *Journal of the History of Ideas* 48, no. 1 (January–March 1987).

Memmi, Albert. *The Colonizer and the Colonized*. Boston: Beacon Press. 1965.

Mendelssohn, Moses. *Philosophical Writings*. Edited by Daniel O. Dahlstrom. New York: Cambridge University Press. 1997.

Mendieta, Eduardo. "Geography Is to History as Woman Is to Man." In *Reading Kant's Geography,* edited by Stuart Elden and Eduardo Mendieta. Albany: State University of New York Press. 2011.

Merlin, Samuel. *The Search for Peace in the Middle East: The Story of President Bourguiba's Campaign for a Negotiated Peace Between Israel and the Arab States*. South Brunswick: T. Yoseloff. 1968.

Mezzadra, Sandro. "En voyage. Michel Foucault et la critique postcoloniale." In *Michel Foucault,* edited by Philippe Artières, Jean-François Bert, Frédéric Gros, and Judith Revel, 352–57. Paris: Éditions de l'Herne. 2011.
Michel Foucault en revues. *La Revue des Revues,* no. 30 (2001).
Miller, James. *The Passion of Michel Foucault.* Cambridge, MA: Harvard University Press. 1993.
Mills, C. Wright. *The Sociological Imagination.* New York: Oxford University Press. 2000.
Milton, Giles. *Samurai William: The Englishman Who Opened Japan.* New York: Penguin Books. 2004.
Moreno Pestaña, José Luis. *Foucault, la gauche et la politique.* Paris: Textuel. 2010.
Morgan, Jamie. "Distinguishing Truth, Knowledge, and Belief: A Philosophical Contribution to the Problem of Images of China." *Modern China* 30, no. 3 (July 2004): 398–427.
Motoori, Norinaga. *Kojiki-Den Book 1.* Translated by Ann Wehmeyer. Cornell East Asia 87. Ithaca: East Asia Program, Cornell University. 1997.
Müller, Martin. "Aspects of the Chinese Reception of Kant." *Journal of Chinese Philosophy* 33, no. 1 (March 2006): 141–57.
Naccache, Gilbert. *Qu'as-tu fait de ta jeunesse? Itinéraire d'un opposant au régime de Bourguiba (1954-1979) suivi de Récits de prison.* Paris; Tunis: Éditions du Cerf/Mots passants. 2009.
Nietzsche, Friedrich Wilhelm. *The Antichrist.* Translated by Anthony M. Ludovici. Amherst, NY: Prometheus Books. 2000.
Nishitani, Keiji. *The Self-Overcoming of Nihilism.* Albany: State University of New York Press. 1990.
Odile Germain, Marie. *Michel Foucault de retour à la BNF.* Chroniques de la Bibliothèque Nationale de France 70, April–June 2014.
Olivier, Lawrence, and Sylvain Labbé. "Foucault et l'Iran: A propos du désir de revolution." *Canadian Journal of Political Science* 24, no. 2 (June 1991): 219–36.
Omri, Mohammed Salah. "The Movement Perspectives: Legacies and Representations." *EurOrient* 38(2012): 149–164.
Othmani, Ahmed. *Une vie militante.* Biographie. Tunis: Déméter. 2012.
Othmani, Ahmed, and Sophie Bessis. *Sortir de la prison: un combat pour la réforme des systèmes carcéraux dans le monde.* Paris: La Découverte. 2002.
Owen, David. *Maturity and Modernity: Nietzsche, Weber, Foucault, and the Ambivalence of Reason.* New York: Routledge. 1994.
Paras, Eric. *Foucault 2.0: Beyond Power and Knowledge.* New York: Other Press. 2006.
Parkes, Graham. "Nietzsche and East Asian Thought: Influences, Impacts and Resonances." In *The Cambridge Companion to Nietzsche,* edited by Bernd Magnus and Kathleen M. Higgins, 356–384. Cambridge, UK: Cambridge University Press. 1996.
Paugam, Guillaume. "De l'Anthropologie à l'Archéologie." *Critique* 65, no. 749 (October 2009): 836–847.
———. "Naissance(s) de la Clinique." *Critique* LVIII, no. 660 (May 2002): 380–90.
Pinguet, Maurice. *Le texte Japon: introuvables et inédits.* Edited by Michaël Ferrier. Paris: Éditions du Seuil. 2009.

———. "Michel Foucault. Les années d'apprentissage." In *Le texte Japon: introuvables et inédits,* edited by Michaël Ferrier. Paris: Éditions du Seuil. 2009.

Pol-Droit, Roger. "Kant et les fourmis du Congo." *Le Monde,* February 5, 1999.

Postel, Danny. *Reading Legitimation Crisis in Tehran: Iran and the Future of Liberalism.* Chicago: Prickly Paradigm Press. 2006.

Piel, Jean, ed. "Michel Foucault du monde entier." Special issue, *Critique* 171–472 (August-September 1986).

Rayward, W. Boyd. "The International Federation for Information and Documentation (FID)." In *Encyclopedia of Library History,* edited by Wayne A. Wiegand and Donald G. Davis, 290–94. New York: Garland. 1994.

———. *The Universe of Information: The Work of Paul Otlet for Documentation and International Organisation.* Moscow: All-Union Institute for Scientific and Technical Information (VINITI). 1975.

Redeker, Robert. "La dernière peau philosophique de Michel Foucault." *Critique* LVIII, no. 660 (May 2002): 391–400.

Reihman, Gregory M. "Categorically Denied: Kant's Criticism of Chinese Philosophy." *Journal of Chinese Philosophy* 33, no. 1 (March 2006).

Revel, Judith. *Foucault, une pensée du discontinu.* Paris: Mille et une nuits. 2010.

Rigby, Peter. *African Images: Racism and the End of Anthropology.* Oxford: Berg. 1996.

Righi, Nicolas. "L'héritage du fondateur? L'histoire des mentalités dans l'école des 'Annales," n.d. Accessed 31 October 2013, www.cairn.info.

Roger, Jacques. "Histoire des mentalités: les questions d'un historien des sciences." *Revue de Synthèse,* July–December 1983, 111–12.

Rodinson, Maxime. "Critique of Foucault on Iran." In Janet Afary and Kevin B. Anderson, *Michel Foucault and the Iranian Revolution: Gender and the Seductions of Islamism.* Chicago: University of Chicago Press. 2005.

Rousseau, G.S. "Whose Enlightenment? Not Man's: The Case of Michel Foucault." *Eighteenth Century Studies* 6, no. 2 (Winter 1972–Winter 1973): 238–56.

Roussel, Raymond. *How I Wrote Certain of My Books and Other Writings.* Edited by Trevor Winkfield. Translated by John Ashbery, Kenneth Koch, Harry Matthews, and Trevor Winkfield. Cambridge, MA: Exact Change. 1995.

Ruf, Werner. "Le bourguibisme, doctrine de politique étrangère d'un état faible." In *Habib Bourguiba, la trace et l'héritage,* edited by Michel Camau and Vincent Geisser (Paris: Karthala, 2004), 455–61.

Sabot, Philippe. "De Kojève à la mort de l'homme et la querelle de l'humanisme." *Archives de Philosophie* 72, no. 3 (2009): 523–40.

———. *Lire "Les mots et les choses" de Michel Foucault.* Paris: Presses universitaires de France. 2006.

Said, Edward W. *Orientalism.* New York: Vintage Books. 1978.

———. "Diary." *London Review of Books* 22, no. 11 (1 June 2000). Accessed 23 April 2017 from http://www.lrb.co.uk/v22/n11/edward-said/diary.

Sakai, Naoki, and Jon Solomon. "Introduction: Addressing the Multitude of Foreigners, Echoing Foucault." In *Translation, Biopolitics, Colonial Difference,* Traces 4, edited by Naoki Sakai and Jon Solomon, 1–38. Hong Kong: Hong Kong University Press. 2006.

———. *Translation and Subjectivity*. Minneapolis: University of Minnesota. 1999
Sartre, Jean-Paul. *Search for a Method*. Translated by Hazel E. Barnes. New York: Vintage Books. 1968.
Schaub, Uta Liebmann. "Foucault's Oriental Subtext." *Modern Language Association* 104, no. 3 (May 1989): 306–316.
Scheiffele, Eberhard. "Questioning One's 'Own' from the Perspective of the Foreign." In *Nietzsche and Asian Thought,* edited and translated by Graham Parkes. Chicago: University of Chicago Press. 1996.
Schönfeld, Martin. "From Confucius to Kant: The Question of Knowledge Transfer." *Journal of Chinese Philosophy* 33, no. 1 (March 2006): 67–81.
Schönfeld, Martin, and Jeffrey Edwards. "Kant's Material Dynamics and the Field View of Physical Reality." *Journal of Chinese Philosophy* 33, no. 1 (March 2006): 109–23.
Sharī'atī, 'Alī. *Marxism and Other Western Fallacies: An Islamic Critique*. Edited by Hamid Algar. Translated by R. Campbell. Berkeley: Mizan Press. 1980.
Shingu, Kazushige. "Freud, Lacan and Japan." *The Letter. Perspectives on Lacanian Psychoanalysis* 34(Summer 2005): 48–62.
Solomon, Jon. "The Experience of Culture: Eurocentric Limits and Openings in Foucault." *Transeuropéennes,* 2013.
Sprung, Mervyn. "Nietzsche's Trans-European Eye." In *Nietzsche and Asian Thought,* edited and translated by Graham Parkes. Chicago: University of Chicago Press. 1996.
Stark, Werner. "Historical and Philological References on the Question of a Possible Hierarchy of Human 'Races,' 'Peoples' and 'Populations' in Immanuel Kant——A supplement." In *Reading Kant's Geography,* edited by Stuart Elden and Eduardo Mendieta. Albany: State University of New York Press. 2011.
Stark, Werner. "Historical Notes and Interpretive Questions about Kant's Lectures on Anthropology." In *Essays on Kant's Anthropology,* edited by Brian Jacobs and Patrick Kain, translated by Jaimey Fisher and Patrick Kain. New York: Cambridge University Press. 2003.
Stauth, George. "Revolution in Spiritless Times: An Essay on Michel Foucault's Enquiries into the Iranian Revolution." *International Sociology* 6, no. 3 (1991): 259–280.
Steckel, Mike. "Ranganathan for IAs," 7 October 2002. Accessed 8 December 2016 from http://boxesandarrows.com/ranganathan-for-ias/.
Stengers, Isabelle, and Robert Bononno. *Cosmopolitics*. Vol. 1. Minneapolis: University of Minnesota Press. 2010.
Sullivan, Roger. "The Influence of Kant's Anthropology on His Moral Theory." *Review of Metaphysics* 49 (September 1995): 77–94.
Szakolczai, Árpád. *Max Weber and Michel Foucault: Parallel Life-Works*. New York: Routledge. 1998.
Takeuchi, Yoshimi. *What Is Modernity? Writings of Takeuchi Yoshimi*. Edited and translated by Richard Calichman. New York: Columbia University Press. 2004.
Tanaka, Stefan. *Japan's Orient: Rendering Pasts into History*. Berkeley: University of California Press. 1993.

———. *New Times in Modern Japan*. Princeton: Princeton University Press. 2004.

———. "Unification of Time and the Fragmentation of Pasts in Meiji Japan." In *Breaking up Time: Negotiating Borders Between Present, Past and Future*, edited by Chris Lorenz and Berber Bevernage. Göttingen: Vandoeck and Ruprecht. 2013.

Toumi, Mohsen. *La Tunisie de Bourguiba à Ben Ali*. Paris: Presses universitaires de France. 1989.

Tu, Wei-ming. "The 'Moral Universal' from the Perspectives of East Asian Thought." *Philosophy East and West* 31, no. 3 (July 1981): 259–67.

Van de Pitte, Frederick, and Lewis White Beck. "Kant as Philosophical Anthropologist." In *Proceedings of the Third International Kant Congress. Held at the University of Rochester, March 30-April 4, 1970*. Dordrecht: Reidel. 1972.

Van Norden, Bryan W, and Robert B. Louden, eds. "'What Does Heaven Say': Christian Wolff and Western Interpretations of Confucian Ethics." In *Confucius and the Analects: New Essays*, ed. Bryan Van Orden, 73–93. New York: Oxford University Press. 2002.

Varisco, Daniel Martin. *Islam Obscured: The Rhetoric of Anthropological Representation*. New York: Palgrave Macmillan. 2005.

Vernant, Jean Pierre. *Les origines de la pensée grecque*. Paris: Presses universitaires de France. 1975. Translated as *The Origins of Greek Thought*. Ithaca: Cornell. 1982.

Veyne, Paul. *Foucault, sa pensée, sa personne*. Paris: Albin Michel. 2008.

Visker, Rudi, and Chris Turner. *Michel Foucault: Genealogy as Critique*. New York: Verso. 1995.

Weber, Max, and Routledge. *The Protestant Ethic and the Spirit of Capitalism*. New York: Routledge. 2005.

Wenzel, Christian Helmut. "Beauty in Kant and Confucius: A First Step." *Journal of Chinese Philosophy* 33, no. 1 (March 2006): 95–107.

Wilkins, John. *An Essay towards a Real Character, and a Philosophical Language*. Menston: Scolar Press. 1968.

Wilson, Holly L. *Kant's Pragmatic Anthropology: Its Origin, Meaning and Critical Significance*. Albany: State University of New York Press. 2007.

Wood, Allen W. *Kant*. Malden: MA: Blackwell. 2005.

———. "Kant and the Problem of Human Nature." In *Essays on Kant's Anthropology*, edited by Brian Jacobs and Patrick Kain, translated by Jaimey Fisher and Patrick Kain. New York: Cambridge University Press. 2003.

———. *Kant's Ethical Thought*. Cambridge: Cambridge University Press. 1999.

———. "Unsociable Sociability." *Philosophical Topics* 19, no. 1 (Spring 1991): 325–51.

Zammito, John H. *Kant, Herder, and the Birth of Anthropology*. Chicago: University of Chicago Press. 2002.

Zamora, Daniel, ed. *Critiquer Foucault: Les années 1980 et la tentation néolibérale*. Bruxelles: Aden. 2014.

Zarka, Charles Yves, ed. *Michel Foucault: de la guerre des races au biopouvoir*. Special issue. *Cités* 2 (2000).

Zeami. *The Spirit of Noh: A New Translation of the Classic Noh Treatise the Fushikaden*. Translated by William Scott Wilson. Boston: Shambhala. 2013.

Zhang, Longxi. "The Myth of the Other: China in the Eyes of the West." *Critical Inquiry* 15, no. 1 (1988): 108–131.

Zhongshu, Qian. "China in the English Literature of the Seventeenth Century." *Quarterly Bulletin of Chinese Bibliography,* December 1941, 113–52.

Zoungrana, Jean. *Michel Foucault. Un parcours croisé: Lévi-Strauss, Heidegger.* Paris: Harmattan. 1998.

ARCHIVES

Bibliothèque Nationale de France, Richelieu site, Paris.

Fonds Michel Foucault. Institut Mémoires de l'Edition Contemporaine (IMEC), St. Germain-la Blanche-Herbe, Caen.

Fonds Othmani. Bibliothèque Documentation Internationale Contemporaine (BDIC), Université de Nanterre.

Index

Abd el Kader, 146
Abe, Sada, 210, 211, 223n96
Adams, William, 214–16, 225n120, 225nn122–25
Afary, Janet, 148, 158n115
Albérès, R. M., 249
Algerian War, 104, 123, 133, 152n15, 157n95, 169, 173, 175, 189n119
Āl-i Aḥmad, Jalāl, 137–38, 155n64
Allen, Amy, 114n1, 158n115
Almond, Ian, 12n23
Althusser, Louis, 171
Amiot, Michel, 120n66
Anabaptists, 129, 135
Anderson, Kevin B., 148, 158n115
Anderson-Gold, Sharon, 93n106
Annales School, 204–5, 222n72
anthropology, 10, 32, 112, 231, 233–34; "anthropological illusion" (anthropologism), 82, 99, 105, 146; "anthropological sleep," 32, 81, 99–100, 109, 115n17; cosmopolitan, 9, 39, 65–66, 71, 75, 77, 83, 88n38, 102, 108, 123, 176, 234, 251–53; "crisis" (end) of, 105–10, 117n38, 118n43; empirical, 9, 68, 69, 73, 77–78, 82, 83, 97, 113, 246; Foucault and, 80–83, 97–105, 109–13, 130, 145–46, 226, 228–29, 233–34, 239, 250–51, 253; goals of, 54, 64–66, 71, 77, 158n115; Kant and, 3–4, 9, 62–83, 118n52, 119n56, 207; as *le regard éloigné,* 230, 232, 241n23; "negative," 113; philosophical, 73, 76, 85n11, 90n70, 91n83, 97. *See also* Foucault, Michel: *Introduction* to Kant's *Anthropology*; Kant, Immanuel: *Anthropology from a Pragmatic Point of View*; Lévi-Strauss, Claude
aphasia, 28
Arabic language, 8, 173, 176, 189n123, 243n57; Tunisian colloquial Arabic, 189n123
archaeology, 9, 250–51
Aron, Raymond, 180n18
Aristotle, 162
Artaud, Antonin, 134
Asukata, Ichio, 200–201, 213
'Ashura, 133, 140, 143, 147, 149, 227
Ataturk, Kemal, 126, 155n70

Bachelard, Gaston, 56–57, 248
Bani Sadr, Abdulhasan, 129
Barbin, Herculine, 130
Barthes, Roland, 218n26
Bataille, Georges, 114n9, 134, 193, 196, 248

Baudelaire, Charles, 36–37, 44n88, 45, 51–52, 71, 237
Baumgarten, Alexander Gottlieb, 63, 84n4
Bazargan, Mehdi, 151
Beau, Michel, 168
Beaucé, Thierry de, 198, 220n41, 220n43
Ben Abed, Aïcha, 187n91
Ben Achour, Habib, 184n62
Ben Jennet, Mohammad, 166, 173
Ben Khader, Noureddine, 187n91, 189n124
Ben Mhenni, Lina, 5, 183n49
Ben Mhenni, Sadek, 5, 183n49
Ben Youssef, Salah, 163, 182n43
Bernasconi, Robert, 117n28
Berque, Jacques, 180n28
Bertrand, Louis, 182n40
Besteman, Catherine, 108
Beuks, Johan, 152n5
Bibliographic Institute of Brussels, 19–21, 33, 41n37
Binswanger, Ludwig, 74, 115n16, 135
biopolitics, 176
Black Panther Party, 171
Blanchot, Maurice, 11n6, 134, 196, 248
Bloch, Marc, 204
Boas, Franz, 108
Bonnefoy, Claude, 248
Borges, Jorge Luis: on cultural relativism, 27–29, 37–38; encyclopedias in, 1–2, 9, 13, 14–22, 24, 28–29, 32, 34, 38, 40n28; on self-identity, 50–52; universalism and, 27
  WORKS: "The Anthropologist," 37–38; "Garden of Forking Paths," 29, 40n28; "John Wilkins's Analytical Language," 1–2, 9, 17–22, 33, 40n26; "Keeper of the Books, The," 41; "Tlön, Uqbar, Orbis Tertius," 29, 41n28
Bosteels, Bruno, 32–33

Bourdieu, Pierre, 2, 218n26
Bourguiba, Habib, 2, 164, 166, 168, 182n43, 182n46, 183n51, 184n58, 185n69, 189n115; modernism of, 163, 175, 190n131, 190n138
Brandt, Reinhard, 90n71
Braudel, Fernand, 180n18
Brière, Claire, 156n89
Brossat, Alain, 12n30
Buddhism, 135, 193, 201, 206, 208–9, 222–23nn80–81, 238. *See also* Zen
Buffon, Georges-Louis Leclerc, Comte de, 117n34, 120n69
Bunzl, Matti, 108, 119n57

Camus, Albert, 155n64, 224n115
Canguilhem, Georges, 2, 10n5, 56–57, 164, 165
Carrette, Jeremy R., 134, 154n46
Caruso, Paolo, 131
Castro, Fidel, 172
Cavallari, Alberto, 123
Caygill, Howard, 63, 85nn9–11, 90n76
Chabert, Jean-Paul, 167
Charfi, Mohammed, 185n66
Cheah, Pheng, 93n94, 101
Cherni, Zineb Ben Saïd, 5, 170–71, 176–77, 188n103
China: Foucault's neglect of, 113; Kant on, 112–13; Western imagination of, 16–17, 22, 24, 32
Chinese encyclopedia concept, 1–2, 9, 13–26, 30–39, 45, 52, 109, 171–72, 178, 195; Chinese scholars on, 34–36
Chinese language: Catholic Church on, 120n69; Foucault on, 23, 28, 32–33
Chinese philosophy, 112, 120n69. *See also* Confucius
Christianity, 26, 126, 134, 140, 146, 193, 244n70, 246; Zen vs., 206, 207, 211–12

classification systems, 15, 19, 21–24, 32–33, 38, 172; Borges on, 29
Clauss, Sidonie, 20
Clavel, James, 215
Clifford, James, 117n38
Club Culturel Tahar Haddad, 161, 163, 187n86
Cohen, Alix, 95n131
Cohn-Bendit, Daniel, 184n62
collective conscience, 203
colonialism (and colonization), 7, 104–5, 127–28, 133, 196, 201, 202, 213–14, 246; "colonizing reason of the Occident," 195; decolonization, 249; Habermas on, 243n50; the Orient and, 195, 202, 211, 216, 234–36, 244n82. *See also* Tunisia: colonialism and
Comaroff, John, 117n35, 118n52
Comte, Auguste, 57, 68, 231
Confucius and Confucianism, 112, 120n73, 121n77, 224n112, 236
Corbin, Henry, 129–30, 138–40, 154n46
cosmopolitanism, 37, 56, 71, 89n60, 109, 177; Kant's "citizen of the world," 51–52, 79–80, 88n46, 113, 160. *See also* anthropology: cosmopolitan
Cottet, Sandrine, 218n21
"crisis of Western thought," 7, 175, 213–14, 230, 238
cultural difference, 25–29, 38–39, 62, 83, 105, 107–10, 246, 251–52; Baudelaire on, 36–37; Geertz on, 118n51; madness and, 45, 51–52. *See also* relativism
culture, 8, 17, 23, 52, 69–71, 99–101, 113, 149, 252; a-prioris of fact and right, 102, 249; classification and, 23–24, 27–28; "common space of culture," 52, 102, 249–50; "cultural collectivities," 111; "cultural facts," 131; cultural identity, 121n77, 196, 249; cultural rollback, 239; Foucault's definitions of, 101–2, 249; Mendelssohn on, 115n22; "state of culture," 102

D'Amico, Robert, 60n42
Damiens, Robert-François, 34
Dauge, Louis, 200
"death of man" thesis, 99, 114n9, 145, 149, 229, 246, 252
de Beauvoir, Simone, 197, 218n26
Defert, Daniel, 3, 5, 33, 91n79, 202–3; in Japan, 198–99, 219n36, 247; on "limit-experience," 196; in Tunisia, 160, 162, 165, 167–68, 171, 175, 180n18
de Gaulle, Charles, 133
Derrida, Jacques, 31, 218n26, 224n110; on Cartesian rationalism, 48–50, 52, 53–54, 58n9, 59n18; on *logos*, 182n38
désarçonné feeling, 212
Descartes, René, 31, 80, 163, 221n53, 250; on language, 18, 20, 40n22, 40n25; on madness (unreason), 9, 28, 45–50, 52–53, 57, 58n8, 246; Western *ratio* and, 52, 62, 246
Detienne, Marcel, 162, 181n36
Dewey decimal system, 41n37
difference, 48, 107–9, 207
Dostoevsky, Fyodor, 51
double concept, 57, 104, 240
Dover, Kenneth James, 182n39
Durkheim, Émile, 146, 241n15
Duvignaud, Jean, 180n28

El Zitouna, 173
"empirico-transcendental doublet," 6, 97
Enlightenment, 74, 89n57, 95n120, 100, 101, 110, 112–13, 115n22; Foucault and, 110–12, 158n115; Kant on, 110, 213

Eribon, Didier, 123, 165
ethnology, 4, 33, 100, 106–7, 114n15, 131, 248–51
experience, 4, 6, 37, 63, 65–68, 74–75, 80, 141, 150; Foucault's definitions of, 134, 177–78; "limit-experience," 7, 39, 46, 57, 74, 82, 93, 122, 146, 150, 193–96, 200, 201, 226, 239; "lived experience" (Husserl), 100; "naked experience," 17, 22; surrealists and, 134, 138; Zen and, 206–8
eyes (and seeing): "academic eye," 37; Nietzsche's optical metaphors, 233; presbyopic project, 249; "scholastic veil," 37

Fanon, Frantz, 137
Febvre, Lucien, 204
Fimiani, Mariapaola, 92n87
finitude, 55, 74–75, 81–83, 101
Finkielkraut, Alain, 124
Fishburn, Evelyn, 30, 43n70
Flaubert, Gustave, 2, 30–31
Foucault, Michel: on being understood, 245; "culturalism" of, 111, 120n66; on encyclopedias, 30–32 (*see also* Chinese encyclopedia concept); *espagnolisme*, 2, 10n5; French Communist Party membership, 2; genetic methodology, 72, 91n77, 91n79; intellectual role, 2, 148; interview style, 4–5; language limitations, 7–8; letter to Georges Canguilhem, 164–65, 184n53; on the penis, 210–11; political orientation, 2–3, 123, 127–28, 133–36, 151n2, 169; psychology interest, 74, 92n87; regressive methodology, 22, 42n41; *reportage d'idées* project, 1, 123–25, 142, 149–50, 158n116; self-admitted ignorance, 61n65; on writing, 99, 245, 248–49, 254n26

WORKS: *The Archaeology of Knowledge* (*L'archéologie du savoir*), 80, 101, 124, 136, 178, 197, 200, 203–4, 249–50; *The Birth of the Clinic* (*Naissance de la clinique*), 197; Collège de France lectures, 9, 103, 162, 181n35, 197, 199, 214; "Des espaces autres," 159; *Discipline and Punish* (*Surveiller et punir*), 34, 130, 176, 247; *Dits et écrits*, 5, 9, 12n27, 129, 203, 253; *History of Madness* (*Folie et déraison*), 1, 10n3, 33, 34, 39, 46, 48, 53, 57, 180, 191n140, 195, 219n31; 1961 preface to, 1, 3, 6, 13, 33, 192, 194–97, 216n3, 245, 247; *History of Sexuality* (*Histoire de la sexualité*), 206, 211, 250; Introduction to Binswanger's *Dreams and Existence*, 74, 115n16, 115n19, 135; Introduction to *Herculine Barbin*, 130; Introduction to Kant's *Anthropology*, 62, 72–81, 86n19, 92n87, 97, 99, 102–3, 112–13, 114n2, 147, 192, 246; *Leçons sur la volonté de savoir*, 162, 181n35; *Le corps utopique, [suivi de] Les hétérotopies*, 179n2; *L'Ordre du discours*, 215; *Mental Illness and Psychology* (*Maladie mentale et psychologie*), 74, 197; *The Order of Things* (*Les mots et les choses*), 1–2, 6, 9, 13–14, 17, 19–23, 28, 31–36, 38–39, 53–57, 62, 81, 83, 97, 104, 113, 139, 145, 163, 165, 196, 197, 202, 205, 240, 247, 250–51; "What Is Enlightenment?" ("Qu'est-ce que les Lumières?"), 110–12
Franchetti, Cody, 222n72
French Communist Party, 2, 175
French Socialist Party, 200–201
French Revolution, 7, 90n64, 135–36, 141, 142
Freud, Sigmund, 98, 194
Frierson, Patrick R., 78

Galinier, Jacques, 119n52
Gandillac, Maurice de, 62
Garfinkel, Harold, 70
Gattégno, Jean, 167, 168
Gauche Prolétarienne, 3
Geertz, Clifford, 31–32, 106–8, 118n46, 118m51
Geismar, Alain, 167, 186n75
geography, Foucault's neglect of, 103–4, 113
Gesner, Konrad, 36
Ghamari-Tabrizi, Behrooz, 157n108
Girtanner, Christoph, 65, 86n25, 116n28
Glucksmann, André, 3, 124
Golden, Arthur, 239
Goldmann, Lucien, 91n77
Gould, Stephen Jay, 35–36
Gracq, Julien, 181n33
Gramsci, Antonio, 190n136
Groupe d'Etudes et d'Action Socialistes Tunisien (GEAST), 163, 170, 183n50, 185n67
Groupe d'Information sur les Prisons (GIP), 3, 174, 177, 191n140
Gusterson, Hugh, 108

Habermas, Jürgen, 151, 243n50
Hafsia, Jélila, 161, 180n24
Han, Béatrice, 33–34
Harris, Marvin, 119n56
Harvey, David, 116n28
Hasnaoui, Ahmed, 171, 173, 188n105, 252
Hasumi, Shiguehiko, 214
Hegel, Georg Wilhelm Friedrich, 49, 58n16, 193, 206, 208
Heidegger, Martin, 74, 91n79, 91n83, 121n78, 134, 213; Japan and, 193, 217n10, 223n93
Herder, Johann Gottlieb, 64, 119n52
Herz, Marcus, 71–72, 86n17
heterotopias, 15, 16, 27–28, 159, 176, 178

historical materialism. *See* Marx, Karl
historicism, 140; historicity, 111, 112, 126
homosexuality, 7, 39, 160, 162, 178; Japanese men's clubs, 198, 220n46
Honneth, Axel, 11n12, 254n24
humanist philosophy, 3, 100, 111, 137; "generalized humanism," 230; "third humanism," 234
Hume, David, 102, 115n17
Hund, Wolf D., 87n25, 116n28
Hungary, Foucault in, 61n65
Husserl, Edmund, 54–55, 100
Hyppolite, Jean, 62

Ibn 'Arabi, 139
imperialism, 111, 127, 175, 213–14, 249. *See also* colonialism
In the Realm of the Senses (Oshima), 210, 211
Iran: Foucault in, 1, 2, 4, 6–8, 83, 114n10, 122–51, 246–47
Ishida, Hidetaka, 5, 217n10
Islam. *See* Shi'ism
Islamic government, idea of an, 136–38, 144

Jacobs, Brian, 89n61
Japan: appeal to French writers, 197, 218n26; "enigma" of, 194, 202, 216; Foucault in, 1, 2, 4–5, 6–8, 52, 55–56, 83, 123, 130–31, 192–216, 226–40, 247–48, 252; "mentality" (*mentalité*) of, 202–5, 216, 222n72, 222n75, 222n77, 232, 234–35, 251; *nihonjinron* field, 236–37, 238; Westernization of, 235–39, 243nn51–53, 244n72
Jesuits in the East, 120n69, 225n123, 225n126
Jullien, François, 205, 207, 222n75, 224n110, 224n113
June '67 protests, 172, 173
Jung, Carl G., 25–26

Kain, Patrick, 89n61
Kamiya, Miyeko, 197
Kang Zhengguo, 35–36
Kant, Immanuel, 7, 33, 54, 57, 128, 148, 151; on China, 112–13, 120n73; cosmopolitanism of, 65, 69, 83, 89n53, 89n60, 102, 108–9, 113, 116n28, 177; Enlightenment and, 110–12, 213; political writings, 89n60; racial views, 70, 86n25, 88n39, 102–4, 111, 116nn26–28; on travel, 70–71, 89n53; women and, 64, 86n20, 103
WORKS: "An Answer to the Question: What Is Enlightenment," 110, 213; *Anthropology from a Pragmatic Point of View*, 3–4, 9, 62–83, 85n11, 92n87, 94n109, 94n117, 97, 99–105, 107–9, 111–13, 116n28, 128, 178, 202; *The Conflict of the Faculties*, 89n64; *Critique of Judgment*, 78; *Critique of Pure Reason*, 73, 75–76, 81–82, 85n10–11, 92n84, 92n87, 94n109; *Essay on Race*, 102; *Groundwork of the Metaphysics of Morals*, 77, 86n35; *Opus Postumum*, 75, 93n92, 93n99; *Physical Geography*, 67, 70, 90n73, 104, 116nn27–28, 119n59
Kawada, Junzo, 244n79, 244n81
Khomeini, Ruhollah, 122, 128, 129, 132–33, 141–45, 154n40; mythification of, 145, 148, 157n95
Kleingeld, Pauline, 116n28
knowledge: genealogy of, 162, 194; Kant and, 33, 64–83 passim, 89n53, 90n71, 92n87, 108, 111–12, 123; power and, 52, 106, 214–15; "will to know," 181n36, 250
Kobayashi, Yasuo, 5, 195, 196, 239
Kojève, Alexandre, 114n9
Kristeva, Julia, 217n12

Kuehn, Manfred, 89n57, 94n109
Kuhn, Franz, 18–20, 40n28

Lacan, Jacques, 218n26, 221n49
La Fontaine, Henri, 41n37
Lange, Antje, 86n20
language, 78–79; as "motherland," 251; "nonplace" of, 32; turn, 80–82; unity and limits of, 15, 20, 22–23, 27–28, 52–53; universal language proposals, 17–18, 24, 38, 41n37
Lapassade, Georges, 167, 168, 187nn89–90
Lawrence ("of Arabia"), T. E., 154n37
Leezenberg, Michiel, 153n32, 156n88
Leibniz, Gottfried Wilhelm, 112, 120n70, 205
Lellouche, Simone Othmani, 164, 165, 170, 172, 184n62
Lévi-Strauss, Claude, 4, 31, 33, 106, 108–9, 114n15, 140, 226, 241n31, 241n33, 242nn45–47, 254n22; comparative mythology and, 250; Japan and, 218n26, 229–39 passim, 241n17, 241n23, 242n36
Lévy, Benny ("Pierre Victor"), 3, 11n8
Lévy-Bruhl, Lucien, 33, 204, 222n72
limit concept. *See* experience; finitude
linguistics, 100
Locke, John, 80
Louden, Robert B., 80, 82, 87n35, 89n58, 90n75
Louis IX (St. Louis), 161
Luxemburg, Rosa, 171

Macey, David, 11n6, 34, 61n65, 124, 178
Madama Butterfly (Puccini), 239, 244n79, 244n81
Madari, Shariat, 129–30, 144
madness, Foucault's conception of, 34, 38, 39, 45–57, 148–49, 194; Kant on, 80; laughter and, 45; poets and, 44n88; in theater, 226–29, 232, 233

Maeda, Yoishi, 197
Makkreel, Rudolph A., 93n100
Mallarmé, Stéphane, 30
Manet, Édouard, 163
Maoism, 163, 172, 188n99
Marchaisse, Thierry, 205, 222n75, 224n110, 224n113
Marcus, George E., 118n43
Marcuse, Herbert, 169
Maruyama, Masao, 199, 200, 203, 248
Marx, Karl (and Marxism), 2–3, 55, 56, 127, 128, 137, 141, 150–51, 158n115, 171, 200–201, 213; *groupusculation,* 170; historical materialism, 3, 100, 101, 194; on religion, 2, 126, 129, 151; sino-castrism, 172; students and Marxism, 2, 164, 165, 169–72, 178
Massignon, Louis, 129, 148
May '68 events, 126, 160, 166–67, 169–70, 172, 174, 176–77, 180n20, 188n96, 189n119
Mead, George Herbert, 88n42
Mead, Margaret, 105
Mendelssohn, Moses, 115n22
Mendieta, Eduardo, 86n20
"mentality" (*mentalité*). *See under* Japan
Mersenne, Marin, Descartes's letter to, 18, 40n22
Miller, James, 151
Milne, John, 237
Mishima Yukio, 211
modernity, 53–56, 111, 178; Baudelaire and, 36–37, 44n88; Iran and, 138, 155n68; Japan and, 153n20, 201–2, 205, 236, 240
modernization, 126, 132, 137–38, 142, 150, 153n20, 155n68, 202, 236
Mohammad Reza Pahlavi, 132, 133, 137–38, 144
Molière, 89n54
Montesquieu, Charles-Louis de Secondat, 120n69
Morse, Edward, 236–37

Motoori Norinaga, 230
mysticism, 140, 148, 206–7, 209

Naccache, Gilbert, 165, 170, 182n44
narcissism, 57
Nasser, Gamel Abdel, 166, 185n69
Naumann, Edmund, 237
Nemoto, C., 210
Nietzsche, Friedrich, 4, 84n1, 98, 130, 160, 162, 163, 171, 237–38, 242n41, 242n43, 246, 252; and the Orient, 192, 194, 206, 216n1, 217n8, 223n81, 232–33, 243n67
nihilism, 237–38
Nishida Kitaro, 237, 244n69
Nishitani Keiji, 237, 244n70, 244n72
Non-aligned movement, 166, 185n68
Nō theater, 198, 226–28, 230

Omori Sogen, 206–8, 209
orientalism, 8, 12n23, 25, 148, 193, 195
Orient–Occident divide, 1–2, 3–4, 6–8, 13, 28, 33, 38–39, 45, 56–57, 136, 150, 192–96, 200–202, 208, 228, 245–47; Japanese scholars on, 195, 211, 237–39, 247
originary concept, 194, 247
otherness, 2, 4, 6, 13, 25, 32, 34, 39, 57, 216, 245, 246, 252–53; Borges on, 50–51, 57; madness and, 52, 54–56
Othmani, Ahmed (aka Reddaoui), 164, 167–68, 170, 174, 186nn71–72
Otlet, Paul, 21, 41n37
Ozu, Yasujirō, 247

Palestinian question, 166, 168, 185n67
Panofsky, Erwin, 222n72
Parham, Baqir, 129
Parsons, Talcott, 83
Perry, Matthew C., 216
Perspectivists. *See* Groupe d'Etudes et d'Action Socialistes Tunisien
phenomenology, 54–55, 100, 115n19

Pinguet, Maurice, 197, 198, 221n52
Platner, Ernst, 64, 65, 72
Plato, 214
Polak, Christian, 5, 198–99, 203, 207, 209, 219–20nn40–41, 248
Pol-Droit, Roger, 119n59
"political spirituality," 7, 133–36, 141–47, 149–50, 154n46, 172–73, 247
positivism, 67, 100–101
postmodernism, 95n117; anthropology and, 106–8, 119n54
power, Foucault's conception of, 10, 130, 134, 153n25, 165, 177, 190n135, 211, 219n38, 247; knowledge and, 52, 106, 214–15
presbyopic project, 249
Priscus, 35
psychoanalysis, 25, 43, 100, 115n16, 221n49

Rabaut Saint-Étienne, Jean-Paul, 135
Rabelais, François, 22, 27
race, 102–4, 164; Kant and, 70, 86n25, 88n39, 102–4, 111, 116nn26–28
Ranganathan, S. R., 42n37
Razgallah, Brahim, 164, 165, 184n56
reflexivity, 29, 68, 71, 79, 83, 102, 249
Reihman, Gregory M., 120n73
relativism, 107, 111–12, 140, 232, 242n37. *See also* cultural difference
religion, 2, 7, 126, 128–29, 206, 246. *See also* mysticism; "political spirituality"; and specific faiths
revolution, 7, 141, 153n26, 214, 224n115
Ricardo, David, 171
Richardson, Samuel, 89n54
Robbe-Grillet, Alain, 2
Roger, Jacques, 222n77
Rousseau, Jean-Jacques, 20

Sabot, Philippe, 114n9, 115n18
Said, Edward, 8, 12n24
Sakai, Naoki, 205, 253n13

Salamatian, Ahmed, 129
Same, the. *See* self-same
Sartre, Jean-Paul, 2, 11n8, 42n41, 123, 160, 175, 180n21, 190n139; Japan and, 197, 218n26
Saussure, Ferdinand de, 194, 197
Schaub, Uta Liebmann, 216n2, 242n49
Scheiffele, Eberhard, 242n43
Schönfeld, Martin, 85n11, 113
Schopenhauer, Arthur, 193, 217n8
self-knowledge, 82–83
self-reflection, 5, 24, 55, 83, 108
self-same, the, 50, 55–56, 57, 238, 240; "the Near and the Same," 55–56; the Same, 14, 39, 57
Serres, Michel, 249
sexuality, 210–11
Sharī'atī, Ali, 137, 138, 142, 155n60
Shingu, Kazushige, 210
Shi'ism, 6, 7, 122–23, 125–26, 128–30, 132–37, 143, 146–50, 154n46, 156n92, 246; Corbin on, 138–40, 156n89
Shinkai, Yasuyuki, 5, 195, 247
Sidi Bou Saïd, 6, 9, 159–62, 167, 176, 181n28
Six-Day War (June War), 163, 165, 185n67
Smith, Adam, 20
socialism, Foucault and, 127–28
sociology, 10, 57, 88n50, 233; Kant's relevance to, 68–71, 77, 95n131
Sollers, Philippe, 217n12
Solomon, Jon, 158n116, 205
Sprung, Mervyn, 217n8, 242n41, 244n73
Stark, Werner, 84n4, 91n84, 116n28
Stauth, George, 150
Stendhal, 10n5
structuralism, 163, 183n48, 197
subject, Foucault on, 134–36, 151; Reason as, 148
suicide, 57
surrealist movement, 114n9, 134, 138

Sweden, Foucault in, 8, 159, 160, 251, 254n26

Takeuchi Yoshimi, 192, 214, 238
Tanaka, Stefan, 243nn51–53, 244n82
taxonomies. *See* classification systems
Thebaid, 161, 180n22
Third World, 2, 127–28, 137–38, 160, 166, 169, 173–74, 176, 177
Thomasius, Christian, 87n32
Tokugawa Ieyasu, 215
torture: in Iran, 151; in Tunisia, 166–67, 176, 184n56, 185n70, 188n103
Touraine, Alain, 128, 153n25
translation issues, 51–52, 106, 205, 209; Foucault and, 5, 60n43, 94n117, 197–98, 203
Trombadori, Duccio, 11n16, 167, 169, 172, 196
Trotsky, Leon, 171
Tunisia: ancient Greece and, 7, 9, 162, 176, 178, 251; colonialism and, 173–79, 214; Foucault in, 1, 2, 4, 6, 7–8, 83, 123, 125–26, 159–79; March '68 events in, 160–61, 166–69, 172–73, 176–77, 184n62, 187n89; media view of, 12n20
Tu Wei-ming, 31–32, 44n82

universalism, 7, 27–29, 38, 99, 110–13, 115n15, 196, 201, 213, 226, 232, 239, 248, 252; madness and, 228–29; Zen and, 206–9

Van de Pitte, Frederick, 85n11, 86n19, 90n71

Velásquez, Diego de, 98
Verdeux, Jacqueline, 149
Vernant, Jean Pierre, 162, 181n36
Vietnam, Foucault and, 127–28, 172
Voeltzel, Thierry, 124, 129

Watanabe, Moriaki, 5, 197–99, 210, 218n28, 220n49, 227, 228, 247, 252
Weber, Max, 88n50, 126, 141, 202, 221n62
Western *ratio*, 1, 3, 8, 13, 27, 33, 57, 192–96, 202, 209, 252–53; Descartes and, 52, 62, 246
Wilkins, John, 17–22, 33, 40n26
Wilson, Holly L., 65, 84n8, 89n59, 90n74
Wolff, Christian, 112, 120n70
women: Hottentot, 102; in Iran, 144, 147–48; in Japanese theater, 227, 240n8; Kant and, 64, 86n20, 103; sex and, 210; in Tunisia, 162, 169, 187n91
Wood, Allen W., 90n71, 98, 114nn5–6
world vs. universe, Foucault on, 75

Yoshimoto, Ryūmei (Takaaki), 208–9

Zammito, John H., 84n4, 85n11, 86n20
Zeami Motokiyo, 227–28, 240n8
Zen, 196, 199, 202–3, 206–9, 212, 232, 239; za-zen exercise, 209
Zhang, Longxi, 34–35
Zoungrana, Jean, 33

www.ingramcontent.com/pod-product-compliance
Lightning Source LLC
Chambersburg PA
CBHW070913030426
42336CB00014BA/2392